ROMANTICISM

ROMANTICISM

Critical Concepts in Literary and Cultural Studies

Edited by
Michael O'Neill and Mark Sandy

Volume IV
Romanticism, Belief, and Philosophy

Routledge
Taylor & Francis Group
LONDON AND NEW YORK

First published 2006
by Routledge
2 Park Square, Milton Park, Abingdon, OX14 4RN

Simultaneously published in the USA and Canada
by Routledge
270 Madison Avenue, New York, NY10016

Routledge is an imprint of the Taylor & Francis Group

Typeset in 10/12pt Times by Graphicraft Limited, Hong Kong
Printed and bound in Great Britain by MPG Books Ltd, Bodmin, Cornwall

British Library Cataloguing in Publication Data
A catalogue record for this book is available from the British Library

Library of Congress Cataloging in Publication Data
A catalog record for this book has been requested

ISBN 0-415-24722-5 (Set)
ISBN 0-415-24726-8 (Volume IV)

M 0027094 bI
Publisher's Note

References within each chapter are as they appear in the original complete work

CONTENTS

VOLUME IV   ROMANTICISM, BELIEF, AND PHILOSOPHY

ACKNOWLEDGEMENTS

The publishers would like to thank the following for permission to reprint their material:

'The Intense Inane' reprinted by permission of the publisher from *Romantic Poets, Critics, and Other Madmen* by Charles Rosen, pp. 31–50, Cambridge, Mass.: Harvard University Press, Copyright © 1998 by the President and Fellows of Harvard College. First published as 'Isn't It Romantic!' *New York Review of Books*, June 14, 1973.

University of California Press for permission to reprint Morton D. Paley, 'Apocapolitics: Allusion and Structure in Shelley's *Mask of Anarchy*', *Huntington Library Quarterly* 54 (1991): 91–109. © 1991, by the Henry E. Huntington Library and Art Gallery. All rights reserved. Reprinted from *Huntingdon Library Quarterly*.

Cambridge University Press and Robert Ryan for permission to reprint Robert M. Ryan 'A Sect of Dissenters', in *The Romantic Reformation: Religious Politics in English Literature 1789–1824*, Cambridge, Cambridge University Press, 1997, pp. 13–42. © Cambridge University Press, reprinted with permission of Cambridge University Press and Robert Ryan.

Taylor & Francis for permission to reprint Paul Hamilton 'The New Romanticism: Philosophical Stand-Ins in English Romantic Discourse', *Textual Practice* 11 (1997): 110–31. www.tandf.co.uk/journals

Studies in Romanticism for permission to reprint Ross Woodman 'Nietzsche, Blake, Keats and Shelley: The Making of a Metaphorical Body' *Studies in Romanticism* 29 (1990): 115–49.

Oxford University Press for permission to reprint Seamus Perry 'Coleridge's Millennial Embarrassments', *Essays in Criticism* 50 (2000): 1–22.

Studies in Romanticism for permission to reprint Lawrence Kramer 'The Return of the Gods: Keats to Rilke', *Studies in Romanticism* 17 (1978): 483–500.

Cambridge University Press and Timothy Webb for permission to reprint Timothy Webb 'Romantic Hellenism', in Stuart Curran (ed.) *The Cambridge Companion to British Romanticism*, Cambridge, Cambridge University Press, 1993, pp. 148–76. © Cambridge University Press, reprinted with permission of Cambridge University Press and Timothy Webb.

Studies in Romanticism for permission to reprint Edward Duffy 'The Romantic Calling of Thinking: Stanley Cavell on the line with Wordsworth' *Studies in Romanticism* 37 (1998): 615–45.

Cornell University Press for permission to reprint Tilottama Rajan 'Introduction', in *Dark Interpreter: The Discourse of Romanticism*, Ithaca, NY: Cornell University Press, 1980, pp. 13–26. Copyright © 1980 by Cornell University. Used by permission of the publisher, Cornell University Press.

Studies in Romanticism for permission to reprint Karen Swann '*Christabel*: The Wandering Mother and the Enigma of Form' *Studies in Romanticism* 23 (1986): 533–54.

Jacobus, Mary, 'Wordsworth and the Language of the Dream.' *ELH* 46 (1979): 618–44. © The Johns Hopkins University Press. Reprinted with permission of the The Johns Hopkins University Press.

Edinburgh University Press for permission to reprint Thomas McFarland 'Coleridge, Prescience, Tenacity and the Origin of Sociology', *Romanticism* 4 (1998): 40–59. www.eup.ed.ac.uk

Disclaimer

The publishers have made every effort to contact authors/copyright holders of works reprinted in *Romanticism: Critical Concepts in Literary and Cultural Studies.* This has not been possible in every case, however, and we would welcome correspondence from those individuals/companies who we have been unable to trace.

INTRODUCTION

Volume IV Romanticism, Belief, and Philosophy

The fourth and final volume in the set brings together twentieth- and twenty-first century critical reflections on Romanticism's many and varied negotiations with religious, philosophical, psychological, and mythological issues. Romantic literature's investment in and testing of the boundaries of subjectivity question and re-interpret religious, philosophical and mythological frameworks that had once assured human agency a definite position in the universal scheme of things. Scepticism about traditional forms of knowledge blends with risings and collapses of political idealism. The result can be an apocalyptic mode which asserts and interrogates the revelatory power of art and religion.

Part 9

Belief, philosophy, and myth

The first reprinted essay, 'The intense inane: religious revival in English, French and German Romanticism' by **Charles Rosen**, reflects on Romantic endeavours to re-inscribe patterns of religious fall and redemption with new meanings. Rosen's 1973 review of M. H. Abrams's study, *Natural Supernaturalism: Tradition and Revolution in Romantic Literature*, and an edition of *Coleridge's Verse: A Selection* by William Empson and David Pirie, is insightful about the 'curious and ambiguous significance' of 'the religious language of the early Romantic writers'. Rosen is sympathetic to Abram's central thesis: that Romantic writers aspired to the restoration of a prelapsarian state, through the successful 'marriage of nature to the mind of man', which resolved spiritual and psychic turmoil by returning human beings to an 'undifferentiated' state of 'being'. However, Rosen finds questionable Abrams's 'pervasive and persistent' application of this religious pattern of fall and redemption. He observes that Abrams does not incorporate models from 'Romantic natural science' (21). He also feels that Abrams's apocalyptic template applies too easily to a whole body of seventeenth- and eighteenth-century European writing. Rosen accepts that religion was of particular interest to Romantic authors. He suggests,

1

however, that Abrams's archetypes need to be measured 'against each poet's relation to religion and morality proper – organized, or at least traditional' (22).

Rosen is closer to the critical views of Empson and Pirie, approving of their conception of 'The Rime of the Ancient Mariner' as enacting 'the awesome consequences of religious guilt' rather than positively affirming, as does Abrams, a redemptive and 'final release' (25) from previous spiritual horrors. Rosen does not share Abrams's sense that Romanticism's appropriation of spiritual patterns of fall and redemption was 'an attempt to salvage the debris of religion torn apart by science and the Enlightenment' (26–7). Radicals such as Blake and the early Wordsworth, and other European Romantics (such as Hölderlin, Schegel, and Novalis), did not 'conserve a traditional theological concept' (27) of salvation. Instead they explored 'the tension between the new meaning and the inevitable residue of the old'. Religious terminology enabled them to 'reconceive of art and literature as a dynamic and endless process', straining after the Hegelian moment when 'humanity realised itself as absolute Mind' (26). Rosen suggests that a condition of self-division is thought of by the Romantics as a religious 'fall from grace' which, inevitably, means that '[a]lienation . . . is synonymous with existence'. In this psychic and spiritual scenario the end stage of the 'circuitous journey' cannot be, as Abrams asserts, 'a renewal of joy and life'; instead, Rosen believes, 'the lost paradise regained is death' (28). There remains a fundamental tension in Romantic rhetoric between 'the hyperbolic language of mysticism' and the 'poetry of despair' (32). Rosen's perception of how the failure of the 'aesthetic doctrine of the Romantics' is 'already acted out within their poetry' (33) chimes with Paul de Man's essay in Volume III and serves as a valuable corrective to Abrams's depiction of 'the early Romantics as hopeful and optimistic' (32). In spite of the force of Rosen's reproofs, Abrams's analysis of Romantic discourse's re-appropriation of religious language and typology was highly influential and remains a seminal study in the field.

In a series of articles culminating in his book-length study *Apocalypse and Millennium in English Romantic Poetry* (1999), **Morton D. Paley** explores in detail how '[t]he poets of the Romantic period drew with great familiarity upon the situations, figures, and language of the Book of Revelation'.[1] M. H. Abrams's central argument, in *Natural Supernaturalism*, that Romantic works secularised Biblical narratives of apocalypse and redemption is an informing influence here. Paley's article, 'Apocapolitics: Allusion and Structure in Shelley's *Mask of Anarchy*' (1991), studies the poem's references to and use of the Book of Revelation. It relates the poem's structure to Shelley's awareness of the difficulty of moving from apocalypse (the overthrow of corruption) to millennium (an imagined new and better order). Paley sees Shelley as using the Book of Revelation 'as a prototype', but as doing so in 'a loose, unsystematic, and even playful manner'. Modern history is persuaded by Shelley's poem to parallel 'that of John's Apocalypse in a complex and sometimes ironical way' (38). If Paley brings out Shelley's indebtedness to John of Patmos's vision, he also convinces us of the Romantic poet's ironising originality.

This originality shows most of all, for Paley, in the poem's structure which, after the introductory stanza, falls on his reading into three sections: the Pageant, the Agon, and the Hortatory Address. The Pageant demonstrates Shelley's command of the 'apocalyptic-grotesque' (38); the Agon his recognition that sudden change defeats adequate representation; and the Hortatory Address his sense that the millennial requires a different kind of poetry from that used in the previous two sections. At the same time, the poem's structure works backwards as well as forwards: only when the ideas conveyed in the Address are fully taken on board 'can the sons of England actuate the myth that precedes it' (43). Paley sees the co-existence of 'pacifist tenors and violent vehicles' in *The Mask* as expressing Shelley's mixed feelings of political 'hope and . . . fear' (44), feelings comparable to the sudden switches of tone and mood in the Book of Revelation. The article, like Paley's book, illuminates the work of a Romantic poet by bringing it into connection with Biblical conceptions that enjoyed a powerful if reworked life in the period. Paley combines contextual awareness with an attention to textual detail, as in his analysis of the 'anaphoric structure' (45) of parts of the Address.

Close if sometimes acrimonious companions, the 'Romantic' and the 'Religious' are alliteratively coupled in the title of **Robert M. Ryan**'s study *The Romantic Reformation: Religious Politics in English Literature, 1789–1824* (1997). Ryan's subtitle pinpoints the connection between religion and politics which is his concern. Whereas M. H. Abrams saw the Romantics as producing a securalised revision of traditional Christianity, Ryan argues for the living force of religious engagement in the poetry of the period. He asserts that the Romantics, with the exception of Coleridge, were 'all concerned much more with the politics of religion than with its metaphysics'. Byron, for example, offers a 'critique of the state religion' that is driven as much 'by belief' as 'by skepticism', and that seeks 'to force Christianity to live up to its self-representations'.[2] The book's emphasis on 'belief' as well as 'skepticism' is unusual in contemporary criticism, but it pays rich dividends as Ryan re-considers what the Romantics thought and felt about religion.

We have included Ryan's first chapter, '"A sect of dissenters"'. In this chapter, Ryan stresses the 'special affinity' between the Romantic period and 'that of the Protestant Reformation in England' (51), an affinity noted by Shelley, Wordsworth, and Keats, among others. The Romantics lived in an age which placed renewed emphasis on the need for religious reform. Catholics and Dissenters, both victims of legal discrimination since the Revolution of 1688, were in the vanguard of 'clamorous political disputes' (56). But while Shelley and Byron were sympathetic to the Catholic cause, the other Romantics were less so. For all the Romantics, it is the claims of so-called rational dissenters that strike the loudest chord, claims that resonate with revolutionary and millennial voices in the period, and Ryan takes his chapter's title from a review in 1802 of Southey's *Thalaba* by Francis Jeffrey in which the critic characterises Southey, Wordsworth, and Coleridge as a '*sect . . . of . . . dissenters*' (quoted 67; the emphases are Jeffrey's).

Ryan sees the Romantic poets as swayed by the 'old radical Protestant insistence' (67) on the right and duty of exercising private judgement. Milton provides a model for the Romantics in his belief that 'religious reformation is a continuing process' (54) with implications for all aspects of life. At the same time, the Romantics not only reassert but also redefine the Miltonic inheritance. For example, Blake attempts to 'revise and rehabilitate Milton' (68) in a poetic endeavour (*Milton*) that involves 'reformation' rather than 'iconoclasm' (69). Wordsworth's Preface to *The Excursion* – in which he passes Jehovah 'unalarmed' – does not, as has been thought, recommend 'naturalistic humanism'. Instead, it repudiates aspects of Milton's 'conception of the Divine' (70). Milton, Ryan remarks, bequeathed more to the Romantics than what Harold Bloom has called 'anxiety of influence' (quoted 71); he also provided them with 'a source of encouragement' and an inspiring model of vocation. The Romantics' sense of the need for 'ongoing reformation' (71) was pervasive, and one of its clearest manifestos can be found in the Preface to Leigh Hunt's 1818 collection of poems, *Foliage*, in which Hunt presents 'the history of English poetry as a record of conflict between superstition and enlightenment, coercion and freedom' (73). But it is in Shelley's *Defence of Poetry* that one finds the most far-reaching account of Romantic religion: in that work, 'denial' of unreformed religion co-exists, Ryan argues, with 'affirmation' of the need for a 'better order of belief' (76).

For his part, **Paul Hamilton** places Romantic belief in a particular philosophical context. Hamilton traces the development of philosophical Idealism from Immanuel Kant to the postmodern pragmatism of Jurgen Habermas, illustrating Romanticism's significant position in the history of Western metaphysics. In 'The New Romanticism: Philosophical Stand-ins in English Romantic Discourse' (1997), Hamilton shows how these recent philosophies play out strategies already embedded in Romantic theory and practice. Hamilton's article reflects the considerable interest this topic has generated in Romantic studies, including three important studies: Andrew Bowie, *From Romanticism to Critical Theory: The Philosophy of German Literary Theory* (1997), Tilottama Rajan, *Deconstruction and the Remainders of Phenomenology* (2003), and Kathleen M. Wheeler, *Romanticism, Pragmatism and Deconstruction* (1993). Hamilton identifies a 'linguistic turn' in twentieth-century thought, in which philosophy shifts its focus from prescribing 'the logical conditions under which linguistic behaviour is meaningful' (82) to a fascination with how truth manifests itself in a particular epoch.

Poststructuralist and postmodern thought has discredited metaphysical speculation and re-located 'transcendental excess' in 'ordinary communication' to 'identify the critical potential in speech itself' (82). Accordingly, Derrida and Habermas (the latter openly admitting the Romantic genealogy of his philosophy) emphasise the importance of difference, so that '[u]nderstanding is . . . no longer a struggle between a subject and an object but a significant agreement over differences' (85). This twentieth-century turn toward philosophical pragmatism is anticipated, for Hamilton, by Romantic negotiations with the tension between Utopian aspirations and reality. Examples occur in the writings of William Godwin, Mary Wollstonecraft, Anna Laetitia Barbauld, and Felicia Hemans (for other perspectives on Romantic women's writing see Volume III). These Romantics adopt a strategy of 'discursive reserve' that contrives to have their theories 'supplemented by a belief in the power of discussion to perform' (87) the Utopian desires of their social and political philosophy. Romantic literature self-reflexively questions the ideal condition to which it aspires. Romantic and post-Romantic thinkers, Hamilton contends, privilege linguistic performance to call into question any hierarchical and unified ordering of experience and reality. Postmodernism's location of the sublime within the fragmentary and discursive is the logical continuation of the Romantic project.

Like Hamilton, **Ross Woodman** locates Romanticism in the wider intellectual context of Western philosophy. In 'Nietzsche, Blake, Keats and Shelley: the making of a metaphorical body' (1990), Woodman reads the poetical invention of a vitally imaginative and metaphoric language in William Blake, John Keats, and P. B. Shelley through the philosophical lens of Friedrich Nietzsche. Woodman's article originally appeared in a special issue of *Studies in Romanticism* (Spring, 1990) that is dedicated to the subject of 'Nietzsche and Romanticism', edited and introduced by Tilottama Rajan (her own critical work is discussed below). The overall ethos of the volume assumes Nietzsche's implicit place in Romantic studies and demonstrates the centrality of Nietzschean ideas to the study of Romanticism. Woodman parallels Nietzsche's concept of the antagonistic Apollonian-Dionysian dynamic with the Romantic conflict between a fixed metaphysical logocentrism and a fluid metaphorical poetics. (For an alternative Nietzschean reading of Keats's *Hyperion* fragments, see the essay by Mark Sandy in Volume I.) Woodman's analysis of the 'metaphorical body' in Blake, Keats, and Shelley is explicitly Nietzschean in its handling of 'the difficulty faced by the poet's own effaced body in finding a metaphorical shape.'[3] In spite of his self-professed anti-Romanticism, Nietzsche's sense of how 'metaphor . . . perpetuates change itself by affirming ceaseless flow' (105) displays a similar Romantic tendency latent in his own thought.

As with his indictment of decadence, Nietzsche's alleged rejection of Romantic sensibility resuscitates (and prolongs) the continuation of

Romanticism. Blake's *Milton*, Keats's *The Fall of Hyperion*, and Shelley's *The Triumph of Life* generate a succession of poetic images and multiple perspectives that perform and anticipate Nietzsche's central ideas about language as a 'mobile army of metaphors, metonyms, anthropomorphisms'.[4] Poetic creation resists the rarefied abstraction of metaphysics and becomes a continual displacement of the bodily reality of suffering 'which in touch with chaos . . . is never allowed to harden into a system' (126). Blake, Keats, and Shelley share Nietzsche's conviction that metaphor 'is the proper and necessary displacement of both metaphysics and the body'. By pre-empting Nietzsche's affirmation of metaphorical flow over metaphysical stasis, these Romantic writings 'also locate Nietzsche himself in the romanticism he too hastily rejects' (132). These resonant echoes between Romantic literature and Nietzsche have produced diverse critical readings of Romantic figures and texts, ranging from Tilottama Rajan's *Dark Interpreter: The Discourse of Romanticism* (1980), to Harvey Birenbaum's *Between Blake and Nietzsche* (1991), and Mark Sandy's *Poetics of Self and Form: Nietzschean Subjectivity and Genre* (2005). For Woodman, a Nietzschean perspective clarifies apocalyptic episodes of *The Fall of Hyperion*, *Adonais*, and *The Triumph of Life*, episodes in which metaphor avoids becoming a fixed metaphysical discourse by suspending its own poetic language and action.

Attentive to the apocalyptic both as an 'end' to the design of history and a formal 'closure or completion' (137), **Seamus Perry**'s essay meditates on 'Coleridge's Millennial Embarrassments' (2000). Perry's approach strikes a fine balance between an appreciation of the 'historical experience' of Coleridge in the late 1790s and the 'formal features' (134) of the poetry that he wrote during the period. M. H. Abrams's thesis that millennial expectations became imaginatively internalised after the French Revolution provides a point of departure for Perry's consideration of the relations between the general historical mood and Coleridge's 'sense of a poem's end' (135). His speculations about the broader historical and theological context of Coleridge's poetry are equally informed by Frank Kermode's reflections on narrative closure and Walter Pater's assessment of Coleridgean aesthetics as 'a happily self-fulfilling prophecy' (137). Perry's central concern is how this 'apocalyptic teleology' and 'millennial frustration' lend to Coleridge's early poetry 'a distinctively checked or embarrassed quality both as to the self-possession of its form, and as to the authority of its meaning' (137).

Coleridge's 'youthful fondness for the sonnet' (139), Perry remarks, exhibits a confident self-belief in 'poetic effect' and 'an imagination dedicated to ending well'. Such confidence in the artistry of finishing a poem is disrupted by 'the obvious embarrassment of millennial expectation represented by the failure in France'. This uncertainty gives to Coleridge's attempts at poetic closure 'a sense of teleology without ending'. These attempts intimate a 'latent revelatory power' (141) that has 'no clear scheme of . . . providential arrangement' (140). 'The Lime-Tree Bower: My Prison' provides one such instance where, in spite of the implied significance of ordinary objects, the visionary is circumscribed and the poem remains at the level of 'a self-justifying act of looking' at the quotidian world. Foregrounding literary history over philosophy, Perry regards these partial numinous moments in Coleridge as anticipating 'the mysteriously suggestive particulars you find in the poetry of Auden' (142). In other poems, like 'Kubla Khan' and 'Westphalian Song', Coleridge unsettles mystical resolution or narrative closure through a playfully parodic framing of their endings. Often Coleridge's 'poetry of non-endings', including 'The Foster Mother's Tale' and 'Christabel', does 'not end, so much as stop' generating the irre-solution of 'uncertain speculation and possibility' (144). Many of Coleridge's poetic endings stage a collapse from providential heights to the contingent and prefigure Auden's mastery of 'a dying fall' (146). Coleridge's poetic treatment of closure seemingly characterises his poetry as ahead of its own time but, as Perry reminds us, these formal properties are the product of a 'transposition into poetic form of an epochal feel' (145–6).

Surveying the wider scene of British and European Romanticism in 'The return of the gods: Keats to Rilke' (1978), **Lawrence Kramer** believes that many Romantic meditations on the absence of a godly presence centre on the 'promise of an apocalyptic reunion of human life with its transcendental origins' (150). The theophanic form in Romantic writing, present in the work of Goethe, Hölderlin, Keats, Shelley, Heine, Rimbaud, Yeats, and Rilke, oscillates between a patiently hopeful invocation of the absent gods and the knowledge that this imagery of gods is redundant and belongs to a bygone age. Nonetheless, motifs of 'the returning gods are an essential element in the phenomenology of the Romantic imagination', and their role, as in Goethe's 'Parzenlied', is 'a measure of human inadequacy in the face of imaginative desire'. It is also often the case that when, as in Rilke and Rimbaud, these gods appear in a theophany (or showing forth of a god) they 'embody the assertion of imaginative power' (151), which is capable of transfiguring the experience of the observing subject, so that 'to see the god is to see *as* a god'. Regretfully, this naming or fixing of the presence of these gods is already to 'have lost the power their presence signifies' (152), as no divine presence can be contained within a poetic invocation.

Consequently, these Romantic theophanies, typified by Keats's 'Ode to Psyche', 'sway back and forth between actual despair and . . . prophetic rapture' (155), evoking divine absence through the immediately intangible presence of 'music, mist, and dream' (156). These images of an absent godly present are normally introduced to promote transcendence, but, invariably, they 'focus the poet's longing on the apocalyptic moment in which the gods are supposed to come forward' (158). Within the theophanic paradigm, the poet's desire for the return of the gods is expressed by cataloguing the gods' 'traditional attributes' (160) and a swerving away from those given attributes in order that the poet might lay claim to them. This aspect is evident in 'Ode to Psyche', where Keats's ritualistic naming of the goddess reflects 'the tropic pattern in theophanic poetry' of 'the necessity for the poet to bind a free or open figure to himself as a subject' (161). The close of 'Ode to Psyche' exemplifies this 'blend of alienation and reassurance' by projecting her theophany into futurity and recalling past vision. Unable to summon forth Psyche's presence in the Ode, Keats assigns her presence to a space 'beyond the borders of the poem' (163). Without the compensations of Wordsworthian memory, these invoked presences of the gods are disembodied and their invoked names are forgotten, unless, as in 'Ode to Psyche', 'the imagination can recover a lost vision by signifying that vision on the threshold of resumption' (166).

Such fascination with breathing new life into ancient mythology reveals the importance of Romantic Hellenism during the period. **Timothy Webb**'s chapter on this subject (1993) is reproduced here for its in-depth, wide-ranging grasp of a 'cultural and literary phenomenon whose existence is widely in evidence yet which remains elusive, problematic and difficult to define with inclusive rigor' (168). The effects of Romantic Hellenism were pervasive, evident in Shelley's *Prometheus Unbound* and *Hellas* (as well as his translations of Homer and Plato), Byron's *Childe Harold's Pilgrimage* and *Don Juan*, and in much of Keats's poetry. The 'interest in Greek art and literature' also manifests itself in the architecture of Neoclassicism, the furniture design of Chippendale (who combined Greek and Gothic with Oriental styles), John Flaxman's Grecian designs 'for the pottery of Thomas Wedgewood' (169), and the political, eventually military campaign for Greek independence from Turkish dominance. The range of these manifestations of Romantic Hellenism explains why it did not achieve 'articulation as a coherent philosophy' (168) or ideology. Early nineteenth-century interpretations of 'Greece or the Grecian model' (169) variously interpreted the similarities and differences between Greek society and the contemporary situation in England, appropriating the example of the ancient civilisation across a whole gamut of political causes from radical to conservative. Modern critical sensibility is alert to how Romantic Hellenism's 'positive achievements can now sometimes be seen less radiantly self-confident and more defiantly and precariously worked' (170) out by artists and writers. Recent book-length studies on this subject include Jennifer Wallace's *Shelley and Greece: Rethinking Romantic Hellenism* (1997) and David Ferris's *Silent Urns: Romanticism, Hellenism, Modernity* (2000).

Keats's 'The Fall of Hyperion', for instance, accentuates a discordant element in Romantic Hellenism and 'depicts a nightmare version of those peaceful Grecian temples pictured by Claude and Poussin' (172) in which the poet struggles to translate Greek mythology into a meaningful poetic form for his own turbulent times. Although Keats's contemporary, Percy Shelley, 'regarded the Greeks as the founders of much that was best in

Western civilisation', he was also 'well aware of the limitations of Athenian democracy' (173) and the inherent danger of translating 'the ancient Greeks into replications of ourselves' (173–4). Yet the Hellenising strain of 'Lines Written among the Euganean Hills' and 'Ode to Naples' caused even Shelley's social conscience, as Webb argues, to veer 'away from the facts of nineteenth-century urbanisation towards an idealized alternative where he can people with his wishes vacancy and oblivion' (175). In contrast to Shelley's idealism, Byron's demystification of Greek mythology through his 'decoding of the Greek language' and his insistence on having 'personal knowledge of [location of the] the plain of Troy' stressed the importance of an immediate and present 'empirical experience of Greece' (176). Unlike Keats or Shelley (who transferred their artistic and emotional commitment readily from Rome to Greece), Byron was passionate in his political allegiance to 'the ideal of Greek independence', but, in terms of literature, he was indebted to 'the examples of Horace and Virgil [which] had been largely discounted by Blake, Keats, and Shelley'. Such contradictions are typical of those 'conjunctions and configurations that mark the history of Romantic Hellenism' (179) as 'a vital and contentious site for the exercise of the contemporary imagination' (192) and disputatious critical interpretation.

These positive and negative responses to the Grecian model within Romantic Hellenism also provide another useful measure of the tension between faith and doubt in Romantic literature. This tension also finds expression as a fluctuation between aesthetic, religious, and political idealism and scepticism. In 'The Romantic calling of thinking: Stanley Cavell on the line with Wordsworth' (1998), **Edward Duffy** re-examines Wordsworth's engagement with the sceptical and the ordinary by reading Wordsworthian poetics through and, as the title's pun suggests, in alignment with the critical thinking of Stanley Cavell, the eminent Harvard aesthetician and philosopher. As a professional philosopher who is 'unguardedly drawn toward romantic texts', Duffy contends, Cavell provides a counter-example to Jerome J. McGann's admonishment that 'professional students of romantic literature must be more guarded against the seductive constructions of their subject' (195). Central to Cavell's account of the complex history of sceptical thought is an attempt to reach a 'diagnosis of how philosophical impositions of our thinking ... deaden us to the world delivered to us in our terms and conditions' (197). In this context, Duffy explains, Cavell conceives of Wordsworth, along with Thoreau and Emerson, as 'calling for a replacement or transfiguring of this ordinary' and routinely experienced 'world of death' (200) through an imaginative re-birth of interest in our actual existences and life.

Romanticism, for Cavell, is 'not some idealizing opium of the dispossessed' but a series of stern exemplars of the moral choices that human agency must make about 'an endless set of things, conditions, terms, histories and responsibilities which ... we have not manifestly lived up to' (205). In this account Romanticism is not, as McGann argues, 'a transcendental displacement of human desire' (quoted 205). Rather, it involves a carefully 'placed and constellated' expression of those desires in life that we have felt 'worthy of remarking and conceptualizing' (205). These claims are further substantiated by Duffy's reading of *The Prelude*'s 'spots of time' as enacting, through complex philosophical retrospection, primal scenes of loss in which Wordsworth as child foundling and grieving son (after his father's unexpected death) found 'emblems of unaccommodated humanity' (211). Wordsworth's remembered losses and disappointments interrupt the progress of his philosophising mind in the act of writing and re-sensitise him to the demands and desires of life and the living. As Duffy writes, 'Wordsworth's recounting of his founding experience of loss carries a recuperative power because at the iconically condensed finding of himself . . . there rings out as internal to this condition a call to go on beyond where he is in the taking of steps toward the finding and recovery of himself' (212). Such Wordsworthian 'spots of time' anticipate Cavell's own valorisation of the 'philosophical power of passiveness' (quoted 219). The early episodes of *The Prelude*'s 'fragmentary snapshots of unbidden memory' grow, for Duffy, into an Emersonian 'constitution of words' (quoted 216).

A similar philosophical adroitness is evident in **Tilottama Rajan**'s theoretically and poetically sensitive approach to the complexities of Romantic discourse. Like Woodman's earlier account, Rajan's essay finds Nietzsche to be a pivotal figure for articulating the interplay between idealism and scepticism in Romantic texts, and for analysing Romanticism's presentation of subjectivity at the level of the writer and reader. Her critical study, *Dark Interpreter: The Discourse of Romanticism* (1980), is concerned with the Romantic movement's deconstruction of its own idealist position. It draws explicitly on Nietzsche's Apollonian-Dionysian duality to demonstrate how '[t]he darker elements in Romantic works are not a part of their organic unity'[5]. Rajan's introductory chapter from the *Dark Interpreter* is represented here as an illustration of the intellectual breadth and subtlety of her critical approach. This approach is always respectful of 'the Romantic poet's sense of the limits of demystification as an attitude to life' (229).

Intelligently adapting the poststructuralism of Paul de Man and Jacques Derrida, and informed by the existentialism of Jean Paul Sartre, Rajan re-orientates critical investigations into 'the darker side of Romanticism' (227). She is sympathetic (see 225–8) to M. H. Abrams's view that Nietzsche's *The Birth of Tragedy* provides a vocabulary for expressing Romantic poetry's secularised version of 'a fall from primal unity into self-division, self-contradiction, and self-conflict as . . . [a] . . . first step along the way toward a higher unity'.[6] But whereas Abrams emphasised the drive to heal the spiritual or psychic rift between the harmonious and the chaotic, the Apollonian and the Dionysian, Rajan stresses irresolution, contradiction, and discord at work in the Romantic 'process of constant self-negation' (*DI*, 136). Still, Abrams's critical intimations of these discordant elements serves as Rajan's point of departure for her examination, through Schopenhauer and Nietzsche, of how Romanticism 'not only secularizes, but also *internalizes* innocence as a psychic defence' which can question its own status as a 'fictive projection of the sentimental consciousness' (232). This self-negating and self-questioning aspect of Romanticism is, for Rajan, an indication 'that the definitions of discourse developed by modern theorists such as Derrida, Heidegger, Sartre, and de Man can already be found in the work of certain Romantic theorists' (228). Rajan's continued interest in German Romantic theory and Romanticism's practical and theoretical strategies for presenting the subjectivity of the reader culminates in her second major study, *The Supplement of Reading: Figures of Understanding in Romantic Theory and Practice* (1990).

Part 10

Subjectivity, psychology, and sociology

Our final three essays in Volume IV, like others in all our volumes, are inter-disciplinary in approach. They interpret Romanticism's treatment of subjectivity as a complex spiritual and psychic site through a variety of fascinating psychological and sociological insights. These approaches often attend to the structural and generic properties of Romantic literature to demonstrate how literary form mirrors and maps the complicated contours of interiority and consciousness.

Karen Swann's article, ' "Christabel": the wandering mother and the enigma of form' (1984), places the construction of identity in relation to social, cultural, and literary conventions as central to her interpretation of Coleridge's poetic fragment. Reading 'Christabel' in conjunction with Burton's *The Anatomy of Melancholy*, Swann's account centres on Coleridge's elusive narrative as a dramatic presentation of hysteria, which teases out the paradox that cultural 'attribution of this condition to feminine bodies is a conventional hysterical response' (239). Christabel's encounter with the preternatural Geraldine and failure to recollect a traumatic event, according to Swann, conform to 'Burton's account of the characteristic symptoms of hysteria'. For Swann, however, the narration of these episodes by 'narrators who are as enigmatic as the women they tell about' and their 'participation . . . in the "feminine" exchanges they describe' keep alive the poem's 'playful suggestion that hysteria cannot be restricted to the *feminine* bodies' (241). Invariably, the narrators of 'Christabel' abandon 'an authoritative point of view' and become engaged hysterically with the present predicament of a character that they are supposed to be relating. The hysterical condition of these narrators perpetuates an atmosphere of fantasy and sets in motion a dream-logic which ensures that 'the reader is impotent to decide the poem's ambiguities from a position outside its fictions'. This disruption at the level of interpretation extends to the literary genre of 'Christabel' which blends stock Gothic conventions with elements of sentimental fiction to 'expose them as the means by which significance is produced and contained' (245); desire is constrained by patriarchal legislation.

Through Coleridge's challenge to his readers to categorise 'Christabel' within a particular genre, poetic and cultural forms emerge not simply 'as the arbitrary, contingent vessel of more enduring meanings' but, in fact, are 'the source and determinate meanings of all meanings, whether the subject's or the world's' (246). In terms of the gendered assumptions underlying cultural forms, 'Christabel' exposes the experience of 'manly authenticity' as a product of mere conventionality and the attribution of 'hysteria to feminine forms [as] a hysterical response to a more general condition' (247). More significantly, 'Christabel' calls into question how literary forms and cultural constructs are supposed to 'produce meaning for the subject' by limiting and controlling our experiences. Coleridge's poetic fragment engenders a state of hysteria within the reader by alerting his audience to the possibility that these regulating forms 'reproduce the indeterminacies they at first appear to limit or control' (249). This indeterminacy is manifest everywhere in Coleridge's narrative, from the ambiguous figures of Christabel and Geraldine to the uncertainty of the Baron's motivation, the enigmatic narratorial voices, and the disruptive poetic form. Read in terms suggested by Lacanian psychoanalysis, Coleridge's Preface underscores the poem's 'double relation to the symbolic order', the order, that, is of social control. Through Coleridge's 'joking treatment of gender and genre', the poem offers 'a compromise between the Law's reificatory strategies and the potentially wanton, disruptive liveliness of passion'. And yet this 'compromise' hints at a more radical insight for Swann: the suggestion that 'the Law itself may be inseparable from the operations of desire' (254) and, thus, subvert itself.

In 'Wordsworth and the language of the dream' (1979), **Mary Jacobus** shares with Swann a psychoanalytic concern about 'the process by which meaning is at once generated and unsettled in *The Prelude*'. The essay charts Wordsworth's poetic treatment, especially in the 'spots of time' episodes, of a movement from a state of '*anxiety* to *motion*, from *motion* to *spectre*, from there to *spectacle*, and finally back to *dream*' (260). Many of the early childhood episodes from *The Prelude* remain significant in Wordsworth's mature mind for their ability to engender a 'life-giving anxiousness' and for their evidence of imaginative activity in which 'the power of the child's anxiety . . . set[s] his imagination to work . . . creating spectral beings out of mountain winds' (263).

The spectral shades and indistinguishable shapes that haunt many of Wordsworth's passages speak of the poet's wish to represent the ineffable. Their shadowy presences become 'intimations of a ghostly life beyond the image which at once blocks it out and conjures it into being'. Such spectral forms are the by-product of Wordsworth's endeavour to monumentalise memory in writing. Wordsworth's chosen autobiographical form enacts how '[l]anguage inscribes loss; lack hollows being into desire; desire perpetuates itself in the symbolic articulations of language' (262). Although many of these spiritual apparitions, or dreams, are symbolic of an expectant ideal, Jacobus also identifies them with 'the "Dark Interpreter" of *Suspiria de Profundis*' (264). She reveals how Wordsworth's most sublimely idealised forms quickly turn into their nightmarish opposites. This process of 'double perception' (261), in which the dream recreates itself in inverted form, 'transforms the sublimely Christianized shepherd from the reflex of Wordsworth's ideal into its antithesis – the ghastly Discharged Soldier . . . the reified Blind London Beggar, or the Arab Quixote' (265). Like De Quincey's 'Dark Interpreter', these Wordsworthian spectres evade the censorship of consciousness to make their anxieties and desires manifest as spectacle in the 'dreamwork'. Conversely, when Wordsworth recalls 'that mingled threat and seduction to the imagination called London', he subsumes 'the spectacle [of the city] into spectrality' in order 'to admit its legitimate pleasures' (267). In *The Prelude*, Wordsworth draws on the power of language and dreams to 'estrange and transfigure' (259) as a means of inscribing non-presences into his retrospective account and as a defence against his own anxieties about non-being. Whether this inscription or psychic defence is apparent as a 'visionary or nightmarish' (260) reverie, Wordsworth's tireless literary (and bookish) allusions to works by Bunyan, Cervantes, Milton, and Pope, to name only a few, erect *The Prelude* as an 'inter-textual edifice' buttressed 'against the violations, seductions, and transformations enacted by the language of the dream' (279).

The last essay in this volume and set unfashionably yet convincingly celebrates coherence rather than splits and fractures. Demonstrating the continuity present in a complex intellectual career. **Thomas McFarland**'s article, 'Coleridge: prescience, tenacity and the origin of sociology' (1998), revises the current critical misconception that the intellectual life of a major Romantic thinker underwent chaotic, disordered and 'constant change'. This misunderstanding has arisen, McFarland suggests, because critics assume that 'the ruinous disintegration of [Coleridge's] personal existence' (299) can be read back into his intellectual habits as a thinker and theorist. McFarland substantiates this view with an example taken from a series of theological lectures given by Coleridge in 1795. The modern critic shows how the analogy between a child's love for its mother and humanity's relationship to God remained as a 'mental formulation' in Coleridge's thoughts until '1820 or later'. During this period of time Coleridge's analogy 'permuted and combined under constant reflection to eventuate in the most distinctive and vivid insistence of the entire *Opus Maximum*' (282). This provides a characteristic instance, McFarland claims, of how Coleridge's mind, sometimes over decades, exhibited an 'extreme ideational tenacity' and 'extreme prolongation of his intellectual attention' matched only 'by the depth of the philosophemes so retained' (284).

Coleridge's meditations on the effect that the behaviour of humans has upon other humans in society also bear 'witness [to] his cultural prescience and intellectual depth'; they 'incorporate the fundamental understanding by which alone the science of sociology is possible' (284). Coleridge's observations intimated important distinctions that could be made between individual and collective consciousness and anticipated areas of investigation conducted by 'the French school of sociologists' (285) that emerged in the 1890s, championed by Marcel Mauss and Emile Durkheim. McFarland demonstrates, through detailed comparison, how even the conclusions of the most mature and advanced work of Durkheim on the *Elementary Forms of the Religious Life* were foreshadowed by Coleridge's life-long reflections on the interaction of church and state. Other areas of Coleridge's writing and thought display a similar foresight, depth, and tenacity; for instance, 'the fundamental division between imagination and fancy . . . had a long provenance in Coleridge's ever-tenacious concern'. Coleridge's working out of his theory of the primary imagination occurred in a 'fifteen year period from 1802 to 1817' (296) and its elaboration was, in fact, 'a reshaping of his earlier preoccupation with necessitarian thought'. Even when Coleridge had intellectually outgrown the necessitarianism of Hartley, Priestley, and Godwin, he did not reject their theories wholesale but 'modified the applicability of their doctrine' and redirected 'their energy into his theory of imagination' (297). Coleridge's sustained interrogation of the doctrine of necessitarianism and his 'magisterial command of . . . Kant' emphatically attest to 'continuity [as] the hallmark of Coleridge's intellectual activity' (299) which has all but been forgotten owing to 'a heightened awareness of Coleridge's psychological desperation' (293). In every sense, McFarland reclaims Coleridge as a rare philosophical intelligence of and beyond his own personal, cultural, and intellectual circumstances.

Coleridge's intellectual prescience points to the importance of Romantic belief, thought, ideology, practice, and authority, all of which have been interpreted and reinterpreted both by contemporary and modern audiences. The vitality of Romantic studies, apparent in the present work, testifies to the rigour with which the literature of the period prefigures present-day hopes and anxieties about the self and the world. Although they were inevitably shaped by their own milieu, Romantic authors wrote for and into a future moment. Romanticism's way of entwining deeply held convictions with self-doubt invites and even anticipates positive and negative interpretations of its varied literary forms. Inheritors and disinheritors of the Romantic enterprise have their voice in our four volumes; cumulatively, they attest to Romanticism's contentious, heartening, and pervasive presence.

Notes

1 *Apocalypse and Millennium in English Romantic Poetry* (Oxford: Oxford University Press, 1999), p. 5.
2 Robert M. Ryan, *The Romantic Reformation: Religious Politics in English Literature, 1789–1824* (Cambridge: Cambridge University Press, 1997), p. 9.
3 Tilottama Rajan, Introduction 'Nietzsche and Romanticism', *Studies in Romanticism* 29 (1990): 7.
4 Friedrich Nietzsche, 'On Truth and Lie in the Extra-Moral Sense,' in *The Portable Nietzsche*. 1968. Edited and translated by Walter Kaufmann (Harmondsworth: Viking-Penguin, 1982), p. 46.
5 Tilottama Rajan, *Dark Interpreter: The Discourse of Romanticism* (Ithaca, NY: Cornell University Press, 1980), p. 19, hereafter *DI*.
6 *Natural Supernaturalism*, p. 255.

Part 9

BELIEF, PHILOSOPHY, AND MYTH

THE INTENSE INANE: RELIGIOUS REVIVAL IN ENGLISH, FRENCH, AND GERMAN ROMANTICISM: M. H. ABRAMS, WILLIAM EMPSON

Charles Rosen

Source: *Romantic Poets, Critics, and Other Madmen* (Cambridge, Mass.: Harvard University Press, 1998), pp. 31–50.

For the young who lived through it, the French Revolution remained a vision of a lost paradise. Chateaubriand was twenty-one in 1789, an impoverished aristocrat forced into the hosiery trade by his debts (when he wrote his memoirs, he omitted this shameful descent into commerce); he never forgot the exhilaration of that dawn when it was "bliss . . . to be alive, / But to be young was very heaven." More than thirty years later, he wrote about the beginning of the revolution in Paris:

> Moments of crisis produce in men a heightening of life. In a society dissolving and reconstructing itself, the struggle of two spirits, the collision of past and future, the mixture of old and new ways of life, make up an unstable compound that leaves no place for boredom. Liberated passions and dispositions reveal themselves with an energy they do not have in a well-ordered polity. The infraction of laws, the freedom from duty, from custom and from propriety, even the perils increase the excitement of the disorder. The human race on holiday takes a walk in the streets, delivered from its preceptors, restored for a moment to the state of nature, and realizing again the necessity of social restraint only when under the yoke of the new tyrants engendered by license. . . .
>
> I could not paint the society of 1789 and 1790 better than by comparing it to the architecture of the time of Louis XII and Francis I, when the Greek orders began to mingle with the gothic style, or

rather by equating it with the collection of ruins and tombs of every century, piled up pell-mell after the Terror in the Cloister of the Augustinian Minors: but the fragments of which I speak were living and varied endlessly. . . .

. . . duels and love affairs, friendships born in prison and the fraternity of politics, mysterious rendezvous among the ruins under a serene sky amidst the peace and poetry of nature, walks apart, silent, solitary, mingled with eternal vows and indefinably tender sentiments, against the muffled din of a world that was vanishing away, against the distant noise of a crumbling society, whose collapse threatened these felicities overshadowed by the events.

In these words there sounds an enduring nostalgia. It is the tone we hear today in the voices of many who were present at the riots of May, 1968, in Paris. They claim the same sense of excitement, of genuine fraternity between strangers in the streets ("here and there a face / Or person singled out among the rest, / Yet still a stranger and belov'd as such"), of enhanced vitality, of energy as eternal delight. The myth of the revolution will die hard. In 1968 the state of nature lasted only a few weeks: in 1789–1790 the redoubled intensity of life burned far more than a year. The betrayal of the revolution was a traumatic blow to the generation that had lived through it and was young enough to hope. These hopes had spread throughout Europe: for the century that followed, the brief glimpse of the possibility of happiness "in the very world, which is the world of all of us," the brief appearance of what Hazlitt called "romantic generosity" dominated politics and art.

In this state of nature that appears unexpectedly at the moment of total corruption and final dissolution, there is a strange innocence, an innocence regained. The human race on holiday has no premonition of the terror that will follow license: for a brief moment, men and women have found once more the grace and naiveté of the savage, of Adam before the Fall. The messianic program of the early Romantics,[1] a program in which politics and art cannot be separated or even distinguished, was to recapture and make permanent that state of nature which had proved to be so transitory.

After the failure, the betrayal even, of the political and social dream of 1789, the Romantic program presented itself in increasingly religious terms, with the Nazarene painters' revival of medieval imagery, the ecstatic cannib-alism of Novalis's vision of Christ's sacrifice, the vocabulary of mysticism that reappears in the poetry of Wordsworth and Coleridge, and the fiercely irrationalist religious and political philosophy of Joseph DeMaistre. It would be a mistake to characterize the religious "revival" of the early nineteenth century as specifically antirevolutionary; the revival had already taken place within the heart of the revolutionary movement, when, under Robespierre, one could be imprisoned for speaking disrespectfully of the deity.

The revolution, in short, had already betrayed itself in reinstating God. The religious language of the early Romantic writers, however, has a curious and ambiguous significance. Two recent and important books touch on this problem: William Empson's selection of Coleridge's verse, in which perhaps the greatest of our critics attempts to rescue Coleridge from priestcraft, and M. H. Abrams's *Natural Supernaturalism*, published in 1971, which deals with the survival and transformation of religious patterns of thought in the Romantic period.

M. H. Abrams, whose *Mirror and the Lamp* is one of the most influential books on the early nineteenth century, is a master of the themes of Romanticism. It is doubtful if anyone has surpassed, or that many have equaled, the range and depth of his reading. His point of departure in *Natural Supernaturalism* is Wordsworth's scheme for the great unfinished poem called *The Recluse*, a poem which was to crown the poet's work and to which the rest of his verse was to stand as chapels to the main body of a cathedral.

From the "Prospectus" Wordsworth wrote for *The Recluse*, Abrams isolates the concept of the spiritual resurrection of mankind by the marriage of nature to the mind of man. For Wordsworth, mind or spirit here has become largely secular: God appears—if at all—only as *within* man's mind, and Abrams recalls a rich seventeenth-century tradition that resists any attempt to place God outside ourselves (the writings of Gerard Winstanley, the leader of a Digger community in Cromwell's time, are particularly striking in their apparent similarity to Blake and Wordsworth). The wedding of man and nature is seen by Abrams as achieving its full meaning as a manifestation of the millennium, a vision of the apocalypse secularized into revolution, but he characterizes this union with nature as a consolation and a substitute for the shattered revolutionary dream.

From here, Abrams is concerned chiefly with Romantic metaphors of alienation—of man from nature, of man from himself. The marriage of nature to the mind of man is a metaphor for the overcoming of this inner and outer division. The most persistent metaphor Abrams finds is that of the "circuitous journey," the vision of a regained paradise, a return through alienation to an original state of "organic" unity, now made transcendent by incorporating and resolving the contradictory forces of the journey itself. The circle is therefore generally a spiral, a return to the same point on a higher level. As the mature mind, in Wordsworth, returns to the child's unconscious acceptance of the world, now transformed by experience, so Hegel's spirit in reaching absolute consciousness attains the static condition, the complete repose of pure, undifferentiated, unalienated being. The juxtaposition of Hegel's *Phenomenology of Mind* with Wordsworth's *Prelude* is perhaps the most brilliant detail of Abrams's book.

The image of the circuitous journey is, indeed, pervasive and persistent. Abrams does not discuss Romantic natural science, but the metaphor has its power there as well. J. W. Ritter, a young scientist who discovered ultraviolet rays and belonged to the Jena circle of the Schlegels and Novalis, delivered a talk to the Munich Academy of Science in 1809 entitled "Physics as Art." He presented the original state of the earth as totally organic, and the present division into organic and inorganic matter as a late and degenerate condition. The earth has died, and the mineral veins of the earth are picturesquely the fossil remains of its former living skeleton. The task of physics is twofold: historical (the reconstruction of the decline into the present state) and apocalyptic (the retransformation of all matter into living organic form). Ritter was curiously enough both a serious scientist who did important work in galvanism and a brilliant, poetic, and erratic writer.

If anything, the image is too pervasive. It cannot be said to define Romantic thought if it characterizes so much else, including *Candide*, that masterpiece of the Enlightenment which is said to represent everything that Romanticism opposed. Like Wordsworth's *Prelude* and Goethe's *Wilhelm Meister*, *Candide* is a *Bildungsroman*, a novel of intellectual development and progress toward maturity, and the garden that Candide cultivates at the end is as much the earthly paradise—the Garden of Eden found again and transformed by experience—as any of Abrams's examples. It is also a "return": Constantinople is not Westphalia, but then Wordsworth's Grasmere is not Cockermouth; nevertheless, the little society of Thunder-ten-Tronckh is reconstituted. Doctor Pangloss philosophizes as before, and Candide is reunited with Cunégonde, grown ugly and ill-tempered but able to cook splendid pastry.

Are the patterns of Romantic thought, as Abrams believes, theological or even religious? These terms can be used loosely. Some years ago Carl Becker's *Heavenly City of the Eighteenth-Century Philosophers* found these same apocalyptic patterns in Voltaire and Helvétius. The influence of eschatology on Marx and of Old Testament morality on Freud are an essential part of the middle-brow vulgarization of these authors. We should be accustomed by now to posthumous attempts to convert the heathen. Nevertheless, if these patterns are to be found wherever one looks (as Abrams finds them from Saint Augustine to Proust), it may be that they are forms deeper or more general than theology, which has used them—as have poetry and science— as part of a repertory of expression.

Abrams, however, has precedent for his view from the Romantics themselves. Wordsworth, for example, spoke easily of "such religious feelings as cannot but exist in the minds of those who affect atheism." This generous view of the meaning of "religious" is found often enough today, if only because the more precise and rigorous sense has come to seem unbearable to so many. But the significance of the early Romantics' use of religion can only be assessed if we measure it against each poet's relation to religion and morality proper—organized, established, or at least traditional.

The extent of the problem may be indicated by the following lines from Benjamin Constant's diary of 1804, when he was in Weimar with Mme. de Stael:

Goethe: Difficulty of all conversation with him. What a pity that he has been caught up in the mystic philosophy of Germany. He confessed to me that the basis of this philosophy was Spinozism. Great idea that the mystic followers of Schelling have of Spinoza, but why try to bring in religious ideas and what is worse, Catholicism? They say that Catholicism is more poetical. "I would rather have Catholicism do evil," says Goethe, "than be prevented from using it to make my plays more interesting."

Goethe has still the grand cynicism of the eighteenth century; a few months later Constant notes about August Wilhelm Schlegel:

... strange system of Schlegel who regrets a religion in which he does not believe, and who believes that one can remake a religion once it has fallen.

As for Friedrich Schlegel, he wrote, "To have religion is to live poetically": the violent dislocation of the concepts of both religion and poetry is evident. Coleridge considered himself deeply religious, and called Wordsworth "at least a semi-atheist," whatever that may mean; but the dirtiest word in Coleridge's vocabulary was "priest," and he included in that category all Protestant (as well as Catholic) ministers who assumed the role of religious *authority.*

Most of the early Romantics came from conservative, Protestant, Pietistic families, from which they derived much of their language and imagery and their views of the world. Their magnification of the purely inward, personal elements in Pietism was turned not only against the "atheistic" Enlightenment—they were all deeply influenced by Hume and Voltaire—but against their own background as well. Their early reading in seventeenth-century mystics like Jakob Boehme provided them with ammunition in this battle on two fronts. The mystical philosophy of the seventeenth century had often been conceived as an attack on organized religion and even as part of a program of social and economic reform. (For example, Winstanley's refusal to accept any Christ outside the inward Christ that was in each man's heart was inextricably bound up with his revolutionary movement to seize the common land of England and turn it over to the poor.) Abrams is right to maintain that the Romantic poets' need of a theological vocabulary was independent of their religious creed or lack of one, but the meaning of that vocabulary cannot be understood except through its relation to organized religion and society.

Empson, on the other hand, is very much concerned with Coleridge's social and religious thought, above all with the changes that his religious creed underwent during his lifetime. Empson is a large-spirited critic, and it pains him to see his poet gradually succumb to the horrors of orthodoxy. To restore Coleridge to himself, Empson and his co-editor, David Pirie, have rewritten the *Ancient Mariner*. Except at one place, they have not actually changed any of Coleridge's words, but they have produced a text that does not look precisely like any of the different versions that Coleridge published. In a way, this serves Coleridge right: he had himself proposed a selection of the great English poets rewritten by himself as a great improvement over the originals; and when he was asked to translate Goethe's *Faust*, he considered whether he should remodel it, adding that it would be even "more easy to compose the whole anew."

Empson and Pirie have divided the changes that Coleridge made to his poem of 1798 into two parts: those that merely refine and clarify the original conception, and those that seriously alter it, and even conceal it behind a smoke screen of Christian allegory. In other words, for Empson, Coleridge afterward "ratted on the poem" and tried to pretend that it was about something else, just as he spent the later part of his life insisting that he had never been a "Jacobin" revolutionary. There are, indeed, serious cuts in the 1800 version of the poem, and the marginal glosses of 1817 give an interpretation based on sin and redemption through suffering that is gravely at odds with the text of 1798. Empson believes that redemption by torture is wicked, and that for God to redeem the human race by torturing His son is even more shockingly wicked; the Coleridge of 1798 and even later was enthusiastically and courageously of the same opinion and risked his career and his livelihood for this belief.

Empson and Pirie's treatment of the text may be high-handed, but any edition with variant readings invites every reader to form just such a text for himself. In their great edition of the *Prelude*, de Sélincourt and Darbishire called upon the reader to form his "ideal text" from the material they provided. However, it is not, strictly speaking, the "ideal" text that Empson and Pirie seek, but the one truest to the original idea of the poem.

Their search implies an idealistic (and Romantic) view of literature in which none of the various stages of the text is the poem itself, but only approaches to it. This is indeed the only coherent view that permits genuinely interpretative criticism. (Only a sacred text cannot be otherwise than it is, and when the form has become totally rigid, the meaning becomes unattainable—i.e. untranslatable and unparaphrasable—and the possibility of interpretation is either zero [the text is a magic formula] or multiplies uncontrollably.) The poem is the idea (Coleridge would have put a capital I) which the text seeks to realize, and which the text may therefore betray and falsify as well as reveal.

This idea of the poem is placed by Empson squarely in the poet's mind, and he equates it with the poet's intention, which is partially misleading. Coleridge knew better when he put the capital I: the poet's intention is itself only an approach to the idea.[2] Empson has (in an earlier essay[3] on the

Ancient Mariner) exploded his own position with an irresistible joke about "four times fifty living men . . . , They dropped down one by one," when he wrote, "I do not believe that there were two hundred of them; Coleridge or the Mariner invents this number to heighten the drama of their all dying at once." As usual Empson is right, four times fifty is clearly an exaggeration, and it is impossible and irrelevant to decide whether the author or the poem is inflating the figure.

Empson treats Coleridge's betrayal of his poetry with generosity and sympathy, and he is wonderfully free of the pious moral airs expressed by recent critics faced with Coleridge's weaknesses. Opium, cowardice, plagiarism, and procrastination make a formidable array, but they seem to have touched Coleridge's nobility of spirit very little in the end. For Empson, indeed, the theme of the *Ancient Mariner* is the very reason that Coleridge betrayed the poem and tried to convince his readers and himself that it was about something else. The theme is a sense of guilt and revulsion from life greater than any possible motivation. The disparity between the shooting of the albatross and the subsequent horrors visited upon the Mariner and the crew is the most terrifying aspect of the poem.

When the Mariner is able for a moment to conquer his disgust for the slimy creatures of the deep and to bless them, it is not true that "at once the terrible spell snaps," as Abrams writes in the wake of the majority of critics. The relief is only temporary when the albatross hung round his neck slides off into the sea and the Mariner is able to pray. Greater penance is still to be exacted from the Mariner, as Empson points out, and even more terrible horrors are to appear. There is never, in fact, any final release: the Mariner is condemned to tell his story obsessively over and over again without obtaining absolution. The poem affirms ambiguously the love that should unite all creatures of the universe and the irrational terror of being unable to sustain and meet that love. Almost as much as anything else, the *Ancient Mariner* warns us of the awesome consequences of religious guilt, and it is in this sense a deeply antireligious poem.

The religious imagery and language of the *Ancient Mariner* are, of course, essential and even obsessive. But Abrams stands things on their heads when he writes:

> The *Ancient Mariner* is neither an allegorical fable nor a symbolist poem. The persistent religious and moral allusions, however, both in the text and in the glosses which Coleridge added to assist the bewildered readers of the first unpublished version, invite us to take the Mariner's experience as an instance of the Christian plot of moral error, the discipline of suffering, and a consequent change of heart.

The Christian plot is not an inward meaning, it is the outer shell. The poem uses religious semi-Christian, semi-pagan narrative patterns openly, and invites us to read into them feelings of a different order. As Coleridge himself wrote about the poem, he treated the supernatural characters "so as to transfer from our inward nature a human interest and a semblance of truth sufficient to procure for these shadows of imagination that willing suspension of disbelief for the moment which constitutes poetic faith."[4] It is to Coleridge's conception of "our inward nature" that the reader's attention is drawn, and to this end the religious images are drained of their specifically religious content and filled with something new.

This is the process of secularization with which Abrams's book deals, and he is deeply aware of its presence without, however, being able to elucidate its action. That is because he appears to claim for his theological forms and images a fundamental and inalterable meaning—a significance which remains constant even when they are reformulated in radically different contexts. What the Romantics discovered, however, was the possibility of stripping forms of their original significance and of giving them a new sense almost diametrically opposed to the original (as Tieck, for example, begins a play with the epilogue).

What they looked for was the tension between the new meaning and the inevitable residue of the old. This was the tension that enabled the Romantics to carry out their program of reconceiving art and literature as a dynamic and endless process that was to reach a static and resolved form only at the point of infinity. For "point of infinity" read "God," and for "God"—as far as that word was given a specific meaning by the Romantics —read nothing more than the immediate use that each writer might have at the moment for Him: the resolution of the dynamic process of life, the realm of the unconscious and the unknowable, humanity realizing itself as absolute Mind, and so forth. In this way, Hegel can be an atheist who talks freely about God and identifies Christ not with Jesus but with Napoleon-Hegel. This free use of language enables Wordsworth to change his religious beliefs over the years without finding the need to alter their expression except in minor details.

The fundamental importance of Spinoza for this period provides an example of these shifts of meaning. For most of the eighteenth century Spinoza was simply an atheist. If you were accused of atheism yourself (as Pierre Bayle and Voltaire were), you could always set up a splendid smoke screen with a violent attack on Spinoza. The break came in 1785 when the German philosopher Jacobi disclosed the great critic Lessing's secret Spinozism. By the last decade of the century, Spinoza had completely changed from an atheist to a "God-intoxicated" philosopher, and it is a question who had been converted, Spinoza or God. To some extent, the religious revival was only a further secularization.

Abrams, nevertheless, views the Romantic movement as a rescue operation, an attempt to salvage the debris of religion torn apart by science and the Enlightenment, to conserve the lost values of religion while giving them an acceptably secular form. "Much of what distinguishes writers I call 'Romantic' derives from the fact that they undertook, whatever their religious creed or lack of creed, to save traditional concepts, schemes and values which had been based on the relation of the Creator to his creature and creation,[5] but to reformulate them within the prevailing two-term system of subject and object, ego and non-ego, the human mind or consciousness and its transactions with nature." But if writers from Goethe to Proust used theological values to save them, what are we to make of the beautiful quotation from Proudhon that Abrams cites?

> [I am] forced to proceed as a materialist, that is to say, by observation and experience, and to conclude in the language of a believer, because there exists no other; not knowing whether my formulas, theological despite myself, ought to be taken as literal or figurative. . . .

(The theological formulas have here been reduced to the status of nouns and verbs, and the process by which they were so neutralized is one of the most revolutionary in the history of style.)

The Romantics inclined often enough to Abrams's view of their work, but what they performed was more often than not a wholesale act of seizure and destruction. Blake's little child contrasts the warm ale-house with the cold church, and says:

> But if at the church they would give us some ale
> And a pleasant fire our souls to regale, . . .

The word "soul" has been almost totally expropriated in order to affirm its absolute identity with the body: yet the meaning of "soul" depended traditionally upon a radical opposition with the body. Blake is not conserving a traditional theological concept but destroying one that his hated many-headed monster, Voltaire-Newton-Gibbon, had been powerless to touch. It cannot be said that Novalis, Hölderlin, and Wordsworth (at least before 1807) were less radical than Blake.

The belief that an earlier concept can remain essentially unchanged in a later reformulation of it is the original sin of the history of ideas. It is especially unfortunate as an approach to the early Romantics, who were the first to insist so fully upon the inseparability of thought and expression. (Language and thought, said Friedrich Schlegel, must in theory be distinguished, but in practice we can only do so when one of them malfunctions.)

Abrams *expounds* ideas in Romantic poetry that lose all vitality when reduced to plain prose that cats and dogs can read. He outlines the concepts of alienation and reconciliation with nature as they were derived from a long theological tradition by Wordsworth and Coleridge, which he believes still useful today, and adds: "These ideas are shared in our time by theologians, philosophers, economists, sociologists, psychologists, writers, critics and readers of *Life* magazine and the *Readers Digest*. . . ." What a crew! Abrams's tone is ironic, but the irony is sadly aimed at the rejection of ideas so universally admired instead of at the reduction of Wordsworth, and us, to so common a denominator.

However vulgar the romantic notion of alienation could become, it was not that of the popular twentieth-century evangelist—and I do not mean to imply that Abrams does not know this, but only that his thesis of Saint Augustine, Wordsworth, and the bereft readers of *Life* reaching out to each other over the ages will not permit him to express it. Alienation played a large role in Romantic thought and it is finally expanded so far as to destroy itself. From Rousseau the early Romantics inherited the idea that self-consciousness is a disease, an alienation of oneself from oneself, a loss of unity. This view of self-reflection was most powerfully delineated in 1794 by Fichte, who influenced all the German and (through Coleridge) the English writers of the turn of the century. As Abrams points out, they regarded "philosophical reflection, the very act of taking thought, . . . as in itself, in Schelling's words, 'a spiritual sickness.'"

This division of the self is, indeed, a fall from grace; the act of reflection is the knowledge of good and evil. But Abrams does not carry it far enough. For Fichte, the ego (the self) does not *exist* except as the act of self-alienation, and comes into being only at the moment of the act. I can be myself only in so far as I am aware of myself as something distinct from the totally subjective, only as my own mind takes a part of itself as an object; otherwise there is no "I." The Fall from grace continuously re-enacted at every moment is the condition of life. Alienation, for Fichte and for Coleridge, is synonymous with existence.

When the concept of alienation is expanded illimitably—is made *absolute*, to use the Romantic term, then the status of the impulse to heal the division, to integrate the ego with itself and with Nature, is threatened. If alienation can be seen as existence itself—the continuous effort to be what one is, to affirm the "I" as distinct from everything else, integration becomes death. In E. T. A. Hoffmann's *Princess Brambilla*,[6] there is a ministerial council meeting at which the treasury of wit is to be replenished for a time of need. The king makes his contribution: "The moment in which a man dies is the first in which his true ego arises," and he drops dead at once.

This is the ambiguity at the heart of the "circuitous journey"; the lost paradise regained is death. Abrams interprets the end of Hölderlin's *Hyperion* as a renewal of joy and life. When the hero gives himself up to Nature after his defeat, his rejection by his father, and the death of his love, that is indeed how Hyperion himself appears to present it. Yet his reconciliation with nature and his new-found joy have a secret and bitter despair:

And yet once more I looked into the cold night of men and shuddered, and wept for joy that I was so blessed, and I spoke words, it seemed to me, but they were like the rushing sound of a fire that flares up and leaves ashes behind.

As Geoffrey Hartman has recently written about a similar identification of the self with Nature by Coleridge: "Nothing is lost by this sublimation except all."[7] Abrams recognizes in *Hyperion* the inevitable return of alienation after this "renewal," but in trying to impose on it his theological doctrine of redemption and resurrection,[8] he does not see that the resurrection itself is a new form of death.

Abrams also omits as irrelevant all mention of the explicitly ironic Romantics like Byron and E. T. A. Hoffmann; but their comic sense is not an aberration from the Romantic tradition but an illumination of patterns implicit in Hölderlin and Wordsworth. Hoffmann's ebullient and fatuous young cat Murr shows how "alienation" can be made to signify almost anything one wants. When he meets his long-lost mother ("come to my paws," she cries) he goes to get her a herring-head he has hidden after dinner. On the way back he gets hungry, but relates this pedantically in the language of Romantic idealistic philosophy: "My ego was alienated from my ego in a strange way so as to remain still my ego and I ate the herring-head."

Alienation is here the instinct for life. In the ironic movement necessary to Romantic art—to Wordsworth as to Byron, to Novalis as to Hoffmann— the "suspension of disbelief" is never a completed act of integration. We accept the supernatural without believing it, we allow what is strange to keep its alien identity, "a stranger and belov'd as such." It is not unity and reintegration, not the return to the lost paradise that is sought, but division and estrangement. In fact the early Romantics conceived the act of poetry as essentially a technique of alienation: for Novalis, it is the power of making the familiar distant and strange; for Coleridge, the "power of giving the interest of novelty by the modifying colors of the imagination."

The uncontrolled expansion of concepts until they referred potentially to everything and therefore to nothing so that their powers of association were completely liberated and magnified was a process repeated until it could seem like a vulgar and maddening trick. "Irony is the form of paradox. Paradox is everything that is both good and great" (Friedrich Schlegel), "Thinking is speaking. Speaking and doing or making are only modifications of one and the same operation" (Novalis), "Truth is Beauty, Beauty Truth" (Keats)—examples are numberless. This technique of expansion contributed to the instability of meaning that made Byron compare the philosophy of August Wilhelm Schlegel to a rosy and agreeable mist cast over everything. But it is a trick based upon a profound comprehension of speech, a realization that there is no possibility of authentic and direct communication without some looseness, some play in the mechanism of language.

This new freedom in the use of meaning is the revolutionary achievement of the early Romantic generation, the men who turned twenty at the time of the French Revolution. "The situation is overripe and stinking and needs to be shaken up," the great linguist and philologist Wilhelm von Humboldt wrote about the contemporary state of poetry, and he tentatively praised the efforts of the Schlegels and Novalis to revolutionize art. "I do not like what they are doing ... but they are the only hope we have." For Hazlitt, the poetry of Wordsworth and Coleridge was the literary analogue to the French Revolution,[9] and he remarked on an amusing image that the infrequency of personification in the poetry of the new school compared with that of Pope and Johnson was a reluctance to bestow the undemocratic dignity of a capital letter.

The newly released power of association created by the whole or partial destruction of the central meaning of words made possible the nonsense verse of *Kubla Khan* and the late poems of Novalis. Empson convincingly says that *Kubla Khan* is about the role of the artist as conqueror, as spokesman for the unconscious desires of his society. But Empson oddly refuses to see the importance of presenting this theme as if it were a vision, as a kind of involuntary nonsense. Coleridge was not, as Empson claims, pretending that he did not know what the poem was about when he added his introductory explanation of the interrupted attempt to write down his dream. *Kubla Khan* is the great Romantic example of the fragment, the created ruin, and the "person on business from Porlock" who broke into Coleridge's inspiration is an essential part of the work. Coleridge's achievement is like a realization of Novalis's contemporary program for writing poems and stories "without sense or logic, but only with associations like dreams or music."

What then was the use of religious frames of thought to men who could be atheists or, like Coleridge when he wrote his great poems, so little a Christian that he refused to accept even Unitarian doctrine? Why did they persist in using religious terms which they often rendered so vague as to accommodate any meaning? A letter of 1803 by Wilhelm von Humboldt may suggest an answer. He wrote about the interrelationship, the "belonging-together" of all intellectual beings, not in a single totality but in

> a unity in which all concept of number, all opposition of unity and
> multiplicity disappears. To call this unity God would be absurd,
> I find, as it throws it outside of the self for no good reason.

This unity which itself swallows up the concept of unity is an explicit image of infinity. Humboldt settles for calling this infinity "Humanity" instead of "God" after rejecting "Universe," "World," and "World-Soul." (It is extraordinary how he could try out different words as if they were hats.)

Most of the Romantics called it "God" without hesitation. The fund of religious imagery and concepts provided a copious (and, at worst, a cheap) source of "innumerable analogies and types of infinity."

This is Wordsworth's phrase for the fundamental virtue of Romantic style; in another place, where he explains the significance of his images, he calls them the "types and symbols of eternity." It is for his generation the basic figure of speech, or, better, figure of thought, since the old rules of rhetoric had been dissolved in a more generalized and fluid concept of language. *Type* and *symbol* (or *analogy*) are not synonymous for Wordsworth: although *type* had still the old meaning of "emblem" or "symbol," it already meant example or model.[10] Images like

> The immeasurable height
> Of woods decaying, never to be decay'd,
> The stationary blasts of waterfalls

are both examples (metonymies) of eternity and metaphors for the secret invariance at the heart of constant mutability. They are therefore examples of what they themselves signify by analogy, embodying that contradiction that Coleridge saw as essential to every symbol, which "partakes of the reality which it renders intelligible . . . abides itself as a living part in that unity of which it is the representative." Such types and symbols of eternity are like the

> . . . Yew tree, pride of Lorton Vale,
> Which to this day stands single, in the midst
> Of its own darkness

These types of infinity are images of freedom. The early Romantic's battle against atheism was essentially against the new authoritarian, religious tyranny of mechanistic thought. The Infinite was a medium in which the imagination could allow for the free expansion of associations, dreams, music—all that the calculating mind held senseless. Yet the early Romantic Infinite is illuminated by the light of common day. As the French émigré Étienne de Sénancour wrote in 1804:[11]

> Love is condemned as a completely sensual affection, having no other principle than an appetite that is called gross. But I see nothing in our more complicated desires of which the true end is not one of the primary physical needs: sentiment is only their indirect expression: Intellectual Man was never anything else than a phantom. Our needs awaken in us the perception of their positive object, *as well as the innumerable perceptions which are analogous to them.* The direct means would not fill life by themselves, but these accessory impulses occupy it fully, *because they have no limits.*

31

The metaphorical activity (the "analogous perceptions") is life itself and cannot be limited or fully determined: the medium of its action is God, to employ the Romantic significance of this much used word. It is in this medium that the individual ego which is only an abstraction rejoins the unconscious and the involuntary that the poets realized they had to master. To this end they abandoned a specific and limited kind of control over meaning to look for a more efficient way of commanding the marginal phenomena of significance that the eighteenth century had appeared to renounce.

That God is the unconscious of humanity is explicit in Wordsworth (although we must be careful not to read back into him Freudian or Jungian meanings). In some lines, unpublished until 1925, he dismisses both passive and active forms of consciousness:[12]

> Such consciousnesses seemed but accidents
> Relapses from the one interior life
> In which all beings live with god, themselves
> Are god, existing in the mighty whole
> As indistinguishable as the cloudless east
> Is from the cloudless west, when all
> The hemisphere is one cerulean blue.

Wordsworth never printed these daring lines written when he was producing his finest poetry: perhaps he would not have subscribed to them some years later. In these lines, the ego is dissolved in the interior life, which is in no sense an individual unconscious: it is the interior life of all beings, and God is here an image of fraternity as well as liberty.

These images of infinity had therefore a political significance as well. When the ideals of the revolution were corrupted, the political vocabulary became corrupt too: to use it without irony was to support betrayal on every front. The vocabulary of mysticism and religion offered refuge, but only briefly. The old traditional meanings soon returned. By 1810 most of the early Romantic writers had abandoned their mixture of free-thinking and mysticism and moved toward orthodoxy.

This is, no doubt, a coarse view of a history that needs more caution, greater reserve: it is offered as a corrective to a portrayal of the early Romantics as hopeful and optimistic. Their poetry is the greatest poetry of despair that survives today, the greatest because entirely untouched by resignation. The messianic revolutionary ideals are kept alive in the hyperbolic language of mysticism because they had been proven hopeless to a generation that refused to accept their final defeat. Not until the 1830s did one find the poignant and melancholy resignation of Tennyson or the magnificent and fatuous optimism of Hugo. The writing of the early Romantics could be sustained for only a brief time; they died young like Novalis, lost courage like Coleridge and Wordsworth, went mad like Hölderlin, or became apologists of the most reactionary regime in Europe like Friedrich Schlegel. The fundamental aesthetic doctrine of the Romantics is an identity of work and life: their failure is already acted out within their poetry.

Notes

Originally written in 1973 as a review of M. H. Abrams, *Natural Supernaturalism: Tradition and Revolution in Romantic Literature* and William Empson and David Pirie, eds., *Coleridge's Verse: A Selection.*

1 By "early Romantic" I mean simply the men who did most of their important work between 1795 and 1815: e.g., Blake, Wordsworth, and Coleridge in England; in Germany the poet Hölderlin, the philosopher Fichte, the critic and philologist Friedrich Schlegel, the poet and philosopher Novalis, the novelists Ludwig Tieck and E. T. A. Hoffmann (the last a half generation later than the others); and, in France, Chateaubriand and Sénancour, author of that bible of French Romanticism, *Obermann* (1804), and the novelist Benjamin Constant. Beyond the fact that certain statements can be made about all of them, I have not found it necessary to assume here that they formed a movement or created a style, nor shall I try to clarify the relations among them.

2 The poet's understanding of his inspiration is not privileged: this is perhaps the oldest critical tradition we have, going back to Plato. For Plato, the poet was the last man to be able to explain his own work. This paradox was already understood then as a hard nut to crack, but essential to literature. But Empson is right to claim what we can reconstruct of the poet's intention as evidence for the meaning of his work. For all Empson's sniping at the Intentional Fallacy (which means largely that the main evidence for the meaning of a poem is the text, whatever the poet may have had in mind), he has a conception of intention grand enough to accommodate any theory of interpretation.

3 *The Critical Quarterly*, 1964.

4 *Biographica Literaria*, Chapter XIV.

5 One of the dogmas of Christianity that Wordsworth disliked most of all was that God created the universe. At least, he felt that one shouldn't talk about it, probably because it was the only thing about God that Voltaire believed.

6 See the comment on this passage by Paul de Man, "The Rhetoric of Temporality," in *Interpretation, Theory and Practice*, Charles S. Singleton, ed. (Johns Hopkins University Press, 1969).

7 "Reflections on the Evening Star," in *New Perspectives on Coleridge and Wordsworth*, Geoffrey Hartman, ed. (Columbia University Press, 1972).

8 Readers are warned by Hölderlin in a preface that if they reads the book for the doctrine they will not understand it.

9 Hazlitt saw this aspect of the poem more clearly than Empson when he said that he could repeat certain lines of *Kubla Khan* forever with delight without knowing what they meant.

10 In spite of the OED, which dates this use much later, English-French glossaries give the meaning "example" as early as 1815. Wordsworth generally uses "type" as an element in a pair ("types and symbols," "type or emblem"), and it is kinder to him to believe it is not always a tautology.

11 *Obermann*, eighth year, Letter LXIII.

12 *The Prelude*, Ernest de Sélincourt and Helen Darbishire, eds. (Oxford University Press, second ed., 1959), p. 535.

52

APOCAPOLITICS: ALLUSION AND STRUCTURE IN SHELLEY'S *MASK OF ANARCHY*

Morton D. Paley

Source: *Huntington Library Quarterly* 54 (1991), 91–109.

The Mask of Anarchy occupies a curious place in the modern criticism of Shelley's poetry. It has been praised as uncharacteristic of Shelley's work by F. R. Leavis,[1] admired for its political content by Richard Holmes,[2] and ignored by Harold Bloom and by Earl Wasserman in their influential studies.[3] There will always of course be disagreement as to the worth of a particular poem, but perhaps most striking in this instance are the reservations expressed by some of those who have written about *The Mask* with the greatest degree of interest. For Thomas R. Edwards, "it is a fine poem, in its earlier parts very nearly a great one," but the clash of attitudes between what Edwards sees as Shelley's "overt political intentions" and his "lurking despair about politics" makes the result a demonstration of "how a certain kind of poetic imagination can damage its own admirable concern for the public world."[4] Although Richard Hendrix takes issue with this conclusion, praising *The Mask*'s "blend of dramatic form . . . with political insight and populist attitudes," he concedes that "the blend was imperfect."[5] Michael Scrivener, who has illuminatingly discussed *The Mask* in relation to popular radical iconography, finds the poem "contradictory, at war with itself, not entirely resolved"; and Stephen C. Behrendt finds in it an "ambivalence of voice [that] is potentially dangerous, for the poem implicitly condones a variety of the violence it explicitly condemns."[6] I suggest that these positive but uneasy views are responses to something deeply embedded in the structure of *The Mask of Anarchy*: the relationship between apocalypse and millenium.

The program of *The Mask of Anarchy* might be described as a rewriting of the book of Revelation in terms of the politics of England in 1819. As Carl Woodring puts it, this poem treats the mode of prophetic dream—vision as apocalypse, a final uncovering and revelation, at first of horror and then of what horror hides. This sequence follows the movement of Revelation from the seven-headed beast empowered by the great red dragon to the victory and marriage of the lamb.[7]

According to this agenda, apocalypse should be followed by the millennial descent of the New Jerusalem, and so it is in what is by far the longest section of the poem. However, the apocalyptic element in the poem comprises a transformation of events actually occurring while the millennial one consists of a future imagined as possible. Each demands and receives a different poetic mode, and although a brilliant transition is made from one to the other, one is left with the disquieting sense that this sequence may not be inevitable.

Shelley's title introduces a sense of ironical inversion characteristic of the poem and especially of the parts I shall call the Triumph and Agon. Shelley knew what a masque is supposed to be and what anarchy is supposed to be: by linking the words on the analogy of, say, *The Masque of Cupid*, he prepares us for the crooked house that he goes on to construct. Both nouns demand scrutiny, as does their syntactical relation.

"Anarchy" is a word with both political and literary associations. In *Paradise Lost* it is associated with the realm of Chaos—"Eternal Anarchy" (2.896), "wild Anarchy" (6.873); and following Milton's designation of Chaos as "the Anarch old," Pope uses "Anarch" in *The Dunciad*.[8] However, in making "Anarchy" characterize the governing institutions of society, Shelley is even closer to Byron's "Imperial anarchs, doubling human woes" in the second canto of *Childe Harold*.[9] In the realm of political discourse, a precedent for transforming the conventional meaning of "anarchy" may be found in Jeremy Bentham's *Plan of Parliamentary Reform in the Form of a Catechism*, first published in 1817.[10] Bentham sarcastically remarks to his imagined Tory antagonist: "The same 'great characters' by which the monster of anarchy has so happily been crushed in France—by these same exalted persons will the same monster be crushed in Britain"; and he continues, in a spirit very much like Shelley's, "In the language of legitimacy and tyranny, and of the venal slavery that crawls under them, *democracy* and *anarchy* are synonymous terms."[11] What Shelley effects is a combination of Bentham's unmasking of "the language of legitimacy" with Byron's ironical reversal of meaning, so that "Anarchy" redounds on the legitimists themselves.

Such a radical transformation is appropriate to a masque, in which we are aware that all the characters are disguised. But what kind of Masque, or Mask, did Shelley have in mind? He seems to have attached the same meaning to either spelling, using "Mask" in manuscript but "Masque" in the sole reference to the title among his letters.[12] (A similar situation exists for Poe's "Masque of the Red Death," where the spelling was "Mask" in the story's first and second publications but then "Masque" in the *Broadway Journal*, of which Poe was an editor.[13]) Either spelling could signify a dramatic performance (*OED*, s.v.), although "Mask" would be the more ambiguous spelling, as in Shakespeare's "Degree being vizarded, / Th'unworthiest goes as fairly in the maske."[14] Stuart Curran has shown that Shelley could have learned about masques from Leigh Hunt's *The Descent of Liberty* / *A Mask* (published in 1815) with its prefatory essay,[15] and Shelley's continuing interest in masque conventions is later displayed in the scene in *Charles the First* called "The Masque of the Inns of Court."

We may say, then, that the primary reference of "Mask" here is to a dramatic performance, as "the Pageant" of line 51 and "the triumph of Anarchy" of line 57 also suggest, but that two other meanings are constantly suggested as well and that any of these may at a given point become the primary meaning: "this ghastly masquerade" (line 27) and the masks worn by Castlereagh and his fellow ministers, for example.[16] Even the preposition "of" creates some semantic wobbling. The syntactical relation can, in addition to suggesting the title of a masque, signify the mask of legitimate authority that Anarchy wears and/or a masquerade hosted by Anarchy. Thus the title immediately introduces a sense of dislocated meanings that characterizes other aspects of the poem as well.

At first *The Mask of Anarchy* may seem to embody anarchy itself. This impression is created in part by its strategy of reversals and of ironical inversions of meaning, in part by the strangely disparate lengths of its structural units. Even so, this ninety-one-stanza poem does have an overall structure, albeit a radically skewed one. It begins with an introductory vision, a single stanza in length, which is followed by a dramatic section that I shall call the Triumph and Agon—the Triumph twenty stanzas long, the Agon twelve. A "bridge" of three stanzas then leads to the longest section of the poem, which I shall call the Hortatory Address. After a two-stanza apostrophe, this section is divided almost geometrically into three parts, as if to call attention to the ungainliness of the previous divisions. That a poem has a plot or plan does not necessarily make it a good poem, but it is important, as a preliminary to further discussion, to realize that *The Mask* does have one.

> As I lay asleep in Italy
> There came a voice from over the Sea . . .[17]

These opening lines with their lulling assonance prepare us for a dream vision of some *locus amoenus*, but our reverie is brutally interrupted by the first line of the next stanza—"I met Murder on the way—." Jarred by this reversal of expectation, our attention is redirected to the beginning. Now those first lines may no longer seem so innocent. Ought the sleeper in Italy to have been awake in England? In compensation or atonement, he is "forth led" to experience and communicate his vision. The sleeper does not seem to comprehend the meaning of what he relates: extraordinary events are re-counted in a flat, quotidian tone, much as in Blake's "The Mental Traveller." This is, as Richard Cronin puts it in his excellent discussion of *The Mask*'s relation to ballad tradition, "the assumed voice of the naive balladeer."[18] The speaker does not, for example, see any reason for Hope's being a "maniac maid," and since "she looked more like Despair," he merely reports her putative identity: "And her name was Hope, she said." The mailed Shape who defeats Anarchy is never identified by the speaker; neither is the "voice" that speaks the last fifty-four stanzas. The reader is left to construe the meaning of what has been said.

The matter-of-factly delivered lines 5–6 introduce another simple—but because simple easy to overlook—aspect of the Triumph that now begins. Murder wears a mask *like* Castlereagh, Fraud an ermined gown *like* Eldon. This is not the usual relation of the disguise to the disguised. To be absurdly simple for a moment: Castlereagh ought to be masked as Murder, not vice versa. Personifications have been reified, taking as their manifestation the iden-tities of British cabinet ministers. (This element would have perhaps been emphasized too literally had Shelley retained the manuscript lines [10v] in which, after Anarchy's overthrow, "Fraud, less quickly[*del.*] to be known / Threw off E——s wig & gown."[19]) Anarchy, however, has no occasional identity but is troped to another representation—"Death in the Apocalypse" —and this double identity is present throughout the Pageant and Agon.

As is widely recognized, these four figures are secularizations of the four riders of the book of Revelation.[20] Anarchy's correspondence to the rider of Revelation 6:8 is indicated explicitly:

> Last came Anarchy: he rode
> On a white horse, splashed with blood;
> He was pale even to the lips,
> Like Death in the Apocalypse . . .
>
> (lines 30–33)

And I looked, and behold a pale horse, and his name that sat on him was death, and Hell followed with him.

So graphic is this image that Donald H. Reiman and Sharon B. Powers suggest the possible influence of Benjamin West's enormous painting *Death on the Pale Horse* (now in the Pennsylvania Academy of Fine Arts).[21] Shelley could indeed have seen this picture exhibited in London before he departed for the Continent in 1817; however, an even better candidate as a pictorial source may be the *Death on a Pale Horse* of John Hamilton Mortimer, as etched by Joseph Haynes. Shelley calls Anarchy "the Skeleton" (line 74), and in Mortimer's design Death has the head and neck of a skeleton, while in West's he is a black figure swathed in a dark gown.[22] Furthermore, Mortimer's treatment of the subject has a sense of *diablerie* that is completely lacking in West's but is consonant with the tone of this part of *The Mask*. Shelley's apocalyptic-grotesque conception also has something in common with James Gillray's caricature print *Presages of the Millennium* where, as in Shelley's "ghastly masquerade," apocalyptic content and contemporary political reference combine in a macabre yet comical way.[23] It should be remembered that prints such as these, though produced long before Shelley's poem, continued to be known by collectors and connoisseurs then as they are today, and there is no reason to limit the history of their reception to the immediate time in which they were produced.

The use of John of Patmos's apocalyptic text as a prototype, which we have seen in the portrayal of Anarchy, continues in a loose, unsystematic, and even playful manner. The "seven bloodhounds" who follow Murder may indicate the seven nations that in 1815 joined England in postponing the abolition of the slave trade,[24] but more generally, they are associated with all the sevens of Revelation. The Destructions who "played" disguised "Like Bishops, lawyers, peers, or spies" (26–29) are analogous to the small flying demons that in the pictorial tradition started by Mortimer hover around the rider on the pale horse like gulls following a fishing boat. (In the Gillray print these become identifiable political figures, Edmund Burke among them.) On Anarchy's forehead the mark of the Beast (Rev. 13:16) is written in a parody of the inscription borne by the messianic rider of Revelation:

> On his brow this mark I saw—
> "I am God, and King, and Law!"
> (lines 36–37)

> And he hath on his vesture and on his thigh a name written, KING
> OF KINGS, AND LORD OF LORDS. (Rev. 19:16)

Much as Blake's Urizen, who announces "One King, one God, one Law,"[25] Anarchy combines elements conventionally associated with the divine with others conventionally associated with the Satanic into a single subversive figuration. The overall effect is of an apocalyptic vision of modern history paralleling that of John's Apocalypse in a complex and sometimes ironical way.

Some of Shelley's phrases from Revelation conflate with other biblical texts. In describing the "Pageant" of Anarchy "Drunk as with intoxication / Of the wine of desolation" (lines 48–49), Shelley is not quite echoing John. In chapter 18 of the book of Revelation, the whore of Babylon has a golden cup, "and all the nations have drunk of the wine of her fornication" (verse 3; see also Rev. 17:2). However, Ezekiel, addressing Jerusalem, prophesies: "Thou shalt be filled with drunkenness and sorrow, with the cup of astonishment and desolation" (Rev. 23:33). The fact that "the wine of desolation" sounds like a biblical quotation rather than a combination of elements both indicates Shelley's success in this mode and prefigures another powerful apocalyptic-political text meant for a wide audience (one that reached the kind of audience Shelley only hoped for in his "Popular Songs"), namely, Julia Ward Howe's "Battle Hymn of the Republic."

Other biblical passages are ironized to underline the Triumph's grotesqueness. Sidmouth is "Clothed with the Bible, as with light" (line 22) in emulation of the Lord in Psalm 104, verse 2, "who coverest thyself with light as with a garment." This ironical parallel is appropriate for the Home Secretary who in 1818 got Parliament to appropriate a million pounds for church-building[26] and in 1819 defended the Peterloo massacre. In his notebook manuscript, Shelley had Sidmouth "Singing Hosannah / With a cold tear in either eye" (23v), but apparently he decided this was excessive, for he canceled the lines. Elsewhere in the Pageant a passage from the Gospels provides material for transmutation. Lord Chancellor Eldon weeps big tears because as a judge he had been famous for weeping while pronouncing the harshest verdicts[27] (like Urizen, who "saw / That no flesh nor spirit could keep / His iron laws one moment. . . . And he wept, & he called it Pity"[28]). But in one of those animated-cartoonlike metamorphoses that characterizes the Pageant and Agon, Eldon's tears

> Turned to mill-stones as they fell.
>
> And the little children, who
> Round his feet played to and fro,
> Thinking every tear a gem,
> Had their brains knocked out by them.
> (lines 17–21)

As Leigh Hunt originally suggested,[29] Shelley is no doubt thinking of the little children of his first marriage, and of Lord Chancellor Eldon, who had distrained him from taking charge of them in 1817, the provocation for "thy false tears—those millstones braining men" in "To the Lord Chancellor" (1817).[30] But in *The Mask* there is another dimension: a macabre echo of Christ and the little children in Matthew 18:6, where Jesus says, "But whoso offends one of these little ones which believe in me, it were better for him that a millstone were hanged about his neck, and that he were drowned in the depths of the sea" (cf., Mark 9:42 and Luke 17:2). In an instance of what Hunt called "the union of ludicrousness with terror,"[31] the millstone that was to punish the transgressor against the child is what causes the child's destruction.

The Triumph of Anarchy continues through line 85, where we are again in the apocalyptic-grotesque world of some of Gillray's caricatures. "Anarchy, the Skeleton" assumes the characteristics of a Regency beau who "Bowed and grinned to every one," and perhaps of that paragon of Regency beaux, the Regent himself, whose "education / Had cost ten millions to the nation" (lines 76–77).[32] Anarchy's agents are sent to seize the Bank of England and the Tower of London, institutions that had allegedly been the object of a plot in 1817, thus providing a pretext for the suspension of habeas corpus.[33] Anarchy himself goes on "with intent / To meet his pensioned Parliament" (lines 84–85). The expression "pensioned Parliament" is especially interesting, for these words occur in one of the radical tracts reprinted in a book that we know was of great interest to Shelley—the Abbé Barruel's *Memoirs of the History of Jacobinism*, translated by Robert Clifford.[34] The Peterloo Massacre seems to have brought to Shelley's mind the potentially revolutionary applications he had previously seen in Barruel's book.[35] However, as *The Mask of Anarchy* is an apocapolitical poem and not a discursive proposal for an association, revolution comes about in a moment.

The instigator of that revolution is a Cassandra-figure, the "maniac maid" Hope, who appears at line 86 and so begins the Agon. It seems beyond coincidence that her cry concludes "Misery, oh Misery!": as Shelley well knew, this was the refrain of Martha Ray in Wordsworth's "The Thorn."[36] This parallel is more than a verbal echo, because Martha Ray is also a "maniac" female. She is furthermore a mother with a dead child, like the iconic figure of the woman whose child was trampled to death at Peterloo.[37] Although Martha Ray was suspected of having killed her child, the narrator's animosity—and presumably the reader's—is directed toward her masculine betrayer, a role assumed in *The Mask* by Anarchy and his all-male crew. Thus the Wordsworthian source is conflated by Shelley with imagery of the sort later displayed in the collaborations of George Cruikshank and William Hone.[38]

The dead children of Father Time (among whom lay Hope herself "naked on a bier" in a canceled MS reading, 7v) in lines 94–96 are analogous both to Martha Ray's child and to the child killed in St. Peter's Fields. (Shelley's most explicit treatment of this theme among the "Popular Songs" of which *The Mask* was to have been part is the "Ballad of Young Parson Richards," in which the parson turns away from his gate a mother with a dying child who is, it turns out, his own.[39]) Father Time is "weak and grey" (line 90), but Anarchy, incorporating the patriarchal "GOD, AND KING, AND LAW," is a seemingly powerful ogre father. In a draft stanza copied by Mary Shelley into both the manuscript notebook (26v) and the intermediate fair Copy,[40] he is the trampler of a figurative child:

> And the earth whereon he went
> A cry   Like a trampled infant sent
> A piercing scream of loud lament.

In the absence of a male both potent and protective, Hope lies "Right before the horses' feet" (line 99) like a Peterloo victim—when a savior appears.

The sudden appearance of "a Shape arrayed in mail" shares with some other parts of *The Mask*, as I have noted, characteristics of an animated cartoon. The reality here is conveyed in a succession of similes which, as so often in this poem, are the primary vehicle of meaning.

> A mist, a light, an image rose,
> Small at first, and weak, and frail
> Like the vapour of a vale:
>
> Till as clouds grow on the blast,
> Like tower-crowned giants striding fast
> And glare with lightnings as they fly,
> And speak in thunder to the sky,
> It grew—
>
> (lines 103–10)

This dramatic modification recalls the approach of the spectre bark in *The Rime of the Ancient Mariner*:

> At first it seemed a little speck,
> And then it seemed a mist;
> It moved and moved, and took at last
> A certain shape, I wist
> A speck, a mist, a shape, I wist!
> And still it neared and neared.[41]

Shelley's images of cloud and storm also reveal a biblical prototype. In I Kings, chapter 18, in the third year of drought Elijah demonstrates the Lord's power to Ahab, sending his servant seven times to the top of Mount Carmel.

> And it came to pass at the seventh time, that he said, Behold, there ariseth a little cloud out of the sea, like a man's hand. And he said, Go up and say unto Ahab, Prepare thy chariot and get thee down, that the rain stop thee not.
>
> And it came to pass in the mean while, that the heaven was black with clouds and wind, and there was a great rain.
>
> (verses 44–45)

All three supernatural figurations begin as vapory configurations—"the vapour of a vale," "a mist," "a little cloud"—and grow into startling

41

realities—Shape, spectre, bark, storm. In *The Mask*, Anarchy is analogous to the tyrannical Ahab, while the role of Elijah, revealing powers greater than those of Ahab's kingdom, belongs to the visionary poet himself.

Three aspects of the giant winged Shape are especially important. Its mail is "brighter than the viper's scale" (line 111), it is associated with the morning star, and it is ungendered. The first two, taken together, are among *The Mask*'s numerous reversals of meaning. The subversion of conventional associations here is like that in the first canto of *The Revolt of Islam*, where after the victory of the blood-red Comet over the Morning Star, "That fair Star fell," and the triumphant Spirit of Evil entered the world to be worshiped, like Anarchy, "As King, and Lord, and God." Consequently,

> his immortal foe,
> He changed from starry shape, beauteous and mild,
> To a dire Snake. . . .[42]

The "planet, like the Morning's" on the Shape's helm, provides a parallel and contrast to the mark on the brow of Anarchy (lines 36–37) and at the same time links the Shape with the Lucifer of Isaiah 14:12: "How art thou fallen from heaven, O Lucifer, son of the morning!" (In manuscript Shelley at one point used the word "Angel" for the Shape but evidently decided this was too explicit.) In a world where Anarchy can personify the institutions of the State, it is appropriate that the savior be represented by the configuration of Lucifer and serpent.

The Shape is almost as indefinite as that "mighty darkness" of *Prometheus Unbound*, Demogorgon, but is in addition without gender, as if the force that brings about apocalyptic transformation must be beyond sexuality. (As H. Buxton Forman points out in his study of the manuscript, Shelley almost made the mistake of referring to the Shape as "her" in the thirty-first stanza but presumably "saw how inconsistent his phraseology was with the carefully guarded mystery of the quality and sex of 'the presence.' "[43]) Attempts to assign an allegorical meaning to this manifestation, from Leigh Hunt's "the description of the rise and growth of Public Enlightenment"[44] to Hendrix's "reborn Liberty,"[45] do not fully describe what is happening because the apocalyptic moment cannot be contained in a single denotative meaning.

The Shape's conflict with Anarchy is even shorter than Demogorgon's with Jupiter, and as decisive. Typical of the violent oppositions of *The Mask* is the outcome in which

> ankle-deep in blood,
> Hope that maiden most serene
> Was walking with a quiet mien. . . .
> (lines 127–29)

The source of all this blood must give the reader pause. Anarchy the Skeleton cannot have supplied it. Even the murderers who, we are told a few lines later, were ground by the hoofs of the white horse, could not have supplied such a deal of blood. It is the not yet named "sons of England" whose blood has "bedewed" the face of their mother Earth (Lines 140–44). This linking suggests the relationship of the Pageant and Agon with the Hortatory Address that follows. The former is the mythologized version of the latter. Only by heeding the Hortatory Address can the sons of England actuate the myth that precedes it.

Linking the Agon with the Hortatory Address is a three-stanza "bridge" that Shelley labored over in manuscript more than any other passage except perhaps for that describing the manifestation of the Shape. As in stanza 1 a "voice" is heard, and again it is of uncertain origin. Although there have been attempts to identify this voice as "the 'power' inherent in nature," or Hope's, or "probably Brittania,"[46] such delimitations once more seem unsatisfactory, for the omission appears both deliberate and effectual. A powerful "as if" clause now enables the recovery of the mother-child relationship that has been absent from the poem so far:

> As if their Own indignant Earth
> Which gave the sons of England birth
> Had felt their blood upon her brow,
> And shuddering with a mother's throe
>
> Had turned every drop of blood
> By which her face had been bedewed
> To an accent unwithstood,—
> (lines 139–45)

In the two following stanzas, the mother-child relationship is reinforced by the continued personification of Earth as female and the address to the "sons of England" as "Nurslings of one mighty Mother" (line 149). (In the notebook, 8r, a strong link would at one point have been established between Earth and the Shape, who in a canceled version of stanza 26 "sprung from the earth.") The kingdom of Anarchy was haunted by the ghosts of dead children and an absent mother ("Misery, oh, Misery!"); this longest section of the poem begins by establishing the seemingly indestructible presences of mother and children.

In addition to their both being addressed by a "voice," the speaker of the beginning of the poem and the men of England have in common their sleep. Called upon to "Rise like Lions after slumber," the men of England are told that their chains had fallen on them "in sleep." "*Sleep*, in Shelley," G. M. Matthews has written, is another over-determined concept which awaits investigation. It may imply what is now known as hibernisation, an artificial state of cold insensibility, or a "detested trance" like that of winter, but winter is also the winter of the world, an era of bondage or apathy in the face of social injustice.[47]

The awakening that is projected has an eschatological dimension affecting both the poet-speaker and the men of England—as at the end of another of the "Popular Songs," "A New National Anthem":

> Sweet as if angels sang,
> Loud as that trumpet's clang
> Wakening the world's dead gang,—
> God save the Queen![48]

In both instances a general awakening suggests the end of the nightmare of history and the dawn of the millennium to follow.

It is now time to consider why, when in this poem the men of England are called upon to oppose their enemies with an anticipation of Gandhian *satyagraha*,[49] the vehicle of awakening should be "Lions after slumber." Although it is possible to see in such a polarization of trope and tenor an "ambivalence"[50] toward revolution, we should be aware of how the contrast contributes to Shelley's apocalyptic scenario. Shelley's thought about revolution does have two aspects, and they appear in virtually all of his major political writings. He hoped revolution would come; he feared it would come violently, in which case it would lead not to millennium but to the return of history upon itself, as at the end of the final chorus of *Hellas*. When he learned "the terrible and important news of Manchester,"[51] both the hope and the fear came sharply to mind. "The same day as your letter came," he wrote to his publisher Charles Ollier,

> came the news of the Manchester work, & the torrent of my indignation has not yet done boiling in my veins. I wait anxiously [to] hear how the Country will express its sense of this bloody murderous oppression of its destroyers. "Something must be done ... What yet I know not."[52]

Had Shelley's hope and his fear not sometimes intermixed, he would indeed have been that angelic figure that he became for some later nineteenth-century readers. As it is, by quoting his own *Cenci*,[53] he indulges a fantasy of violent revenge: Beatrice Cenci says the quoted words after being raped by her father, and what she does is to bring about his murder. The savage nature of the trope in line 151 (to be repeated in the last stanza of the poem) may image such retributive fantasies, in apparent conflict with Shelley's belief that violence would only bind its perpetrators into an ever more violent cycle of "blood for blood—and wrong for wrong" (line 195), and that apocalypse would not then be followed by millennium. Such polarizations of pacifist tenors and violent vehicles in *The Mask* are one aspect of the dramatic reversals and striking, even shocking, contrasts that characterize the poem as a whole. This is yet another link with the Apocalypse of St. John, in which the visions of the millennium and of the New Jerusalem are juxtaposed with evocations of terrible violence.

The organization of *The Mask of Anarchy* has so far seemed to be devoid of any sense of predetermined proportion. We have seen that after an introduction only four lines long come the Triumph and Agon, assymetrically divided into twenty- and twelve-stanza units. Then, after a three-stanza "bridge," the Hortatory Address starts with two stanzas each in turn beginning "Men of England, heirs of Glory" These are followed by a disquisition on the nature of freedom that occupies the rest of the poem and that displays an almost geometrical architecture, one which is further reinforced by the rhetorical features of each of its sub-units. Such symmetry is appropriate to the millenarian vision that informs the Hortatory Address. If, as Woodring suggests, the poem leads from the triumph of the Dragon and Beast to "the victory and marriage of the lamb," the latter demands a different kind of poetry to convey a sense of millennial peace emerging from the horrors that precede it.

In their paper entitled *Shelley's Socialism*, delivered to the Shelley Society in 1885,[54] Edward Aveling and Eleanor Marx Aveling (Karl Marx's daughter) placed one of Shelley's most salient characteristics under the heading "His Understanding of the Real Meaning of Words."[55] Their first two examples are "Anarchy" and "Freedom." The Hortatory Address is in the Avelings' sense an essay on the real meaning of words. It begins its answer to "What is Freedom?" first by defining the present condition as slavery, then by showing what freedom really is. Each of these two sections, as Stuart Curran points out, is thirteen stanzas long.[56] The remainder of the poem moves to fill the mental space between these two divisions by showing how to get to freedom from slavery. This third part is precisely the sum of the preceding two plus one stanza, the additional stanza being the repetition of stanza 38, beginning "Rise like Lions after slumber," at the very end. Each of these three subsections is, moreover, governed by a different type of predication, and each is bound together by a different, appropriate anaphoric structure.

The stanzas immediately following "What is Freedom?" are characterized by predications of *being* followed by infinitives. "'Tis to" plus an infinitive occurs six times in the eight stanzas comprising lines 160–96, five of these at the beginning of a stanza. With stanza 48 this type of rhetorical structure culminates with "Then it is to feel revenge. . . ." "What is? . . ." 'Tis to . . . Then it is" creates a feeling of inexorable cause and effect, of Shelleyan Necessity. The end of stanza 47, "Blood is on the grass like dew" (line 192), looks back to the figuration in lines 141–42, where it is as if Earth's face had been bedewed with blood. This conjunction is reminiscent of Tertullian's declaration to the Roman officials that "We become more numerous every time we are hewn down by you: the blood of Christians is seed."[57] Shelley's evocation of self-sacrifice seems to precipitate the extended analogy of the Englishman and Christ in lines 197–204, after which the entire movement is concluded and summarized in a stanza that begins with another variant of the "'Tis to" anaphora: "This is Slavery. . . ."

"What art thou Freedom" at the beginning of stanza 52 is a marker leading us to expect a sequence of answers as in the section following "What is Freedom?" thirteen stanzas before. The "thou" in this question anticipates a new organizing anaphora. The twelve following stanzas feature "thou art" seven times, "thou art not" once, and "art thou" once. Six of these begin stanzas. The change from "it is" to "thou art," with its transition from an inanimate to an intimately personal grammatical subject, prepares the way for the millennial transformation of the human universe.[58]

The last movement of the address, beginning with stanza 65, once more shifts into a new organizing anaphora with "Let a great Assembly be / Of the fearless and the free" (lines 262–63).[59] As the subject changes from what Freedom is to how it can be actualized, predication moves from the declarative mode to the imperative. The construction "Let" followed by a verb is found eleven times from line 262 on. Nine of these occurrences begin stanzas. Concomitantly we encounter other vital imperatives—"Be," "Stand," "Look, "Shall." Such monosyllabic initial predications also make the four-beat lines they introduce "headless,"[60] which both emphasizes the imperative nature of the verbs and calls our attention to the "voice" speaking the lines. In this way a sense of increasing momentum is created, reinforced by a subsection in which the gathering of participants is rendered by the anaphoric "From the" that begins stanzas 67, 68, and 69 and that also occurs in stanza 70. At line 295 the beginning of the third movement is virtually reiterated in "Let a vast assembly be," and the poem plunges ahead to the confrontation between the people and their oppressors.

The military's attack is rendered in remarkably bloody imagery, while the people's weapon is, significantly, speech. This essential opposition is rendered in the simile "Be your strong and simple words / Keen to wound as sharpened swords" (lines 299–300). Once more, nonviolent tenor and violent vehicle are polarized, with the image in the latter now ironically reflecting the literally envisioned "fixed bayonets" and "horsemen's scimitars" to come. And once more the people's weapon is a voice, associated as in stanza 36 with an effusion of blood:

> And that slaughter to the Nation
> Shall steam up like inspiration,

Eloquent, oracular;
A volcano heard afar.
(lines 360–63)

It is a powerful revolutionary image, which is parallel to

the realm
Of Demogoron, and the mighty portal,
Like a volcano's meteor-breathing chasm,
Whence the oracular vapour is hurled up. . . .[61]

The voice that came over the sea to the poet, the voice of Hope, the voice of Earth, the voice that speaks the entire Hortatory Address, the voice of a bleeding people—all these concenter in a single metaphor, making it seem as if the repetition of stanza 38 at the conclusion were changed in a great chorale:

"Rise like lions after slumber
In unvanquishable number—
Shake your chains to earth like dew
Which in sleep had fallen on you—
Ye are many—they are few."

Thus concludes the Hortatory Address, which contrasts as sharply with the Triumph and Agon in structure as it does in tone. Up to line 134 *The Mask* speaks in a sardonic-macabre voice—Hunt's "union of ludicrousness with terror." Here the violent transformations of biblical and other texts stylistically parallel the plot's violent metamorphoses and are appropriate to its apocalyptic nature. There follow, as we have seen, three transitional stanzas (lines 135–46) that mime, in a series of rapid enjambments, the process they describe. "Shuddering with a mother's throe," apocalypse gives birth to millennium. Consequently, the carefully plotted, deliberate rhetorical organization of the fifty-three stanzas from line 156 to the end projects a secularized version of Revelation 20:4:

I saw the souls of them that were beheaded for the witness of Jesus, and for the word of God, and which had not worshipped the beast, neither his image, neither had received his mark upon their foreheads, or in their hands; and they lived and reigned with Christ a thousand years.

If a sense of radical dislocation between the two main parts of the poem persists, that is perhaps less a fault in the poem than an expression of the unsettled nature of the relationship between apocalypse and millennium in Shelley's vision of history itself.

47

Notes

Research for this paper was done while I was a Fellow of the John Simon Guggenheim foundation, to which grateful acknowledgment is made. I am also indebted to Donald H. Reiman and Jerrold Hogle for helpful criticisms.

1 F. R. Leavis, *Revaluation: Tradition and Development in English Poetry* (New York, 1947), 228–30.

2 Richard Holmes, *Shelley: The Pursuit* (London, 1976), 532–39.

3 Harold Bloom, *Blake's Apocalypse* (New Haven, 1959); Earl Wasserman, *Shelley: A Critical Reading* (Baltimore, 1971).

4 Thomas R. Edwards, *Imagination and Power: A Study of Poetry and Public Themes* (London, 1971), 161–68.

5 Richard Hendrix, "The Necessity of Response: How Shelley's Radical Poetry Works," *Keats-Shelley Journal*, 27 (1978): 68.

6 Michael Scrivener, *Radical Shelley* (Princeton, 1982), 199; Stephen C. Behrendt, *Shelley and His Audience* (Lincoln, Nebr., 1989), 199.

7 Carl Woodring, *Politics and English Romantic Poetry* (Cambridge, Mass., 1970), 266.

8 The use of "Anarch" by Milton and by Pope is noted by Donald H. Reiman, *Percy Bysshe Shelley* (New York, 1969), 168.

9 Byron, *Complete Poetical Works*, ed. Jerome J. McGann, vol. 2 (Oxford, 1980), 58. Shelley uses "Anarch" in this subversive sense in a number of poems, including "Lines Written Among the Euganean Hills" (line 152) and *Hellas* (lines 318, 879, 934).

10 This is evidently the book Shelley had in mind when he wrote of his own *Philosophical View of Reform*, "It is intended for a kind of standard book for the political reformers, like Jeremy Bentham's something, but different & perhaps more systematic" (Letter to Leigh Hunt, 26 May 1820, *The Letters of Percy Bysshe Shelley*, ed. Frederick L. Jones [Oxford, 1964], 2:201).

11 *Works of Jeremy Bentham*, ed. John Bowring (Edinburgh, 1843), 3:436a, 447b.

12 Letter to Leigh Hunt, 14–18 November 1819, *Letters*, ed. Jones, 2:152. "Masque" is the spelling of the first edition, edited by Leigh Hunt: *The Masque of Anarchy* (London, 1832). Reiman suggests that either Hunt or his publisher Moxon may have considered the spelling "Mask" obsolescent in 1832. See *The Manuscripts of the Younger Romantics*, vol. 2, *Percy Bysshe Shelley: The Mask of Anarchy*, ed, Donald H. Reiman (New York and London, 1985), xv.

13 See *The Complete Poems and Stories of Edgar Poe*, ed. Edward H. O'Neill (New York, 1946), 2:1079.

14 *Troilus and Cressida*, I.iii.83–84. For editorial discussion, see the New Variorum Shakespeare, vol. 26, ed, Harold N. Hillebrand (Philadelphia and London, 1953), 53.

15 See Stuart Curran, *Shelley's Annus Mirabilis* (San Marino, Calif., 1975), 187–90.

16 Kenneth Neill Cameron calls attention to *The Examiner*'s expression "Men in the Brazen Masks of Power" in an editorial on the Peterloo Massacre published on 29 August 1819 (*Shelley: The Golden Years* [Cambridge, Mass., 1974], 625 n. 8).

17 Unless otherwise indicated, citations of Shelley's poetry refer by line numbers to *Shelley's Poetry and Prose*, ed. Donald H. Reiman and Sharon B. Powers (London and New York, 1977).

18 Richard Cronin, *Shelley's Poetic Thoughts* (London, 1981), 43. See also Edwards, *Imagination and Power*, 162; and Hendrix, *Shelley's Radical Poetry*, 33.

19 All quotations of Shelley's draft MS are from his manuscript notebook in the Henry E. Huntington Library, and grateful acknowledgment is made to the Library for permission to refer to it. A facsimile edition of this manuscript is now available in *The Manuscripts of the Younger Romantics*, vol. 4, *The Mask of Anarchy Draft Notebook*, ed. Mary A. Quinn (New York and London, 1990).

20 See, for example, Carlos Baker, *Shelley's Major Poetry: The Fabric of a Vision* (Princeton, 1948), 61; and Heiner Schwinning, "Der Maskenzug der Anarchie," *Gulliver/Deutsche-Englische Jarbucher*, 1 (1976): 76.

21 *Shelley's Poetry and Prose*, ed, Reiman and Powers, 302 n. 8.

22 See Morton D. Paley, *The Apocalyptic Sublime* (New Haven and London, 1986), 18, 184–86.

23 Cf. Woodring, *Politics in English Romantic Poetry*, xiii, xiv, where a parallel between Gillray's print and Shelley's *Swellfoot the Tyrant* is suggested.

24 See G. M. Matthews's note in *Shelley: Selected Poems and Prose* (Oxford, 1964), 197.

25 See *The Complete Poetry and Prose of William Blake*, ed. David V. Erdman (Berkeley and Los Angeles, 1982), 72.

26 See *Shelley: Selected Poems and Prose*, ed. Matthews, 197.

27 See *inter alia* Woodring, *Politics in English Romantic Poetry*, 266; and Cameron, *Golden Years*, 34.

28 *Complete Poetry and Prose of Blake*, ed. Erdman, 81–82.

29 Preface to *The Masque of Anarchy* (London, 1832), 4.

30 Hendrix, "Shelley's Radical Poetry," 54.

31 Preface to *The Masque of Anarchy*, 4. Reiman (*Manuscripts of the Younger Romantics: The Mask of Anarchy*, 70) observes that Hunt first wrote "humour with terror" but changed the word in proof. Another instance of the quality Hunt had in mind would have been, had Shelley retained it in the final poem, the frisking of Murder's bloodhounds in the MS notebook.

32 See P. M. S. Dawson, *The Unackowledged Legislator* (Oxford, 1980), 206; Scrivener, *Radical Shelley*, 207.

33 See *Shelley: Selected Poems and Prose*, ed. Matthews, 197.

34 Robert Clifford, "Note" appended to volume 4 of his translation of the *Memoirs* (London, 1798), 17.

35 Of course both Barruel and Clifford were bitterly hostile to revolution, but this did not prevent Shelley from separating his wheat from their chaff. On Shelley's interest in the *Memoirs*, see Walter Edwin Peck, "Shelley and the Abbé Barruel," *PMLA*, 37 (1921): 347–53; Cameron, *Golden Years*, 321, 411; and Holmes, *The Pursuit*, 242.

36 The verbal parallel with "The Thorn" is noted by Reiman, *Manuscripts of the Younger Romantics: The Mask of Anarchy*, 15.

37 See Holmes, *The Pursuit*, 532.

38 Cf. George Cruikshank's (later) "Victory of Peterloo," rpt. in Woodring, *Politics in English Romantic Poetry*, 22; see also Scrivener, *Radical Shelley*, 201–3.

39 Cameron points out the relevance of a letter by Sir Francis Burdett in the *Examiner*, urging the English "not to stand idly by while tyrants 'rip open their mother's womb'" (*Golden Years*, 625 n. 8).

40 For details see *Shelley and His Circle*, ed. Donald H. Reiman, vol. 6 (Cambridge, Mass., 1973), 892–94.

41 *The Poems of Samuel Taylor Coleridge*, ed. Ernest Hartley Coleridge (London, 1960), 192.

42 See stanzas 26–28, lines 360, 367–69, 378 (Shelley, *Poetical Works*, ed. Thomas Hutchinson, 2d ed., corrected by G. M. Matthews [London, 1973], 46).

43 *Note-books of P. B. Shelley, Deciphered, Transcribed, and Edited* (Boston, 1911), 2:30, 37.

44 Preface to the first edition, v.

45 Hendrix, "Shelley's Radical Poetry," 58. Also cf., "the spirit of Hope, mingled with the spirit of direct action," in Paul Foot, *Red Shelley* (London, 1980), 176–77, and "the goddess-figure of Liberty," in Jerrold Hogle, *Shelley's Process: Radical Transference and the Development of His Major Works* (New York, 1988), 137.

46 Cameron, *Golden Years*, 348; Cronin, *Shelley's Poetic Thoughts*, 47, 49, 43; and Scrivener, *Radical Shelley*, 205.

47 G. M. Matthews, "A Volcano's Voice in Shelley," *Shelley: Modern Judgments*, ed. R. B. Woodings (London, 1968), 177.

48 Shelley, *Poetical Works*, 574.

49 Gandhi's word meaning "truth-firmness" as distinguished from mere passive resistance seems appropriate here. See *Autobiography: The Story of My Experiments with Truth* (New York, 1983), 284. Gandhi once recited *The Mask of Anarchy* as an illustration of his own principles; see John Pollard Guinn, *Shelley's Political Thought* (The Hague, 1969), 127.

50 See Scrivener, *Radical Shelley*, 210. Very close to my own view is Cronin's characterization of the poem's "precariously threatened situation" in which the poet's consciously assumed stance is "threatened by the violently hating revolutionary who lurks within the poem" (*Shelley's Poetic Thoughts*, 50).

51 Letter to Thomas Love Peacock, 9 September 1819, *Letters*, ed. Jones, 2:119.

52 6 September 1819, ibid., 117.

53 As noted by Jones, ibid., the quotation is from III.i.86–87 (see *Shelley's Poetry and Prose*, ed. Reiman and Powers, 263).

54 Published in 1888; republished London and West Nyack, 1979. This lecture is the source of the statement by Karl Marx that "those who understand them and love them rejoice that Byron died at thirty-six because if he had lived he would have become a reactionary bourgeois; they grieve that Shelley died at twenty-nine, because he would always have been one of the advanced guard of socialism"; see 1979 ed., 16.

55 Ibid., 33.

36 Curran, *Shelley's Annus Mirabilis*, 192–93.

57 *Apology*, trans. Sister Emily Joseph Daly, in *The Fathers of the Church* (New York, 1950), vol. 10, chap. 50, 125.

58 This is, of course, close to the central argument of Bloom's *Shelley's Mythmaking*, although, as I mentioned, *The Mask of Anarchy* is not discussed there.

59 Ronald Tetrault has interestingly distinguished this type of "optative" *let* from other let-constructions in this part of the poem. See *The Poetry of Life: Shelley and Literary Form* (Toronto, 1987), 205–7.

60 See Curran, *Shelley's Annus Mirabilis*, on Shelley's "acephalic tetrameter" and its association with the rhyming speeches of masques.

61 *Prometheus Unbound*, II.iii.1–4. On this passage, see Matthews, "A Volcano's Voice in Shelley," 162–95.

53

'A SECT OF DISSENTERS'

Robert M. Ryan

Source: *The Romantic Reformation: Religious Politics in English Literature 1789–1824* (Cambridge: Cambridge University Press, 1997), pp. 13–42.

We owe the great writers of the golden age of our literature to that fervid awakening of the public mind which shook to dust the oldest and most oppressive form of the Christian Religion. We owe Milton to the progress and development of the same spirit; the sacred Milton was, let it ever be remembered, a Republican, and a bold enquirer into morals and religion. The great writers of our own age are, we have reason to suppose, the companions and forerunners of some unimagined change in our social condition or the opinions which cement it. The cloud of mind is discharging its collected lightning, and the equilibrium between institutions and opinions is now restoring or about to be restored.

(Percy Bysshe Shelley, Preface to *Prometheus Unbound*)[1]

Shelley's perception of an intimate, necessary connection between politics and religion as forces for social change and his assumption that imaginative literature participated in the enterprise of political and religious reformation were shared by other writers of the time, even by those who did not sympathize with the radical politics that colored Shelley's optimism. The special affinity he perceived between his own time and that of the Protestant Reformation in England was also noticed by the other Romantics. William Wordsworth remarked on the resemblance between his own era and that of the first English Protestants, who had lived, he wrote, in an age "conspicuous as our own / For strife and ferment in the minds of men; / Whence alteration in the forms of things / Various and vast."[2] And like Shelley, John Keats saw the poets of his own time taking their rightful place in the vanguard of "a grand march of intellect" that would continue the liberalization of religion left unfinished by the Reformation. Keats honored Wordsworth, in particular, as the prophet of a more enlightened faith, one more concordant with human nature than Milton's Protestantism had been.[3]

> Here I must think Wordsworth is deeper than Milton – though
> I think it has depended more upon the general and gregarious
> advance of intellect, than individual greatness of Mind ... The
> Reformation produced such immediate and great benefits, that
> Protestantism was considered under the immediate eye of heaven,
> and its own remaining Dogmas and superstitions, then, as it were, re-
> generated, constituted those resting places and seeming sure points
> of Reasoning ... Milton, whatever he may have thought in the
> sequel, appears to have been content with these by his writings – He
> did not think into the human heart, as Wordsworth has done – Yet
> Milton as a Philosopher, had sure as great powers as Wordsworth –
> What is then to be inferr'd? O many things – It proves there really
> is a grand march of intellect –, It proves that a mighty providence
> subdues the mightiest Minds to the service of the time being, whether
> it be in human Knowledge or Religion.[4]

Keats's Milton is rather different from Shelley's "bold enquirer into morals
and religion," that impatient visionary who not only prophesied but actively
abetted revolution in the religious and political orders. To Keats Milton
seems a more passive product of the spirit of his age, one who remained
content with a dogmatic, superstitious faith that he was incapable of seeing
beyond. But both Keats and Shelley found in Milton an obvious illustration of their common conception of Britain's religious history as involving
a progressive refinement of doctrine and morals, a liberalization in which
poets in particular took positions of leadership not only as articulators of
contemporary beliefs but as agents of continuing religious change. Shelley
saw the great writers of his own age as driven by the same "spirit" that
accomplished the Reformation; Keats understood Wordsworth to have
been raised up by a "mighty providence" to help purify his countrymen's
religious sense, illuminating a path that younger poets could follow.

   It was not coincidental that Shelley and Keats arrived at similar visions
of the English Reformation as a continuing process in which poets bore
special responsibilities and in which Milton had played an exemplary role.
This complex of ideas is not only suggested by the events of Milton's life;
it is articulated frequently in that poet's writings. Church reform was a
central issue in the quarrel between King and Parliament in which Milton
participated so prominently. Although the English Reformation had reached
a temporary resolution in the Elizabethan Settlement, the more radical Protestants never fully accepted the compromise with Catholic tradition that
established the Church of England and they continued to demand a more
complete reformation in doctrine, discipline, and liturgy of the kind John
Calvin had effected at Geneva. The attempt of William Laud, Archbishop
of Canterbury under Charles I, to increase episcopal power and revive Catholic traditions in liturgy and church furnishing made the need for a radical

reformation even more urgent in the eyes of Charles's Puritan opposition. Milton articulated their position in his first published prose work, *Of Reformation Touching Church Discipline in England: And the Causes That Hitherto Have Hindered It* (1641), in which, after reviewing the reasons why the English Church had not been properly "rectified" by the reforms of Henry VIII, Edward VI, and Elizabeth I, he urged Englishmen to "cut away from the publick body the noysom, and diseased tumor of Prelacie, and come from Schisme to *unity* with our neighbour Reformed sister Churches."[5]

As the political crisis of the 1640s deepened, Milton's conception of reformation changed. After episcopal governance was legally abolished in 1643 it quickly became apparent that bishops had not been the only obstacles to religious progress in England. When the newly empowered Presbyterians issued an ordinance prohibiting the publication of books without the prior approval of a board of censors, it was clear that presbyters could be as obscurantist and coercive as prelates. Milton's response in *Areopagitica* (1644) was to argue that the English Reformation was a continuing process on which no one should try to impose a premature conclusion. The Reformation of the sixteenth century was only one phase in a movement that had begun in England two centuries earlier with John Wycliffe, at whose example the German and Swiss reformers "lighted their Tapers." Although Wycliffe was "the first Restorer of buried truth," his own country had not yet experienced the fullness of reformation enjoyed by other European states. Milton's objection to the Licensing Order was precisely that it denied the need and prevented the means for further reformation:

> The light which we have gain'd, was giv'n us, not to be ever staring on, but by it to discover onward things more remote from our knowledge. It is not the unfrocking of a Priest, the unmitring of a Bishop, and the removing of him from off the *Presbyterian* shoulders that will make us a happy Nation, no, if other things as great in the Church, and in the rule of life both economicall and politicall be not lookt into and reform'd, we have lookt so long upon the blaze that *Zuinglius* and *Calvin* hath beacon'd up to us, that we are stark blind.[6]

Reformation involves more than ecclesiastical purgation; even the radical "rectifications" of Zwingli and Calvin are now perceived as involving too limited a conception of reform. Milton's Reformation has become a broader cultural process, one that has not only doctrinal but political and economic change in view: "For the property of Truth is, where she is publickly taught, to unyoke & set free the minds and spirits of a Nation first from the thraldom of sin and superstition, after which all honest and legal freedom of civil life cannot be long absent." In the ecclesiastical disturbances of his time Milton saw signs that "God is decreeing to begin some new and great period in his Church, ev'n to the reforming of Reformation it self."[7]

This work of national reformation was too important to be left to ordained ministers, whatever the cut of their cloth. *The Reason of Church Government*, an essay that has been widely read since its publication for its autobiographical content, recounts the mental process by which Milton determined that his own literary talent should be dedicated to the service of religious reform. Convincing himself that "the completion of England's reformation would bring with it the long-sought release of his poetical powers,"[8] Milton decided that his own God-given talent could be employed with equal justification in the arena of religious controversy as in the composition of poetry. Since literary genius is the gift of "that eternall Spirit who can enrich with all utterance and knowledge, and sends out his Seraphim with the hallowed fire of his Altar, to touch and purify the lips of whom he pleases," the divine calling of the poet provides credentials at least as legitimate as those bestowed by canonical ordination for addressing religious issues in the public forum: "These abilities, wheresoever they be found, are the inspired gift of God rarely bestow'd . . . and are of power beside the office of a pulpit, to imbreed and cherish in a great people the seeds of vertu and publick civility."[9]

Here is the Milton of Shelley and Keats (and Blake and Wordsworth also) illustrating in his own life the principle that religious reformation is a continuing process with consequences not only in the theological sphere but in politics and economics as well, and inviting and encouraging others to apply their talents to the ongoing work of reform. Keats, an admirer of Milton's "delectable prose,"[10] could have borrowed his concept of a grand march of intellect presided over by a mighty providence directly from *Areopagitica*:

> When God shakes a Kingdome with strong and healthfull commotions to a generall reforming . . . God then raises to his own work men of rare abilities, and more then common industry not only to look back and revise what hath been taught heretofore, but to gain furder and goe on, some new enlightn'd steps in the discovery of truth. For such is the order of Gods enlightning his Church, to dispense and deal out by degrees his beam, so as our earthly eyes may best sustain it. Neither is God appointed and confin'd, where and out of what place these his chosen shall be first heard to speak.[11]

The Romantic poets had reason to believe that the same historical tendency, the same reformational spirit was working in their own time to bring some "unimagined change" in the religious opinions that cemented the social order. They saw in contemporary events signs that their own time might be as remarkable an era in English religious history as the ones that brought the Tudor Reformation and the Civil War. This expectation was not poetic fancy. The need and the opportunity for comprehensive religious reform were acknowledged by public figures representing a broad range of experience and theological opinion. Of course, the precise nature of this necessary reformation was understood differently according to the varying social agendas of those who expected it. The breadth of the spectrum is illustrated in two of the most influential books of the 1790s – Thomas Paine's *The Age of Reason* (1794) and William Wilberforce's *A Practical View of the Prevailing Religious Systems of Professed Christians* (1797). Paine, who had perceived that the social revolution outlined in *The Rights of Man* would require a fundamental change in the ideological underpinnings of the political order, and who identified organized Christianity as the chief abettor of repressive government, called for "a revolution in the system of religion [in which] human inventions and priestcraft would be detected; and man would return to the pure, unmixed, and unadulterated belief of one God, and no more."[12] Wilberforce's *A Practical View*, which was, after Burke's *Reflections*, the most influential book of the decade among the upper classes,[13] and was intended, in part, as a response to Paine, saw the national salvation as contingent on a return to orthodox, vital Christianity – as distinct from the "dry, unanimated religion . . . professed by nominal Christians."[14] Although Paine and Wilberforce were worlds apart in their vision of what a future society should look like, they resembled each other in their understanding of the need for a purification of the national religion of England and in the belief that their own time was ripe with opportunity for such a reformation.

Aside from the example of the French Revolution, which made all social structures seem vulnerable to change, two recent developments encouraged contemporary observers to expect or fear that a dramatic transformation might be occurring in the character of the national religion and in the political and social order it helped to sustain. Those events were the campaign for religious liberty being waged throughout the country by Protestant Dissenters and the remarkable nationwide rebirth of Christian faith and piety that became known as the Evangelical Revival.[15] Both phenomena involved resistance to coercion in the religious sphere and an insistence on the primary importance of authentic personal experience; both, therefore, tended toward subversion of traditional religious authority, with profound consequences for what Shelley called "the equilibrium between institutions and opinions." For a period of approximately three decades, the decades in which Romantic poetry flourished, religion in England seemed to abandon its character as a guarantor of social stability and to become, as it had during the sixteenth and seventeenth centuries, a force for potentially revolutionary change. In 1643 Milton had commended the "pious forwardness among men, to reassume the ill-deputed care of their Religion into their own hands again."[16] At the turn of the nineteenth century admirers and critics of such forwardness often commented on the similarities between Milton's time and their own.[17] Before continuing my account of how the Romantic poets participated in the reformational activity of their time, it will be useful to consider further the historical context that conditioned their thinking.

Throughout the Romantic period, the most clamorous political disputes in England were provoked by marginalized religious groups attempting to gain a larger share of political and economic power. Demands by Roman Catholics for relief from the severe political, economic, and cultural disabilities inflicted by the Penal Laws had been quiescent since an effort to moderate the laws provoked the Gordon Riots in 1780, but they were revived by the Act of Union with Ireland in 1800 and became the most explosive political issue in Britain in the early years of the century. Disputes over the "Catholic Claims" forced William Pitt's resignation in 1801, brought down the Whig ministry of "All the Talents" in 1807, and kept the Whigs out of power afterward until new pressure for Catholic Emancipation precipitated the political crisis that resulted in passage of the 1832 Reform Bill.[18] The Catholic Question, one might note in passing, embroiled Wordsworth in years of anti-popery campaigning, provoked Coleridge's *On the Constitution of Church and State*, and provided the subject of Byron's second speech in the House of Lords. However, it was not Catholics but Protestants who fomented most of the domestic agitation during the crucial decade of the 1790s in which British Romanticism first emerged as a cultural force. As the decade began, the most contentious political issue in England was the campaign to repeal the laws excluding Protestant Dissenters from full participation in the public life of England.

When the Interregnum following the death of Charles I ended in the accession of his son to the throne, those religious communities in England that refused to conform to the discipline and liturgy of the restored Church of England were subjected to punitive laws limiting their freedom of worship and imposing other civil and cultural disabilities. After the Revolution of 1688, an Act of Toleration permitted Protestant Nonconformists to worship as they desired but continued to restrict their civil rights. Throughout the eighteenth century the officially recognized Dissenting sects – Presbyterians, Baptists, Congregationalists, and Quakers – had been excluded by law from full participation in national and local government, as well as from various other educational and social opportunities.[19] Although the discriminatory laws were erratically enforced and the penalties were routinely abrogated, Dissenters officially remained second-class citizens, prevented from taking degrees at Oxford and Cambridge and from being legally married or buried by their own ministers, and sometimes subjected to petty, capricious tyranny by Anglican officials with whom they came in contact. This low-grade persecution kept alive the Dissenters' old heritage of intellectual resistance until it flared up again in the years 1787–1796, invigorated by a new wave of religious revivalism and inspired by events in France. Between 1787 and 1791, the Dissenting sects joined forces in three successive, increasingly militant attempts to win parliamentary repeal of the discriminatory laws under which they suffered. In what would now be called a national lobbying effort, the Dissenters organized themselves in towns and cities throughout the country, coordinating their local efforts through an interdenominational committee in London, to apply pressure in Parliament for repeal. Their ultimate aim – to change the religious character of the nation by breaking the legal monopoly of the Church – involved a dual effort to free religion from institutional control and to bring it into accord with a broadly liberal political program. This campaign for liberation from the tyrannies of pre-scription and privilege put religious freedom at the top of the national political agenda, impinging on the consciousness of people at every level of society.[20]

As the repeal campaign intensified, its object changed from a request for increased legal toleration to a demand for religious liberty as a natural right. The Dissenters had been appealing to abstract rights since the campaign began in 1787, but their vocabulary showed some new French seasoning when in January 1790 the central Repeal Committee resolved "that every test calculated to exclude [Dissenters] from civil and military offices on account of religious scruples is a violation of their rights as men and citizens of a free state, inconsistent with the principles of the constitution of this country and repugnant to the genuine spirit of true religion."[21] The echo of *"droits de l'homme et du citoyen"* was provocative, but not more so than the appeal to a truer religion than the one professed by the Established Church of England. The rhetoric of reformation was becoming more explicit, and criticism not only of the Church's privileges and revenues but even of its doctrines and liturgy was becoming part of the national debate.

While the majority of Dissenters involved in the campaign were ortho-dox, the most prominent spokesmen for the cause were "rational dissenters" (Joseph Priestley's term for anti-trinitarian nonconformists), particularly members of the newly distinct denomination of Unitarians. They had more at stake in the struggle than others, since their heterodox beliefs were not protected even under the terms of the Toleration Act of 1689 and were further penalized by the Blasphemy Act of 1698, which criminalized denial of the Trinity. Perhaps on that account they were the most audible in their demand for a continued Reformation and devoted much attention to preparing a new "correct" translation of the Bible as well as a revision of the Prayer Book. Even after the failure of the repeal campaign they were confident enough in their growing strength to petition Parliament again in 1792 for relief from their legal disabilities. Their persistent efforts finally bore fruit in 1813 with passage of the Trinity Act, which legalized Unitarian worship.[22]

The repeal campaign of the early nineties failed, largely because the Dis-senters' organized pressure tactics provoked a hostile response from the Anglican community, a reaction that culminated in the "Church and King" riots of 1791 in which the homes and chapels of Dissenters in many parts of England were destroyed. The agitation on both sides became so tumultu-ous that one historian of Dissent has called the repeal campaign "England's French Revolution."[23] It seemed to many that not since England's own revolution of the 1640s had religious disturbances posed such a threat to the stability of the social order. The Dissenters were challenging, as the Puritans before them had done, the legitimacy of the religious Establishment that made up an essential component of the British Constitution and a vital prop of the monarchy in particular. Religion, it bears repeating, had always been the most powerful solvent of political structures in Britain. Now, against the backdrop of the French Revolution, the old argument over "divine right" was being renewed in the ecclesiastical sphere, a more dangerous arena than the legislative forum because passions ran higher, certainties were more absolute, and consequences were, by definition, of greater moment, since they affected one's eternal life and not merely one's earthly pilgrimage. Faith and piety gave to political commitment the intimacy of a subject for meditative prayer and the urgency of a religious obligation – a situation that in Britain had always been pregnant with consequence for the order of power. Not surprisingly, the old association of "sectaries" with the regicide of 1649 was recalled frequently in the heated rhetoric of the day.

In purely political terms (setting aside the domestic effects of the war with France) the repeal controversy may be said to have had a more profound effect on public life in Britain than the French Revolution itself. The controversy dominated national politics for ten years years, from 1787 to 1796, and the issues and emotions raised by the campaign foreshadowed and in some ways shaped the debate over the French Revolution, creating ideological divisions that ran through British politics for decades afterward. The reactionary "Church and King" emotion provoked by the repeal campaign was easily redirected at "Jacobin" radicals when they succeeded the Dissenters as public critics of the Constitution. In fact, the national network that had agitated for repeal provided much of the infrastructure for later radical movements in politics.[24] In other words, the British counter-revolution may be said, paradoxically, to predate the French revolution, since it originated in a domestic religious dispute that began two years before the Estates General convened in Paris.

The repeal campaign generated the heated political climate in which, on November 4, 1789, the Presbyterian minister Richard Price delivered his provocative *Discourse on the Love of Our Country* at a meeting of a society founded to commemorate the English Revolution of 1688. Price, a "rational dissenter," was a leading spokesman for the cause of repeal and his address to the Revolution Society was primarily intended to rally enthusiasm for the campaign, including for that purpose a call for reformation of the national Church and elimination of "the defects (may I not say the absurdities?) in our established codes of faith and worship." In his celebrated "Nunc Dimittis" peroration, Price linked the repeal campaign in England with the political and religious changes then being effected in France: "And now, methinks, I see the ardour for liberty catching and spreading; a general amendment beginning in human affairs; the dominion of kings changed for the dominion of laws, and the dominion of priests giving way to the dominion of reason and conscience. Tremble all ye oppressors of the world! Take warning all ye supporters of slavish governments and slavish hierarchies! Call no more (absurdly and wickedly) REFORMATION, innovation."[25]

Literary historian H. N. Brailsford designated November 4, 1789 as the beginning of the French Revolution in England,[26] because it was Price's discourse that provoked Edmund Burke's *Reflections on the Revolution in France and on Proceedings in Certain Societies in London Relative to that Event*. The second part of Burke's title, often elided, indicates that the book was a response to domestic as well as foreign provocation, and his attack on Richard Price suggests that it was the religious content and tone of Price's reformational "sermon" that especially antagonized him. The *Reflections* characterize Price as a "political Divine," a "spiritual doctor of politics," and an "arch-pontiff of the *rights of men*" who along with other "apostolic missionaries" had been spreading a new "political gospel"; he is compared twice with the Reverend Hugh Peters, who was executed as a regicide in the seventeenth century. Burke was obviously evoking the 1640s when he expressed his fear of revolution, "the signals for which have so often been given from pulpits."[27]

Burke did his best to turn the debate on the French Revolution into a religious argument. He was astute enough to sense very early what historians now see clearly, that the Revolution's most serious tactical error was its attack on the Catholic Church, beginning with the confiscations and desecrations of ecclesiastical property in November 1789.[28] Judging by the amount of space he gives to them in the *Reflections*, these depredations seem to have outraged him more than any other activity of the revolutionaries. They "rankled in his mind," a contemporary observer commented, "and tainted by infection the general current of his thoughts."[29] "Irreligious" and "unhallowed" became for him broad terms of political disapproval,[30] and he began to characterize the war against France as a crusade: "We cannot, if we would, delude ourselves about the true state of this dreadful contest," he said in 1793. "*It is a religious war*. It includes in its object every other interest of society as well as this; but this is the principal and leading feature. It is through the destruction of religion that our enemies propose the accomplishment of all their other views."[31] On the domestic front, Burke seldom missed a chance to associate the preservation of the political order in Britain with the welfare of the national Church. He said in *Reflections* that the people of England "know, and what is better we feel inwardly, that religion is the basis of civil society, and the source of all good and comfort." Englishmen "do not consider their church establishment as convenient, but as essential to their state . . . the foundation of their whole constitution, with which, and with every part of which, it holds an indissoluble union. Church and state are ideas inseparable in their minds, and scarcely is the one ever mentioned without mentioning the other."[32] Whether or not this assessment of the country's sentiments was accurate, Burke worked very hard to forge just such an identification between Church and State in the national consciousness and to defend the ecclesiastical establishment as an indispensable barrier against revolution.[33] The strategy was successful; religion became an increasingly important factor in the revolutionary debate, one that grew in significance as the prevailing revolutionary ideology in France became more militantly anti-Christian.

So the political argument that divided Britain in the 1790s was initially and remained in important senses a religious debate. Every prescription offered for the national welfare, whether radical or reactionary, had its religious ingredient. This fact has tended to be overlooked by some literary historians when they analyze Romanticism as an expression of the spirit of the age. The poets' increasing concern with religious matters was not a retreat from social activism; it was an energetic engagement in some of the central public policy debates of the era. The issues of religious authority and religious authenticity were at the heart of current events during the Romantic period, as they were close to the heart of the literary movement itself.

The repeal campaign generated throughout England an urgent reexamination of the nation's religious character, helping to create a national climate of intellectual unrest, of spiritual dissatisfaction and inquiry and desire. This mood of religious discontent and expectancy was reflected also in the evangelical revival that had been taking place in the country since the middle of the eighteenth century but which reached new levels of intensity in the 1790s, becoming what one historian called "the greatest revival of religious faith since the middle ages,"[34] and contributing to the sense of crisis in the public religious sphere. The connection between the repeal campaign and the revival is not often noted, because the best-known spokesmen for repeal, such as Richard Price and Joseph Priestley, were "rational dissenters" – liberal and even heterodox in their beliefs, while the revival was orthodox in tendency. But there was a remarkable spirit of ecumenical cooperation among Dissenters at this time, and much of the energy behind the repeal campaign, especially at the provincial level, came from orthodox Dissent.[35]

The revitalization of Christian faith and piety initiated by Wesley in the 1740s and its eventual spread to the middle and upper classes in the form of Church Evangelicalism is sufficiently well known that it does not need to be reviewed here.[36] What has not so often been discussed was the special political character given to the revival by the secession of the Methodists from the Church of England after Wesley's death in 1791 and the simultaneous quickening of religious fervor among the older Dissenting sects, especially the Independents and the Baptists, who suddenly rediscovered in the 1790s the duty of converting the rural population of England to a more vital Christian faith and piety. The new attention to domestic evangelism seems to have arisen partly as an afterthought to the fervor for foreign missions that emerged rather suddenly among the Dissenters in the early 1790s. As the Baptist minister Robert Hall recalled later, "A zeal for the conversion of pagans had occasioned a powerful reaction at home, by producing efforts, hitherto unexampled, toward carrying the Gospel into the darkest corners of the kingdom."[37] Imitating procedures that the Methodists had developed earlier in the century, the Dissenting revival of the 1790s was conducted mainly by itinerant preachers, many of them haphazardly educated laymen, who emphasized the experience of conversion to a saving faith more than doctrinal formulations or disciplinary codes.[38] At first the Methodists and other Dissenters concentrated on bringing religious ministry to places where the national Church provided none, but they eventually began challenging the regular clergy on their own ground, building alongside the parish structure and in opposition to it the alternative religious order suggested by the distinction still preserved in Britain between "chapel" and "church." The result was a suddenly expanded and increasingly homogeneous nonconformist religious culture that had in common primarily its sense of separation from the Established Church.

Cultural historians until recently have been inclined to describe the evangelical revival in Britain as a conservative force protecting Britain from radical political change.[39] While this may be an accurate enough description of the revival's final effect, in the 1790s and the years immediately following it was possible, indeed common, for contemporaries to see the revival as a dangerously destabilizing force in society and a threat to the established political order. The increase in the proselytizing activity of the older Dissenting communities called attention to what had been a previously unregarded aspect of the growth of Methodism – the massive disaffection from the Established Church that it had discovered and then stimulated, especially among the lower classes. When the spiritual revival spread to Dissent in the 1790s it added new intensity of religious fervor to the old heritage of political alienation; Anglican clergymen who had tended to ignore or deride the Methodists had to take more seriously a newly invigorated Dissent with its tradition of defiance of the established political and ecclesiastical order.

Christianity provided the central principle of cohesion in British society and the primary ideological rationale for submission to authority. It was within the sphere of religion, therefore, that class conflict might arise in the most dangerously destabilizing manner, as what ought to have been a common religious ideology became susceptible to radically differing political interpretations, driven by high intensities of zeal. Insofar as subservience had a religious sanction, insubordination that appealed to a higher religious rationale was the most dangerous kind of all. As the historian Theodore Maynard observed, "Religion, though it normally exerts a conservative influence on culture, also provides the most dynamic means of social change. Indeed one might almost go so far as to say that it is only by religion that a religious culture can be changed."[40] The millenarianism that tended to accompany religious revivals was, as J. F. C. Harrison has pointed out, an ideology of change: "it focused attention on the great changes which were currently taking place in these last days, and promised a vast transformation of the social order when all things would be made new. Men and women who were looking eagerly for a new heaven and a new earth could not but be consciously aware that the future would be utterly different from the present."[41] Such enthusiasm was truly dangerous because it induced a kind of recklessness that trusted Providence to pick up the pieces after apocalyptic events had run their course.

There was a more immediate threat to the social order in the revival's tendency to encourage disaffection from the Established Church, which in many parts of Britain was the most visible embodiment of the national government. Historian J. C. D. Clark has pointed out that the average person in England at the time had very little to do with the political power structure centered in London but had continual contact with the religious arm of the ruling order:

> The agency of the State which confronted him in his everyday life was not Parliament, reaching out as a machinery of representative democracy: elections were infrequent, contests less frequent still, the franchise restricted, and access to MPs minimal for most electors. The ubiquitous agency of the State was the Church, quartering the land not into a few hundred constituencies but into ten thousand parishes, impinging on the daily concerns of the great majority, supporting its black-coated army of a clerical intelligentsia, bidding for a monopoly of education, piety, and political acceptability.[42]

While it was routinely asserted that the Church of England lived under the protection of the State, in practice the reverse was true: the government depended on the Church to ensure the subservience, if not the loyalty, of the people. The Church created, more effectively than either the judiciary or the military could, a climate of respect for law and order. It was at the parish level that deference and obedience were taught as the standard of acceptable deportment and a manifestation of the divine order. In some areas the clergy and the criminal justice system were identical, since clergymen constituted a large proportion of the justices of the peace.[43] But even in their more routine priestly roles the clergy served a law-enforcement function. When the local landlord, whether nobleman or gentleman, took his pew in the parish church on Sunday morning and received the blessing of the parson, one could see in them a synecdoche of the national power structure – Church and State united for mutual advantage and protection in a hierarchical society where power derived from birth and educational privilege.

Infringement of the clergy's influence at this local level constituted, then, a potentially serious subversion of the political order. The rapid growth of alternative, nonconformist religious communities involved a radical alienation of the poor from the hegemonic systems into which they had been born. When the defections from the national Church began noticeably to increase during the French revolutionary period, the political danger became apparent to the more alert churchmen. As the Bishop of Chester complained, "Every addition [nonconformity] makes to the number of its supporters alters the proportion existing in the country between the monarchical and democratic spirit."[44] And Samuel Horsley, Bishop of Rochester and leader of the hierarchy's conservative wing, also suspected that the revival had a subversive political agenda:

> In many parts of the kingdom new conventicles have opened in great numbers, and congregations formed of one knows not what denomination. The Pastor is often, in appearance at least, an illiterate peasant or mechanic . . . It is very remarkable, that these new congregations of non-descripts have been mostly formed, since the Jacobins have been laid under the restraint of those two most salutary statutes, commonly known by the names of the Sedition and Treason bills. A circumstance which gives much ground for suspicion, that sedition and atheism are the real objects of these institutions, rather than religion . . . The Jacobins of this country, I very much fear, are, at this moment, making a tool of Methodism.[45]

The notion that the "gagging acts" had redirected Jacobins into second careers as village preachers is comical but not entirely paranoid. Many Dissenting preachers, even quite orthodox ones, publically maintained "Jacobin" principles and allegiances right through the 1790s, and much of the radical agitation in the years that followed, such as that of the "Tolpuddle martyrs" and the Pentrich uprising, was led by Methodist activists.[46] Bishop Horsley's concern was justified in more general senses too. In a country whose Parliament each year still solemnly and penitentially commemorated the execution of Charles I, no one could predict confidently the direction a new revival of religious enthusiasm might take; improperly channeled religious passions created political hazards, as the Civil War had memorably demonstrated.

What made the widespread defections of the 1790s even more culturally remarkable was that these new conversions away from Anglicanism were individual assertions of religious independence, of personal choice in the spiritual realm. In the sixteenth century if uneducated people became Protestants it was usually a matter of enforced conformity with the religious policy of their political rulers. The disaffections from the Church that occurred in late eighteenth-century England had no such leadership from the top. Believers were converted one by one, usually by members of their own class who had been sent to them as lay preachers by the local Methodist connection or one of the older Dissenting sects. In this case, conversion away from the local parish church meant conversion into a temporary state of religious freedom, with liberty to choose from a range of sectarian options. The Methodists themselves soon after Wesley's death began to fragment into separate denominations, each appealing to a different set of political or theological predispositions. And this new kind of religious liberation could mean not only a transfer of allegiance from church to the chapel of one's choice; it could mean repudiation of all religious affiliation. For many, Methodism and the other revivalist sects provided a halfway house on the road to secularism or religious indifference, an increasingly common destination in those years for those who had been invited to think for themselves in matters of religion.[47]

To look upon the religious revival of the 1790s primarily as a counter-revolutionary force, then, is to underestimate its vitality as a destabilizing, liberating, and renovating cultural movement. Rather than encouraging political or intellectual subordination, the revival was, for a time, a potent force for intellectual liberation and political empowerment. A number of social historians have suggested that it was in their religious life that the British lower classes were first liberated, released from their previously determined place in the social order, and invited to assume positions of authority that made use of hitherto untried talents. For Alan Gilbert, the revival "offered particular social groups not just other-worldly salvation, but also a welcome escape from anomie and a more or less legitimate means of affirming social emancipation from old deferential relationships. But both these latter functions were of maximum significance only during the late-eighteenth-, early-nineteenth-century hiatus between the destruction of one cultural system and its replacement by another."[48]

This period of religious volatility did not endure very long; by the 1820s the various Dissenting denominations were reasserting doctrinal and disciplinary control over their numerous new converts, moving religious services from fields and barns into newly constructed chapels under the supervision of ministers who were more professional and conventional in demeanor than the earlier field preachers had been, and British Nonconformity began to take on that coercive, repressive character for which it was known later in the century. But during the time we call the Romantic period, public religion in England was in a transitional state that offered hope and apparent opportunity for genuine change in the spiritual temper of the country. This was the spirit of the age that conditioned British Romanticism, a spirit of religious spontaneity and innovation, and this destabilizing, liberalizing impulse was not confined to the sphere of religion only but had broad social, economic, and political implications as well.

The buoyant, optimistic temper of Nonconformist religion in the 1790s may be seen in the public expressions of sympathy with which Dissenters of all doctrinal persuasions greeted the French Revolution in its first years.

The libertarian sentiments generated during the repeal campaign and the religious optimism that accompanied the revival encouraged a positive response to the outbreak of the Revolution, which was welcomed not only as striking a mortal blow against the Catholic Church and thus bringing apocalyptic cheer to the hearts of all good Protestants, but also as signifying a promising change for the better in human nature generally, a development that boded well for their newly invigorated missionary efforts at home and abroad. Millennial expectations generated by the revival greeted the Revolution as part of the shaking of the old order necessary for the construction of the new. Religious zeal and political optimism thus went hand in hand – a conjunction that Wordsworth illustrated in *The Excursion* when the Solitary was inspired by the good news from France to resume the clerical ministry he had earlier abandoned and, for a time, "from the Pulpit zealously maintained / The cause of Christ and civil liberty, / As one; and moving to one glorious end."[49] Such sympathies, it bears repeating, were expressed not only by "rational" Dissenters such as Priestley and Price but by orthodox Nonconformists as well. One of the most fearlessly outspoken of these, the Baptist preacher Robert Hall, repudiated Burke's efforts to sanctify the counter-revolution and demonstrated in his 1791 tract *Christianity Consistent with a Love of Freedom* that religious zeal could be recruited equally well on the radical side. Hall, like Richard Price, welcomed the Revolution as a work of God:

> The empire of darkness and of despotism has been smitten with a stroke which has sounded through the universe. When we see whole kingdoms, after reposing for centuries in the lap of their rulers, start from their slumber, the dignity of man rising up from depression, and tyrants trembling on their thrones ... these are a kind of throes and struggle of nature, to which it would be a sullenness to refuse our sympathy. Old foundations are breaking up; new edifices are rearing ... That fond attachment to ancient institutions and blind submission to opinions already received, which has ever checked the growth of improvement ... is giving way to a spirit of bold and fearless investigation. Man seems to be becoming more erect and independent. He leans more on himself, less on his fellow-creatures. He begins to feel a consciousness in a higher degree of personal dignity, and is less enamoured of artificial distinctions ... The devout mind will behold in these momentous changes the finger of God, and, discerning in them the dawn of that glorious period, in which wars will cease, and antichristian tyranny shall fall, will adore that unerring wisdom, whose secret operation never fails to conduct all human affairs to their proper issue, and impells the great actors on that troubled theatre, to fulfill, when they least intend it, the counsels of heaven, and the prediction of its prophets.[50]

It is hard to distinguish religious from political exhilaration here. Biblical faith added an apocalyptic resonance, a heightened sublimity, to the politics of the day, representing them *sub specie aeternitatis* as a moment in the history of salvation.

One cannot help noticing the resemblance between the religious aspirations expressed by liberal preachers like Hall and the exalted vision of human potential that one finds in much Romantic poetry. Remove the more specific theological vocabulary and the passage above might have been written by Shelley or the younger Wordsworth. Like Hall, Wordsworth also discovered a higher degree of personal dignity in the commonest of people, a dignity that did not depend on artificial distinctions. The fall of the empire of darkness, the awakening of humanity from slumber, and the rearing of new social edifices constitute the central narrative of Blake's *Jerusalem*. In optimistic moments Byron, Shelley, and Keats thought they saw, or hoped they saw, blind submission giving way to bold investigation in the mental life of mankind. Whether by affinity or consanguinity, the ideology of Dissent and the Romantic ideology show signs of a close familial relationship. And however much they insisted on their unique visions and definitions of national salvation, poets who held out to their contemporaries the promise of "a new Earth and new Heaven, / Undreamt of by the sensual and the proud"[51] were working the same territory as the religious revivalists – who, for their part, could have described their mission in the terms that Wordsworth used to characterize his own effort: to "arouse the sensual from their sleep / Of Death, and win the vacant and the vain / To noble raptures."[52]

In 1802, in the first notice taken by a professional critic of what we now call the English Romantic movement, Francis Jeffrey sensed a connection between this new development in literature and the religious agitation being felt at that time. In a review of Robert Southey's *Thalaba*, he wrote,

> The author who is now before us belongs to a *sect* of poets, that has established itself in this country within these ten or twelve years, and is looked upon, we believe, as one of its chief champions and apostles. The peculiar doctrines of this sect, it would not, perhaps, be very easy to explain; but, that they are *dissenters* from the established systems in poetry and criticism is admitted, and proved, indeed, by the whole tenor of their compositions. Though they lay claim, we believe, to a creed and a revelation of their own, there can be little doubt, that their doctrines are of *German* origin, and have been derived from some of the great modern reformers in that country. Some of their leading principles, indeed, are probably of an earlier date, and seem to have been borrowed from the great apostle of Geneva . . . The disciples of this school boast much of its originality, and seem to value themselves very highly, for having broken loose from the bondage of ancient authority, and re-asserted the independence of genius.[53]

In his attempt to characterize this new group of writers (Wordsworth, Coleridge, and Lamb are mentioned as well as Southey), Jeffrey chooses an analogy from the religious politics of his day. The poets are, he says, a *sect* of *dissenters* (the italics are his own) from established systems, who have liberated themselves from "the bondage of ancient authority." At one level the comparison is playful: writing at a time when a revival of religious enthusiasm among marginal groups was attracting national attention, Jeffrey is parodying the kind of theological scrutiny to which Nonconformists were being subjected when he finds the German origins of the new doctrines in "reformers" like Kotzebue and Schiller rather than in Martin Luther and cites Rousseau instead of Calvin as the Genevan inspiration. Beneath the jocularity, however, there are more serious reasons why Jeffrey would have associated the new poetry with religious dissent.

In one sense, the association was already established critical practice, one that began in 1798 when the *Anti-Jacobin Review* attacked Southey, Coleridge, and Lamb as "Jacobin poets" and lumped them together with Joseph Priestley and other liberal Dissenters.[54] Jeffrey had some knowledge of the poets' personal connections with the Dissenting communities in London, Bristol, and Cambridge. Coleridge's involvement in such circles, including his own brief career as a Unitarian preacher, was no secret, and Southey's relations with Dissenters in Bristol were also well known. But beyond what he knew of their personal backgrounds, Jeffrey thought he saw in these writers a complex of attitudes that had become associated with religious Nonconformity in England, especially as it was now being transformed by the religious revival. Having separated themselves from "the catholic poetical church," and abandoned "the establishments of language" this new "sect of dissenters" were affecting "simplicity and familiarity of language," translating, as the revivalists did, lofty conceptions into vulgar diction. The poets resembled Dissenters too in their "discontent with the present constitution of society." In all, Jeffrey's comparison of the Romantics with religious nonconformists was not so whimsical a conceit as it may appear to us, separated by two centuries from its cultural and political context. In 1802, Dissent provided the most familiar example on the domestic scene of rebellion against intellectual coercion, setting a pattern which any other movement for cultural innovation might be seen as imitating. By having "broken loose from the bondage of ancient authority, and re-asserted the independence of genius," the Romantics were repeating, consciously or not, the old radical Protestant insistence that in the most important aspects of life individual intuition, or private inspiration, was of more importance than doctrines defined by authority and sanctified by custom.

It was, then, perhaps not accidental that the birth of the Romantic movement in England coincided with a national struggle for religious freedom, the freedom to define the ultimate meaning of human life independent of traditional or legislated definitions. Just as the repeal campaign became a struggle for spiritual liberty against institutional coercion and the tyranny of prescription and privilege, the revival in its earlier stage encouraged the rejection of older religious formulations and disciplinary codes. At the beginning of the repeal campaign in 1787 Richard Price predicted, "The human mind must soon be emancipated from the chains of Church authority and Church establishments, for the liberality of the times has already loosened their foundations."[55] Fifteen years later, this longing for spiritual emancipation was being observed even among the most orthodox Anglicans. In one of the earliest episcopal comments on the phenomenon of Church Evangelicalism, the Bishop of Oxford warned these enthusiasts that "while they bring everything within private suggestion, they encourage in Religion the very principle, which in Politics has proved so fatal to the peace and good government of states; being no other than giving the reins to private opinion, in opposition to public authority."[56] Consciously or not, the Romantic poets found themselves adopting the agenda of the religious reformers of their time when they themselves directed their energies toward creating a climate of spiritual freedom that would liberate religion, at least, from the control of repressive institutions.

Celebrating in his own time "this pious forwardness among men, to reassume the ill-deputed care of their Religion into their own hands again," Milton wrote in *Areopagitica*: "Now the time seems come, wherein Moses the great prophet, may sit in heav'n rejoycing to see that memorable and glorious wish of his fulfill'd, when not only our sev'nty Elders, but all the Lords people are become Prophets."[57] "Would to God that all the Lords people were Prophets," echoed William Blake, as he began his remarkable attempt to revise and rehabilitate Milton in the epic poem he named for him. That Blake shared Milton's sense of the English Reformation as unfinished business may be seen in Plate II of *Europe*, which depicts King George III wearing the papal tiara – an emblem not only of the pernicious union of Church and State against which Blake waged relentless mental warfare but also of the inadequacy of the Reformation in Britain. The English Church under George III was still as corrupt and benighted, still as repressive and as much in need of reform, as it had been under papal domination.[58] In *Milton* one can find a less polemical, more touching emblem of the Romantic reformation when Milton, having joined himself to Blake, recants his own erroneous theology and struggles to reshape in a more human form the image of Urizen, the authoritarian, punishing Father he had portrayed in *Paradise Lost*. Milton confronts his God at Peor, a place where the Israelites worshipped false divinities (Num.25):

Urizen emerged from his Rocky Form & from his Snows . . .
And met him on the shores of Arnon; & by the streams of the brooks
Silent they met, and silent strove among the streams, of Arnon
Even to Mahanaim, when with cold hand Urizen stoop'd down

And took up water from the river Jordan: pouring on
To Miltons brain the icy fluid from his broad cold palm.
But Milton took of the red clay of Succoth, moulding it with care
Between his palms: and filling up the furrows of many years
Beginning at the feet of Urizen, and on the bones
Creating new flesh on the Demon cold, and building him,
As with new clay a Human form in the Valley of Beth Peor.[59]

This is not iconoclasm; it is reformation in a quite literal sense. Milton does not pull down and destroy the image of Urizen. Upon a hardened image of God he spreads fresh clay, susceptible to new representations of the Divine Vision. Meanwhile Urizen attempts to impose his control over the prophet in a parody of baptism, specifically the baptism at the Jordan in which God claimed paternal authority over Jesus (Matthew 3:13–17). Blake illustrates this confrontation between creative and ossified religious vision on Plate 18 of *Milton* (the plate I have used as frontispiece). In that richly ambiguous illumination one sees an image of the Romantic religious enterprise – a struggle which is almost an embrace, an assault that is an effort to support and rejuvenate the tottering victim, who must be revived and renewed because his decrepitude is dangerous and his death a threat to something valuable in human existence.

"Milton! thou shouldst be living at this hour," Wordsworth wrote, appealing to Milton as a standard against whom to measure the religious as well as the political and literary deficiencies of his own society at a time when "altar, sword, and pen . . . have forfeited their ancient English dower." His own most ambitious attempt to address his country's religious condition, *The Excursion*, was prefaced by an acknowledgement that he would need to surpass even Milton, "Holiest of Men," if he was to succeed in articulating a new religious vision adequate to the needs of his own contemporaries. He invokes Milton's muse:

> Urania, I shall need
> Thy guidance, or a greater Muse, if such
> Descend to earth or dwell in highest heaven!
> For I must tread on shadowy ground, must sink
> Deep – and aloft ascending, breathe in worlds
> To which the heaven of heavens is but a veil.
> All strength – all terror, single or in bands,
> That ever was put forth in personal form –
> Jehovah – with his thunder, and the choir
> Of shouting Angels, and the empyreal thrones,
> I pass them unalarmed. Not Chaos, not
> The darkest pit of lowest Erebus,
> Nor aught of blinder vacancy – scooped out

> By help of dreams, can breed such fear and awe
> As fall upon us often when we look
> Into our Minds, into the Mind of Man –
> My haunt, and the main region of my Song.[60]

This passage has been read as a proclamation of naturalistic humanism,[61] but such an interpretation requires decontextualizing the lines from their prefatory position in *The Excursion*, a poem that is usually lamented as a retreat from naturalistic humanism. But Wordsworth is more interested in mythopoesis here than in doctrine. He is not repudiating Milton's belief in a noumenal order, but only the "personal form" in which Milton clothed his conception of the Divine.

The challenge of finding an adequate language for religious expression is an important part of the "argument" of the poem that follows, an argument that is articulated most plainly in Book 4, which traces the history of humanity's attempts since the Fall to find an appropriate language for its religious insights. During the history of Israel, the Wanderer says, 'Jehovah – shapeless Power above all Powers,/ Single and one, the omnipresent God" manifested his Presence unmistakably "By vocal utterance, or blaze of light,/Or cloud of darkness, localized in heaven."[62] In the absence of such direct perception of Divinity, fallen humanity's religious sense attempted in various ways to articulate its religious intuitions, and Wordsworth reports the results in his survey of ancient mythologies – that poetic *tour de force* which so impressed John Keats. Wordsworth's point is that human religious language, however sublime in power, must always be inadequate to express the inexpressible. A year after publishing *The Excursion* he wrote, "The religious man values what he sees chiefly as an 'imperfect shadowing forth' of what he is incapable of seeing. The concerns of religion refer to indefinite objects, and are too weighty for the mind to support them without relieving itself by resting a great part of the burden upon words and symbols." The more concrete these words and symbols, the less suitable they are to signify the Ineffable. "The anthropomorphitism of the Pagan religion subjected the minds of the greatest poets in those countries too much to the bondage of definite form; from which the Hebrews were preserved by their abhorrence of idolatry. This abhorrence was almost as strong in our great epic Poet, both from circumstances of his life, and from the constitution of his mind."[63] But even Milton had surrendered too much to "the bondage of definite form," and his successors were responsible for continuing the purification of religious language.

Enlightenment thinkers had argued persuasively that religion needed to be more philosophical than the kind of "vulgar superstition" which depended on concrete images and personages – e.g., the Biblical faith that had provided Milton with the material for his poem. Wordsworth's prospectus to *The Excursion* suggests that Milton's own concretions, his shouting angels, etc., now needed to be left behind by poetry. In his comparison of Milton and Wordsworth, Keats had criticized Milton for resting content with the dogmas and superstitions of Protestantism and praised Wordsworth for thinking more deeply into the human heart. Keats observed that humanity, having matured since the seventeenth century, now demanded a more sophisticated religion, one that had no need for palpable, named mediators or of the dogmas and superstitions associated with them.[64] Keats found in Wordsworth's "Prospectus" a forceful expression of the Romantic program of religious reformation through literature. Its bold balance of reverence and iconoclasm, dismissing Jehovah while submitting humbly to "the law supreme of that Intelligence which governs all," led Keats to conclude that Wordsworth was, in religious matters at least, "deeper" than Milton.

All the Romantic poets found *Paradise Lost* wanting in its attempt to answer definitively the great religious questions it raised. As Stuart Curran has observed, "Blake would never have written *Milton*, nor Shelley *Prometheus Unbound*, nor Byron *Cain*, nor Keats *Hyperion*, if *Paradise Lost* had been definitive. All these works are ultimately theodicies – justifications of the ways of God to man – and each attempts a new, more modern, more humane, or more inclusive vision than Milton's."[65] Each new generation of poets had to incorporate its vision of ultimate truth in new forms and fresh language. Religious poetry, like religious doctrine and discipline, must undergo continual revision to serve the changing needs of a maturing humanity.

And so, while all the Romantics struggled under "the burden of the past" and "the anxiety of influence," one major source of intimidation, the example of Milton, was also a source of encouragement.[66] The need for a continued reformation, which Milton himself had articulated, encouraged the hope that poetry still had new, historically important work to do under the direction of "a mighty providence" that reveals new truth to each generation. That hope contributed to Shelley's optimism about his own generation's literary opportunities: they would represent a new, critical phase in the ongoing reformation. The poets were consoled not only by the prospect of work to be done, but by the realization that such work was inevitably incomplete in any one generation.

As they undertook their mission of rehabilitating the religious imaginations of their countrymen, the writers of the period took considerable pains to demonstrate their qualifications for this work of national reformation. Wordsworth late in life articulated most clearly the Miltonic belief that poets could act as effectively in matters of the spirit as those who were canonically ordained to the work:

> Though Pulpits and the Desk may fail
> To reach the hearts of worldly men;
> Yet may the grace of God prevail
> And touch them through the Poet's pen.

71

That is the Wordsworth of 1841, but he was sounding the same note a quarter century earlier when he claimed in the Appendix to his 1815 *Poems*, "Poetry is most just to its own divine origin when it administers the comforts and breathes the spirit of religion."[67] And ten years before that, reminiscing about his life in a still earlier period, he was already presenting himself in the character of a kind of field preacher:

> To the open fields I told
> A prophecy; poetic numbers came
> Spontaneously, and clothed in priestly robe
> My spirit, thus singled out, as it might seem,
> For holy services.[68]

One has little difficulty accumulating evidence of this tendency of the Romantic poets to ordain themselves ministers of the word, charged with the task of bringing the means of redemption to a community that had lost its way morally and spiritually. They all repeated in one form or another what the Bard proclaimed in *Milton*: "Mark well my words! they are of your eternal salvation."[69] Each of them found the public religion of his country to be deficient – a partial vision, at best, of a larger truth – and took it as his mission to chastise, to purify, or to redefine Christianity so that it might better reflect its own authentic ideals and serve more effectively as an instrument of social reform. From Blake's "Bible of Hell" in 1794 to Byron's *Cain* and Shelley's *Hellas* in 1821, all grappled with the national religion in a broad-scale attempt at changing its character.

Among the Romantics, Byron was the least comfortable about laying claim to any sort of religious magisterium, but such authority was nevertheless generally conceded to him, if only in negative terms. John Wilson of *Blackwood's* was not being simply perverse when he said of Byron, "the chief power of his poetry is its religion."[70] In 1823 the Evangelical minister James Kennedy said to the author of *Cain*, "whatever you do or say is of infinite importance to the church."[71] Byron's theological pronouncements were taken seriously enough to be considered a political as well as a religious danger. Fear of his destabilizing views can be observed even in a liberal periodical like the *Edinburgh Review*, when it suggested that *Cain* should be banned because of its undisciplined theological speculations:

> We think . . . that poets ought fairly to be confined to the established creed and morality of their country, or to the *actual* passions and sentiments of mankind; and that poetical dreamers and sophists who pretend to *theorize* according to their feverish fancies, without a warrant from authority or reason, ought to be banished the commonwealth of letters.[72]

The concluding allusion to Plato's *Republic* is revealing. In a political order dominated by a religious ideology, those who challenged the official national creed were a menace to society. It was just this insistence on proclaiming religious doctrine "without a warrant from authority" – their tendency, in short, to behave like a sect of dissenters – that made the Romantics most worrisome politically. While none of the other Romantics defied orthodox opinion with the public audacity of Byron and Shelley, or the private audacity of Blake, even partisans of the national Church like the older Wordsworth and Coleridge refused totally to surrender their religious independence. Even they could endorse the sentiment if not the rhetorical style of Leigh Hunt when he wrote: "I declare that I do not believe one single dogma, which the reason that God has put in our heads, or the heart that he has put in our bosoms, revolts at."[73]

Hunt, who devoted much of his energy through a long life to the struggle for religious liberty, left one of the clearest statements of the Romantic understanding of literature as a crucial arena for this struggle in the preface to his 1818 volume, *Foliage*, which surveyed the history of English poetry as a record of conflict between superstition and enlightenment, coercion and freedom. A central element in Hunt's program for modern poetry was resistance to the darkening shadow of Evangelical religion, which the *Examiner* had been combatting since its founding in 1808.[74] The same theme appears later in the volume in the poem "To Percy Shelley, on the Degrading Notions of Deity." For Hunt, bad religion perverts the aesthetic sense as well as the moral sense:

> What wonder, Percy, that with jealous rage
> Men should defame the kindly and the wise,
> When in the midst of the all-beautiful skies,
> And all this lovely world, that should engage
> Their mutual search for the old golden age,
> They seat a phantom, swelled into grim size
> Out of their own passions and bigotries,
> And then, for fear, proclaim it meek and sage!
> And this they call a light and a revealing![75]

The Romantics all saw themselves as charged with a mission not only to continue the liberalization of religion that began in modern times with the Reformation, but also to fight against any counter-reformational tendencies that appeared in their own society. The Romantic conception of literature as the organ of reformation made them especially alert to any attempt to use literary art in an effort to reverse the progress of religious liberalization. In *The Spirit of the Age* William Hazlitt accused the conservative *Quarterly Review* of an intention "to pervert literature, from being the natural ally of freedom and humanity, into an engine of priestcraft and despotism."[76] Like

Shelley and Keats, Hazlitt saw an intimate relationship between the spirit of reformation and that which inspired great literature and he was always on the alert when literature was employed for reactionary purposes. He detected, for example, in Coleridge's 1816 "Lay Sermon" just such a counter-reformational tendency:

> The whole of this Sermon is written to sanction the principle of Catholic dictation, and to reprobate that diffusion of free inquiry – that difference of private, and ascendancy of public opinion, which has been the necessary consequence, and the great benefit of the Reformation . . . [Coleridge], or at least those whom he writes to please . . . would give us back all the abuses of former times, without any of their advantages; and impose upon us, by force or fraud, a complete system of superstition without faith, of despotism without loyalty, of error without enthusiasm, and all the evils, without any of the blessings, of ignorance.[77]

To conclude this preliminary overview I return to Shelley, who poses the severest challenge to my thesis since he is the most ostensibly irreligious of all the Romantics. But although he contemptuously rejected the Christian faith of his contemporaries he never willingly surrendered the religious arena to those more conventional in their beliefs than he. On the contrary, he persistently claimed for himself as poet a privileged status as an articulator of eternal truth and an instrument of moral good.[78] Like Wordsworth he gave the poet not only the title of prophet but even that of priest; poets, he said, were "priests of an unapprehended inspiration" whose verse "participates in the eternal, the infinite, the One."[79] Poets are "teachers, who draw into a certain propinquity with the beautiful and the true that partial apprehension of the agencies of the invisible world which is called religion" (p. 482). All great poetry provides a record of authentic religious revelation: "What were our consolations on this side of the grave – and what were our aspirations beyond it – if Poetry did not ascend to bring light and fire from those eternal regions where the owl-winged faculty of calculation dare not ever soar?" (p. 503) And Shelley went so far as to assert that "the office and character of a poet participates in the divine nature as regards providence, no less than as regards creation" (p. 492). Poets serve in every generation as teachers, guardians, and protectors, assisting mankind to see the truth and pointing out the way (or ways) to salvation.

By the time he wrote the *Defence* Shelley had outgrown many of his cruder prejudices against religion; he had come to see Christianity not as the source of despotism and superstition so much as the victim of those tendencies that conspire in every age to extinguish the "poetical principle" from which religion derives whatever value it may possess (pp. 495–6). It is the responsibility of poets to help restore that vital principle so that religion may become a more beneficent force in society. Of all the Romantics, Shelley had the clearest vision of the relationship connecting literature and religious reform. I began this chapter by quoting one of his remarks on the subject. He makes a similar observation in *A Philosophical View of Reform* when he speaks of the English Reformation as a time when

> the exposition of a certain portion of religious imposture drew with it an inquiry into political imposture and was attended with an extraordinary exertion of the energies of intellectual power. Shakespeare and Lord Bacon and the great writers of the age of Elizabeth and James the 1st were at once the effects of the new spirit in men's minds and the causes of its more complete development.[80]

What is noteworthy here is not only the priority Shelley gives to religious reform as a stimulus for political change but also the mutually invigorating relationship he perceives between reformation and literary achievement. Great literature is inspired by change in the religious order and then goes on to become itself an impetus for continuing religious reform.

As "hierophants of an unapprehended inspiration" (p. 508), poets are often better qualified to undertake the work of reformation than those who are professionally committed to the religious enterprise. Shelley relegated even the father of Protestantism to a subordinate role in the history of religious reform when comparing his achievement with that of one great poet in particular: "Dante was the first religious reformer," Shelley wrote, "and Luther surpassed him rather in the rudeness and acrimony, than in the boldness of his censures of papal usurpation" (p. 499). The line of poet-reformers runs from Plato through Dante and Milton to the poets of Shelley's own day:

> We live among such philosophers and poets as surpass beyond comparison any who have appeared since the last national struggle for civil and religious liberty. The most unfailing herald, companion, and follower of the awakening of a great people to work a beneficial change in opinion or institution, is Poetry.
>
> (p. 508)

The poet-philosophers of the Romantic period, Shelley believed, were committed to finding the right answers to "those obscure questions which under the name of religious truths have been the watch-words of contention and the symbols of unjust power ever since they were distorted by the narrow passions of the immediate followers of Jesus from that meaning to which philosophers are even now restoring them."[81] In that sentence, its quick progress from denial to affirmation so typical of Shelley's range of response in this matter, one finds a summary of the Romantic determination to reform the religious life of the time by penetrating the corruptions and distortions of the national religion so that a better order of belief might be discerned and restored.

Notes

1 *Shelley's Poetry and Prose*, ed. Donald H. Reiman and Sharon B. Powers (New York: Norton, 1977), p. 134.
2 *The Excursion* 7: 1009–12. In *The Poetical Works of William Wordsworth*, ed. Ernest de Selincourt and Helen Darbishire (Oxford: Clarendon Press, 1949), 5: 263.
3 On this "religion of the heart" that, unlike Christianity, did not "affront our reason and humanity," see *The Letters of John Keats*, ed. H. E. Rollins (Harvard University Press, 1958), 2: 103, and my *Keats: The Religious Sense* (Princeton University Press, 1976), pp. 171–72, 202–5.
4 *Letters* 1: 281–82.
5 *Complete Prose Works of John Milton*, vol. 1: *1624–1642*, ed. Don M. Wolfe (Yale University Press, 1953), p. 598.
6 *Complete Prose*, vol. 2: *1643–1648*, ed. Ernest Sirluck (Yale University Press, 1959), pp. 549–50.
7 *Complete Prose* 1: 853, 2: 553.
8 Arthur E. Barker, *Milton and the Puritan Dilemma 1641–1660* (University of Toronto Press, 1942), p. 19.
9 *Complete Prose* 1: 820–21, 816.
10 *Letters* 1: 255.
11 *Complete Prose* 2: 566.
12 *The Age of Reason*, ed. Moncure Daniel Conway (New York: Putnam, 1896), p. 23.
13 "Everyone talked of it, everyone was attracted by its eloquence, everyone admitted the benevolence and talents and sincerity of the author." Introduction to *A Practical View* (1797 rpt. New York: American Bible Society, 1830), pp. 18–19.
14 *A Practical View*, p. 313.
15 "Evangelical" was a name of broad signification that was used originally to designate those who claimed to take the gospels as a rule of life, irrespective of their denominational affiliation. There were Evangelicals among the Dissenters as well as in the Church, but the word came to be applied more particularly to the party within the Anglican Establishment whose piety and conduct marked them as spiritual heirs of John Wesley and George Whitefield, although they did not follow the Methodists out of the Church.
16 *Complete Prose* 2: 554.
17 See Joseph Nicholes, "Revolutions Compared: The English Civil War as Political Touchstone in Romantic Literature" in *Revolution and English Romanticism: Politics and Rhetoric*, ed. Keith Hanley and Raman Selden (New York: St. Martin's, 1990), pp. 261–76.
18 J. C. D. Clark provides a most coherent account of the unsettling impact of the Catholic Question on British politics in this period.
19 The most thorough recent study of the history of Dissent in England is Michael R. Watts, *The Dissenters*, vol. 1: *From the Reformation to the French Revolution* (Oxford: Clarendon Press, 1978).
20 Detailed accounts of the repeal campaign may be found in Anthony Lincoln, *Some Political and Social Ideas of English Dissent 1763–1800* (1938; rpt. New

York: Octagon, 1971); Richard Burgess Barlow, *Citizenship and Conscience: A Study in the Theory and Practice of Religious Toleration in England During the Eighteenth Century* (University of Pennsylvania Press, 1962); and Ursula Henriques, *Religious Toleration in England 1787–1833* (University of Toronto Press, 1961).

21 Thomas W. Davis, ed., *Committees for Repeal of the Test and Corporation Acts, Minutes, 1788–90 and 1827–28* (London Record Society, 1978), pp. 19, 43.

22 G. M. Ditchfield, "Anti-trinitarianism and Toleration in Late Eighteenth Century British Politics: The Unitarian Petition of 1792," *Journal of Ecclesiastical History* 42 (1991): 31–67. For the continual pressure for reform brought by the Unitarians throughout the Romantic period, see Frida Knight, *University Rebel: The Life of William Frend, 1757–1841* (London: Gollancz, 1971).

23 Lincoln, *Political and Social Ideas of Dissent*, p. 249.

24 See G. M. Ditchfield, "The Parliamentary Struggle over the Repeal of the Test and Corporation Acts, 1787–1790," *English Historical Review* 89 (1974): 563.

25 Richard Price, *Political Writings*, ed. D. O. Thomas (Cambridge University Press, 1991), pp. 183, 195–96.

26 H. N. Brailsford, *Shelley, Godwin and Their Circle* (New York: Holt, 1920), p. 1.

27 *The Writings and Speeches of Edmund Burke*, vol. 8: *The French Revolution 1790–1794*, ed. L. G. Mitchell (Oxford: Clarendon Press, 1989), pp. 61–62, 64, 66, 76, 116–17.

28 "Perhaps no single action of the revolutionary governments caused greater resentment among Frenchmen than the policy toward the Church." Charles Breunig, *The Age of Revolution and Reaction, 1789–1850* (New York: Norton, 1970), p. 22.

29 [Anonymous], *Temperate Comments upon Intemperate Reflections or, A Review of Mr. Burke's Letter* (London: J. Walter, 1791), p. 47.

30 See, for example, *Writings and Speeches* 8: 117.

31 "Remarks on the Policy of the Allies" (1793) in *Writings and Speeches* 8: 485.

32 *Writings and Speeches* 8: 141, 149.

33 See, for example, *Letter to Richard Burke, Esq.* (1792), in *Writings and Speeches* 9: 647–48.

34 Harold Perkin, *Origins of Modern English Society* (1969; rpt. London: Routledge, 1991), p. 203.

35 W. R. Ward, "The French Revolution and the English Churches," *Miscellanea Historiae Ecclesiasticae* 4 (1970): 75–76. On cooperation among Dissenters see also J. E. Cookson, *The Friends of Peace: Anti-War Liberalism in England, 1793–1815* (Cambridge University Press, 1982) and Barlow, *Citizenship and Conscience*, pp. 256, 259, 272.

36 Some recent studies include Gordon Rupp, *Religion in England 1688–1791* (Oxford: Clarendon Press, 1986), pp. 325–485; Boyd Hilton, *The Age of Atonement: The Influence of Evangelicalism on Social and Economic Thought, 1795–1865* (Oxford: Clarendon Press, 1988); and David Bebbington, *Evangelicalism in Modern Britain: A History from the 1730s to the 1980s* (Winchester, MA: Allen & Unwin, 1989).

37 *The Miscellaneous Works and Remains of the Rev. Robert Hall, with a Memoir of his Life, by Olinthus Gregory and a Critical Estimate of His Character and Writings by John Foster* (London: Bohn, 1846), p. 476.

38 See Alan D. Gilbert, *Religion and Society in Industrial England: Church, Chapel and Social Change, 1740–1914* (London: Longmans, 1976); Deryck W. Lovegrove, *Established Church, Sectarian People: Itinerancy and the Transformation of English Dissent, 1780–1830* (Cambridge University Press, 1988); W. R. Ward, *Religion and Society in England 1790–1850* (London: Batsford, 1972) and "The

Baptists and the Transformation of the Church, 1780–1830," *Baptist Quarterly* 25, no. 4 (Oct. 1973): 167–84.

39 The historian Elie Halévy is usually credited with establishing the notion that religion acted as a counter-revolutionary force in Britain. For a review of responses to Halévy, see Elissa S. Itzkin, "The Halévy Thesis – A Working Hypothesis? English Revivalism: Antidote for Revolution and Radicalism 1789–1815," *Church History* 44 (1975): 47–56. The argument has received more careful scrutiny in E. P. Thompson, *The Making of the English Working Class* (1963; New York: Pantheon, 1964), Bernard Semmel, *The Methodist Revolution* (New York: Basic Books, 1973), and A. D. Gilbert, "Methodism, Dissent and Political Stability in Early Industrial England," *Journal of Religious History* 10 (1979): 381–99. A sophisticated analysis of the political impact of evangelical religion, particularly Methodism, may also be found in Perkin, *Origins of Modern English Society*, pp. 196–207, 347–62.

40 *Religion and Culture* (London: Sheed and Ward, 1948), p. 59. In Bruce Lincoln's terms, the "religion of the status quo" was apparently becoming a "religion of resistance," which could too easily become a "religion of revolution." See Bruce Lincoln, "Notes toward a Theory of Religion and Revolution" in *Religion, Rebellion, Revolution* (London: Macmillan, 1985), pp. 266–92.

41 *The Second Coming: Popular Millenarianism 1780–1850* Rutgers University Press, 1979), p. 222.

42 *English Society 1688–1832*, p. 277. Coleridge noticed the political significance of a ubiquitous clergy as a "germ of civilization" transplanted "to every parish throughout the kingdom," a situation which patriots "cannot estimate at too high a price." *Biographia Literaria*, ed. James Engell and W. J. Bate (Princeton University Press, 1983), 1: 227.

43 The number of clerical magistrates increased markedly from the 1790s to the 1820s. Anthony Russell, *The Clerical Profession* (London, SPCK, 1981), pp. 32–41, 146–67.

44 Quoted by Ward, *Religion and Society*, p. 54.

45 *The Charge of Samuel Lord Bishop of Rochester to the Clergy of His Diocese, Delivered at his Second General Visitation in the year 1800* (London: Robson, 1800), pp. 19–20.

46 Two recent books that have demonstrated convincingly the relationship between religious and political radicalism in the 1790s are Iain McCalman's *Radical Underworld: Prophets, Revolutionaries and Pornographers in London, 1795–1840* (Cambridge University Press, 1988) and Jon Mee's *Dangerous Enthusiasm: William Blake and the Culture of Radicalism in the 1790s* (Oxford: Clarendon Press, 1992). See also C. B. Jewson, *The Jacobin City: A Portrait of Norwich in its Reaction to the French Revolution 1788–1802* (London: Blackie, 1975), 52, 87, 138.

47 See Perkin, *Origins of Modern English Society*, pp. 196, 203, 353–64.

48 *Religion and Society in Industrial England*, pp. 145–46. See also McCalman, *Radical underworld*, p. 57; R. F. Wearmouth, *Methodism and the Working-Class Movements of England, 1800–1850* (2nd edn., London: Epworth press, 1947), pp. 7–8; and Gerhard Lenski, *The Religious Factor: A Sociological Study of Religion's Impact on Politics, Economics, and Family Life* (Garden City, NY: Doubleday, 1961), pp. 300–1.

49 Leslie Chard observed that, except for his brother Richard, "all of [Wordsworth's] known associates in the spring of 1793 were Dissenters, and his thought of that time has many striking similarities to Dissenting ideas." *Dissenting Republican; Wordsworth's Early Life and Thought in Their Political Context* (The Hague: Mouton, 1972), p. 122.

50 *Miscellaneous Works*, pp. 153–55.

51 Coleridge, "Dejection: An Ode," lines 69–70, in *The Poems of Samuel Taylor Coleridge*, ed. Ernest Hartley Coleridge (Oxford University Press, 1961), p. 366.

52 "Prospectus" to *The Excursion*, lines 60–62. The temperamental affinities between British Romanticism and the Evangelical Revival have been examined by other scholars, most recently Richard Brantley in *Wordsworth's "Natural Methodism"* (Yale University Press, 1975) and *Locke, Wesley, and the Method of English Romanticism* (University of Florida Press, 1984).

53 *Edinburgh Review* 1 (Oct. 1802), p. 66. *The Romantics Reviewed: Contemporary Reviews of British Romantic Writers*, ed. Donald H. Reiman (New York: Garland Press, 1972), Part A, vol. 2, pp. 415–17.

54 See William Haller, *The Early Life of Robert Southey 1774–1803* (1917; rpt. New York: Octagon, 1966), pp. 268–75.

55 *Sermon on the Evidence of a Future Period of Improvement in the State of Mankind* (London, 1787), p. 27.

56 John Randolph, *A Charge Delivered to the Clergy of the Diocese of Oxford* (Oxford, 1802), p. 11.

57 *Complete Prose* 2: 256.

58 David Erdman identifies the papal eminence as George III in *The Illuminated Blake* (Garden City, NY: Doubleday/Anchor, 1974), p. 169.

59 *Milton* 18: 51–19: 3–14, in *The Complete Poetry and Prose of William Blake*, ed. David V. Erdman (revised edn., New York: Doubleday/Anchor, 1988), p. 112.

60 "Prospectus" to *The Excursion*, 1814 edition, ed. Jonathan Wordsworth (New York: Woodstock Books, 1991).

61 E.g. by Harold Bloom in *The Visionary Company: A Reading of English Romantic Poetry* (New York: Doubleday, 1963), pp. 132–36.

62 *The Excursion* Book 4, p. 169.

63 Essay, Supplementary to the Preface to *Poems* (1815). *The Prose Works of William Wordsworth*, ed. W. J. B. Owen and Jane Worthington Smyser (Oxford: Clarendon, 1974), 3: 65, 34–35.

64 *Letters* 1: 281, 2: 103. See also *The Complete Works of John Keats*, ed. H. B. Forman, 5 vols. (1901; rpt. New York: AMS, 1970), 3: 268, for Keats's remarks on "the abstract adoration of the Deity."

65 Stuart Curran, "Blake and the Gnostic Hyle: A Double Negative," *Blake Studies* 4 (1972): 117–33.

66 See Walter Jackson Bate, *The Burden of the Past and the English Poet* (Belknap Press of Harvard University Press, 1970) and Harold Bloom, *The Anxiety of Influence: A Theory of Poetry* (New York: Oxford University Press, 1973). For rebuttals to Bloom, see Joseph A. Wittreich, *Angel of Apocalypse: Blake's Idea of Milton* (University of Wisconsin Press, 1975), and Lucy Newlyn, *Paradise Lost and the Romantic Reader* (Oxford: Clarendon, 1993).

67 *Prose Works* 3: 64.

68 *The Prelude* (1805) 1: 59–63.

69 *Milton* 2: 25. In Erdman, *The Illuminated Blake*, p. 96.

70 "Aird's Religious Characteristics," *Blackwood's* (June 1827), p. 677.

71 *His Very Self and Voice: Collected Conversations of Lord Byron*, ed. Ernest J. Lovell (New York: Macmillan, 1954), p. 444.

72 *Edinburgh Review* 36 (Feb. 1822), p. 438. In *The Romantics Reviewed*, B-2: 931.

73 *The Autobiography of Leigh Hunt*, ed. J. E. Morpurgo (London: Cresset, 1949), p. 451.

74 The first volume of the periodical ran a series of articles attacking "the intolerant disciples of the merciless Calvin, the gloomy Methodists." *Examiner*, May 15,

1808, p. 301. For an overview of Hunt's struggle against the religious establishment see my *Keats: The Religious Sense*, pp. 40, 51–53, 71–78, 86–94.

75 *Foliage* (London, 1818), p. cxxii.

76 *The Complete Works of William Hazlitt*, ed. P. P. Howe (London: Dent, 1930–34), 11: 124.

77 *Complete Works* 16: 105–6.

78 *The Defence of Poetry*, in *Shelley's Poetry and Prose*, ed. Reiman and Powers, pp. 485, 488. Shelley's *Defence* provides most of the material for the discussion that follows; to simplify documentation I have included page references to the Reiman–Powers edition within in the text.

79 *A Philosophical View of Reform* in *The Complete Works of Percy Bysshe Shelley*, ed. Roger Ingpen and W. E. Peck (New York: Scribner's, 1926–1930), 7: 20.

80 Ibid., 7: 7.

81 Ibid., 7: 9.

54

THE NEW ROMANTICISM: PHILOSOPHICAL STAND-INS IN ENGLISH ROMANTIC DISCOURSE

Paul Hamilton

Source: *Textual Practice* 11 (1997), 110–31.

To read English literature written in the Romantic period through emergent and then dominant idealist philosophies has for some time appeared simplistic and reactionary. It's all been done before, hasn't it, from Coleridge onwards? Such philosophies appear to favour canonical lyric poetry and so lock into place a familiar canon of English Romantic poetry. The philosophers empower poetry to save philosophy from its inability to grasp conceptually its own ideals. Equally, literature that does not have this expressive, symbolic function lacks philosophical valorization and is consequently disqualified from serious consideration. In practice, a simplistic aesthetic, unresponsive to the complex variety of Romantic period writing, prescribes what is to count as genuine artistic production.

Nowadays, literary critics of Romanticism have mostly given up excoriating its philosophical sublimation of real issues and just get on with interpreting the neglected archives. But philosophers, too, habitually revise their own traditions; they have also sought to sidestep this binary opposition and to see that philosophical aspiration and textual practice might always have been much closer than their idealist predecessors officially conceded. The independence of philosophy then seems as much at risk as does the aesthetic it prescribed, now happily no longer constraining scholarship. But the absorption of philosophy by textual practice means that literary scholarship must still take on board the philosophical impulse of the period and not, in revenge, issue its own exclusion order on idealism. A remedial attempt to record the transactions between a soluble philosophy and an absorbent writing has to respond to interpretative challenges that can arise almost anywhere. First, though, the philosophical revisionism has to be appreciated before the diffuse textual negotiations it makes possible can be observed.

I. Theories

It must be almost uncontroversial to claim that much mid- to late-twentieth-century philosophy can be characterized by the significance it attributes to language. The 'linguistic turn', as it is usually called, takes very different forms in different traditions. Without prejudice to their disagreements, one can say that these different traditions agree that to attribute theoretical authority to discourse is also to reflect upon the status of philosophy. For those who approve the linguistic turn, philosophy no longer independently prescribes the logical conditions under which linguistic behaviour is meaningful. It relinquishes this anachronistic imperiousness for a role more in keeping with modernity, one modestly allowing the logic of discourse to predetermine the limits of sensible philosophical speculation. Philosophical clarification must, in Wittgensteinian phrase, leave things as they are. Richard Rorty's philosopher can no longer privilege her insights over the practical knowledge of language-users. At best, ancillaries to Foucault's genealogists, philosophers assist in the job of describing and comparing the ways in which truth is discursively produced at different times. And so on.

This provocation offered to philosophy by discourse becomes especially controversial when we try to account for change or progress. The linguistic turn, as I have just described it, sounds conservative: philosophy's task appears now to be to reconstruct or stand in for the undoubted rationality of the status quo. Philosophy abandons its purchase on the universal, an ideal against which discursive practice could always be found wanting or to which it always aspired. Idealism of that sort is discredited; but proponents of the linguistic turn sensitive to the charge of conservatism must therefore relocate the idealizing impetus to change in the discourses now designated the only proper sphere of philosophical interpretation. Change in thought must then be something one does: a kind of action, not a kind of speculation; possible discursive behaviour, not an abstract proposal. For Georges Bataille, opposing the 'restricted', conservative economy of his day, 'No one can say without being comical that he is getting ready to overturn things: he must overturn, and that is all.'[1] Jurgen Habermas's own critique of Bataille in *The Philosophical Discourse of Modernity* finally concedes the power of Bataille's poetic practice as an erotic writer to realize in his reader's experience a heterogeneous excess eluding the philosophical 'tools of theory'.[2] But it is a quotidean, practical realm that Habermas himself envisages absorbing transcendental excess when he resituates the idealizing impulse in unconditioned and normative idioms we unavoidably use in ordinary communication. 'Counterfactual presuppositions become social facts.'[3] Tensions between our ideals and our actual existence no longer license metaphysics but identify the critical potential in speech itself.

Kant's late guide to Enlightenment divisions of knowledge, *The Contest of the Faculties*, significantly foreshadows this compromise. There he argues for a separation of intellectual and political powers: more specifically, he tries to divide intellectual responsibilities in such a way as to free philosophy from the constraints of government and leave government untouched by philosophical critique. Philosophy, the lower faculty, pronounces upon the truth or falsity of the higher theological, legal or medical faculties. This might seem to issue a challenge to the various doctrines that a government licenses these faculties to promulgate, but which philosophy finds false. Kant, however, argues that such conflict between philosophy and government is illusory because the pragmatic, utilitarian grounds for wishing unphilosophical institutions to flourish are of a different order from those legitimating philosophical critique. 'The Government', as Hans Reiss summarizes Kant, 'never protects the higher faculties because their public doctrines, opinions and statements are true.'[4]

Nevertheless, Kant (who after the publication of *Religion Within the Bounds of Reason Alone* had suffered from the censorship of Frederick William of Prussia) obviously wants there to be possible 'a legal conflict of the higher faculties with the lower faculty'.[5] The government is to propagandize through the professions, supporting their higher status, while encouraging the public debate of philosophical questions in case a new discovery turns out to be to its profit. It can only articulate its policies through statutes of these state organs or 'faculties' that philosophical criticism may show to be 'dangerous' or 'unsuitable' (p. 55). Kant's government, therefore, maintains a kind of *reserve* in its acceptance of such 'writings' or statutes that legitimate the discourses of the faculties pronouncing on legality, physical well-being and the ultimate questions of religion. Equally, philosophy only comes into play, politically, if its criticisms are adopted for use by the higher faculties for unphilosophical reasons of political expediency. Nevertheless, such changes in policy undeniably follow discoveries resulting from philosophy's search after ideal, universal truth and so in this case fit Habermas's reduction of idealizing counterfactuals to social facts. Kant engineers the same straddling of logical and social categories so as both to reactivate philosophy at a discursive level in the modern state and to ascribe a progressive direction to discursive action.

In the tradition founded on revision of his major texts, Kant's later anticipation of Habermas's pragmatism tends to get overlooked. Kant's three earlier *Critiques*, while clearly mapping divisions of experience – scientific, moral and aesthetic – are also concerned to imply the integrity of that experience. The desired unity is embodied, for Kant, in just that philosophical consciousness that can indeed review experiential variety from a single viewpoint and consequently can criticize infringements of one area of jurisdiction by another. The difficulties for Kant's scheme, difficulties that generate post-Kantian critique of his own *Critiques*, come when he tries to enunciate this unified subject of philosophical consciousness without inserting it into one of the experiential areas it has to lie outside for its disinterested criticism to be possible. How can we know what this transcendental ego is like without reducing it to an empirical object of science? Alternatively, if it is claimed that the philosophical viewpoint experiences itself instead in moral imperative or aesthetic feeling, we are still left with the problem of saying what it is that recognizes itself in these experiences. Every time Kant tries to specify the subjectivity that has made possible his philosophical divisions of experience he appears obliged to objectify it in terms belonging to one of those divisions it is meant to transcend. At best he can be defended for having deliberately left the thing in mystery or obscurity (*Dunkelheit*), an aporia tragically constitutive of our essential homelessness in any world we can describe. And for Heidegger, of course, here lies the crucial failure of nerve in idealism, the moment where it cannot acknowledge the larger Being it has disclosed beyond its own powers of ratiocination.[6]

From Kant's immediate follower, Fichte, to Derrida and Habermas, philosophers have been offering alternatives to Kant's problematic account of self-knowledge as a subject knowing an object. Despite their differences, Habermas and Derrida equally participate in the linguistic turn of contemporary philosophy. They both continue to preserve the otherness of self from scientific, moral or aesthetic prescription by refocusing philosophy on the construction of the self not in reflective self-consciousness but in language. The perpetual self-differing that produced an infinite regress in Kant's philosophy is permissible as the *différance* generating Derrida's grammatology. The otiose transcendentality of the Kantian self is put to work in the ideal aspirations Habermas characteristically believes we have to attribute to ordinary language in order to make sense of it as communicative action.

Habermas is more useful for my purposes here because latterly he finds his linguistic turn anticipated in the Romantic period, most strikingly by Humboldt. Wilhelm von Humboldt, Habermas believes, replaced the eighteenth-century divisions of knowledge, which fragmented rather than mapped a unified subject, with a diversity of linguistic practices. Negotiation between these practices can be rational without this rationality being obliged to appear paradoxically as some unrepresentable, transcendental subject in whom they all inhere. The idea of negotiation indicates sufficiently for Habermas a respect for differences, an individuality preserved on both sides of the table because in each case it is in excess of agreed compromises and so realizes an idealistic, progressive impulse. The sentence from Humboldt on which Habermas seizes to exemplify this post-metaphysical thinking retrieves individuality as an inescapable feature of ordinary communication and so supplements an otherwise entirely structuralist approach. When we communicate, we have different intentions, interests and so forth, yet we can agree, we can be meaningful to each other. 'For this reason', writes Humboldt, 'all understanding is always simultaneously non-understanding, and all accord in thoughts and feelings is simultaneously a parting of the ways.'[7] Understanding is therefore no longer a struggle between a subject and an object but a significant agreement over differences, potential change, necessary for communication to take place. A working model replaces a theoretical possibility. Kant's contest of faculties rather than his critiques of self-consciousness becomes the paradigm.

The kind of Romanticism described by Humboldt's methodological shift in the framing of experience is therefore an *alternative* to the reactionary ideology normally associated with idealism, and rightly attacked by a succession of thinkers, from Heine and Marx to contemporary new historicists. The rhetorical strategies we as literary critics or cultural historians habitually try to decipher grow richer in meanings when we keep this in mind. Ideological dispute yields up more secrets of its workings, that is, if we look for this contemporary refiguring of individual difference from an absolute otherness into a discursive reserve necessary for communication between different individuals to be possible. 'Reserve', as I commend it throughout this discussion, links surplus, unspoken linguistic competence to respect for the individuality of one's interlocutor – a discursive ethics, as Habermas might optimistically claim, which is progressive because it continuously increases communicative (and, one might add, literary) resources. Initially this may look like the birth of a fairly simple hermeneutical confidence; in practice, the negotiations are complex and fascinating.

The production of orderly maps of the faculties raised difficulties for late Enlightenment philosophers trying to define the owner of the map. Kant had clearly seen this problem as it applied to past projections. A footnote to *Contest* says of Plato's *Atlantis*, More's *Utopia*, Harrington's *Oceana* and Allais's *Severambia* that 'It is the same with these political creations as with the creation of the world: no-one was present at it, nor could anyone have been present, or else he would have been his own creator' (p. 188n.). But the same objection applies to Kant's *Critiques*: the subject writing them is, by definition, producing the only possible knowledge of herself and so must already be in them, but as if created by another self, equally hers, outside them. Kant sometimes appears to repeat the error, the Encyclopaedic error it might be proper to call it, he seeks to criticize. The movement beyond this error, though, incurs its own difficulties. We are now rid of that comic embarrassment Bataille attributed to 'a vast project' whose 'announcement . . . is always its betrayal', or its subsumption by the conditions of definition it purported to circumscribe. But we are left with the description of experience as a miscellany of discourses whose negotiations are often much more oppositional and much less in the service of communication than Humboldt or Habermas appears to allow. Maybe they are right to think that discourses are nevertheless obliged to share ideal aspirations simply in order to be discursive; I don't wish to debate that here. I do wish to suggest that much writing in the Romantic period that concerns itself with the dispositions of different discourses often prefers the obliquities of theorizing through discursive practice to systematic philosophical abstraction.

This syndrome is exhibited at different levels. To recognize it helps us to get a purchase on otherwise nebulous shifts in writing practice, such as those that dissolve philosophy in the poetry of Wordsworth and Coleridge, and then poetic philosophy in the sageness of Carlyle, Arnold, George Eliot, Ruskin and further Victorian practitioners of edifying discourse. The poverty of philosophy endows their anti-theoretical, prosaic versatility with responsibilities and ambitions originally exemplified by philosophy's meta-discursive range. But pure philosophy can be redeployed in different, local, less well-noticed ways in the Romantic period whenever traditions of interpretation or conceptual inheritances are reviewed. Once it is realized that a lack of *explicit* concern for relations between different kinds of experience – knowledge, labour, gender – may belie a *practical* engagement with those questions in discourses remote from transcendentalism, then the relocation of what were once explicitly theoretical debates becomes visible, and the continuing pertinence of these debates about a general economics of experience becomes legible.

This is not to say, in defiance of the facts, that the transcendental tradition does not flourish, and that Kantian idealism and its developments are stopped in their tracks. At the beginning of his *Phenomenology*, Hegel seeks to establish the impossibility of describing immediate consciousness without invoking general terms. Amongst other things, this is a formal reduction of Kant's problem of describing a consciousness existing outside any conceptual scheme. But Hegel's presentation of Kant's crux as a misunderstanding of how language is obliged to work has encouraged, not dissipated, subsequent concern for the individuality his generalizations smoothly efface. Hegel stifles the need for a view of language which, like Humboldt's, will honour particular resistances to hegemonic schemes while acknowledging the necessity of living under their conceptual dispensations. Humboldt, Schelling and Schleiermacher do concede this point and, as a result, can be rehabilitated by contemporary philosophers as Romantic precursors of post-modern singularity.[7] Hegel, though, erases particularity in the interests of tidiness and system, arguing on the side of a traditional map of existence, allowing only for the evolution of new boundaries within its restricted economy. He notoriously neglects the untidiness of particular pressure groups who are provoked by their material conditions to partisan dissent. He ignores them to an extent that invites Marx's verdict in *The German Ideology*: when reality is depicted philosophy of Hegel's kind has ceased to exist.

English thinkers on the grand scale look more open to the intellectual shift of focus I am describing, perhaps because they are less successfully grand or systematic than Hegel. Coleridge, from within both an idealist and a common-sense tradition, registers the pressure to acknowledge the untidiness of discursive conflict as the arena where philosophical debate about the categories of experience is to be conducted. He usually refers to his *Logic* as the 'Elements of Discourse'. The larger project to which it was intended to belong he can describe as an 'Anti-Babel', an attempt to discipline obstreperous 'logoi' under a single, unifying 'Logos'. De Quincey's Spinozistic ambition of correcting the human intellect is still more obviously fragmented into energetic polemic of immense discursive variety: the range of 'disciplines' that, as Jo McDonagh has recently emphasized, is achieved at the expense of overall intellectual organization. As McDonagh surmises, this phenomenon could concur with Foucault's claim that 'at the beginning of the nineteenth century a new arrangement of knowledge was constituted' in which historical and linguistic awareness were at a premium. De Quincey's pathological stylistics, to follow John Barrell's readings here, would then give good grounds for the accompanying scepticism Foucault believed also to be producing the period's conviction that language was an opaque, not a transparent, medium, a new object of knowledge rather than the invisible purveyor of knowledge.[8]

It is hard, certainly, to separate the power of words from notionally different ideological interests that nevertheless could not have been stated in any other way. Foucault's point is recycled in recent claims, from late de Man to Derrida's book on Marx, that there has been an ideological critique inherent in deconstruction all along; but the awareness that language might therefore have its own input into ideological debate need not support an anachronistic, dehistoricized uniformity of critique. I hope that my story so far of the fate of metaphysical divisions of experience suggests a more optimistic and defensibly empathetic retrospect. Imprisonment in a form of words obliges us to use a discourse as the tool of debate; it also implies a slack that might evoke other words not explicitly present in the debate, words whose exclusion is a negotiated compromise, an individual reserve of expression, one silently conceded at the time, there for later changes (progressive, one hopes) in reading to uncover.

II. Examples

Examples of this discursive reserve must therefore, by definition, be graspable only in various idealizing practices and not be susceptible to philosophical abstraction and definition. The philosophical reconstructions they facilitate only stand in for and will be superseded by the ideal end-points aimed at by communicative action.[9] To begin with a relatively obvious example, William Godwin's systematic thinking is supplemented by a belief in the power of discussion eventually to perform what his system desires – an understanding no longer bound by existing institutions. In *Political Justice*, Godwin declares himself unable to think of an example of social intercourse that does not leave both participants 'better' than before.[10] Is 'better' grasped inside or outside ideas of justice current in Godwin's day? Godwin's answer in *Political Justice* is ambivalent in that he suggests that the logical conclusion of following the rational principles partly embodied by existing social institutions is the dissolution of those institutions. The end may be utopian; the means are practical and emphatically begin with things as they are, fostering the rationality immanent in current practices. When Godwin is satirized, as he is by Edward Dubois in *St. Godwin* (1800), for opposing 'all political and moral order',[11] his anarchic ideal is strategically (and comically in Bataille's sense) detached from its practical implementation by the satirist. While this tactic is unfair, it is nevertheless true to the end-point desired by Godwin's provisional use of his contemporary discursive framework. Dubois's unfairness, though, makes him overlook *St Leon*'s own satire on the idea of taking up a position, *ab extra*, from which the moral order might be 'overcome': an unreal position as illusory, the novel implies, as the advantages of the philosopher's stone or a knowledge of alchemy, which can only be invisaged in secret. On the other hand, *St Leon*'s emphasis on the social affections, in line with changes to the third edition of *Political Justice*, need not contradict the final aim of *Political Justice* to achieve a rational state unimpeded by current institutions, moral, political, legal and so on. The paradox here is captured in that 'unreserved communication' desired by *Political Justice* (p. 288). Godwin there despises an inwardness that, like *St Leon*'s alchemical lore, does not seek outward expression; but the communication guaranteed by discourse can only be adequate to an unreserved inwardness, a private judgement, if it exceeds or subverts current standards of publicity (p. 315). To champion communication as an overriding aim, therefore, is to breach the jurisdiction of positive institutions. For the Godwin of *Political Justice*, to generalize one's opinion successfully is to 'increase the stock of political knowledge', not to assimilate opinion to orthodox concepts. The published ending of *Caleb Williams* famously presents this enlightened optimism, the long-awaited scene of dialogue between Caleb and Falkland, as constituting not so much an out-of-court settlement as a dispensing with legal arbitration altogether. The sacrifices involved in such absolutism, Falkland's death and Caleb's loss of 'character', show Godwin's awareness of the dangers in anticipating the ideal truthfulness to which the logic of communication leads. Equally, the unpublished ending indicates that the suppression of this utopian rational impulse depletes human beings of something fundamental to their ordinary sanity.

For Godwin, as for Wollstonecraft, discursive initiatives (also known as unwelcome publicity) create radical possibilities out of the same means by which ordinary communication is assured. The contradiction in theorizing an ideal subject still free to critique its own episteme disappears. Its puzzling metaphysics is replaced by a plausible reserve in communication between individuals, a reserve that both specifies their particular differences and the pragmatics by which they actually communicate. Godwin's theory and novelistic practice repudiate that absolute Romantic subjectivity, the role of

'St Godwin' in which he was cast by opponents like Dubois; he avoids the comedy of *St. Godwin*'s transcendental or arbitrary superiority to things as they are, opting instead for a radicalism expressed through the dynamics of dialogue. The strain put on attempts to honour both the utopianism and the pragmatics of communication produces the split, the two endings of *Caleb Williams* that cannot be entertained at the same time. Whichever ending Godwin had published would have been shadowed, cryptically, by the other possibility his theory of communication held in reserve.

Cryptography is worth bearing in mind if evaluating the terms of public argument during the Romantic period when that argument draws on or represents constituencies that do not share its language. The Revolutionary debate, as represented by Burke and Paine, can seem an exclusive affair: an argument about political theory, a confrontation between Burke's Romantic idealism and Paine's Lockean empiricism. Ruled out of court by both their arguments is the wealth of impolite pamphleteering accompanying and provoked by their dispute. If, however, Paine's arguments are read as a cryptic attack on the economy within which formal constitutional debate in Britain traditionally operated, then we should be able to detect at work in his polemic the discursive variety wider than the ostensible terms of his enquiry. Political theory would then be visibly prescribed by the language in which it is conducted, rather than itself be empowered to pass judgement on the admissibility of forms of writing. As Olivia Smith and others have demonstrated, the traditional hierarchy of debate prevailed. Pitt's 'terror' largely succeeded in its censorship. But it is still arguable that the dispute rocked conservative apologists because it mobilized current demotics and their different discursive traditions against the weakening notion of a single viewpoint from which the true map of faculties, disciplines and so on could be charted or, to use Blake's word, 'chartered'.

Radicalism of Tom Paine's kind holds this kind of cryptic opposition in reserve. Directed against the accommodation of inherited inequity, it is for that reason directed against a mixed economy in politics of any kind. This antagonism opposes him to a government, as he 'ludicrously' styles it, 'of *this, that and t'other*'.[12] His distaste for compromise obviously targets Burkean conservatism. It also reflects on that older tradition favouring a 'balance of powers', one that, growing out of Harrington's *Oceana* (1656), could allow his editor of 1700, John Toland, to describe England as a republic in the frame of a monarchy, and one that Wordsworth surely must assume when he sketches his 'perfect *Republic* of Shepherds and Agriculturists' living, nevertheless, 'in the midst of a powerful *empire* like an *ideal* society' (my emphases) in his *Guide to the Lakes* first published in 1810.[13] As early as his defence of the American Revolution in *Common Sense* (1776), though, Paine suspected such notions of a mixed English constitution, branding their compromises as having 'all the distinctions of a house divided against itself' (p. 7), and clearly distrustful of the efficacy of their pragmatic idealism.

Already he is discarding the domestic, familial metaphor Burke will use to figure the working relationship obtaining between different ranks of society. Paine regards the synchronic existence of monarchy, aristocracy and democracy as anachronistic rather than pragmatic or progressive. These different political characters are to be properly explained by his own diachronic narrative. There each kind of government succeeds the other in a progress from legitimation by superstition, then by power, to a final and convincing corroboration by the rationalization of common social interest in deference only to the rights shared by all men. The halting of progress to institutionalize coexistence of different kinds of government can only be politic in a sense that favours the less rational, whose interest deserves to be superseded.

Paine tells us that 'it is in [Burke's] paradoxes that we must look for his arguments' (p. 62). The demystification, then, of Burke's paradoxical tolerance of constitutional diversity reveals his actual argument to champion a political interest over the rational grounds for its removal, and so, by definition, to support a despotic interest. Paine's plain-speaking, by contrast, creates and enfranchises a wider audience of men using their private judgement in the manner so feared by Burke's parliamentarianism. But Paine's meliorist narrative does not simply call for more participation, as his analogy of political republicanism with 'the republic of letters' might suggest (p. 166); the asymmetry of democratic and hereditary interest is too pronounced for that. Democratic inclusiveness has to cater for languages, customary practices and world-views that blow apart hierarchical understanding mapped from the top down. Paine's writing therefore can retain a cryptic opposition connected to the artisanal background that gives him access to this asymmetrical, proletarian culture. It sometimes emerges in the main line of his attack, especially in the way he drives Burke's own hereditary argument to a logical conclusion prior to the authority it wishes to conserve. Burke's pursuit of historical legitimation stops short of that original state in which the rights of man become visible. The language in which Paine chooses to describe Burke's strategy is strongly inflected with a Dissent much more radical than the enlightened words preached in the Old Jewry by Richard Price. Burke's opportunistic attenuation of historical possibility (a fault he himself will ascribe to Bedford in *Letter to A Noble Lord*) provokes Paine to echo seventeenth-century Leveller opposition to political closure or enclosures. 'But Mr. Burke has set up a sort of political Adam in whom posterity are bound forever; he must therefore prove that his Adam possessed such a power or right' (p. 57). This same Adam's restrictive politics is also the target of *The True Levellers' Standard Advanced: or, The State of Community opened and Presented to The Sons of Men* (1649). The *Standard* attacks an exclusive inheritance or primogeniture and the corresponding property rights that later flesh out Burke's understanding of constitutional liberties as 'entailed inheritance':

And since the coming in of the stoppage, or the A-dam, the earth hath been enclosed and given to the elder brother Esau, or man of flesh, and hath been bought and sold from one to another; and Jacob, or the younger brother that is to succeed or come forth next, who is the universal spreading power of righteousness that gives liberty to the whole creation, is made a servant.[14]

Paine echoes the communism of Everard and Winstanley in order to counter Burke's conversion of legislator into testator to justify heredit-ory succession. For Paine directly to suggest we turn the world upside down would, once again, risk being comical. Blake, or E. P. Thompson's antinomian Blake, was prepared to risk ridicule and obscurity and openly tries to turn his Dissenting legacy into a system offering an alternative to cultural staple, resort or recourse. Despite having occasionally 'lost heart', as Morton Paley puts it, evidenced by his modified 'Address to the Public' at the start of *Jerusalem* (Plate 3), his radicalism appears of a different order to that of primarily Enlightenment polemicists and respectors of private property like Price and Paine.[15] Nevertheless, Paine's discourse cryptically mobilizes a political vision unconfined by apparently inescapable political divisions. In *his* vision of a shareholders' society, 'Every man is a proprietor in society, and draws on the capital as a matter of right' (p. 79). This is closer to opposing the 'divided house' of Burke's constitution with the Levellers' 'one house of Israel . . . taking the earth to be a common treasury' than it is to invoking the scholars and philosophers backing Price's claims – Milton, Sidney, Harrington, Hoadley – characters just as likely to appear in Wordsworth's political sonnets of 1802. Eventually the fact that Paine stops short of advocating Leveller ideology aligns his cryptic entertainment of its idiom to the exercise in pragmatic containment practised by the Putney debates; but even comparison with the generals of the New Model Army obviously exceeds anything Price's ideals could invite. Paine's radicalism hits more significant limits in his gendered scorn of titles – 'the counterfeit of woman' (p. 89). He is in turn corrected by the parallel Wollstonecraft draws between titles and the politically degrading construction or 'character' of woman as possessing 'the arbitrary power of beauty'.[16]

'Let it not be concluded that I wish to invert the order of things', we are told in *Vindication of the Rights of Woman* (p. 109); but we know from recent Romantic scholarship that feminism can be counter-revolutionary and not the less feminist for that. Men might enforce the 'reserve' required of women by popular eighteenth-century conduct books, but they could not prescind its convergence with the radical 'reserve' I have been describ-ing. Feminist radicalism, more than other types of radicalism, seems able to work within given economies of experience, partly because there was so much work to be done simply to get on cultural terms with men before thinking of exceeding those terms of reference. Elizabeth Hamilton, for example, has a character in *Memoirs of Modern Philosophers* (1800) unanswerably, one imagines, cite Jesus Christ as the 'one philosopher' who 'placed the female character in a respectable point of view'; the same Christianity, though, validates 'the order of Providence'.[17] Thirteen years later, in *A Series Of Popular Essays, Illustrative Of Principles Essentially Connected With The Improvement Of The Understanding, The Imagination, And The Heart*, the conservative acceptance of the map of experience offered by traditional eighteenth-century faculty psychology does not prevent her from criticizing Blackstone's notorious refusal of legal personhood to wives: Hamilton calls it 'a gratification of the selfish principle' by which 'for ages an heiress was considered in no other light than a promissory note'.[18] Hamilton ascribes this abuse to '*a propensity to magnify the idea of self*', whose perpetrators she then cautiously exculpates by allowing that the fault develops unconsciously, irrespective of conscious desire or affection (pp. 271–2). But this care to refrain from letting her feminist discovery interfere with established psychology nevertheless allows an autonomy to feminist resistance more visible in a post-Freudian age when unconscious alternatives to conscious explanation can no longer look discreet and unchallenging in the way that Hamilton wants. By not having to be observant of the checks and monitors belonging to established models of experience, Hamilton's analysis of the unconscious begins to set its own agenda. Its unconscious target, male self-magnification, invites her feminism on secret missions, invisible to normal jurisdiction and law-enforcement. Elizabeth Hamilton still thinks she is doing God's work; Christianity's founding philosopher inaugurates feminism; consciousness-raising is all that is called for in her Christian society, in contrast to the conversion of 'the barbarian' to which she nevertheless compares modern, European treatment of 'the sex'. Nevertheless, her gendered division of knowledge constructs the unconscious sphere of feminist critique so as to produce a reserve or difference from public meaning in which a feminist identity can now take shape. Her critical difference now makes a virtue of that 'exclusion of "woman"' which Michele Le Doeuff argues to be 'consubstantial with the philosophical' from the eighteenth century onwards.[19] For Le Doeuff, 'philosophy is just the formal idea . . . that admissible modes of thought cannot be undefined'.[20] But Hamilton cleverly makes the *inadmissibility* of her 'unconscious' evidence stand in for the *ideal*, still unrealized quality of a Christian perfection: that full, integrated consciousness, towards which her society would claim to be striving.

III. Failure and success

What we read into female reserve can be a controversial business. Angela Leighton's revelatory book, *Victorian Women Poets: Writing Against the Heart*, illuminates how women Victorian poets come to write against their allotted place in the accepted map of experience, partly in reaction to the unworldly rectitude of sensibility and sincerity practised by Romantic precursors like Felicia Hemans, Laetitia Elizabeth Landon, and, one might add, by prosaic theorists like Elizabeth Hamilton. Jerome McGann, in his pathbreaking *The Poetics of Sensibility*, reads back into Romantic women's poetry one of the reactions Leighton attributes to later Victorians – in her words, 'an existential emptying of [sensibility] from within'.[21] This 'poetry of loss' (McGann's soubriquet now) by draining writing of reference leaves high and dry for our better inspection conventions and communities of feeling instead of the objects they supposedly map. Unworldliness ceases to signal sentimental self-indulgence; for the world put aside creates the space from which we can view critically our construction of it. This optimism is perhaps advisedly tempered by a return to Leighton's scepticism. Otherwise the critic ends up commending poems, as Kingsley Amis does Hemans's 'The graves of a household', for being 'superficially superficial', consecrating the shallowness we can't give up.[22] On this male charity towards female superficiality Norma Clarke relevantly remarks, in her analysis of the hostility Hemans met with from the women of the Wordsworth household: 'It was not difficult to regard sewing as a higher achievement than writing. . . . What was harder was to notice how these values came from the mouths of those whose shirts had to be sewn by hand at home.'[23] Or there is Leighton's unhappiness with Marlon Ross's liberalization of literary–critical standards to favour Hemans, turning, she thinks, 'historical differences of gender (Hemans is a woman and therefore dutiful, self-denying and wary of poetic vocations) into rules of aesthetic value' (p. 20).

These critical responses show different calculations as to the significance of a female reserve lying behind women's deployments of the discourses of knowledge, gender and labour. Where McGann sees a critical distance, Leighton tends to diagnose dissociation, which only modulated into criticism later on in the century. To show that the stakes here are different from male idealizations of women, and the creation of a discursive surplus within erotic literary traditions from Petrarch to Rousseau, we might briefly mention the startling example of Hazlitt's *Liber Amoris*, a kind of grotesque parody of *La Vita Nuova*, but one that ultimately excoriates its own inability to make coherent that slack or give in its own language created by its abundant discontent with its given forms of knowing. I want to suggest that by contrast with Hazlitt's stylistic dead-end there is a robustness in women Romantic poets' reserve that valorizes the progressive subjectivity about whose power McGann and Leighton have their nuanced disagreement, but concerning whose activism neither seems to be in doubt.

To understand the depth of the self-critique of the language of *Liber Amoris*, we have to appreciate the policing of the escapes that might have been open to the eroticized object (S) of the narrator's (H) imagination. Had Hazlitt been able to criticize sufficiently the literary tools he lends, with some irony, to his narrator, then the young woman, S, might have been able to elicit alternatives, however cryptic, to the constructions H incessantly puts upon her behaviour. He does, it is true, sometimes express strong literary scepticism. Contemporaneous with some of the mid-life crisis described in *Liber Amoris* is Hazlitt's article in *The London Magazine* of June 1821, 'Pope, Byron and Mr. Bowles', where he declares that it is 'the conflict between nature and the first and cheapest resources of art, that constitutes the romantic and the imaginary'. The unreadability of S to the infatuated H means that nature drops out of the picture and one is left with the self-confessed 'first and cheapest resources of art'. The novella is subtitled 'the new Pygmalion', thematizing this lack of an original and the tawdriness of the arts substituted for her. However, unable to do anything with such literary reserve, H ends up in a parodic critique of literariness that turns out to be another fantasy of possessing S. He rents the whole of Southampton Buildings, where he and her family live, in order to offer S the freedom from class and economic circumstance that his idealizing but reactionary literary accommodations of her had professed but of course failed to provide.

The other escape from the literary constructions baffling the relationship between H and S would be downwards, dropping out of the polite register. There is a famous kitchen conversation alluded to in *Liber Amoris*, when the servant Betsy gives back to H the books he had lent to S, an allusion incomprehensible without the letter to P. G. Patmore (one of the letters to him and others drawn on by *Liber Amoris*) which details Hazlitt's own eavesdropping. The offending conversation was prompted by the thought of 'what a sight there would be' if the trousers of one of Hazlitt's fellow-lodgers at Southampton Buildings were to fall down. Hazlitt's frantic conclusion is: 'can there be any doubt, when the mother dilates this way on codpieces and the son replies in measured terms, that the girl runs mad for size?' Sarah, Hazlitt's real-life obsession, says something 'inaudible, but in connection', but the whole incident remains inaudible within *Liber Amoris*. Again, the lack of an original explanatory context doesn't so much tell the story of Pygmalion as frustratingly perform it. H's confession pretends to a Rousseauistic honesty, but primly censors itself in such contrast to the innovative discursive confidence of Rousseau's divulging of childhood likings for being spanked, for masturbation, and for urinating in Mme Clot's cooking pot when she was at church – all within a few pages of beginning his *Confessions*. A realism based on knowing imprisonment within images cannot fail to sound post-modern to our ears. The dilemma of *Liber Amoris*, though, lies precisely in the way that the novella does not redeem through artistic transformation the letters on which it is based, not because the difference between art and nature does not exist, but because the discourses of both are so impoverished.

The same tale can be told of the 'little image' of Napoleon that H gives as a present to S and then breaks on the ground in a rage on its return. H gives S the little statue of Napoleon because it reminds them both of hopeless allegiances: in his case the continuation of French Revolutionary hopes in Napoleon, in her case the likeness of a former lover. Her unfaithfulness to H here in this nostalgia is his only, eagerly seized on guarantee that she can be faithful. Since the logic of representation, of being an image of something, cannot be given up, it seems immaterial whether the image in question is in pieces or not. And *Liber Amoris* works for its defenders because its disorder simulates a kind of egalitarianism, 'a democratic erotic moment', Michael Neve calls it, in which because you can't get anything right you can't get it wrong either.[24] As he tells Patmore in another letter written in the cheap vein of *Liber Amoris*, 'For a man who writes such nonsense, I write a good hand.'[25]

The effective deployment of literary reserve contrasts strikingly with all this tortuousness. Anna Laetitia Barbauld's poem 'The rights of woman' is now canonical. It is anthologized in collections by Roger Lonsdale, Jerome McGann, Jennifer Breen and in the *Norton Anthology*. The poem presents the constraints on female emancipation in an extraordinarily knowing way. Written in 1795, it presents an alternative to feminist writing coming out of a Painite framework, like Wollstonecraft's. It mixes cynicism and radicalism, eschewing heterosexual friendship, yet ending in a notion of sexual mutuality. The last line's explosion of the poem's earlier cynicism, apparently with all the force of Blakean innocence, is, however, partly muffled by the recollection, surely solicited as well, that women lose legal personhood in marriage at this time. On the way, Barbauld manages to show that if men believe their own propaganda about women they concede to them a power that it was the purpose of their rhetoric to exclude, one generating aggressive successes in a military, masculinist idiom. Barbauld, in short, manages to criticize complacency, conformity and radical transcendence all at once. Her ambiguities do not concede discursive bankruptcy but orchestrate the senses in which material circumstances will have to change before a new, coherent culture of ideas about gender politics can arise. This is not a poetry of loss of referent, relying on post-modern charity in later interpreters, but a poetry whose multivalencing of the current referent, woman, figures the power to change the referent because narrator and referent are here the same – woman. Discursive versatility and interior distancing already reconfigure their object by being another version of it. The constructions of woman the poem takes as its object are belied by the constructive woman – the new woman – whose creative manipulation of them the reader admires in the poem's subject.

The poem calls for this subject to be given the social, practical, material existence justified by her demonstrated superiority to conventional objectifications of women. However, as Marx saw, idealism is infinitely elastic in its capacity for self-critique because such critique is always internal to the philosophy that mounts it. Barbauld's poem dramatizes a comparable discursive imprisonment, showing that it is the very discourses it employs that need to be displaced for the material implications of this new woman to be gathered. To stay with an idealist subject/object paradigm of self-knowledge here would be to describe as a constitutional aporia of self-consciousness a situation that cried out for practical remedies. This constructive rather than incoherent (Hazlitt's) or aporetic (Kantian) reserve concerning the words she is obliged to use distinctively shapes Barbauld's other poetic productions. She is fascinated by the rhetorical possibilities of reticence both in political action and in personal expression. Her early pro-Wilkes poem, *The Times* (late 1760s), compares the physical but articulate violence lamented by Cicero's *Catiline* (*O tempora! O mores!*) favourably with the unstated corruption of George III's rule through bribery and placemen: 'Then, then exclaim "Oh hapless Times indeed";/For deeper is the wound that does not bleed'.[26] And her much later lines 'On the death of the Princess Charlotte' (1817?) similarly home in on the unspoken misery of Charlotte's Prince Regent father. Unfashionably, the poem argues that his apparently unnatural indifference to his daughter's fate merits not the popular contempt it got but an even greater effort of readerly sympathy. This attractiveness, though, leaves him a vulnerable figure because so removed by his strangely inexpressive grief from the common circle of values and meanings whose legitimate representative he, as Royalty, is supposed to be.[27] Barbauld's sympathy is obliquely republican.

Barbauld's most notorious poem, entitled *Eighteen Hundred and Eleven*, and published a year later, provoked a review from the *Quarterly* so vicious that it reputedly dissuaded Barbauld from the further publication of poetry.[28] John Wilson Croker is supposed to have succeeded in censoring her where he later failed with Keats; and, as in his criticism of Keats's *Endymion*, he reveals himself to be a reader politically disqualified from responding to the expressive reserve with which writers of his period might deploy traditional poetic tropes and structures. Barbauld's diagnosis of an *annus horribilis* in British history is full of aesthetic double-takes and figurative entrapments whose inescapability provokes the reader to feel more sharply how differently things actually could be under another political dispensation. The cumulative effect of the war with France since 1793 is the departure of prosperity from Britain: 'The golden tide of Commerce leaves thy shore', its light 'streaming westward', emigrating along with enlightened British intellectual and cultural hegemony, 'Science and the Muse' (p. 154).

There are three kinds of scepticism built into this initial gloomy frame of reference. First of all, the British traditions whose passing Barbauld laments are clearly controversial: their composition partly from archives of intellectual dissent (Locke, Paley, Thomas Clarkson, Sir William Jones) compromises other constituents that a Croker would prefer to read as politically conformist. Milton, here, must be a Puritan, James Thomson, a patriot poet writing against the political establishment. Second, the *demise* of this mixed loyalist and oppositional heritage turns out to be its *dissemination* in other cultures, lands and societies – an appropriation and recycling elsewhere that most effectively signals the tradition's lasting value. If readers can just put aside national prejudices for a moment, and with them the partisanship sustaining the war, then the loss of national culture deprecated by the poem can be reinterpreted as an international gain. The poem's final call, after all, will be to replace cultural imperialism with a commonwealth of ideas inspiring the still colonized nations of America, the world of Columbus, to gain their freedom. Third, the privileged point of view from which the poem reviews the sequence of history and the successive ruins of empire is variously figured as that of 'a Spirit' or 'The Genius': a 'capricious', 'vagrant Power' which now appears too arbitrary to offer a convincing gloss on the logic of cultural and commercial exchange (pp. 158–9).

The figure puzzled the poem's first readers, and its progress while following 'the march of Time' scarcely imparts to history a notion of progression. Croker is witty at its expense in the same way that he is about Barbauld's pretensions to be a political commentator, a *'dea ex machina'*. His marrying of the figure's implausibility to the political viewpoint he cannot countenance is a good reason for betting that they are *not* equivalent.[29] But if explanation is definitely not located in this transcendental overview, then it has to be found in the particularities that such a high horse loftily soars above. We are returned to the discourses of art, war, wealth and commerce, which can 'destroy the fruits they bring' and know 'no second spring'. This inherent obsolescence, however, is tied to their self-serving, nationalistic modes whose limitations, the poem's stance implies, can be overcome by a reciprocal, more communal attitude towards the spread of civilization. Otherwise our identity will perish with a London Barbauld imagines sunk in future ruin. The alternative is to free identity from a fixed patriotism and tie it instead to a cultural centre of gravity that will settle wherever civilization renews itself. Chauvinistically regarded, in other words, the individual cycle of mercantile and aesthetic fulfilment is doomed to decay and frustration: 'But fairest flowers expand but to decay;/The worm is in thy core, thy glories pass away' (pp. 160–1). Focused by a militant national interest, the poem does seem to mark, as William Keach rightly points out, 'a decisive break with the meliorist historical perspective' to which 'the progressive Dissenting ideology that motivates all [Barbauld's] work . . . had previously been attached'.[30] By contrast, and more plausibly, we can read the poem as open to the disseminating values of the *internationale* typical of the early optimism of the 'friends' of the French Revolution, Richard Price's 'citizens of the world' whose enthusiasm Kant located in a progressive 'moral disposition of the human race'.[31] *Eighteen Hundred and Eleven* optimistically predicts the recrudescence of what it values elsewhere, surviving local extinctions.

Reflexively, therefore, the poem has reservations about the received, transcendental viewpoint common to writings as different as Dr Johnson's

Juvenilian satire, *London*, or Volney's *Les Ruines*, the viewpoint from which such surveys are traditionally conducted towards pessimistic conclusions. History as successive ruination is acceptable to the *Quarterly* when it appears, deceptively, as classical, tragic travelogue in Byron's *Childe Harold*, whose first canto is favourably reviewed in the preceding number of the same volume. Again, Barbauld's elusive reserve in her use of poetic privilege suggests the alteration in political attitude and national outlook needed if that overview is not to be mechanically determined to tell a story of cyclical destruction, inevitable decay and cultural supersession – the same story over and over again. For to describe instead the preservation and resurgence of liberties cherished by the Good Old Cause, the imperialist assumptions of a Croker ('We had hoped . . . that the empire might have been saved without the intervention of a lady-author') and their aesthetic correlatives ('. . . in a quarto, upon the theatre where the great European tragedy is now performing') are precisely what must change.

Barbauld's cosmopolitanism is common to moderate sympathizers with the French Revolution such as Price and Kant. Kant's republican ideal, as he emphasized in *The Conflict of The Faculties*, signified the best of all constitutions with which 'to banish war, the destroyer of everything good'. Barbauld shares Kant's difficulties in persuading his readers that republican pacifism is the conceivable endpoint towards which current national strife might be leading. By way of illustrating his embarrassment, Kant tells one of his rare jokes about an over-optimistic doctor whose reassurances finally can only persuade his patients that they are dying of improvement.[32] The more influential texts of Kant's critical philosophy, though, emphasize the impossibility of the sensuous appropriation of ideas of reason such as the cosmopolitan republic: a perpetual estrangement of the ideal from the real, which Lucien Goldmann correctly defined as 'tragic'.[33] Barbauld's scepticism, by contrast, does not so much answer to a logical requirement as constitute a call to the remedial action enjoined by her strictures on war and profiteering. Barbauld's ambivalent poetic presentation of the viewpoint from which the cosmopolitan ideal ought to be seen unfolding invokes the transformation required – and a practicable one if Croker's indignation at her 'party pamphlet' is to be credited – if people are to shed the nationalism and accompanying bellicose behaviour impeding that ideal and rendering it implausible. Were people to start believing in it, then the latent meaning of *Eighteen Hundred and Eleven* could surface: the poem would now expose and satirize the interests keeping tragic pessimism in place. Progress rather than repeated tragedy must be the repressed norm against which Barbauld's capricious spirit of genius of history looks an unlikely nemesis, chimerical and fanciful. Barbauld's literary reserve invokes a political unconscious circumscribing the tragic construction of history with which, her poem's intertextuality suggests, she is obliged to deal. As with the subject of 'The Rights of Woman', this alternative history demands readers who, understanding its significant reticence, will stand in for the new society that will let it speak.

In conclusion, I hope we can now understand better why Habermas could think that philosophy, from the Romantic period onwards, begins to stand in for and interpret those unconditioned idealisms silently embedded in discursive practice. So understood, philosophy has nothing to say on its own; nor does it enjoy the privilege of prefiguring the unreserved communication for which discourse strives. It simply holds a place in our attention for those idealizing elements in which are secreted discursive desiderata that cannot at present be more fully articulated. There are clear (if unexpected) similarities in this position to Lyotard's revamping of a Kantian sublime to figure a post-modern reach for the unrepresentable – a philosophical entertainment of what 'will have been'. Habermas, though, eschews all such aesthetic solutions; perhaps he risks being too systematic in his optimism where Lyotard is arguably still too Romantic in his.

Accordingly, when we consider a selection of the actual transactions between philosophy and writing of the Romantic period, we have to recognize both that their sense may emerge from ways in which they *criticize* aestheticization, and that these criticisms are still powered by the same idealistic, progressive impulse that the aesthetic had tried to monopolize and sublimate. Released from aesthetic institutionalization, writing refigures its critical impulse, but varies it with each literary example, each stand-in for a better dispensation. Failure to generalize theoretical and political vision is thus still redeemed by local examples – a particularity with which Romantic aesthetics supplemented philosophy, yes, but with which post-modern thinkers (as different as Foucault, Lyotard and Habermas) have continued the work of Barbauld and others to oppose the hierarchical distinctions idealism had otherwise been used to keep in place.

Notes

In revising this paper I have been greatly helped by reactions to different versions of it tried on English departments at Southampton, York and Birkbeck College, as well as by conversations with Ken Hirschkop and Peter Dews, although in ways they all might not recognize.

1 Georges Bataille, *The Accursed Share: An Essay on General Economy*, Vol. 1, *Consumption*, trans. Robert Hurley (New York: Zone Books, 1988), p. 9.
2 Jurgen Habermas, *The Philosophical Discourse of Modernity*, trans. Frederick Lawrence (Cambridge: Polity Press, 1987), pp. 286–7.
3 Jurgen Habermas, *Postmetaphysical Thinking: Philosophical Essays*, trans. William Mark Hohengarten (Cambridge, MA: MIT Press, 1992), p. 47.
4 *Kant's Political Writings*, ed. with an Introduction and notes by Hans Reiss, trans. H. B. Nisbet (Cambridge: Cambridge University Press, 1977), p. 176.
5 I. Kant, *The Conflict of The Faculties (Der Streit der Fakultaten)*, trans. and Introduction by Mary J. Gregor (Lincoln and London: University of Nebraska Press, 1992), p. 53.

6 See in Germany, for example, Manfred Frank's *Der Unendliche Mangel an Sein: Schelling's Hegelkritik und die Anfange der marxischen Dialektik* (Frankfurt am Main: Suhrkamp, 1975), and for English developments of Frank's thought see Andrew Bowie, *Aesthetics and Subjectivity* (Manchester: Manchester University Press, 1992) and *Schelling and Modern European Philosophy: An Introduction* (London: Routledge, 1993) as well as Peter Dews's 'Deconstruction and German Idealism: a response to Rodolphe Gasche's *The Tain of the Mirror*', in *The Limits of Disenchantment: Essays on Contemporary European Philosophy* (London: Verso, 1995), pp. 115–51.

7 Habermas, *Postmetaphysical Thinking*, p. 48.

8 Michel Foucault, *The Order of Things*, trans. Alan Sheridan (London: Tavistock Publications, 1970), pp. 262, 300. See Jo McDonagh, *De Quincey's Disciplines* (Oxford: Clarendon Press, 1994).

9 See Jurgen Habermas, 'Philosophy as stand-in and interpreter', in *Moral Consciousness and Communicative Action*, trans. Christian Lenhardt and Shierry Weber Nicholsen (Cambridge: Polity Press, 1990), pp. 15–16.

10 William Godwin, *Enquiry Concerning Political Justice And Its Influence On Modern Morals And Happiness*, ed. Isaac Kramnick (Harmondsworth: Penguin, 1985), p. 301.

11 [Edward Dubois], *St. Godwin: A Tale Of The Sixteenth, Seventeenth, And Eighteenth Century By Count Reginald De St. Leon* (London, 1800), p. 233.

12 Thomas Paine, *Political Writings*, ed. Bruce Kuklick (Cambridge: Cambridge University Press, 1989), p. 137.

13 James Harrington, *The Oceana and other Works of James Harrington, with an Account of his Life by John Toland* (1700); see J. G. A. Pocock's edition of Harrington's *Political Works* (Cambridge: Cambridge University Press, 1977), pp. 141–3; William Wordsworth, *Guide to the Lakes*, ed. Ernest de Selincourt (Oxford: Oxford University Press, 1977), pp. 67–8; see Nigel Leask's discussion of Commonwealth influences on Wordsworth and Coleridge in *The Politics of Imagination in Coleridge's Critical Thought* (London: Macmillan, 1988), Part I.

14 *The True Levellers' Standard Advanced*, in Gerard Winstanley, *The Law of Freedom and Other Writings*, ed. Christopher Hill (Harmondsworth: Penguin, 1973), p. 79.

15 Morton D. Paley, *The Continuing City; William Blake's* Jerusalem (Oxford: Clarendon Press, 1983), pp. 6–7.

16 Mary Wollstonecraft, *Vindication of the Rights of Woman*, ed. Miriam Kramnick (Harmondsworth: Penguin, 1982), p. 103.

17 [Elizabeth Hamilton], *Memoirs of Modern Philosophers*, 3 Vols. (London: 1800), I, p. 198.

18 Elizabeth Hamilton, *A Series Of Popular Essays, Illustrative of Principles Essentially Connected With The Improvement Of The Understanding, The Imagination, And The Heart* (Edinburgh, 1813).

19 Michele Le Doeuff, *The Philosophical Imaginary*, trans. Colin Gordon (London: Athlone, 1989), p. 111.

20 Ibid., p. 115.

21 Angela Leighton, *Victorian Women Poets: Writing Against the Heart* (New York and London: Harvester Wheatsheaf, 1992), p. 299; J. J. McGann, *The Poetics of Sensibility* (Oxford: Clarendon Press, 1996).

22 Quoted with approval by Peter W. Trinder in *Mrs Hemans* (Cardiff: University of Wales Press, 1984), p. 2.

23 Norma Clarke, *Ambitious Heights: Writing, Friendship, Love – The Jewsbury Sisters, Felicia Hemans, and Jane Welsh Carlyle* (London and New York: Routledge, 1990), p. 65.

24 'Introduction' to *Liber Amoris, or The New Pygmalion*, new introduction by Michael Neve (London: The Hogarth Press, 1985), p. xii.

25 *The Letters of William Hazlitt*, ed. H. M. Sikes, W. H. Bonner and G. Lahey (New York: New York University Press, 1978), p. 269.

26 *The Poems of Anna Laetitia Barbauld*, ed. William McCarthy and Elizabeth Kraft (Athens and London: University of Georgia Press, 1994), p. 27.

27 Ibid., pp. 174–6.

28 Ibid., pp. 152–61.

29 *Quarterly Review*, VII (1812), pp. 309–13.

30 William Keach, 'A Regency prophecy and the end of Anna Barbauld's career', *Studies in Romanticism*, 33: 4 (Winter 1994), p. 577; James Chandler provides an excellent discussion of the complexities of the stadial view of history Barbauld would have inherited from the Scottish Enlightenment in an unpublished paper given at Exeter University's conference on 'Anachronism', and to be published in his forthcoming book, ch. 2 of *England in 1819*. Particularly helpful here is his highlighting of her posthumously published letters 'On the Uses of History', which reinforces her relativism ('*When* is a relative term') and her insistence on a global perspective with which to understand 'One consoling idea . . . [our] tendency towards amelioration', *A Legacy for Young Ladies, Consisting Of Miscellaneous Pieces In Prose And Verse By The Late Mrs Barbauld* (London, 1826), pp. 148, 134.

31 Kant, *Conflict*, p. 153.

32 Op cit., p. 169.

33 L. Goldmann, *Immanuel Kant*, trans. Robert Black (London: New Left Books, 1971).

55

NIETZSCHE, BLAKE, KEATS AND SHELLEY: THE MAKING OF A METAPHORICAL BODY

Ross Woodman

Source: *Studies in Romanticism* 29 (1990), 115–49.

That impulse toward the formation of metaphors, that fundamental impulse of man, which we cannot reason away for one moment—for thereby we should reason away man himself—is in truth not defeated nor even subdued by the fact that out of its evaporated products, the ideas, a regular and rigid new world has been built as a stronghold for it.

"On Truth and Falsity in their Ultramoral Sense"

Essential to any reading of Nietzsche is the recognition of his distinction between the artist and the priest as warring impulses within himself. The artist seeks to construct a provisional self not by reference to any pre-existent model but out of the will to metaphor arising out of the chaos of nature present as nerve-stimuli or what Blake calls "Nervous fibres" (*Jerusalem* 98: 37).[1] The will to metaphor may be defined as Nietzsche describes "the Will to Power": the will to inhabit one's metaphorical invention of oneself. The priest, on the other hand, arrests metaphor into a system of belief which he declares to be permanent, immutable, binding and true. Such a system by virtue of being fixed is also dead. God as the archetypal maker of system, a hierarchical universe in which everything, including man, has its assigned place, is by his very logocentrism a dead God not unlike Shelley's Jupiter or Keats's fallen Titans. The recognition of his death—the release of an inchoate nature from the delusion of his grasp—restores man to the primacy of his experience and action which in *The Birth of Tragedy* he calls Dionysus. Apollo as the representation of Dionysus is the illusion of an identity which imposes a provisional form and meaning upon a nature not to be subdued. As the metamorphosis of nature into language, metaphor thus designates, as Eric Blondel points out, "the separation between body and thought."[2] This separation, Nietzsche suggests, is the very foundation of culture understood as the *opus contra naturam*. Man's metaphorical break with nature involves a coming to terms with a consciousness or will to consciousness that in its drive toward autonomy and control is so alien to nature that it renders man in relation to it a sickness, an aberration. Language constitutes a break, a fissure, a representation that is other than what is represented which is nevertheless unknowable except as it is represented. Cast out of nature by a consciousness alien to it, he suffers the pain of alienation which is the pain of his own cast-out body, a body invaded by consciousness and subjected to its control.[3] Metaphor, as Blondel aptly describes it, is a "quasi-*hysterical* and displaced language: it is the body's symptomatic *conversion* into language" (152).

Body as linguistic embodiment, as Helen Keller's discovery of water as the word "water," is the "symptomatic *conversion*" of a nerve-stimulus into a percept which Nietzsche in "On Truth and Falsity in their Ultramoral Sense" calls a "first metaphor."[4] Before making this discovery of metaphor (the imposition of a name upon the nameless), Helen Keller had lived as an animal devoid of language in an environment of nerve-stimuli in which words were simply signals provoking an encoded or learned response. When in what Blake calls a moment "less than a pulsation of the artery" (*Milton* 28[30]: 62), she made the mutation from the animal to the human state described by Nietzsche in that same essay as "out of one sphere right into the midst of an entirely different one" (178), she began her systematic metaphorical transformation of an animal environment into a human world. The conversion of an animal signal into a human sign, the word "w-a-t-e-r" spelled out by Ann Sullivan onto the palm of Helen Keller's free hand as the sensation of cold water from the pump rushed over her other one, startled her into a human awareness which her physiological condition had managed to block. "She dropped the mug," Ann Sullivan reported, "and stood as one transfixed. A new light came into her face. She spelled 'w-a-t-e-r' several times."[5] This instant of creation, one that Blake explores in *Milton* and to a lesser degree in those other works which celebrate the illumination of the Word, defamiliarizes the moment in order to recover it. Ololon, for example, descends in *Milton* "to Los & Enitharmon / Unseen beyond the Mundane Shell / Southward in Miltons track" (*Milton* 35[39]: 46–47). Blake, like Helen Keller, is liberated from his "Vegetated portion" (*Milton* 36[40]: 22)—the "Mundane Shell" of encoded response—by the power of the Word transforming a signal, a "pulsation of the artery," into a sign that expands to a symbol carrying him momentarily as a poet into the Nietzschean realm of the *Übermensch*. The sign marks the direction of "Miltons track." That track itself shapes its metaphorical way in the image of Milton taking the "red clay of Succoth" and "moulding it with care / Between his palms." Beginning "at the feet of Urizen," he "creat[es] new flesh on the Demon cold, and build[s] him / As with new clay a Human form . . ." (*Milton*

19[21]: 10–14). Blake, now imaged as Milton moving through his vegetable body beginning at the left foot, thus releases himself and Milton from the dead metaphor ("the Demon cold") they had both become. In doing so, however, he subjects the safety and repose of what Nietzsche in "On Truth and Falsity" calls "congelation and coagulation" to an "original mass" of "fiery liquid" (184). He replaces the lamb with the tiger, which is for Nietzsche the original form of the lamb; Blake's lamb, in Nietzsche's view, arises from "the fact that man forgets himself as subject, and what is more as an *artistically creating* subject" (184). Man, that is, forgets that he creates himself; what he calls God is, for Nietzsche, the arrested image of his own mind.

For Nietzsche the creation of "new flesh on the Demon cold" is the work of the "*Übermensch*: man constructing himself to become like Nietzsche in *Thus Spake Zarathustra* his own work of art, which is to say his endlessly evolving aesthetic self understood as a metaphorical body in a ceaseless state of "Mental Fight." For Nietzsche, as for Shelley, the highest form of this metaphorical action is music understood as a perpetual flow of sound each note of which becomes the metamorphosis of the previous one. The "crawling glaciers" (frozen or canonized music) that pierce Prometheus in the first act of Shelley's lyrical drama "with the spears / Of their moon-freezing chrystals" (*Prometheus Unbound* (*PU*) 1.31–32) become in the fourth act "clear, silver, icy, keen" notes of Mozartian music (*The Magic Flute*?) that "pierce the sense and live within the soul / As the sharp stars pierce Winter's chrystal air" (*PU* 4.190–93).[6] Shelley in his final act celebrates "the Omnipotence / Of music"; the "inspired voice and lute" languish, leaving "responses" to "wind and roll" through "the deep and labyrinthine soul" (*PU* 1.802–5). Precisely in the languishing of Shelley's music, a languishing which Nietzsche heard in the music of Wagner, lay for Nietzsche the decadence of romanticism. That decadence he described as "the conviction of an absolute untenability of existence when it comes to the highest values one recognizes; plus the realization that we lack the least right to posit a beyond of an in-itself of things that might be 'divine' or morality incarnate."[7]

In *Prometheus Unbound*, the metaphorical union (the androgyne) of Asia and Prometheus is in marked contrast to the failure in "The Triumph of Life" to put new flesh on the dead metaphor that Rousseau has become. In the fragment found after Shelley's drowning the failure would appear to reside, at least in part, in what was for Nietzsche Shelley's romantic desire to find safety and repose in metaphysics, to escape by means of a delusory transcendence the ceaseless flux that is as metaphor Shelley's Chariot of Life. "Rousseau gains shape, face or figure only to lose it as he acquires it" writes Paul de Man in "Shelley Disfigured" (49).[8] The decisive factor in that loss, he argues, "its decisive textual articulation," is the "disfigurement of Shelley's body, burned after his boat capsized and he drowned off the coast of Lerici," a disfigurement that leaves the reader with a "defaced body . . . present in the margin of the last manuscript page" to become "an inseparable part of the poem." The final test of reading thus depends for de Man "on how one reads the textuality of this event, how one disposes of Shelley's body" ("Shelley Disfigured" 66–67). An even more Nietzschean test of reading would be how one disposes of the poem's metaphysics (itself for Nietzsche a dead body) which, as in *Adonais*, encourages an interpretation of Shelley's drowning as an apocalyptic gesture in which he rejects the world out of a desire to flee back with the "sacred few" to their "native noon" ("The Triumph of Life" 128–31).

Like the metaphorical "old root" still growing to "strange distortion" ("The Triumph of Life" 182–83) in which Shelley first encounters Rousseau's body as a result of Rousseau's delusory yearning for a primary pre-linguistic state of nature, Shelley's own effaced body finds no fit metaphorical shape within the fragment as it stands. What de Man calls "the endless prosopopoeia by which the dead are made to have a face and a voice which tells the allegory of their demise and allows us to apostrophize them in our turn" ("Shelley Disfigured" 68) thus becomes yet another reading of a text which Shelley himself was not prepared to decipher. Precisely in that indecipherability, described by Shelley as "thoughts which must remain untold" ("The Triumph of Life" 21), resides for Nietzsche, as for his uncanny disciple de Man, the indecipherability of life as text, the multiple perspectives of which, as in a Cubist painting, celebrate as fiction what otherwise in their absence might easily be mistaken for truth. In announcing the death of God, Nietzsche affirms the multiplying of perspectives that together illuminate the absence of a center to which in their configurations they nevertheless appear to point.

Nietzsche's perspectivism rejects the nihilism attributed to the absence of a center that opens an abyss. Like Blake and Shelley before him, he rejects the God of the golden compasses who in Milton's epic sends Messiah into the abyss to circumscribe chaos by reducing it to an immutable order. An immutable order, both Blake and Shelley argue, reduces a mythical creation to a dead metaphor, a reduction undertaken by Urizen in Blake's poetry and by Jupiter in Shelley's lyrical drama. Opposing the static or stationing action of Milton's God, Blake and Shelley bring to their reading of Milton's epic a new perspective which remains new only to the degree that it releases into perpetual mobility those that already exist. Nietzsche's notion of "*amor fati*"—"that one wants nothing to be different, not forward, not backward, not in all eternity"[9]—is here helpful for an understanding of this radically metaphoric reading of life. Metaphor, for Nietzsche, ultimately changes nothing because, unlike metaphysics, it perpetuates change itself by affirming ceaseless flow. Where all is change, there is, ironically, nothing to change, "not in all eternity." Apocalypse in the poetry of Blake and Shelley thus becomes in the context of "*amor fati*" less a celebration of political revolution than an affirmation of revolution's vitally metaphorical nature.

105

Keats's problem in *Hyperion*, like Shelley's and the reader's problem in "The Triumph of Life," is the disposal of the dead understood as a shift from metaphysics to metaphor. What can he do with the "gray-hair'd Saturn" sitting "quiet as a stone" which left the air about him so still that not even a "light seed" could be lifted from "the feather'd grass" and the stream flowing by "voiceless, still deadened more / By reason of his fallen divinity (1.4–12)?"[10] He cannot leave him as an "old root which grew / To strange distortion out of the hill side" because to do so would be to canonize a metaphor rather than renew it by carrying it along in that process of perpetual metamorphosis, which is in essence what metaphor is. A dead body undisposed of, left for dead, is a dead metaphor. It is what Derrida calls a "white mythology" which images a failure of the imagination, the life of which is perpetual metamorphosis or an everlasting flow of impressions through the mind. Shelley powerfully affirms this flow in the opening lines of "Mont Blanc" when they are read aloud as the expulsion of a single breath. The lines so uttered become an *apologia* or declaration of himself not as an individuated person with a fixed metaphysical identity, but as a poet whose identity is a perpetual flux, which Keats realized was, from a metaphysical point of view, no identity at all (". . . it is not itself—it has no self,—it is every thing and nothing" [*Letters* 27 October 1818]). Resisting metaphysics in favor of metaphor, Keats affirms the flow when in *Hyperion* he substitutes chaos for the gods as the origin of life. "Thou art not the beginning nor the end," Oceanus tells Saturn:

> From Chaos and parental Darkness came
> Light, the first fruits of that intestine broil,
> That sullen ferment, which for wondrous ends
> Was ripening in itself.
>
> (*Hyperion* 2.190–94)

For Nietzsche, Blake, Keats and Shelley, language and poetry are born of "intestine broil" ripening as it were in the body's "sullen ferment," the "volcano's meteor-breathing chasm" to which Asia and Panthea are carried by "the sound" (*PU* 2.1–3).

Crucial therefore to an understanding of the shaping of a metaphorical body overcoming the fearful, often unexpected, confrontation with an inert or dead one (a metaphysical freeze) is the removal of golden compasses which God keeps in storage to circumscribe the abyss. Once removed, the abyss itself stands open as, for example, it stands open to Panthea and Asia who have been borne by a sound (Nietzsche's spirit of music) to the "mighty portal" of Demogorgon's cave. Asia enters that cave much as in Blake's *Milton* Milton enters Blake's left foot at the metatarsal. Like Demogorgon's cave, Blake's body in *Milton* is a place of physiological, pre-linguistic energy waiting to be transformed into a "vitally metaphorical" body which, like "a prismatic and many-sided mirror" (*Defence* 491), collects, divides and reproduces what Shelley will call "the One." This Platonic temptation to absorb the "many" metaphors that "change and pass" into the Neoplatonic "One" that "remains" (*Adonais* 460) is, for Nietzsche, the danger confronting what he considered decadent romantics like Shelley and Wagner. By exploring the work undertaken in the cave of Demogorgon and in the body of Blake, I will attempt to relate Nietzsche's replacement of the dead god of metaphysics with a "vitally metaphorical" one (such as his Zarathustra) to the poetic act of creation that in romanticism, and particularly here in Shelley's *Prometheus Unbound* and Blake's *Milton*, constitutes the proper action of the romantic imagination.

1

In turning from a mythological account of the Dionysian origins of language in his first published work, *The Birth of Tragedy*, to what may be called a psychosomatic account, Nietzsche, among other things, set out to read the painful symptoms of his own body not by an identification with the suffering Dionysus, an identification to which in his final madness he would return to make of his insanity a kind of divine intoxication, but by understanding with Schopenhauer's help language as the representative images of bodily processes. Blondel accurately describes Nietzsche's view of language as the "quasi-*hysterical* . . . symptomatic *conversion*" of the body itself, a "meta-phorical" displacement of its "sullen ferment" or "intestine broil." Creativity, for Nietzsche, derives from pain; it is impossible for him to conceive how in the absence of bodily decrepitude creativity can occur. Art, he suggests, feeds upon the agony of the body—an agony that signals its death—to create a metaphorical body that is, among other things, a celebration of pain as the trumpet of resurrection. In another, more sinister, sense, however, the metaphorical body constitutes, as de Man suggests, a confrontation with the face of death itself. "Nihilism [nothingness] stands at the door: whence comes this uncanniest of all guests" (7), asks Nietzsche in the opening sentence of *The Will To Power*.

It is precisely this celebration, triumph and confrontation that Nietzsche identified with Greek tragedy, which he read as the Dionysian text of life. In their denial of the Dionysian text, Socrates and Christ, Nietzsche asserted, were the enemies of life. Viewed in one of its offered perspectives, Shelley's "The Triumph of Life" anticipates Nietzsche by imaging "the sacred few" (which includes Socrates and Christ) fleeing from the on-rushing Chariot of Life back to their "native noon" (131). Rousseau, however, though himself defeated, would, like Nietzsche after him, not have Shelley withdraw from the wretched spectacle. He would rather have him engage his own still-living, though corpse-haunted, body, which in *Adonais* he is prepared, unlike Keats in *The Fall of Hyperion*, to abandon, and turn again "actor . . . in this wretchedness" ("The Triumph of Life" 306). If he does then Rousseau might find a way out of the condition into which he has sunk. There may be metaphorical life in the "old root" ("The Triumph of Life" 182) yet capable of a new growth beyond its present distortion.

The possibility of new growth arising out of an "old root" haunts the relationship between Shelley and Rousseau in his final fragment. Some such possibility set within a very different mythical framework haunts Keats's fragment, *Hyperion*. In order to "die into life" (3.130), Keats suggests in *Hyperion*, the poet must forsake metaphysics, the ontology of Being, in favor of metaphor, the ceaseless turmoil of Becoming. Thus as the fragment breaks off, Apollo, imaging Keats in his struggle to break free of Milton, takes leave of "pale immortal death." "Wild commotions," shake the "immortal fairness of his limbs" as with "fierce convulse" (3.124–30) he enters, or is about to enter, a new metaphorical body which, because he is still perhaps too much in awe of Milton's gods, Keats could not construct. In that kind of failure, Nietzsche located what he considered the decadence of romanticism. Though moving toward it, Keats stopped short of Nietzsche's death of God.

"What is a word?" Nietzsche asks in "On Truth and Falsity in their Ultramoral Sense." "The expression of a nerve-stimulus in sounds" (177), he replies. In *The Birth of Tragedy Out of the Spirit of Music* (which was Nietzsche's title in its first edition) Nietzsche identifies these sounds— Rousseau's impossible "*language of children before they begin [have learned] to speak*" analyzed by Jacques Derrida in *Of Grammatology*[11]—with Dionysus and the Dionysian musician. It is, for Derrida, precisely the language which Rousseau identified with the state of nature, a state which writing could not enter because it lacked for Shelley's Rousseau the "purer nutriment" ("The Triumph of Life" 202). As writer, Shelley's Rousseau had to endure a "disguise" which "stain[ed] that within which still disdains to wear it" (204–5). Whether Shelley can himself accept the "stain" that ink brings to the white sheet, having himself come in *Adonais* to the brink of rejecting it ("even whilst we speak / Is it not broken?" 285–86]) may indeed constitute the "thoughts that must remain untold" 21) which become perhaps the "trance of wondrous thought" (41) which at once binds him to Rousseau and, as in *Adonais*, "lure[s] [him] to the brink" (*Adonais* 423). Clearly, he is not yet fully prepared, nor is Rousseau prepared, to dispose of him in the way that he finally disposes of Keats in *Adonais* where by the poem's end he is perhaps prepared to sacrifice metaphor to a dubious metaphysics. A metaphysical defense of his own suicide which would allow him in Keats's fate to weep his own hovers, as it were, on what de Man in "Shelley Disfigured" calls "the margin of the last manuscript page" (67) of "The Triumph of Life." Again in such a metaphysical defense Nietzsche would find the romantic enactment of that "will to nothingness" that yet remains a will.

The agony of composition (Apollo dying into life), which the romantic metaphorically enacts under a thin disguise of joy or a metamorphosis into joy, is a confrontation with the sickness of the body. The pen wars with the flesh, composition wars with a physiological process, words carry across to the page the painful stab wounds that as nerve stimuli penetrate the body. The music of the final act of *Prometheus Unbound*, its clear crystal notes that penetrate the sense and settle in the soul, are first "the spears / Of moon-freezing chrystals" piercing the agonized body of the bound Prometheus. "The perfect brightness and cheerfulness, even exhuberance of the spirit, reflected in [*The Dawn*]," writes Nietzsche in *Ecce Homo*,

> is compatible in my case not only with the most profound physi-
> ological weakness, but even with an excess of pain. In the midst
> of the torments that go with an uninterrupted three-day migraine,
> accompanied by laborious vomiting of phlegm, I possessed a
> dialectician's clarity *par excellence* and thought through with very
> cold blood matters for which under healthier circumstances I am
> not mountain-climber, not subtle, not *cold* enough.
>
> (223)

In *The Fall of Hyperion* Keats makes a similar confession. Moneta, his chastising Muse, is an "immortal sickness which kills not," progressing as she does deathwards "to no death" (*The Fall of Hyperion* 1.258–61). If Keats is to write his epic, he must strive against the "numbness" that as "a palsied chill" ascends his limbs and grasps his throat to put out "those streams that pulse beside [it]" (*The Fall of Hyperion* 1.122–25). Finally, in perhaps his last serious lines, "This living hand, now warm and capable," he holds out to the reader his "living hand" that is still "warm and capable / Of earnest grasping," warning the reader that if it "were cold / And in the icy silence of the tomb," it would "so haunt [his] days and chill [his] dream-ing nights" that he would "wish [his] own heart dry of blood" (1–5) so that blood might stream again in Keats's veins. The relationship between Shelley and Rousseau, I suggest, is not unlike this gothic relationship between Keats and his reader. Will Shelley "wish [his] own heart dry of blood" that Rousseau's veins might stream again? Some such wish may inform Shelley's treatment of the dead Keats in *Adonais*.

2

Nietzsche's Dionysus has much in common with Wordsworth's image of the infant Hartley Coleridge who makes "a mock apparel" of sounds, fit-ting their "breeze-like motion" to "unutterable thought" ("To H.C." 2–4).[12] He is "felt in the blood" ("Tintern Abbey" 28). The freezing of the blood, cutting the head off from the feelings and the instincts (Wordsworth's "independent intellect" [*The Prelude* 11. 244]), describes, among other things, Nietzsche's rejection of Socrates whose philosophy, as presented by Plato, enacted for Nietzsche the Apollonian usurpation of Dionysus which encouraged the hardening of metaphor into a metaphysical system. Greek tragedy, Nietzsche argues, emerged from the sacred dance and song identified with the worship of Dionysus even as Wordsworth's poetry, as in "The Idiot Boy" for example, emerged from the "breeze-like motion" of "unutterable thought." When Shelley argues in his *Defence of Poetry* that "poetry is connate with the origin of man" (480), he describes that origin in terms of "the motions of the dance" and "the melody of the song" by which men "in the youth of the world" imaginatively construct a "vitally metaphorical" world arising out of their own bodies moving in continuous rhythmical intercourse with natural objects (480–82), a view which he may in part have derived from his reading of Wordsworth's 1800 Preface to the *Lyrical Ballads*. When Greek tragedy lost touch with its origins in the sacred dance and song it died even as for Blake and Shelley Wordsworth as a poet died once his poetry, particularly *The Excursion*, lost touch with his "vitally metaphorical" child.

Like Nietzsche, Blake as a poet was deeply grounded in the psychosomatic processes of his body which under the control of Urizen became, like the body of Shelley's Prometheus under the control of Jupiter, a labyrinth of imprisoned energy arthritically experienced as ceaseless pain. The "red Globule of Mans blood," (*Milton* 29[31]: 19) in a single pulsation of which "the Poets Work is Done: and all the Great / Events of Time start forth & are concievd" (*Milton* 29[31]: 1–2), becomes, when subjected to "the palsied chill" of Urizen, Orc's "incessant howls burning in fires of Eternal Youth, / Within the vegetated mortal Nerves" (*Milton* 29[31]: 29–30). Orc appears to suffer from rheumatoid arthritis.

In the "Optic vegetative Nerves," sleep is transformed to death. The "Nerves of the Nostril" become "Opaque & Indefinite," the Opaque becoming Satan and the Solid Adam. Indeed, only "the Nerves of the Ear" remain open "for the Nerves of the Tongue are closed" (*Milton* 29[31]: 29–39). The world of sense, except the ear (music), suffers "the cruelties of Demonstration" which narcissistically mirror "Mathematic power" (29[31]: 36–38). The result, as Blake describes it in *The [First] Book of Urizen*, is Urizen's "Book/ Of eternal brass," written in "solitude" in his "strong [arthritic] hand." It consists of

> One command, one joy, one desire,
> One curse, one weight, one measure,
> One King, one God, one Law
> (2.32–40)

Milton in *Paradise Lost* (*PL*) is, according to Blake, the prisoner of Urizen. The Messiah who created the world with his "golden Compasses" (*PL* 7.225)[13] is "the Governor or Reason" who cast out "Desire" (*Marriage of Heaven and Hell* [*MHH*] 5). In truth, however, Messiah fell when "on the Wings of Cherubim," he rode "in Paternal Glorie . . . / Farr into *Chaos*, and the World unborn" (*PL* 7.218–20). Far from casting out Desire, he created the world with it by forming "a heaven of what he stole from the Abyss" (*MHH* 5). Energy or Desire, Blake argues, is "the only life and is from the Body"; Reason is its "bound or outward circumference" (*MHH* 4). Reason and Energy are not, therefore, opposed even as for Nietzsche Apollo and Dionysus in *The Birth of Tragedy* are not opposed: Apollo is the representation of Dionysus; Reason is the representation of Energy. Milton, however, in his creation myth failed, according to Blake, fully to mirror the vitally meta-phorical action of his imagination. In the representation of his creative mind he fell back upon the "cruelties of Demonstration" to construct with his Newtonian compasses a false or perverse image based upon "Mathematic power," rendering "the divine Saviour" a "Ratio of the five senses" (*MHH* 5). He created, that is, natural religion governed by mathematical law.

If, however, Milton was in need of Blake to rescue him from the math-ematical confines of Urizen, Blake at Felpham living in the cottage of his patron, William Hayley (the cottage appears in Plate 40 of the Trianon facsimile of *Milton* where Blake is walking in his garden with Ololon de-scending), was equally in need of Milton. For both of them a new beginning, a new discharge of energy, was needed. Blake's account of Milton walking about "in Eternity / One hundred years, pondring the intricate mazes of Providence / Unhappy tho in heav'n" (*Milton* 2: 16–18) found its counter-part in Blake walking in his garden at Felpham where Blake's "Vegetated portion" had been taken on Los's "firy whirlwind . . . / To display Natures cruel holiness: the deceits of Natural Religion" (*Milton* 36[40]: 21–25), even as in *Paradise Lost* Milton had been nightly taken by the virgin Urania to the throne of God where she dictated to him slumbering his "unpremeditated Verse" (*PL* 9.23).

The problem for Blake was that Urania-Ololon, who now descends into his garden as she descended nightly from Heaven to the sleeping Milton, is a vir-gin who initially as virgin displays "Natures cruel holiness." As vehemently as Nietzsche after him, Blake rejects the holiness of chastity; he sees in it the repression of Dionysian energy which turns the vital metaphors that constitute poetic tales into the dead one that constitute forms of worship. "At length," Blake concludes in a manner that anticipates Nietzsche, "they [the "ancient Poets"] pronounced that the Gods had orderd such things" (*MHH* 11).

Unlike Milton receiving the nightly visitations of Urania while he slept, Blake is awake when Ololon descends searching for Milton whom she knows has been "driven from Eternity" (*Milton* 37[41]: 3) into Blake's body. This act she herself in some sense performs ("terrified at my Act / In Great Eternity" [*Milton* 37[41]: 2–3]) when Blake commands her as a daughter of Beulah to come into his hand and descend "down the Nerves of [his] right arm" (*Milton* 2: 5–6). Ololon, that is, has emerged "from out the Portals of

111

[Blake's more lustful] Brain" (*Milton* 2: 7) still terrified of the Paradise she has left. Now located in the writing hand of Blake, Ololon must become the pen as sword in Blake's and Milton's ceaseless fight to build Jerusalem. She must, and does, in Blake's brain cast off her virginity to unite with Milton (who has himself removed his Puritan robes) so that the true apocalyptic form of his descent can at last be realized. She now descends, not as a frightened virgin, but in true Nietzschean fashion: "In clouds of blood, in streams of gore, with dreadful thunderings / Into the Fires of Intellect that rejoic'd in Felphams Vale / Around the Starry Eight" (*Milton* 42[49]: 9–11). The "rural pen" has "stain'd the water clear"; the staining acts as a linguistic deferral which, so long as it is affirmed, prevents the hardening of metaphor into a metaphysical system.

3

Nietzsche's reading of Christianity as "the will to nothingness pronounced holy" finds its Blakean counterpart in "Natures cruel holiness" to which Christianity had been Deistically reduced when its energy was circumscribed by Milton's Urizenic God of the golden compasses. The result was a subjugation of the body's energy to "Mathematic power," a reduction of the "Divine Saviour" to a "Ratio of the five senses." To release Jesus from that dead metaphor was in Blake's metaphorical view to raise him from the dead through a radical process of defamiliarization described by Shelley as "before unapprehended relations" (*Defence* 482). He would, that is, confront his readers not with the enlightened behavior of the neo-classical Jesus, but with the cruel horrors that behavior concealed. Like Prometheus crying out against the Spectre version of himself as the crucified Christ, Blake's reader is led to reject as a curse the metaphorical nightmare to which Deism had reduced the Savior who now, with Milton's help, sought in Blake's "Vegetated body" the resurrection long denied. Thus as Milton is about to enter Blake's body, he cries out

> . . . O when Lord Jesus wilt thou come?
> Tarry no longer; for my soul lies at the gate of death.
> I will arise and look forth for the morning of the grave.
> I will go down to the sepulcher to see if morning breaks!
> (*Milton* 14[15]: 18–21)

The sepulchre is at once the left foot of Blake and the foot of Urizen where Milton begins his metaphorical "track," moulding "new flesh on the Demon cold," shaping in the vegetated body of Blake the "Human body" that was for both poets the imaginative form of the Incarnation.

Milton entering Blake's body renders it a scene of reading; Milton in the body of Blake dismantles his own epic in order, with Blake's help, to recreate it. Blake's body is "the morning of the grave," the "sepulcher" where "morning breaks." It is thus as a scene of reading a scene of "self-annihilation" undertaken by Milton "lest the Last judgment come & find [him] unannihilate" (Milton 14[15]: 22–23).

The dis-eased life of Blake's physiological body thus becomes Milton's "Selfhood, which must be put off & annihilated away / To cleanse the Face of [his] Spirit by Self-examination" (*Milton* 40[46]: 36–37). This cleansing by "Self-examination" constitutes the dismantling of *Paradise Lost*, liberating it from the whited sepulchre it had become as the imagination was subjected to a system of belief. "When will the Resurrection come; to deliver the sleeping body / From corruptibility" (*Milton* 14: 17–18), cries Milton locked like the Christ of Christian orthodoxy in the sepulchre of a dead poem now seen as Blake's sick body. By making his sick body a metaphor of Milton's Urizenic epic, Blake restores the epic to what in the Nietzschean sense is its primal metaphorical scene: the linguistic displacement of bodily pain.

At Felpham Blake suffered from continuous stomach ailments which in *Milton* become the metaphorical action of a vast digestive machine called Bowlahoola that is similar in its mythical role to the belly of the whale where Jonah undergoes a partial transformation through the release of repressed energies. Francis Bacon, Blake later told John Linnell (1 February 1826), would have prescribed certain medicines for "a cold in my stomach," a cold which he claimed descended upon him not only at Felpham but whenever he was exposed to the damp air of Hampstead, Highgate, Hornsea, Muswell Hill, Islington, and all places north of London, districts which loom large in *Jerusalem* as places under siege in his own body that propelled him to write. (Nietzsche suffered equally from damp air and, like Blake, catalogued in *Ecce Homo* the geographical sites of his agony which in Nietzsche's case settled in the intestines where, he suggests, the German spirit originates [240].) Calling Bacon a "Liar," Blake told Linnell that medicinal matter against stomach colds was an "ostentatious Exertion against . . . Eternal Existence itself, because it is a Mental Rebellion against the Holy Spirit, & fit only for a Soldier of Satan to perform" (*Letters* 154). A stomach cold, "excruciating while it lasts," is the operation of the Holy Spirit calling upon Albion to awaken from the sleep of Ulro even as pain called upon Nietzsche. ("All prejudices come from the intestines," writes Nietzsche in *Ecce Homo*. To settle into them "is the real *sin* against the holy spirit" [240].)

Like Nietzsche, then, Blake experienced the substitution of a living metaphorical body for a sick one in a psychosomatic rather than metaphysical way. The energy of the body is for Blake the life of the Holy Spirit. Whenever the Holy Spirit is divorced from the body, he argues in *The Marriage of Heaven and Hell*, "a system" is formed "which some [take] advantage of & enslav[e] the vulgar by attempting to realize or abstract the mental deities from their objects" (*MHH* 11). The "objects" of the "mental deities" do not belong to the metaphysical realm of pure ideas which Plato, transcending the body, describes. They are the psychosomatic processes of the human body itself. They are "what passes in [man's] members," his "earthly lineaments" (*Milton* 21[23]: 9–11), though, as Blake explains, "man cannot know / What passes in his members till periods of Space & Time / Reveal the secrets of Eternity" (*Milton* 21[23]: 8–10).

Blake's Los as "the Spirit of Prophecy, the ever apparent Elias," is "Time's swiftness / Which is the swiftest of all things" (*Milton* 24[26]: 71–73). He takes Blake in his "firy whirlwind" to Felpham and there reveals "the secrets of Eternity" as they pass "in his members" (Plate 47 in the Trianon facsimile is a full-page illustration which portrays Blake kneeling, his head turned toward the groin of Los whose legs are spread within a wheel of fire.) Divorced from that "firy whirlwind" all things in time become "eternal torment" which is for Blake the torment of Christ's body and his own, a torment which his poetry metaphorically explores. Thus the powerful Los whose "locks flourish like the brows of morning" (*Milton* 24[26]: 70) becomes again and again the dismembered or crucified Los of *Jerusalem*. Los, perceived in his mortal state, is reduced to endless duration described by Shelley's Prometheus as "wingless, crawling hours" that move at the writhing pace of "crawling glaciers" piercing his flesh with "moon-freezing chrystals" (*PU* 1.31–32). To that "eternal torment" of frozen or repressed energy which Blake calls Selfhood Milton had been reduced by Urizen in *Paradise Lost* even as Blake had been reduced to it by Hayley at Felpham.

Blake focuses upon torment. In *Jerusalem* he sits "day and night," his hand trembling "exceedingly upon the rock of ages" as he calls upon the Savior to "annihilate the Selfhood in me" (5: 16–22), a process that continues until the poem's end. His task, like Nietzsche's, is to reveal torment as the crucible of creation. Sudden apocalyptic breakthroughs of "Time's swiftness" emerge from the painful consolidation of error, from an endlessly extended moment imprisoned in sheer duration like the mindless ticking of a clock whose maker has disappeared. Apocalypse is present in its absence or negation. It inhabits the freezing of the blood, a hand, like Wordsworth's, locked in arthritic pain, a body locked in death which is nevertheless, like Shelley's Rousseau, conscious of its condition.

Only when the agony of the body is thus metaphorically displayed as the scene of writing can man experience the reduction of himself to his "Vegetated portion" subject to "Natures cruel holiness: the deceits of Natural Religion." In the agony of linguistic contraction resides the expansion of consciousness itself. When released from the delusion of a metaphysics that would rob pain of physiological sensation, the God of natural religion inhabiting the language of abstraction is exposed as the Satan who would subject man to the eternal curse the emblem of which is the crucified Christ. That curse Blake, like Keats in *The Fall of Hyperion*, enacts as a numbness of the senses ("I strove hard to escape / The numbness" [*The Fall of Hyperion* 1.127–28]), a death of the body imaged in the recurrent guise of Urizen stooping down

114

and taking up the icy waters of the Jordan and "pouring on / To Miltons brain the icy fluid from his broad cold palm" (*Milton* 19[21]: 8–9). Its counterpart is Jupiter piercing Prometheus with "moon-freezing chrystals."

Blake's dis-eased body metaphorically enacts its psychosomatic condition in the slow composition of his epic vision as it painfully, sometimes plotlessly, unfolds in *The Four Zoas*, *Milton*, and *Jerusalem*. Like Shelley's "The Triumph of Life," it remains a broken body sustained by the absence of a wholeness which, like a torso, adumbrates as absence some metaphysical pre-existent state identified as essence. That hypothetical state posited by existence as the consciousness of itself—the unified body of the four Zoas in a state of perfect equilibrium—would, if metaphysically realized as in Plato, incarnate for Blake the tyranny inherent in any system as system. Blake, like Keats in *Hyperion*, perhaps confronted this tyranny when in imitation of *Paradise Lost* he conceived of *Milton* as a twelve-book epic, his two-book version becoming a deliberate act of dismemberment not unlike Nietzsche's aphoristic dismemberment of an Urizenic God in his ceaseless effort to enact his death, an enactment which paradoxically, as Alexander Nehamas points out, makes "his presence as an author literally unforgettable" and prevents "his readers from overlooking the fact that his views necessarily originate with him."[14] Blake's dismembering style works in the same way: it forces the reader to recognize Blake as the creator of what in destroying he himself constructs. Blake's God, like Nietzsche's, is his own imagination. Thus, when Milton entering Blake's body declares that he is annihilating his Selfhood, he means that he is annihilating the collective system ruled by Satan which constitutes Selfhood. He is giving himself over to his own painful bodily processes as the surest sign of his individuality.

What as a poet Blake *can* do as opposed to what the mind left to itself *would* do isolates the essential difference between metaphor and metaphysics. The mind released from the body would create a metaphysical system. Bound to the physiological processes that are "Bowlahoola thro all its porches" ("The Bellows are the Animal Lungs: the Hammers the Animal Heart / The Furnaces the Stomach for digestion" [*Milton* 24[26]: 54–59]), metaphysics becomes again metaphor, a linguistic mirroring of "what passes in [man's] members," his "earthly lineaments." What passes in Blake's "members" is Milton rewriting *Paradise Lost*, making use of Blake's "Bellows," "Hammers" and "Furnaces." Annihilating the Selfhood is for Blake, as for Jonathan Swift, a thunderous digestive process that includes the "excrementitious" (*Jerusalem* 88: 39).

Except as inspired by Los entering Blake as his "Vehicular Form" (*Jerusalem* 53: 1), Blake falling unconscious upon his path a "moment" as "Terror struck in the Vale" (*Milton* 42: 24–26), Blake cannot see the life of his own body. He must, rather, be taken out of his own body a "moment" in order to perceive its operations. The soul, however, is not distinct from the body; it is a perspective on the body, the body's metaphorical perception of itself.

The paradox of knowing and not knowing, which is the paradox of inspiration, protects the mind in the process of metaphor-making from the metaphysical delusion of a knowledge or system alien to it. Blake's metaphorical reading of his own bodily processes is his reading of *Paradise Lost*. The epic thus becomes in Blake's radical reading of it a diagnosis of Milton's psychosomatic illness for which Blake's own writing provides a remedy. Though he describes in three separate contexts Milton's descent into the metatarsus of his left foot, he insists that he "knew not that it was Milton" (*Milton* 21[23]: 8). He did not, that is, know the psychosomatic effect of his reading of *Paradise Lost*. He did not, that is, know at a conscious level the responses of his own body (nerve-stimuli) which presented themselves as metaphors. He did not know that Milton's epic had in his reading of it become his own body's "symptomatic *conversion* into language" which, because of his love of Milton, worked as healing metaphors. Healing metaphors are, for Blake, eternal life.

By insisting that the body is the form of the imagination, its processes the creative activity of the imagination itself, Blake sought to overcome the dualism that conducted not only to a false morality but to the body's death. "Energy," he declares in anticipation of Nietzsche, "is the only life and is from the Body" (*MHH* 4). His war, like Nietzsche's war, was not therefore against the senses but against mental abstraction as the extinction of them. His task was not denial but enlargement. Like Nietzsche, he enacted that enlargement physically as pain—the cry of a fixed body against the agony of its psychic expansion—and metaphorically as pleasure—the release of a defamiliarizing metaphor from the confines of a familiar one. He sought, that is, and again like Nietzsche, to transform the "fires of hell" into "the enjoyments of Genius" (*MHH* 5). His purpose was "salutary and medicinal" (*MHH* 14).

Firmly grounded in a celebratory affirmation of the creative processes of the body, Blake's healing metaphors, infused with the "mercy of Eternity" and partaking of "Time's swiftness" (Los's "firy whirlwind"), are a "quasi-hysterical" conversion of sexuality and sexual orgasm into metaphors of "Cominglings: from the Head even to the Feet" (*Jerusalem* 69: 43). Such embraces constitute "the lineaments of Gratified desire," which, writes Blake, "In a wife I would desire" (Erdman 474). Such "lineaments" constitute Blake's metaphorical body, Albion united with his bride, Jerusalem, Milton united with Ololon, Blake united with Catherine in that "moment" in his garden when Jesus descends, the "Clouds of Ololon folded as a Garment" around his limbs (*Milton* 42[49]: 11–12).

The poet, Blake suggests, is inspired by the "Daughters of Beulah" who lead the poet into "soft sexual delusions / Of varied beauty" (*Milton* 2: 1–4) unless the poet, like Blake in *Milton*, takes charge by connecting them to "the Portals of [the] Brain" (*Milton* 2: 7). He must not remain bound as Ovid's Hermaphroditus remained bound to the water nymph, for in that binding resides the lingering presence of Satan as hermaphrodite. Satan as Blake describes him is the creator of "Female Space" which "shrinks the Organs / Of life till they become Finite and itself seems Infinite" (*Milton* 10[11]: 6–7).

In a manner that anticipates Nietzsche's ambivalent attitude to women, Blake's Satan in *Milton* stupifies "the masculine perceptions / And [keeps] only the feminine awake" (*Milton* 12[13]: 5–6). Reduced to his "Vegetated portion," man becomes a hermaphrodite. Thus Milton standing "on the verge of Beulah" enters "his own Shadow" which he describes as "A mournful form double: hermaphroditic: male & female / In one wondrous body" (*Milton* 14[15]: 37–38). The Shadow as "male & female / In one wondrous body" is also in its rich metaphorical elaboration Milton's fusion with his sixfold Emanation, his three wives and three daughters who serve Urizen even as Blake's wife, Catherine, served in her illness the Satanic purposes of Hayley.

Milton entering his hermaphroditic body is thus Milton entering the body of Blake which at Felpham was reduced to "the earth of vegetation" (*Milton* 14[15]: 41) on which now he writes. Reduced to his "Vegetated portion" by the dictates of Hayley working in alliance with his sick wife, Catherine, Blake had been reduced by pity and gratitude to turning over to Satan "the Harrow of the Almighty" lest "Satan should accuse him of / Ingratitude" (*Milton* 7: 10–12). By colluding with Blake's wife, Hayley had bound Blake in a "mournful form double."

The apocalyptic transformation of this "mournful form double" to become a renewal of the Biblical metaphor of the descent of New Jerusalem "prepared as a bride adorned for her husband" (Revelation 21: 2) is apparent in the final image of Ololon's many-faceted descent into Blake's garden at Felpham. She descends as the bride of the apocalypse, her wedding garment folded round the burning limbs of "One Man Jesus the Saviour" (*Milton* 40[47]: 11). Overpowered by the thunderous announcement of descent, at once threefold (sexual) and fourfold (human), Blake falls "outstretched upon the path / A moment" (*Milton* 42[49]: 25–26). In that "pulsation of the artery" in which, writes Blake, "the Poets Work is Done: and all the great Events of Time start forth & are concievd" (*Milton* 29[31]: 1–2], Blake's epic is conceived, its entire vision appearing as a "Column of Fire in Felphams vale" (*Milton* 42[49]: 22) in which he and his trembling wife are for an instant consumed.

Blake, like Nietzsche after him, avoids the anagogic consummation overtaking Shelley in the closing stanzas of *Adonais* and in the final lines of *Epipsychidion* ("I pant, I sink, I tremble, I expire!"). Instantly Blake's soul "returnd into its mortal state / To Resurrection & Judgment in the Vegetable Body," his wife, Catherine, "trembling by his side" (*Milton* 42[49]: 26–28). Blake is unwilling to separate the descent of New Jerusalem as bride from either Milton's sexual union with his twelve-year-old bride, Ololon, or his own trembling wife giving herself at last to her husband, Blake having

invited Ololon into his cottage to attend her. He will not substitute metaphysics for metaphor, a form of worship for a poetic tale. The "litteral
expression" of the Bible, Blake suggests, is metaphor, Ololon's wedding
garment "written within and without in woven letters" (*Milton* 42[49]: 13).

By thus locating as metaphor "Resurrection & Judgment in the Vegetable
Body," Blake anticipates in attitude as well as in style Nietzsche's notion of
"great healthiness." It is, Nietzsche writes in *The Joyful Wisdom*,

> the ideal of a spirit who plays naively (that is to say involuntarily
> and from overflowing abundance and power) with everything that
> has hitherto been called holy, good, inviolable, divine; to whom the
> loftiest conception which the people have reasonably made their
> measure of value would already imply danger, ruin, debasement, or
> at least relaxation, blindness, or temporary self-forgetfulness; the
> ideal of a humanly superhuman welfare and benevolence, which
> may often enough appear *inhuman*, for example, when put by the
> side of all past seriousness on earth, and in comparison with all past
> solemnities in bearing, word, tone, look, morality and pursuit,
> as their truest involuntary parody,—but with which, nevertheless,
> perhaps *the great seriousness* only commences, the proper inter-
> rogation mark is set up, the fate of the soul changes, the hour-hand
> moves, and tragedy *begins*. . . .[15]

If metaphor is, as Nietzsche suggests, the linguistic displacement of
nerve-stimuli, metaphysics is a further displacement of metaphor into a
system that releases consciousness from the body to become an autonomous self-sustaining activity. Precisely in the affirmation of metaphysics as
twice-removed from the body lay for Nietzsche as for Blake his criticism
of all self-sustaining logocentric systems grounded in "the Body of
Death . . . perfect in hypocritic holiness" (*Milton* 13[14]: 25). The perfected
death of the body whether into nature (Shelley's Rousseau) or into super-
nature (Shelley's Keats) images for Blake the killing desire of the mind to
a firm as Urizen or Jupiter its own omnipotence. In that logocentric
movement toward the infinite dwells for Nietzsche the roots of every
metaphysical system which *Thus Spake Zarathustra*, like Blake's *Milton*,
parodies within the framework of what Nietzsche in *Ecce Homo* calls a
"physiological presupposition" of "the *great health*" (298). "For a typically
healthy person," he, like Blake, insists,

> conversely, being sick can even become an energetic *stimulus* to life,
> for living *more*. This, in fact, is how that long period of sickness
> appears to me *now*: as it were I discovered life anew, including
> myself. . . . I turned my will to health, to *life*, into a philosophy.
>
> (*Ecce Homo* 224)

While Blake declared well before Nietzsche the death of God, agreeing in advance with his assessment of orthodox Christianity (the religion of the Elect) as "the will to nothingness pronounced holy," he nevertheless sought, like Nietzsche in *Thus Spake Zarathustra*, to enact a radical metaphorical resurrection by means of that most dominant of romantic metaphors critically scrutinized by Mary Shelley in *Frankenstein*: the making of a new human body. Blake's "Eternal Great Humanity Divine" (*Milton* 2: 7) is the fourfold man of Eden propelled by his "Sexual Threefold" Chariot. Each of his "Human Nerves of Sensation" faces a separate direction expanding to "the bound or outward circumference" to which his "Sexual Threefold" Chariot conducts. His "Body of Death" is thus driven "outward . . . in an Eternal Death & Resurrection" which is its perpetually renewed life "among the Flowers of Beulah." South stands "the Nerves of the Eye," east "the Nerves of the / Expansive Nostrils," west "the Parent Sense of the Tongue" and north "the labyrinthine Ear." These vastly extended senses, Blake argues, reduce to a "Vacuum" the "excrementitious" husk that is his own physiological corruption entered by Milton when he descended into his left foot. The excremental process thus becomes a metaphor of "Self-Annihilation" which to those locked in the "Husk & Covering" (Blake's "Covering Cherub") is a mere "Vacuum" (*Jerusalem* 98: 12–23). For those readers of Blake's *Milton*, however, who are prepared to follow in "Miltons track" through the vegetable body of Blake, the vacuum to which that body is reduced becomes Blake's critical reading of *Paradise Lost*. The vacuum is now perceived as what Blake variously calls the "Negation" or "Spectre," "the Reasoning Power in Man," the "false Body," the "Incrustation over [the] Immortal / Spirit," the "Selfhood, which must be put off & annihilated alway" (*Milton* 40[46]: 34–36). The vacuum becomes, that is, the Sepulchre of Christ now perceived as an empty tomb. It is the defended "Lie" of the Bard's Song by which Satan "may be snared & caught & taken" (*Milton* 8: 48). It is Milton's critical self-examination of Urizen that conducts in Blake to "Self-Annihilation."

Christ returning in the apparel of Ololon, which is Blake's illuminated text, carries in its woven letters the grotesquerie of the physiological body in the process of being transformed into a new metaphorical state. It thus enacts the awakening of Blake to a consciousness of his own "Resurrection & Judgment in the Vegetable Body." This new metaphorical body images a psychosomatic process in which "every Word and every Character / [Are] Human according to the Expansion or Contraction, the Translucence or / Opakeness of Nervous fibres" (*Jerusalem* 98: 35–37), According to their translucence or opaqueness, time and space vary, governed as they are by these "Nervous fibres" which as "Human Nerves of Sensation" converse "together in Visionary Forms dramatic" (*Jerusalem* 98: 15–38). "Human Nerves of Sensation" conversing together are "cominglings" from head to foot. As "Visionary Forms dramatic" they constitute Blake's resurrected metaphorical body.

Over against Blake's gothic body carrying as metaphor its psychosomatic pain stands a mild and loving Jesus. In *Jerusalem*, he makes as "the Good Shepherd" seeking and finding his lost Albion a few scattered appearances, reminding the reader of what the text itself would have us forget: Blake's song is "mild" (*Jerusalem* 4: 5). Despite this assurance, Albion marches against him in his "deadly Sleep of Six Thousand Years" only to be taken by surprise "like a Serpent of precious stones & gold" dazzling around his "skirts" (*Jerusalem* 96: 10–12). Only through the shaping of the anti-Christ (Blake's text as the Serpent) can the true Christ appear even as only through defending a lie can the truth emerge. In this ceaseless struggle, words and characters contract and expand, are opaque or translucent, like the "Nervous fibres" from which they spring.

The lie resides in the congealing of the text into a system. The "red Globule of Mans blood," the pulsation of the poet's artery in which the work of six thousand years is done, linguistically congeals as an illuminated woven text into "the Dead Corpse of Sinais heat / Buried beneath his mercy Seat." "O Christians, Christians," cries Blake in his Prologue to *For the Sexes: The Gates of Paradise*, "tell me why / You rear it on your altars high" (9–10). Blake is here crying out against the inevitable contraction of his soul to that portion of itself perceived by the five senses, a contraction which reduces the risen Christ to a "Dead Corpse" lying on a Druid-Christian altar where his "shrieks" are preserved "in cups of gold" ("The Mental Traveller" 12). He is crying out against the death of metaphor, a death that overtook Milton's epic and continues to threaten Blake's own.

Bursting the bounds of his contracting and opaque senses against which he has struggled in his treatment of Los and Albion, Blake in the concluding plates of *Jerusalem* returns to the risen Savior standing over Blake in the opening lines of the epic. Responding to the Savior's dictation, his contracted "Organs of Perception" expand "in Visions, / In new Expanses . . . / Creating Space, Creating Time according to the wonders Divine / Of Human Imagination" (*Jerusalem* 98: 29–32). By virtue of this metaphorical expansion, Blake apprehends new relations among his senses which, when contracted, remain "unapprehended" (*Defence* 482). His expanded "Organs of Perception" walk "To and fro in Eternity as One Man reflecting each in each & deeply seen / And seeing" (*Jerusalem* 98: 39–40). What they see is the risen Savior of the opening lines incarnate in the metaphorical body of Blake's epic, which is now the body of "the Earth" and all "the Living Creatures of the Earth" "Humanize[d] / In the Forgiveness of Sins according to the Covenant of Jehovah" (*Jerusalem* 98: 44–45). In this vision of a fully human world ("All Human Forms identified even Tree Metal Earth & Stone" (*Jerusalem* 99: 1–2]) resides Blake's "mild song."

The Nietzschean counterpart of Blake's Savior is Dionysus who is perhaps best described as a "pulsation of the artery" transformed by the imagination into a "vitally metaphorical body" most nearly realized by Nietzsche in *Thus Spake Zarathustra*. That metaphorical body, which Blake describes as a poetic tale, is, for Nietzsche as for Blake, always in danger of hardening into a system, which is to say becoming the slave of its own representation. Perhaps for this reason, Zarathustra continues to wait for the emergence of the *Übermensch*, assuring his disciples as he lectures them in the cave that they are themselves not yet ready. The danger of Apollo, who for Keats as for Nietzsche must "die into life," is that he may usurp the darkness rather than reveal it. For Blake, as for Nietzsche, the light is in the darkness; the imagination brings darkness to light through an expansion of the senses. Blake's "Body of Death" is driven "outward" in *Jerusalem* to rejoice in its fourfold unity even as Nietzsche's ravaged body is driven outward in *Thus Spake Zarathustra* to rejoice in the coming of the *Übermensch*. What, above all, Blake and Nietzsche share in common is the ceaseless making and unmaking of a "vitally metaphorical" body out of the sickness of a dying one. Blake describes that ceaseless "Mental Fight" as "an Eternal Death and Resurrection" (*Jerusalem* 98: 20). In *Milton*, he images "Eternal Death" as "the rotten rags of Memory" (*Milton* 41[48]: 4) which Milton in the body of Blake must cast off in order to release himself from his "siren daughters," his "Sixfold Emanation" scattered through the deep in torment. Resurrection, on the other hand, is their human form who is Ololon. It is, therefore, the weaving of Ololon's wedding garment, the new garment of the imagination. That wedding garment, Milton's resurrected body, is the text itself "written within and without in woven letters" (*Milton* 42[49]: 13).

As the spectral form of the Resurrection "Eternal Death" is the memory. Ololon's wedding garment, present in "the Fires of [Blake's] intellect that rejoic'd in Felphams Vale" (*Milton* 42[49]: 8), settles with time into a metaphysical system to become "the rotten rags of Memory." Those "rotten rags," Blake further explains, are the "Natural Effect" of a "Spiritual Cause" which as "a Delusion / Of Ulro" usurp the "Spiritual Cause" itself (*Milton* 26[29]: 44–46). The "rotten rags of Memory" whick Blake opposes to inspiration even as Milton in *Reason of Church Government* opposes "dame memory and her siren daughters" (526) to the Holy Spirit, thus become "a ratio of perishing Vegetable Memory" (*Milton* 26[29]: 46) to which the soul is reduced when bound to linear time.

4

Nietzsche shares Blake's view of memory as the graveyard of metaphor. In "The Use and Abuse of History," Nietzsche begins with a meditation on a herd of grazing animals which, he writes, "lives *unhistorically*; for [the herd] 'goes into' the present, like a number, without leaving any curious remainder." "But," he continues man is always resisting the great and continually increasing weight of the past; it presses him down, and bows his shoulders; he travels with a dark invisible burden that he can plausibly disown, and—is only too glad to disown in converse with his fellows in order to excite their envy. And so it hurts him, like the thought of a lost Paradise, to see a herd grazing, or, nearer still, a child, that has nothing yet of the past to disown, and plays in a happy blindness between the walls of the past and the future.[16]

The "happy blindness" of the child from which de Man's title, *Blindness and Insight*, derives is for Nietzsche the divine intoxication of the Dionysian, an intoxication that Wordsworth describes when he compares himself in "Tintern Abbey" not to Nietzsche's grazing herd but to a "roe" whose linguistic oblivion is in Nietzsche's view tragically destroyed by the poet's simile of himself "bounding o'er the mountains . . . / Wherever nature led" ("Tintern Abbey" 67–70). Returning more than once to Derrida's account of what de Man calls "Rousseau's bad faith toward literary language, the manner in which he depends on it while condemning writing as if it were a sinful addicition"[17] (which is the issue of writing confronted in "The Triumph of Life"), de Man explores in "Literary History and Literary Modernity" the same problem in Nietzsche and declares it to be the problem of modernity itself. Because the biology of the animal is present in the physiology of the man, there may be moments when, as in Dionysian ecstacy, "he re-establishes contact with his spontaneity [his red globule of blood] and allows his truly human nature to assert itself" (*Blindness and Insight* 146). "Moments of genuine humanity," de Man therefore concludes in his account of Nietzsche,

> thus are moments at which all anteriority vanishes, annihilated by the power of an absolute forgetting. Although such a radical rejection of history may be illusory or unfair to the achievements of the past, it nevertheless remains justified as necessary to the fulfillment of the human condition and as the condition for action.
>
> (147)

De Man, however, tends to ignore here both the creative role of "anteriority" and the fact that human physiology exists as psychically experienced. Far from "vanishing" in the manner he describes, anteriority is present as a degenerative condition within the physiological body, the consciousness of which not only separates man from the animal (nature having for Nietzsche a genetic memory without consciousness), but becomes for him the very condition of creativity. Blake's "pulsation of the artery" is also in its vegetable form an encounter with mortality out of which springs the spontaneous necessity of a metaphorical body. "One pays dearly for immortality," writes Nietzsche in *Ecce Homo*, "one has to die several times while still alive" (303). "Born 28 Nov 1757 in London & has died several times since," writes Blake signing his name. And in *Jerusalem*, as Enitharmon dissolves away, "in gnawing pain from Los's bosom in the deadly Night," he, suspended over her, shoots forth "Self-living" a "red Globule of blood trembling beneath his bosom / . . . Feeding it with his groans & tears day & night without ceasing" (17: 51–56).

In *Prometheus Unbound*, Shelley moves toward a perpetually absent moment the deferred nature of which is the movement toward it. It is the absent moment "at which all anteriority vanishes," annihilated by the power of an absolute forgetting. By invoking the Phantasm of Jupiter, a figure which, like Nietzsche's nature, is without consciousness, Prometheus is able to recall the curse without re-membering it; his recalling becomes a revoking which cancels out what he hears. In obedience to Prometheus's command the Phantasm arises "Why have the secret powers of this strange world," he asks,

> Driven me, a frail and empty phantom, hither
> On direst storms? What unaccustomed sounds
> Are hovering on my lips, unlike the voice
> With which our pallid race holds ghastly talk
> In darkness? And proud Sufferer, who art thou?
> (*PU* 1.240–45)

The "unaccustomed sounds . . . / hovering on [his] lips" are indeed within Prometheus "an awful whisper" that rises up as an "inorganic voice" which "scarce like sound . . . tingles through the frame / As lightning tingles, hovering ere it strike" (*PU* 1.132–34). They are, in short, nerve stimuli that remain a sound to which no meaning is yet attached. They are akin to what Julia Kristeva calls the semiotic: the pre-linguistic unorganized rhythmic pulsations that survive inside language as an echo of what no longer exists as language or never was language.[18] "Speak the words which I would hear, / Although no thought inform thine empty voice" (1.248–49), Prometheus commands the Phantasm. The Earth responds by warning the echoes of the mountains, woods, haunted springs and prophetic caves to remain mute. Prometheus is, as it were, cancelling a dead metaphor even as in the added fourth act Shelley will cancel the "dead Hours" (*PU* 4.12), returning both to a forgotten form of sleep which the "infirm hand" of "Eternity," "Mother of many acts and hours" (*PU* 4.565–66), could revive or awaken by freeing the serpent. By the end of the third act, the fame of Jupiter's world is a shadow without substance, "ghosts of a no more remembered fame" (*PU* 3.4.169). It stands "not o'erthrown, but unregarded now" (3.4.179). "Where is the Spectre of Prophecy where the delusive Phantom / Departed," cries Blake in the concluding lines of *The Four Zoas*.

123

Prometheus, I suggest, is excreting a dead metaphorical body shaped by his opposition to Jupiter, a body which has become, in Nietzsche's words, "truth," which is to say, "a sum of human relations which became poetically and rhetorically intensified, metamorphosed, adorned, and after long usage seem to a nation fixed, canonic and binding" ("On Truth and Falsity in their Ultramoral Sense" 180). It has become, that is, Nietzsche's despised Christian morality, even as Prometheus' firm and patient opposition to Jupiter becomes through time and habit the very basis upon which what Shelley calls Jupiter's "undoubted triumph" rests. Precisely in the dissolution of that canonical body born of hate resides the possibility of creating a new and "vitally metaphorical" one. It involves the affirmation of illusion, Nietzsche's "*amor fati*," that alone can release man from the tyranny of truth.

That affirmation resides in Shelley's lyrical drama in Demogorgon who may be described as the metaphor-making power viewed simply as a power or metaphoricity itself. In itself "ungazed upon and shapeless—neither limb, / Nor form—nor outline" (*PU* 2.4.5–6), it is nevertheless felt by Panthea to be "a living spirit" who can assume whatever form the "human mind's imaginings" ("Mont Blanc" 143) project onto it. Indeed, as to what it is "as a living spirit" "each to itself," Asia confesses, "must be the oracle." (*PU* 2.4.123). To call it "eternal Love" is to initiate a metaphorical action appropriate to the name. The rocks binding Prometheus are instantly "cloven" (*PU* 2.4.129) and the car of the Hour, previously one among the many of the "wingless, crawling hours" (*PU* 1.48), instantly appears to take Asia to Prometheus. The naming thus carries the revelation which naming carried for Helen Keller. Another, checking "its dark chariot by the craggy gulf" (*PU* 2.4.143), ascends to "wrap in endless Night heaven's kingless throne" (*PU* 3.4.148). The past as past is being cancelled in accordance with Nietzsche's conviction, shared by Goethe, that a man must be "without knowledge" and forget "everything in order to be able to *do* something" (*Blindness and Insight* 147). In forgetting Jupiter, rejecting his knowledge of him, leaving Demogorgon to dispose of him (obliterating a worn-out metaphor in favor of a vital one), he is, in Nietzsche's words, "unfair toward what lies behind and knows only one right, the right of what is now coming into being as the result of his own action" ("The Use and Abuse of History" in de Man's translation [147]).

Shelley enacts this radically Nietzschean stance by turning the action over to Asia and her sisters who belong to the realm of dream described by Shelley in his *Defence of Poetry* as "beyond and above consciousness" (486). That realm includes the abyss itself upon which, for Nietzsche and the romantics, creation depends. Shelley first presents Asia in the oceanic world of Prometheus' own soul which has been contaminated by three thousand years of "sleep-unsheltered" (*PU* 1.12), hate-filled hours. Those hours, now as a paralyzed force, a dead metaphor ("Black, wintry, dead, unmeasured; without herb, / Insect, or beast, or shape or sound of life [*PU* 1.21–22]), gradually rise within him as a strange cacophony of sounds which initially announces the appearance of the Phantasm of Jupiter. Beyond that, however, it announces the rising up of a new metaphor out of the sounds (nerve-stimuli) themselves, Jupiter's "Ai! Ai!" (*PU* 3.1.80), for example. As the Phantasm approaches, "awful thoughts, rapid and quick," sweep "obscurely through [Prometheus'] brain like shadows dim." "I feel / Faint," he declares, "like one mingled in entwining love, / Yet tis not pleasure" (*PU* 1.146–49). So opaque has the pain-ridden soul-body of Prometheus become ("pain, pain, ever, forever" [1.23]) that Asia and the Phantasm remain indistinguishable from each other within it. By the end of the act, however, the sounds, gradually purified by the cleansing spirits vibrating in the "liquid lair" (*PU* 1.687) as music, become Coleridge's "strong music in the soul" ("Dejection: an Ode" 60).[19] Because Asia is still in exile, however,

> Only a sense
> Remains of them, like the Omnipotence
> Of music when the inspired voice and lute
> Languish, ere yet the responses are mute
> Which through the deep and labyrinthine soul,
> Like echoes through long caverns, wind and roll.
> (*PU* 1.802–7)

Shelley in his *lyrical* drama is turning to what Nietzsche considered its origins: music as the metaphor of "primal unity," the body as a living organism or cosmos which carries within the Apollonian *principium individuationis* an "augury of restored oneness." Significantly, Prometheus will disappear entirely in the second act, as indeed will both he and Asia in the added fourth act in which not only Time as "the dead Hours" is borne "to his tomb in eternity" (*PU* 4.13–14), but the cosmos itself existing as a metaphorical spell is dissolved by Demogorgon acting as a Prospero abjuring his "rough magic." Demogorgon himself, it should thus be noted, is not language; he is a "universal sound" which may appear as language. "There is a sense of words upon my ear—," declares Ione. "A universal sound like words . . . O list!" replies Panthea as Demogorgon, "rising out o' Earth, and from the sky / . . . and from within the air," begins to speak (*PU* 4.510–18) from a source which is, in Wordsworth's words, "far hidden from the reach of words" (*The Prelude* 3.187). Shelley, it would appear, is affirming the nihilistic perspective upon which, among all the others, Nietzsche will insist. He will not, as Shelley will not, allow us to embrace an illusion as truth by forgetting that it is an illusion. Like Nietzsche, Shelley is determined to keep his language "vitally metaphorical" by not allowing it to become canonical. The drama thus becomes more and more lyrical ("I am the inventor of the *dithyramb*," writes Nietzsche of *Thus Spake Zarathustra* in *Ecce Homo* [306]). Even Apollo, whom Shelley in his drama identifies with natural law, must stand aside in wonder as the sun postpones its rising until noon, until, that is, the high noon of the imagination. That high noon is the "restored oneness" of Asia and Prometheus, which in Nietzsche's vision of Greek tragedy is realized by the third Dionysus who, as Dionysus Zagreus, endured the dismemberment necessary to the consciousness of that unified body which Nietzsche, prior to its dismemberment and restoration, metaphorically identified with the grazing herd.

5

In "Potentiality in *Prometheus Unbound*," D. J. Hughes explores in considerable depth Shelley's metaphor of the "mind in creation" as a "fading coal" awakened to a "transitory brightness" (*Defence* 503–4) by arguing that Shelley's characteristic strategy is to resolve the actual into its potential in such a way that the potential is never allowed to reify itself in the actual. Precisely in this way the "vitally metaphorical" nature of language at its source is never allowed to lose its vitality. By remaining in touch with chaos, it is never allowed to harden into a system. Demogorgon presides. The result, Hughes suggests, is a "pure present, beyond time," identified as "the pre-existent" (or what forever exists) which, while "appearing to press forward toward futurity . . . does so not that a new existent may emerge, but that a new Potentiality may sustain itself; it mirrors the mind freed from the causal, purified, transformed."[20] As the "feeble shadow" of a pure present (Shelley's original conception), the mythos thus contains both Nietzsche's "*amor fati*" and eternal recurrence. "Then Go O dark futurity," declares Urizen as he shakes off his "aged mantles" into the fires of his "radiant Youth" from which he arises naked,

> I will cast thee forth from these
> Heavens of my brain nor will I look upon futurity more
> I cast futurity away & turn my back upon that void
> Which I have made for lo futurity is in this moment.
> (*The Four Zoas* 9: 180–83)

Urizen, like Prometheus after the interpenetration of Asia, has purified the "heaven of [his] brain" so that he no longer looks upon a futurity forever receding in the endless anteriority of linear time which Blake calls "the void." The mind, "freed from the causal," is mirrored in an epic or lyrical drama freed from what Shelley in his *Defence of Poetry* calls "a catalogue of detached facts, that have no other connection than time, place, circumstance, cause and effect" (485). Precisely these connections constitute Blake's "Natural Effect" masquerading as a "Natural Cause." They are what Shelley, paraphrasing Bacon, calls in his *Defence of Poetry* "the moths of a just history" that "eat out the poetry of it" (485).

The "pure present" is Blake's "pulsation of the artery," which Nietzsche identifies with Dionysus and which finds its most immediate metaphoric expression in music and dance understood as the heart beat of life itself. The metaphoric body of that heart beat present for Nietzsche in the Greek chorus is the most immediate and at the same time the highest affirmation of life, an affirmation in radical contrast to Christianity with its crucified God. "I never failed," Nietzsche writes of Christianity in his "Attempt at Self-Criticism" (which he added to a new edition of *The Birth of Tragedy* published in 1886),

> to sense a *hostility to life*—a furious, vengeful antipathy to life itself: for all of life is based on semblance, art, deception, points of view, and the necessity of perspectives, and error. Christianity was from the beginning, essentially and fundamentally, life's nausea and disgust with life, merely concealed behind, masked by, dressed up as, faith in "another" or "better" life. Hatred of "the world," condemnations of the passions, fear of beauty and sensuality, a beyond invented the better to slander this life, at bottom a craving for nothing, for the end, for respite, for "the sabbath of sabbaths" —all this struck me, no less than the unconditional will of Christianity to recognize *only* moral values, as the most dangerous and uncanny form of a "will to decline"—at the very least a sign of abysmal sickness, weariness, discouragement, exhaustion, and impoverishment of life.[21]

Nietzsche condemns what in retrospect he considered the romanticism of *The Birth of Tragedy*: the rejection of "the Now" in favour of "a coming generation" who will create an *"art of metaphysical comfort"* and exclaim with Faust: "Should not my longing overleap the distance / And draw the fairest form into existence?" To this—and by direct reference to "that Dionysian monster who bears the name of Zarathustra"—he replies: "No! you ought to learn the art of *this-worldly* comfort first; you ought to learn to laugh, my young friends, if you are hell-bent on remaining pessimists. Then perhaps, as laughers, you may some day dispatch all metaphysical comforts to the devil—metaphysics in front" (26).

Hughes's discussion of potentiality in *Prometheus Unbound* too easily, I suggest, aligns itself with a Platonic anamnesis that resides in Being rather than a Nietzschean absence of Being. Shelley as poet is metaphorically at war with the metaphysician in himself. Thus in his Preface to his lyrical drama he assures his critics that if he lives "to accomplish what I purpose" (135) he will take Plato rather than Aeschylus as his model. As a poet, however, his chief concern is continuously to defeat what in his *Defence of Poetry* he calls "the curse which binds us to be subjected to the accident of surrounding impressions" (505) by creating ever new "before unapprehended" relations among them. Once a relation (that is, a metaphor) is apprehended it tends as an apprehension to become fixed. Once fixed, Shelley argues in his *Defence of Poetry* "the words which represent [before unapprehended relations] become through time signs for portions or classes of thoughts instead of pictures of integral thoughts; and then if no new poets should arise to create afresh the associations which have thus been disorganized, language will be dead to all the nobler purposes of human intercourse" (482). Metaphysics deals with "classes of thoughts"; metaphor deals with "pictures of integral thought." Metaphor "create[s] afresh" what metaphysics renders "dead."

The pattern of dissolving the actual back into the potential, annihilating creation in the very process of creation, identifies each pulsation of the artery as the coming forth of the work itself. To freeze the work in its coming forth is, in Keats's powerful image in *The Fall of Hyperion*, "to put cold grasp / Upon those streams that pulse beside the throat" (1.124–25), even as Urizen in Blake's *Milton* pours "the icy fluid from his broad cold palm" onto "Miltons brain" (19[21]: 9). Each succeeding pulse beat is in this sense the rebirth of the poet which is in part what Shelley suggests about the mind in creation awakened by an "invisible influence" to a "transitory brightness." The "invisible influence" is the body itself, the red globule of blood each pulsation of which constitutes eternity or what Nietzsche calls "Now." To enter that eternity time must be abolished in the manner which Shelley, in his lyrical drama struggles in vain to enact, composition in time rendering the timeless (the poet's "original conception") a "feeble shadow." "Prometheus shall arise / Henceforth the Sun of this rejoicing world: / When shall the destined hour arrive?," Asia asks Demogorgon in the oracular cave to which she and her sister have been carried by a "sound." "Behold," Demogorgon replies as "the rocks are cloven" (*PU* 2.4.105–9). To "behold" is to convert a pulsation into a metaphor. To "behold" is to render the future the Blakean "Moment: a Pulsation of the Artery" (*Milton* 29[31]: 3). "Time's swiftness" (*Milton* 24[26]: 72) releases whatever has been arrested. Without the swiftness of metaphor "all were eternal torment" (*Milton* 24[26]: 73). The speed of metaphor, which is the movement of the imagination, is the "mighty motion" of Demogorgon's breathing in Shelley's added fourth act metaphorically imaged by Shelley as feet which wear "sandals of lightning" and wings "swift as thought" (*PU* 4.90–91). Blake binds himself to that motion (Los's "firy whirlwind") when Milton, entering Blake's left foot, turns "all this Vegetable World" into a "bright sandal formd immortal of precious stones & gold." Stooping down, Blake binds it on "to walk forward thro Eternity" (*Milton* 21[23]: 13–15).

Rejecting a metaphysics of presence which would substitute a Platonic form for a psychosomatic process (metaphysics as a corpse), Nietzsche denies any notion of a reality behind or above the phenomenal world, beyond, that is, breathing, movement, and sound. Reality is what appears, though to make claims for it as "truth" is to reject the perspectivism of appearance itself understood as illusion confirming its own illusoriness. "The Thing-in-itself (it is just this which would be the pure ineffective truth)," Nietzsche writes in "On Truth and Falsity in their Ultramoral Sense,"

> is also quite incomprehensible to the creator of language and not worth making any great endeavor to obtain. He designates only the relations of things to men [Shelley's "before unapprehended relations of things"] and for their expression he calls to his help the most daring metaphors. A nerve-stimulus, first transformed into a percept! First metaphor! The percept again copied into a sound! Second metaphor! And each time he leaps completely out of one sphere right into the midst of an entirely different one.
>
> (178)

It is precisely this process—nerve-stimulus to percept, percept to sound—that Shelley enacts in the rising of the Phantasm of Jupiter.

Nietzsche affirms the perpetual making-unmaking of a "vitally meta-phorical" body as the action proper to man as man. Withdrawal from that ceaseless "Mental Fight," from his own aesthetic nature, constitutes nihilism, a will to extinction rather than creation. Shelley, as Hughes will argue, is not affirming nihilism in this sense. As a poet, he may be in the final analysis (though this is not Hughes's point) as anti-Christian and anti-Platonic as Nietzsche. The illusory nature of the metaphorical body wrought for Shelley by spell and incantation to become what Tilottama Rajan in *Dark Interpreter* calls an "existence with only the fiction of essence"[22] constitutes its life rather than its death, a death decreed for Shelley, as for Nietzsche, by the canonization of the Word in, among other things, the doctrine of the Incarnation which Shelley's Jupiter is determined to institute in order to render his reign eternal. His "fatal Child," though "unbodied now," "floats" between himself and Thetis, "felt although unbeheld / Waiting the incarnation" (*PU* 3.1.44–46). The Shelleyan words —"unbodied," "floats," "felt," "unbeheld"—echo the opening lines of his "Hymn to Intellectual Beauty": "The awful shadow of some unseen Power / Floats though unseen among us." To incarnate that "unseen Power" is to transform metaphor into truth, which is precisely what Jupiter, like Blake's Urizen, is determined to do. It is to freeze the blood, to reduce Rousseau to an "old root" or the Visionary in *Alastor* to "mouldering bones" covered by a "pyramid / Of mouldering leaves in the waste wilderness" (54–55). It is also to bind Prometheus to a precipice in a ravine of icy rocks.

Music for Shelley, as for Nietzsche, is the essential means of unbinding. Prometheus is released by music from his frozen state. The lyricism of Shelley's drama is its action. "Assuming that music has been correctly termed a repetition and a recast of the world," Nietzsche writes in *The Birth of Tragedy*,

> we may say that [the Dionysian artist] produces the copy of this primal unity as music. Now, however, under the Apollonian dream inspiration, this music reveals itself to him as a *symbolic dream image*. The inchoate, intangible reflection of the primordial pain in music, with its redemption in mere appearance, now produces a second mirroring as a specific symbol or example. The artist has already surrendered his subjectivity in the Dionysian process. The image that now shows him his identity with the heart of the world is a dream scene that embodies the primordial pain, together with the primordial pleasure, of mere appearance.
>
> (49)

One example must suffice to illustrate in Shelley's lyrical drama the way in which music constructs as from its own sound a "*symbolic dream image*" much in the manner that, for Nietzsche, Greek tragedy arises from the chorus as from a womb. That music, itself a metaphoric substitution of a pulsation of the artery, carries Panthea to Asia on the wings of her dream of Prometheus. "I am made the wind / Which fails beneath the music that I bear / Of thy most wordless converse" (*PU* 2.1.50–52), she tells Asia upon her arrival as the psychic carrier of the "wordless converse" between Asia and Prometheus, a converse not unlike the one Wordsworth also chose as his "heroic argument." "O Heavens!," Wordsworth writes,

> how awful is the might of souls,
> And what they do within themselves while yet
> The yoke of earth is new to them, the world
> Nothing but a wild field where they are sown.
> This is, in truth, heroic argument.
>
> (*The Prelude* 3.180–85)

Panthea then tells Asia that in her "*symbolic dream image*" the

> . . . pale, wounded-worn limbs
> Fell from Prometheus, and the azure night
> Grew radiant with the glory of that form
> Which lives unchanged within, and his voice fell
> Like music which makes giddy the dim brain
> Faint with the intoxication of keen joy.
>
> (*PU* 2.1.62–67)

The "glory of that form" inhabits "a pulsation of the artery." "I saw not—heard not—moved not," she tells Asia,

—only felt
His presence flow and mingle through my blood
Till it became his life and his grew mine
And I was thus absorbed—until it past
And like the vapours when the sun sinks down,
Gathering again in drops upon the pines
And tremulous as they, in the deep night
My being was condensed, and as the rays
Of thought were slowly gathered, I could hear
His voice, whose accents lingered ere they died
Like footsteps of far melody.

(*PU* 2.1.79–89)

As an emerging vital metaphor arising from icy cliffs, Prometheus here becomes the flow of Panthea's blood which absorbs them both into what Coleridge calls the

. . . one Life within us and abroad,
Which meets all motion and becomes its soul,
A light in sound, a sound-like power in light,
Rhythm in all thought, a joyance every where.

("The Aeolian Harp" 26–29)

That "one Life within us and abroad," present "Now" in every pulsation of the artery "equal in its period & value to Six Thousand Years," is precisely what both Blake and Shelley celebrate in a language so "vitally metaphorical" that it must continually renew itself through its own dissolution. In the cave of Demogorgon, Asia declares that only "eternal Love" is free of "Fate, Time, Occasion, Chance and Change" (*PU* 2.4.119–20). Recounting her first dream to Asia, Panthea says at its conclusion:

Thy name,
Among the many sounds alone I heard
Of what might be articulate; though still
I listened through the night when sound was none.

(*PU* 2.1.89–91)

Asia grows impatient with the inadequacy of Panthea's rendering of musical sound as articulate speech ("his voice fell / Like music which makes giddy the dim brain / Faint with intoxication of keen joy" [*PU* 2.1.65–67], she tells Asia). "Thou speakest," says Asia, "but thy words / Are like the air. I feel them not." She then adds: ". . . oh, lift / Thine eyes that I may read his written soul" (*PU* 2.1.109–11). The lifting of Panthea's eyes so that in them Asia may read the "written soul" of Prometheus wonderfully images

131

a metaphorical curtain going up on Shelley's psychodrama, Nietzsche's *"symbolic dream image,"* which "the highly refined imagination of the more select classes of poetical readers" (Preface to *Prometheus Unbound* 135) is invited by Shelley to see.

To assist us in our seeing, we may, I suggest, profitably turn to Nietzsche's understanding of metaphor as the displacement of the body, of music as "primal" even as the pulsation of the artery is primal, and of the *"unhistorical"* as a "'go[ing] into' the present, like a number, without leaving any curious remainder." Thus, though Nietzsche will later distinguish between the romantic and the Dionysian, we may, by focusing as does Nietzsche himself upon metaphor as the proper and necessary displacement of both metaphysics and the body, not only recognize what Nietzsche calls Dionysus in the work of Blake and Shelley, but also locate Nietzsche himself in the romanticism he too hastily rejects.

Notes

1 All references to Blake's poetry and prose are taken from *The Collected Poems and Prose of William Blake*, ed. David V. Erdman; commentary Harold Bloom (Berkeley: U of California P, 1982). All references to Blake's letters are taken from *The Letters of William Blake*, ed. Geoffrey Keynes (London: Rupert Hart-Davis, 1968).

2 "Nietzsche: Life as Metaphor." *The New Nietzsche: Contemporary Styles of Interpretation*, ed. David B. Allison (New York: Delta, 1977) 151.

3 The body-in-pain, it should be noted, is itself what Nietzsche calls a "first metaphor." Pain awakens a mute body locked in oblivion, like the grazing herd described by Nietzsche in the opening paragraphs of "The Use and Abuse of History," into a metaphoric embodiment that is language. Once metaphorically embodied it is subject to the potentially endless transformations of ceaseless flux bestowed upon it by the imagination. A metaphorical body is, for Nietzsche, a body in process, forever rising and falling. Priesthood would arrest that process; its defining act is crucifixion. When Nietzsche concludes *Ecce Homo* with the words *"Dionysus versus the Crucified"* he is yet again distinguishing between artist and priest, aesthetic and religious, suspended disbelief and belief

4 *The Complete Works of Friedrich Nietzsche*, ed. Oscar Levy, trans. Maximilian A Mügge (New York: Russell & Russell, 1964) 2: 178.

5 *The Story of My Life* (New York: Airmont, 1965) 187.

6 All references to Shelley's poetry and prose are taken from *Shelley's Poetry and Prose*, ed. Donald H. Reiman and Sharon B. Powers (New York: Norton, 1977).

7 *The Will to Power*, trans. Walter Kaufmann and R. J. Hollingdale (London: Weidenfeld and Nicolson, 1968) 9.

8 *Deconstruction and Criticism* (New York: Continuum, 1969).

9 *On the Geneology of Morals* and *Ecce Homo*, trans. Walter Kaufmann (New York: Vintage, 1967) *Ecce Homo* 258.

10 All references to Keats's poetry are taken from *The Poetry of John Keats*, ed. Jack Stillinger (Cambridge: Harvard UP, 1978). All references to Keats's letters are taken from *Letters of John Keats*, ed. Robert Gittings (London: Oxford UP, 1975).

11 *Of Grammatology*, trans. Gayatri Chakravorty Spivak (Baltimore: Johns Hopkins UP, 1976) 247 ff.

12 All references to Wordsworth's poetry, excluding *The Prelude*, are taken from *Poems*, ed. John O. Hayden (Harmondsworth: Penguin, 1977). All references to *The Prelude* are taken from *The Prelude 1799, 1805, 1850*, ed. Jonathan Wordsworth, M. H. Abrams, and Stephen Gill (New York: Norton, 1979).

13 All references to Milton's poetry and prose are taken from *The Student's Milton*, ed. F. A. Patterson (New York: Appleton-Century Crofts, 1933).

14 *Nietzsche: Life as Literature* (Cambridge: Harvard UP, 1985) 37.

15 *The Complete Works of Friedrich Nietzsche*, ed. Oscar Levy, trans. Thomas Common (New York: Russell & Russell, 1964) 10: 352–53.

16 Ibid, 5: 6–7.

17 "The Rhetoric of Blindness: Jacques Derrida's Reading of Rousseau," *Blindness and Insight: Essays in the Rhetoric of Contemporary Criticism* (Minneapolis: U of Minnesota P, 1971) 114.

18 *Revolution in Poetic Language*, trans. Margaret Waller (New York: Columbia UP, 1984) 25–30.

19 All references to Coleridge's poetry are taken from *The Poems of Samuel Taylor Coleridge*, ed. E. H. Coleridge (London: Oxford UP, 1960).

20 *SiR* 11 (1963): 115.

21 *The Birth of Tragedy* and *The Case of Wagner*, trans. Walter Kaufmann (New York: Vintage, 1967) 23.

22 *Dark Interpreter: The Discourse of Romanticism* (Ithaca: Cornell UP, 1986) 54.

56

COLERIDGE'S MILLENNIAL EMBARRASSMENTS

Seamus Perry

Source: *Essays in Criticism* 50 (2000), 1–22.

What connections can be made between the formal features of the poems Coleridge first wrote in the later 1790s and his historical experience? My attempt to link the provoking idiosyncrasies of these poems with Coleridge's experience of his times follows the recommendation made in several places recently – that we could do with some sort of rapprochement between 'close reading' and the contextual 'placing' of literary texts which has become so prominent a feature of the scene.[1] The likely shortcomings of a quite unqualified historicism are nicely illustrated by Christopher Caudwell's suggestion that the eighteenth century heroic couplet mirrored or emulated the prevailing mode of Augustan society, 'the bourgeois class in alliance with a bourgeoisified aristocracy in the epoch of manufacture',[2] but however good the point about the heroic couplet as a form, it is very blunt-fingered when it comes to particular lines. Historicism's approaches to poetic form have often conjured it into a higher abstraction in this way, 'thematising' it, and so returning it to the less recalcitrant (for the historicist) realm of paraphraseable content or subject-matter.[3] Even if, at some theological level, historical determinism were true, the theory that describes it must claim so elevated a level of generality that, however minutely explanatory in principle, one suspects that in critical practice it could not fall to neglect as somehow epiphenomenal the formal realities of specific texts.

Strong determinism (like Caudwell's Marxism) dissolves the apparently independent and volitional subjective world into the concretely *real* reality of the outside, material world; and much recent criticism of the Romantics has treated their poems similarly, as things of the interior to be fed back into the properly determining context of their historical moment. But the antithesis between a subjective, literary inner world and a material, historical outer is too severe for my Coleridgean argument here: the 'history' that shapes Coleridge's poems, while necessarily gathering strength from external events, is already an internal affair. Although he occasionally wrote public responses to particular incidents, what matters is the imaginative impact upon his poetry of an *idea* of history – or, more precisely, of the epochal feel created when a certain idea of history gets disproved by what happens to happen. In Coleridge, this feeling doesn't get discussed as a theme, but registers its presence in more implicit ways; and this may not be unusual: 'Any good poet can focus for us this vivid sense of the life of his own time', Barbara Everett has written, but he will 'embody his time for us only if we read him as a poet and not as a crypto-historian'.[4] The examples she gives of more appropriate objects for an historically minded reading are Marvell's metres, Browning's syntax, Larkin's imagery; my example is Coleridge's sense of a poem's end.

The formative Coleridgean sense of history I have in mind, entertained but then fruitfully thwarted by events, is millennial, inevitabilist, and sure that the necessary cataclysm is imminent. It is itself an example of the brand of historicism attacked by Popper, which holds that history has '*laws or trends*', a shape or a destiny or a pattern which it is bound to fulfil, a quasi-philosophical notion which, as Popper observed, allies itself very easily with kinds of revolutionary Utopian politics.[5] Some of Coleridge's early poems enthuse about such an historical scheme; but it is the subsequent *embarrassment* of such Utopian, millennial expectations which many of his greatest poems implicitly register – the later thwarting of a once sincerely held belief in a scheme of historical inevitability. When Christopher Hill speaks of other poets' 'experience of defeat' he has especially in mind millennially-minded Republican poets living on into the Restoration;[6] there might be an analogy as well with some figures of the 1960s, when times were changing, and their translation to the 1970s, when the only thing to do was to keep on keeping on. My own preferred parallel would be with left-wing English poets of the 1930s, Auden especially, who, however firmly card-carrying his individual brand of Marxism actually was, habitually imagined his time when topically minded in apocalyptic terms. 'Waiting for the end, boys, waiting for the end', was Empson's smack at Auden, 'It has all been filed, boys, history has a trend, / Each of us enisled, boys, waiting for the end';[7] and waiting for the end was exactly what Coleridge and his circle were doing for much of the mid-1790s too. 'The hour is nigh', as Coleridge says in 'Religious Musings';[8] so Auden prays in 'The Orators', 'Not, Father, further do prolong / Our necessary defeat'.[9] It is when such expectant hopes of imminent redemptive catastrophe collapse, or when they fall into dark doubt – which in both Coleridge's and Auden's case was rather quickly – that the great poetry begins to appear. As Auden recollected,

> We hoped; we waited for the day
> The State would wither clean away,
> Expecting the Millennium
> That theory promised us would come:
> It didn't.[10]

Coleridge's reconsideration of what he had been doing in his radical phase, which dates from late 1796 or early 1797, provoked him, like Auden, to look back on 'a low dishonest decade', and evidently to think of some of his earlier political verse, as Auden did of his, 'as trash I am ashamed to have written'.[11]

But the collapse of millennial hope can effect subtler things than such abashed, belated self-censoring. The most distinguished account of a deeper relationship between poetry and millennial expectation remains that of M. H. Abrams, put forward in his great essay, 'English Romanticism: The Spirit of the Age', and then at length in *Natural Supernaturalism*. (Abrams's sympathetic interest in this experience is, one might guess, at least partly the result of his own generation's similar experience.)[12] 'The formative age of Romantic poetry was clearly one of apocalyptic expectations, or at least apocalyptic imaginings', Abrams says;[13] and after the historical failure of those expectations with the disaster of France, millennial ambitions are internalised and become attributes of the imagination, so that 'a new heaven and a new earth' become (for example) a dowry received when the mind weds nature, rather than the attributes of a new political settlement. 'The millennial pattern of thinking [. . .] persisted', Abrams says, but 'with this difference: the external means was replaced by an internal means for transforming the world' (*Natural Supernaturalism*, 334).

Abrams's account mostly focusses on the brave new Romantic theology of imagination (as if confirming Hulme's view that Romanticism was 'spilt religion', though without Hulme's disapproval); but the thesis might have implications too for poetic form. This sort of link by analogy, or by micro-cosm, between historical vision and aesthetic theory is best described in Frank Kermode's *The Sense of an Ending*, which explores the 'link between the forms of literature and other ways in which, to quote Erich Auerbach, "we try to give some kind of order and design to the past, the present and the future"', and especially the way that certain conceptions about art cor-respond with, or adopt, divine habits of thinking about the end of all things; narratives, Kermode's primary interest there, are given mini-providences of their own to work out, 'in concordance with remote origins and predictable ends'.[14] A faith in (or at least, a deep attraction to) teleological schemes of divinely guided historical inevitability gives rise, by analogy, to the inter-woven notions of poetic form and meaning that, drawn into a theory, we might recognise as Coleridge's 'organicism': the idea that the art-work has an intrinsic, purposive oneness of design and achievement, and (if a perfect work) comes to attain its necessary shape through a kind of happily self-fulfilling prophecy. As Pater glossed this Coleridgean ideal, while disliking what he saw: 'an energetic unity or identity makes itself visible amid an abounding variety'. Like the cosmic scheme of historical inevitability which it emulates in miniature, this aesthetic doctrine dissolves agency into necessity ('the artist has become almost a mechanical agent'), and Pater wanted instead to stress the choices of artistry and individual handiwork.[15] Admittedly, such parallels simplify an intricate historical picture: apocalypticism (the belief that revelation is imminently due at the cataclysmic end of the present order) and millennialism (the expectation of Christ's thousand-year personal reign, due to follow the Apocalypse) are properly quite distinct;[16] and neither need imply in principle any particular sort of Utopian politics. But what is relevant here is less the specifically paradisal or Utopian end-point to the apocalyptic teleology, than the sense of an *ending*, the sense that history has an *end*, at all. And 'end' here has two interrelated senses, both of which translate into poetics: first, a sense of closure or completion; and second, a sense of purposiveness or unity of design, as in 'built with an end in view'. The first would relate most obviously to questions of form, and the second to content, especially the relationship the various contents of a poem have to the overall meaning of the work.

We can certainly see in much Romantic theory the translated millennialism that Abrams describes and Pater disputes (though whether that is an adequate summary of Coleridge's wider thinking about poetry is another matter); but the frustration of the necessary teleological schemes doesn't result only in promising to make good in art what has gone bad in history. We can see as well the experience of millennial frustration translated more directly into the shaping of particular poems – where, in a quite unwishful and unconsoled manner, it precipitates poetry with a distinctively checked or embarrassed quality both as to the self-possession of its form, and as to the authority of its meaning. These characteristics might amount to an instinctive or unwitting criticism of organicism (unwitting because the doctrine wasn't explicitly worked out, by Coleridge at least, for some years); and they distinguish a poetry which approaches its ends in a spirit of reluctance or scepticism or even comic disavowal, rather than with any quasi-millennial confidence.

Millennial thinking was perfectly respectable at the time. Both young Coleridge's most formative influences, Hartley and Priestley, were millennial thinkers (as was Milton).[17] Hartley was rather vague about dates,[18] but Priestley's interest was much more topical, with a catching mixture of excitement and foreboding: 'The more I think on the subject, the more I am persuaded that the calamitous times foretold in the Scriptures are at hand'.[19] Self-declared 'a compleat Necessitarian', historical necessity was redeemed for young Coleridge (as for his mentors) by its being recast as Providence: 'a Necessitarian – and (believing in an all-loving Omnipotence) an Optimist'.[20] (Coleridge glossed 'Optimist' in his notebook: 'by having no will but the will of Heaven, we call in Omnipotence to fight our battles!').[21] Developments in science (including those made by Priestley) contributed to the sense that the times were somehow pivotal – 'Millenium [*sic*], an History of', Coleridge planned in the notebook, 'as brought about by a progression in natural philosophy' (*Notebooks*, i.§133) – but it was pre-eminently the Revolution in France that, as Priestley told John Adams, 'was opening a new era in the world and presenting a near view of the millenium [*sic*]'.[22] The times, as Priestley's friend Richard Price (Burke's target in the *Reflections*) concurred, 'are auspicious'.[23]

Things auspicious must be interpretable as signs: to live knowingly in an apocalyptic epoch is to be an exegete of history's implicit symbolism. Priestley's 1794 fast-day sermon, inspired by Hartley's millennial pages, took Matthew 3:2 as its text ('Repent ye, for the kingdom of heaven is at hand!'), and scrutinised current affairs with an eye on Revelation, discerning their apocalyptic trend: 'That those great troubles, so frequently mentioned in the ancient prophecies, are now commencing, I do own I strongly suspect . . . and the events of the last year have contributed to strengthen that suspicion'.[24] In this sense, Coleridge's 'Religious Musings' is a thoroughly Priestleian poem: a poem about current affairs at one level, yet shot through with the wording and imagery of Revelation, and full of what Priestley calls 'The certainty of this great catastrophe'.[25] When Coleridge writes, 'Ev'n now the storm begins', a note in *Poems* (1796) helpfully reads, 'The French Revolution' (l. 315 and n.1.; *Poetical Works*, i.121); and the argument at the start of the poem makes the point even more hopefully: 'The present State of Society. The French Revolution. Millenium [*sic*]. Universal Redemption. Conclusion' (*Poetical Works*, i.108, n.1). Such interpretative confidence stems from a conviction of historical inevitability – the knowledge that, in Morton Paley's words, 'It will all happen as a result of the fulfilment of a pattern embodied in history';[26] and this sense of an all-encompassing pattern makes everything that occurs symptomatic of the ordering purpose of God. As Priestley's sermon shows, it is an inbuilt tendency of millennial vision to see particular events in the world as important because divinely symbolic.

Coleridge's later, self-consciously tangled doctrine of the symbol reworks the double vision that he discovered in the millennial culture of his youth: the symbol, 'while it enunciates the whole, abides itself as a living part in that Unity, of which it is the representative'.[27] The theory proposes a sympathetic balancing-act of particular and general; but the hold on particularity can prove very tenuous, when faced with so strong an impetus to envisage things as evidences of the gathering 'Unity' for which they stand. '[A]ll that meets the bodily sense I deem / Symbolical', Coleridge declares in 'The Destiny of Nations', which might be taken (and sometimes Coleridge took it) as an incentive to bypass the provisions of a corporeal 'sense' attuned merely to 'this low world' (ll. 18–19; 20: *Poetical Works*, i.132). '[T]he Great / Invisible (by symbols only seen) / With a peculiar and surpassing light / Shines from the visage of the oppressed good man', we learn in 'Religious Musings' (ll. 9–12: *Poetical Works*, i.109), which is mystical and ennobling, though noticeably reluctant to enter into things from the good man's oppressed point of view. It is Coleridge's visionary penchant for the ideal that gives 'Religious Musings' its heaving cast of capitalised abstractions and rousing stereotypes, all serving to dragoon diverse and particular human experience into the general cases of allegory: 'Disease that withers manhood's arm, / The daggered Envy, spirit-quenching Want, / Warriors, and Lords, and Priests' (ll. 213–15; *Poetical Works*, i.117), and so forth. Coleridge's theoretical disposition to dash for abstraction is not hard to detect – *Biographia* tells us that one of the imagination's tasks is 'to idealize' (*BL*, i.304) – and this is the late formalisation of an instinct. We can occasionally see such interpretative idealising happening before our eyes in his early verse, as the mundane is conjured into what it stands for: 'our Cot o'ergrown / With white-flower'd Jasmin, and the broad-leav'd Myrtle, / (Meet emblems they of Innocence and Love!)' ('The Eolian Harp', ll, 3–5; *Poetical Works*, i.100).

Besides encouraging a certain spiritualised remoteness from the quotidian, a lingering millennial preference for the end over the present means also implies an idea of form. Verses describing the progress of the providential universe are honour-bound to evoke feelings of the ineluctable, but any poem inspired by the example of millennial vision might aspire to a kind of inevitable rightness, a point which Coleridge (and Wordsworth) would continue to invoke as a criterion of poetic excellence: 'it would be scarcely more difficult to push a stone out from the pyramids with the bare hand, than to alter a word, or the position of a word, in Milton or Shakespeare, (in their most important works at least)'.[28] That is a later development in Coleridgean theory (and exemplifies Abrams's grand thesis), but Coleridge had long experienced a more intuitive sense of a poem's necessary order. Such order would find its naturally clinching test when poems come to their close. Once 'Religious Musings' has reached 'Universal Redemption' in its account of the last things, it is only appropriate that it should come to its own 'conclusion' (what else is there to say?); but this is only a special example of a more generally alerted interest in how poems end, which a mind theologically preoccupied with the confident sense of ending would be bound to experience.

Coleridge's early poetry is often drawn to forms that allow it to finish well and truly: his youthful fondness for the sonnet, in which he finds an especially intense kind of formal *'oneness'* (*Poetical Works*, ii.1137), for example, might be attributed to the special opportunity for resolution offered by its final couplet.[29] Indeed, the last lines of his sonnets are frequently *about* endings – often of an apocalyptic temper – and while you couldn't say that such triumphant conclusions are especially successful, there's no mistaking that they're certainly *ends*:[30] 'Seize, Mercy! thou more terrible the brand, / And hurl her thunderbolts with fiercer hand!' ('Pitt', ll. 13–14: *Poetical*

Works, i.84); or, 'And thou from forth its clouds shalt hear the voice, / Champion of Freedom and her God! rejoice!' ('To Earl Stanhope', ll. 13–14; *Poetical Works*, i.90); or, 'For lo! the Morning struggles into Day, / And Slavery's spectres shrink and vanish from the ray!' ('La Fayette', ll. 13–14: *Poetical Works*, i.82). Given such emphatic company, 'Religious Musings' closes more quietly than might be expected, but it still completes itself with utter resolution, in a self-involving confluence of light and water, where 'influence' retains its full sense of 'in-flowing':

> As the great Sun, when he his influence
> Sheds on the frost-bound waters – The glad stream
> Flows to the ray and warbles as it flows.
> (ll. 417–19: *Poetical Works*, i. 125)

The last things in a poem devoted to the excitement of last things, as well as the last verses in their volume (*Poems* (1796]), these lines bear their inevitable weight with surprising delicacy: the diverse elements enact a gentle dissolution, blending one into another and acquiring each other's characteristics. The last line's flowing return to its own beginning enacts in miniature what the last lines manage as a whole: what Coleridge calls, describing his revision to the end of 'Frost at Midnight', a 'rondo, or return upon itself'.[31] The completion of a circle, whose end is in its beginning, like the snake with its tail in its mouth, 'for ever flowing into itself', was one of Coleridge's favourite figures for the imagination's perfect work, things contributing impeccably to the achievement of their own self-fulfilling end;[32] and he remained drawn to that sense of wrought closure as a reader: 'Nothing were ever more admirably made out than the figure of the Compass', he wrote next to 'A Valediction Forbidding Mourning'.[33]

These sorts of poetic effect are the finished virtues of an imagination dedicated to ending well; but they become troubled in Coleridge's art as the millennial confidence that inspired them is troubled. Kermode dates an avant-garde disinclination to indulge the consoling plots of ending to the scientific advances of the late eighteenth and early nineteenth centuries – to works like the geology of Hutton, who found 'no sign of a beginning – no prospect of an end'.[34] The most immediate source for a loosening conviction of the authority of endings for the Coleridge circle was the obvious embarrassment of millennial expectation represented by the failure of France. E. P. Thompson described the Romantic radicals as swapping their millenarianism merely for what he called a 'chialism of despair'; but their poetry reveals a much more interesting, paradoxical, and double-minded predicament: the sense of a teleology without ending, a surviving intuition of the significance or portentousness of objects and events, but without any clear scheme of the providential arrangement into which they might justly fit. The twin aspects of a literature of ending that I have described persist, but changed: the sense of representativeness, of latent revelatory power, now lacks any interpretative conviction about what that might be, and a continuing preoccupation with formal endings is accompanied by an apprehension of their evasiveness or arbitrariness. These may not be prominent features of Coleridgean theory, but they do distinguish Coleridgean practice and characterise his most original poetry. It is a cast of mind in which (to adopt T. S. Eliot's phrase) one has the experience, but misses the meaning – though not the possibility of meaning, or the ghost of a meaning. 'Religious Musings' is very emphatic about its meaning, which is what tempts it into such strident and abstract apostrophe: it cracks the code of contemporary events with great command, but denies us anything we might ordinarily recognise as experience. Coleridge's major poetry, on the other hand, is often unclear about its 'meaning' but generous in its provisions of 'experience', investing the particulars of that experience with a possibility or an aura of meaning which somehow declines to resolve itself into plain statement.

This combination contributes to Coleridge's distinctively modern brand of religious verse. An intuition that the world is indeed symbolical, but only tentatively or mysteriously so, grows into the structure of the later conversation poems, in which apparently innocent details, introduced merely as part of the scene, become themselves the focal point of spiritual attention and gradually acquire a portentous but uninsistently prophetic air, which the poem returns to, though hardly expounds, in its last lines. This is the kind of progress one finds pre-eminently in 'Frost at Midnight', from the owlet's cry amid the frost, to the modulated, entirely implicit, profundity of the last paragraph (as published in its later text: *Poetical Works*, i.242). The lack of any precise scheme of significance grants a sort of ordinary numinousness to objects, which Wordsworth's verse, at once deeply religious and wholly non-denominational, goes on to use to best advantage. The effect is more remarkable still in 'This Lime-Tree Bower'. Here, the natural description to which we are treated in the setting of the poem, while structurally justified by the immanence of its religious symbolism, yet feels as though it has a materiality or individuality in excess of that putative function:

> Pale beneath the blaze
> Hung the transparent foliage; and I watch'd
> Some broad and sunny leaf, and lov'd to see
> The shadow of the leaf and stem above
> Dappling its sunshine! And that walnut-tree
> Was richly ting'd, and a deep radiance lay
> Full on the ancient ivy, which usurps
> Those fronting elms, and now, with blackest mass
> Makes their dark branches gleam a lighter hue
> Through the late twilight.
> (ll. 47–56: *Poetical Works*, i. 180–1)

The theology insists that these appearances are still symbolical; but the verse implies and maintains, instead of visionary exegesis, a self-justifying act of looking, staying at the level of the ordinary. In a fully achieved poetry of ending, like the ideal poetry Coleridge later attributes to Milton, every thing contributes, each an obedient means, to the final end; while in the idiosyncratic best of Coleridge, as Geoffrey Grigson once remarked, 'we are given means in prodigious quantity and quality'.[35] Grigson describes a poetry that has (fruitfully) lost sight of a predominant end in view: its object of celebration is not some informing unity of design, but a natural plurality which embarrasses that vision; its literary form of choice is not the clinching form of the sonnet, but the digressive spaciousness of the 'conversation' poem.

Instead of a poetic inevitability, things in the poem governed by the trend or end of the whole, what we experience is more like contingency, or accidence, or freedom: a redundance which the poetry doesn't worry about correcting into pertinence. The effect seems to anticipate the mysteriously suggestive particulars you find in the poetry of Auden: 'Well? // As a matter of fact the farm was in Pembrokeshire' (*English Auden*, 87). Usually, Auden's free-floating significants are darkly ominous, rather than innocently self-gratifying, though they retain a certain reckless delight: 'Just as his dream foretold, he met them all: / The smiling grimy boy at the garage / Ran out before he blew his horn [. . .] The deaf girl too / Seemed to expect him at the green chateau', and so on (*English Auden*, 148). Portentousness can take darker or possibly nightmarish forms in Coleridge too, as seen to best advantage in the so-called 'supernatural' poems – although the question of how much that occurs in those poems is genuinely supernatural is precisely the secret of their puzzling successes. 'The Ancient Mariner' and 'Christabel' are both full of details we know to be resonant but for which we have no authoritative interpretation: 'Perhaps it is the owlet's scritch / For what can ail the mastiff bitch?' (ll. 152–4; *Poetical Works*, i. 221). The matter is intensified and made more complex, most successfully in 'The Ancient Mariner', by the device of a narrator, himself largely in the dark about the significance of what has occurred to him, but – equipped with a needy and resourceful eye for omens – ever-busy in suggesting that significance attends events we might otherwise accept as simply contingent. Even the connection between killing the albatross and the ensuing disasters proves remarkably tenuous once you look for it, and there are many other such ill-fittings. The exegetical energy of the Mariner (and of the editorial glosses in the margin) cannot conceal a superfluity of experience – the 'unmeaning miracles' in the poem that Lamb conceded to Southey[36] – which the teleological meaning proposed will not properly comprehend.

If a loosening specificity of omen-watching, or sign-deciphering, is one aspect of what I am identifying as a post-millennialist sensibility, then a hesitancy about the finality of a poem's ending is, naturally, another. Yeats (himself a keen theorist of history's necessity) once spoke in a letter of the moment in which 'a poem comes right with a click like a closing box', a bringing of its diverse elements to a oneness which Geoffrey Hill has called a type of 'atonement'.[37] Coleridge's post-millennialist poetry, by contrast, is haunted by endings it will not indulge, or cannot pull off. (As often with Coleridge, success is close-cousin of failure.) 'Kubla Khan' is the most sensational case: an ending triumphantly achieved, but then turned into an ironical inadequacy. It ends where distinguished precedent has had poems end (in 'Paradise'), and everything about the life of its last lines makes them feel definitively final (a circle is completed; 'close' is cleverly insinuated as we near the close):

> Weave a circle round him thrice,
> And close your eyes with holy dread,
> For he on honey-dew hath fed,
> And drunk the milk of Paradise.
> (ll. 51–5; *Poetical Works*, i. 298)

But the poem comes after its 'Preface', which (playfully?) denies it any of the firm resolution that our ears so confidently deduce: 'all the rest had passed away like the images on the surface of a stream into which a stone has been cast' (*Poetical Works*, i.296). 'Kubla Khan' is a showy piece of non-achievement; but the experimentalism that distinguishes many of Coleridge's poems repeatedly delights in not 'coming right': concentrating its energies on teasingly odd or somehow abortive endings, the poetic mind resigns its God-like, atoning duties, as though ruined by its fidelity to a different kind of experience. A prefatory note to the little 'Westphalian Song' drew particular attention to '[t]he turn at the end':

> When she asks, 'What! Is he sick?'
>   Say, dead! – and, when for sorrow,
> She begins to sob and cry,
>   Say, I come tomorrow.
> (ll. 5–8; *Poetical Works*, i.326)

That's little more than a teasing sting in the tail, but other Coleridgean poems go out of their way to 'turn' in more imaginative ways. The labouring 'Hexameters' sent to the Wordsworths in Germany, having interrupted themselves to apologise for missing things (*'There was a good deal more, which I have forgotten . . .'*), complete themselves in an isolated couplet sadly confessing incompleteness: 'You have all in each other; but I am lonely, and want you!' (ll. 35–6; *Poetical Works*, i.305). Meanwhile, 'The Devil's Thoughts' ends, altogether appropriately, with 'general conflagration' (l. 70; *Poetical Works*, i.323); but, as if parodying the millennial conclusiveness of his earlier mode, there is no conflagration: the devil has mistaken General

Gascoigne's (or Tarleton's: see *Poetical Works*, i.323, n.1) florid complexion for that terminal event.

Other poems do not end, so much as stop. 'The Foster Mother's Tale', for instance, scarcely ends at all, neither happily nor sadly, but amid uncertain speculation and possibility; not as a good 'tale' should: 'And all alone, set sail by silent moonlight / Up a great river, great as any sea, / And ne'er was heard of more: but 'tis suppos'd, / He liv'd and died among the savage men' (ll. 78–81; *Poetical Works*, i.184). 'Christabel' is famously inconclusive: consider the end of the so-called 'Conclusion to part II'.

> Perhaps 'tis tender too and pretty
> At each wild word to feel within
> A sweet recoil of love and pity.
> And what, if in a world of sin
> (O sorrow and shame should this be true!)
> Such giddiness of heart and brain
> Comes seldom save from rage and pain,
> So talks as it's most used to do.
>   (ll. 670–7; *Poetical Works*, ii.235–6)

It is a rum kind of 'Conclusion' anyway: the poem springs on us a sudden change of subject-matter ('A little child, a limber elf': l. 656), which can only relate to the poem it supposedly concludes in some tangential or metaphorical way. (Coleridge obliquely attempts to justify his own audacious obliquity by commenting: 'Perhaps 'tis pretty to force together / Thoughts so all unlike each other': ll. 666–7.) This non-concluding fragment boasts a forlorn inconclusiveness of its own too. Notice how adroitly Coleridge allows its rhymes to unravel: the conclusion begins by chiming in couplets, but its incongruous inconclusion peters out in stretching quatrains, like an undoing sonnet – from AABB, to ABAB, to the tenuous cohesion of ABBA, the rhyme-scheme used to such brilliantly inconclusive effect in 'In Memoriam'. The effect is less throwaway than trail-off, rhyme's certainty coming adrift, but leaving a ghostly sense of its former cohesiveness – a deliberate version of what Coleridge found in one of Daniel's epistles: 'how rhymes may be *wasted*, and the Poet have all the restraint & trouble, while the Reader has none of the effect – except indeed now & then a perplexed suspicion of a *jingle*' (*Marginalia*, i.44).

Coleridge's poetry of non-endings is always alert to the possibilities of rhyme, because rhyme enacts in miniature the fulfilment of expectation: it boasts a little historical inevitability of its own; so that, when weakened or dissipated, it can have a peculiar, *sotto voce* potency. 'The Nightingale', like much of his poetry, complicates an excitedly vital nature-mysticism with feelings of subdued stasis and despair, and it manages to end in a kind of audible stalemate.

144

>   He knows well
> The evening-star; and once, when he awoke
> In most distressful mood (some inward pain
> Had made up that strange thing, an infant's dream –)
> I hurried with him to our orchard-plot,
> And he beheld the moon, and, hushed at once,
> Suspends his sobs, and laughs most silently,
> While his fair eyes, that swam with undropped tears,
> Did glitter in the yellow moon-beam! Well! –
> It is a father's tale: But if that Heaven
> Should give me life, his childhood shall grow up
> Familiar with these songs, that with the night
> He may associate joy. – Once more, farewell,
> Sweet Nightingale! once more, my friends! farewell.
>   (ll. 97–110; *Poetical Works*, i. 267)

Coleridge again introduces the idea of a 'tale', only to decline such narrative duties with a self-dismissive turn ('Well!'); the story he offers is touchingly inconsequential, driven by an entirely personal sense of enchantment, the excitement of which barely registers in the confusion of narrative and immediate tenses (from 'woke' and 'hurried' to 'Suspends' and 'laughs'). In the two last lines, Coleridge steps forward as a gracious leave-taker, but the verse works assiduously to undermine the finality of his departure. Redundantly non-rhyming five times on 'well' in the complete last paragraph, the poem finishes, as if trying to end well, in reiteration: 'Once more, farewell, / Sweet Nightingale! once more, my friends, farewell'. The buoyant spirits in the poem say: you could not get more resoundingly finishing a rhyme for 'farewell' than 'farewell'. But darker feelings in the poem say: such repetition hasn't the progressiveness of confident optimism, the embracing of change that every proper rhyme involves; it is a kind of dawdling or lingering, as though of one unwilling or uncertain how to leave, unsure what is going to happen next – so, retrospectively, discovering a poignant neediness in the rather theatrical ominousness of 'if that Heaven / Should give me life'.

Charles Burney's description of 'The Ancient Mariner' as 'the strangest story of a cock and a bull that we ever saw on paper' was not sympathetic, but not obtuse.[38] The cock and bull story that Burney has in mind appears at the close-which-is-no-ending of *Tristram Shandy*, a book of great importance to Coleridge; and something of the same quality attends the close-which-is-no-ending of 'The Ancient Mariner'. E. M. W. Tillyard is regularly scolded for saying that 'The Ancient Mariner' is not a political poem;[39] and if we wish to correct him again, this sense of an ending denied might be another way in which the poem betrays its political moment. For such a resistance to closing, I am suggesting, is the transposition into poetic form of an epochal feel. The poem doesn't end with a clinching couplet or the explanation of some implicit symbolism or an apostrophe to the agencies of imminent change, but like this:

> He went like one that hath been stunned,
> And is of sense forlorn:
> A sadder and a wiser man,
> He rose the morrow morn.
>
> (ll. 622–5; *Poetical Works*, i. 209)

Everything here alludes to the moralistic conclusiveness of ballad literature while disrupting it. To go *like* one stunned and forlorn is not to *be* either of those things, so how *was* he affected? The stanza's inconsequence mirrors the poem's at large: if one is bereft (forlorn) of sense, how can one at once be 'wiser'? If indeed 'wiser', does he rise the morrow morn sadder and wiser than the night before *because* of what he has learnt? Or does he rise the morrow morn because, as a sadder and wiser sort of man, he is able to carry on after such grisly and dispiriting encounters? Even the rhymes, which have worked so absolutely throughout the poem, contrive a para-rhyme (man/morn), at this supposedly conclusive moment, insinuating to the ear an incompletely resolved quality while apparently going about the business of finishing off.

Again, although the mood is very different, it is perhaps no coincidence that Auden, who (like Coleridge) typically starts his poems with such grabbing virtuosity, similarly chooses to end some of the most interesting of them with a dying fall, a calculated collapse from providence into contingency, as though reluctant to claim too presumptuously assured a sense of his poetry's own finish. 'Not in Baedeker', for instance, is a brilliant damp squib of a poem about life proving a damp squib:

> One September Thursday two English cyclists
> Stopped here for a *fine* and afterwards strolled
> Along the no longer polluted stream
> As far as the Shot Tower (indirectly
> Responsible in its day for the deaths
> Of goodness knows how many grouse, wild duck
> And magnificent stags) where the younger
> (Whose promise one might have guessed even then
> Would come to nothing), using a rotting
> Rickety gallery for a lectern,
> To amuse his friend gave an imitation of
> Of a clergyman with a cleft palate.
>
> (*Collected Poems*, p. 423)

Such a poem exemplifies very well Barbara Everett's acute description of Auden's characteristic mode: '"a loosely-cohering amalgam of brilliant, idiosyncratic details"' which is not likely to boast 'formal or organic unity' as its outstanding characteristic.[40] You might read that as a conscious inversion of the self-necessitating organisation marking Coleridge's ideal poem, and so the very crux of Auden's anti-'Romanticism'. What Auden comes to embrace as an anti-aesthetic poetic vocation, Coleridge experiences less than willingly, even while theorising the kinds of wholeness to which his own poetry cannot in good faith rise. Auden can afford to be more brazen than Coleridge in his sense of no ending – or so one might think, but consider how Coleridge exploits the opportunity for incoherence afforded by the conversion of his contributions to 'Joan of Arc' into 'The Destiny of Nations'. The reconstituted poem ends perfectly at a millennial pitch, with talk of 'Fit instruments and best, of perfect end: / Glory to Thee, Father of Earth and Heaven!' But then, after a break and a separation line, it perplexingly goes on:

> And first a landscape rose
> More wild and waste and desolate than where
> The white bear, drifting on a field of ice,
> Howls to her sundered cubs with piteous rage
> And savage agony.
>
> (ll. 470–4; *Poetical Works*, i.148)

A lost fragment, this gets lost in itself too, absorbed in its brilliant arctic simile, which is about being lost on an icy fragment. In the 1817 *Sibylline Leaves*, this final fragment (about what happened 'first') comes last in the book, so it appears, nicely, with one word beneath it: 'FINIS'. It is as though Coleridge is going out of his way to parody the confident finality of 'Religious Musings', which had ended his 1796 book with such millennial resolution ('Religious Musings' is suppressed in *Sibylline Leaves*). It is Coleridge's most sprightly play with endings that are no end, and may imply something of wider significance about Coleridge's career. Several scholars have lately argued that Coleridge's writing life is longer and more various than usually credited; but nothing rivals the sudden mass and brilliance of the great four or five years; and even when poetry flares up later, it is very often when Coleridge is returning to themes or even to actual texts (like the 'Destiny of Nations' lines) from the great period. The repeated revisions of 'The Ancient Mariner' alone occupied a vast amount of his poetic life, and the eccentric characteristics of those poems remained a kind of taproot to which his imagination periodically returned for sustenance, as, while continuing to operate magnificently in prose, it faltered in poetry, intimidated by the enormous demands his aesthetic theorising placed upon it.

Coleridge's poems, like any others, are a possible subject for historicist criticism; but they are also a sort of allegory of its perplexities. As the historicist critic seeks to return the particulars of literary works to their determining external cause, so Coleridge's early millennial habits of mind instinctively sought to identify things with the larger purposes which they symbolised; and as any literary text resists its complete absorption back into the history that (purportedly) determines it, so the eccentric individuality of particulars in Coleridge's post-millennialist poems affirms a wilful resistance to their poetic destiny. A natively historicist disposition keeps encountering styles of freedom: the diversity and accidence, which historicism seeks to reform, makes itself the secret subject of his poetry, and establishes an implicit comedy of irresolved embarrassment as its most characteristic mode.

Notes

1 Pre-eminently, Susan 'Wolfson's call for 'a contextualized formalist criticism': *Formal Charges. The Shaping of Poetry in British Romanticism*, (Stanford, 1997). Paul Magnuson advocates 'historical close reading': *Reading Public Romanticism*, (Princeton, 1998). A similar programme underwrites James Chandler's *England in 1819*, (Chicago, 1998).

2 *Illusion and Reality. A Study of the Sources of Poetry*, (1937; 1947; repr. 1977), p. 99.

3 e.g. 'Tintern Abbey' 'registers *in its form* (in its lyric sublimity), the connection between the meditative and isolated self and the scene of writing': Marjorie Levinson, 'Revisionist Reading: An Account of the Practice', *Studies in the Literary Imagination*, 30:1, (1997), 119–40, p. 123.

4 *Poets in their Time. Essays on English Poetry from Donne to Larkin*, (1986), p. vii.

5 *The Poverty of Historicism*, (1957; 1960; repr., 1976), pp. 36, 71–6.

6 *The Experience of Defeat. Milton and Some Contemporaries*, (1984).

7 'Just a Smack at Auden': *Collected Poems*, (1955; repr., 1969), pp. 62, 63.

8 'Religious Musings', l. 308: *The Poetical Works of Samuel Taylor Coleridge*, ed. E. H. Coleridge, (2 vols.; Oxford, 1912), i.120.

9 'The Orators': *The English Auden: Poems, Essays and Dramatic Writings 1927–39*, ed. Edward Mendelson, (1977), p. 109.

10 'New Year Letter': *Collected Poems*, ed. Edward Mendelson, (1976), p. 175.

11 'September 1, 1939': *English Auden*, p. 245; Auden's note (quoted as a condition for reprinting some famous early poems) in the prefatory pages to *The Penguin Book of Thirties Verse*, ed. Robin Skelton, (Harmondsworth, 1964). Coleridge seems to have felt something similar about poems like the sonnet on pantisocracy, or the sonnets to Godwin and Southey, or the lines to Tooke (none of which was collected in his lifetime).

12 *Natural Supernaturalism. Tradition and Revolution in Romantic Literature*, (1971), pp. 333–4 – where the lines from 'New Year Letter' are quoted as evidence of 'the spiritual biography of Auden's own generation, and mine'.

13 'English Romanticism: The Spirit of the Age', in Northrop Frye (ed.), *Romanticism Reconsidered. Selected Papers from the English Institute*, (N.Y., 1963) 26–72, p. 37.

14 *The Sense of an Ending. Studies in the Theory of Fiction*, (N.Y., 1967), pp. 93, 56.

15 *Appreciations[;] with an Essay on Style*, (1889; Library edition, 1910; repr., 1920), pp. 79, 80.

16 'Millennialists' might be further distinguished from 'millenarians': see Peter Kitson, 'Coleridge, Milton and the Millennium', *The Wordsworth Circle* 18, (1987) 61–6, p. 61.

17 See Kitson, pp. 63–5.

18 David Hartley, *Observations on Man*, (1791; facs. repr., 2 vols.; Poole, 1998), ii.380.

19 Priestley to Lindsey and Belsham, (1795); quoted in Morton D. Paley, '"These Promised Years": Coleridge's "Religious Musings" and the Millenarianism of the 1790s', in Keith Hanley and Raman Selden (eds.), *Revolution and English Romanticism. Politics and Rhetoric*, (Hemel Hempstead, 1990), 49–65, p. 56.

20 *The Letters of Samuel Taylor Coleridge*, ed. Earl Leslie Griggs, (6 vols.; Oxford, 1956–71), i.137, 145.

21 *The Notebooks of Samuel Taylor Coleridge*, ed. Kathleen Coburn, (4 double vols. to date; 1957–), i.§22.

22 Adams to Jefferson; quoted in Clarke Garrett, 'Joseph Priestley, The Millennium, and the French Revolution', *Journal of the History of Ideas*, 24, (1973) 51–66, p. 51.

23 Richard Price, *A Discourse on the Love of our Country*, (1789), quoted in François Piquet, 'Shadows of Prophecy: Blake and Millenarian Ideology', *Yearbook of English Studies* 19, (1989) 28–35, p. 30.

24 'The Present State of Europe compared with Antient Prophecies', in Joseph Priestley, *A Farewell Sermon*, (1794; facs. repr., Spelsbury, 1989), p. 18.

25 Ibid. p. 30.

26 Paley, p. 57.

27 *Lay Sermons*, ed. R. J. White, (Princeton, 1976), p. 30.

28 *Biographia Literaria*, ed. James Engell and W. J. Bate, (2 vols.; Princeton, 1983), i.23.

29 Although Coleridge characteristically introduces the idea (in the 'Preface' to *Poems* [1796]) to apologise for his own sonnets' lack of such '*oneness*'.

30 To end a poem with talk of an end is a common form of authoritative closure, according to Barbara Herrnstein Smith, *Poetic Closure. A Study of How Poems End*, (1968; repr., Chicago, 1970), pp. 172–5.

31 Coleridge's marginalia, quoted by B. Ifor Evans, 'Coleridge's Copy of "Fears in Solitude"', *TLS* 1733, (18 April, 1935), p. 255.

32 Hazlitt's reconstruction of Coleridge's conversation, *London Magazine*, (1820); quoted by John Beer, *Coleridge the Visionary*, (1959), p. 5.

33 *Marginalia*, ed. H. Jackson and George Whalley, (3 vols. to date; 1980), ii.223.

34 Quoted by Marilyn Gaull, *English Romanticism. The Human Context*, (N.Y., 1988), p. 210.

35 *Blessings, Kicks, and Curses. A Critical Collection*, (1982), p. 85.

36 Roy Park (ed.), *Lamb as Critic*, (1980), p. 216.

37 *The Lords of Limit. Essays on Literature and Ideas*, (1984), p. 2 (where Yeats is quoted).

38 J. R. de J. Jackson (ed.), *Coleridge. The Critical Heritage*, (1970), p. 56.

39 *Five Poems 1470–1870*, (1948), p. 80.

40 *Auden*, (Edinburgh, 1964), p. 3.

57

THE RETURN OF THE GODS: KEATS TO RILKE[1]

Lawrence Kramer

Source: *Studies in Romanticism* 17 (1978), 483–500.

When Keats showed him the "Hymn to Pan" from *Endymion*, Wordsworth dismissed the poem as "a pretty piece of paganism." From various passages in Wordsworth's own work, we can surmise that his objection was not to the presence of classical gods in Keats's poem, but to Keats's apparent lack of awareness that the gods were *dated*: once an authentic product of the imagination, they had long since become no more than shopworn tropes. Yet even Wordsworth could feel a nostalgia for the gods when his own time seemed devoid of imaginative life:

> So might I, standing on this pleasant lea,
> Have glimpses that would make me less forlorn;
> Have sight of Proteus rising from the sea;
> Or hear old Triton blow his wreathèd horn.[2]

The appearance of Proteus and Triton in "The World Is Too Much With Us" touches on a longing for the classical gods that runs throughout the Romantic tradition in poetry. That longing is not at all a casual thing, and it turns up in many major texts. Keats's "Ode to Psyche" comes to mind at once, a poem that insists on bringing Psyche back despite the recognition—Wordsworth could not have said worse—that the nineteenth century is an age too late for the "fond believing lyre." Likewise, in that great pagan poem suggestively named "Brot und Wein," Hölderlin holds out the elusive promise of an apocalyptic reunion of human life with its transcendental origins. The form of that promise, felt in an endlessly patient waiting, is the possibility of the return of the gods; and the form of the waiting itself is a yearning for the gods' immediate presence. Clearly, there are some Romantic poets who want the gods to return, and to return in direct theophany—despite the fact that the gods are dead, the leftover imagery of a former age. At various moments, Goethe, Hölderlin, Keats, Shelley, Heine, Rimbaud, Mallarmé, Yeats, Rilke, Pound, Stevens, Lawrence, and others all find the gods in such theophanies, in a distinctively "theophanic" form of poetry, leaving us to recognize that the returning gods are an essential element in the phenomenology of the Romantic imagination. The purpose of this essay is to identify the modern mythology that Romantic poetry constructs to receive the gods, and to define the peculiarities of the genre— the theophanic poem—in which the return of the gods takes place.

I

As M. H. Abrams reminds us, the Romantic experience of imaginative illumination usually involves a sense that time has been transcended, a sense that the present moment is a kind of eternity.[3] One way of describing what the imagination achieves in such moments is to say that it lifts the self briefly into the condition of the gods. Eternal and unchanging, the gods are embodiments of the timeless time that the imagination experiences in vision. Human in form, they experience human joys, but without the temporal limitations that make all imaginative heightening only a seeming eternity. The gods, as Goethe puts it, feast eternally at golden tables and stride from peak to peak;[4] their existence is a perpetual lifting of experience into overflowing imaginative presence. They are forms of the imagination abounding, and without bound; the spirit, as Hölderlin explains, blooms eternally for them.[5]

Seen from a distance, as they are for example in Goethe's "Parzenlied," the gods act as a measure of human inadequacy in the face of imaginative desire, and may provoke either despair or a Promethean rebelliousness. When they appear in theophany, though, the gods embody the assertion of imaginative power. They appear, says Rilke, where the heart beats a path into some soundless pause in the day; and within that pause one can "hear" what a laurel feels when a butterfly brushes its leaves.[6] Growing up in the gods' arms, writes Hölderlin, one could understand the stillness of air and learn love from the flowers;[7] and if the gods would only return to live among men, human hands would bless the things they touched and vision become an everyday matter.[8] In Rimbaud's "Génie," the divine form who is "l'amour, mesure parfaite et réinventée, raison merveilleuse et imprévue, et l'éternité" combines the mind's fertility and the vastness of the universe ("fecondité de l'esprit et immensité de l'univers") into the present moment within the mind's "open house" ("la maison ouverte").[9] And at the climax of Pound's *Pisan Cantos*, Aphrodite's eyes appear to the poet in his tent, while what those eyes see—"sky's clear / night's sea [and] / green of the mountain pool"—at once becomes the poet's vision.[10] Here, as elsewhere, to see the god is to see *as* a god: to transfigure experience to the highest degree of imagination. The gods themselves, in theophanic moments, appear simply as reflections of the strong imagination that is lifting experience into vision.

But the imagination that sees the gods is never strong when it sees them. Remembering or desiring the imaginative power embodied in theophany, the theophanic poet and his poem call the gods by name; and as Hölderlin explains, one does not call the gods by name if one is in their arms.[11] To name them, to fix them as a poetic image, is already to have lost them, or rather to have lost the power that their presence signifies.[12] This distressing paradox, which lies at the heart of Romantic theophany, can be clarified by making a necessary distinction between theophany as a poetic form and theophany as a thing in itself. In its own right, theophany is an immediate experience, an outburst of imaginative power so full as to disclose the gods' presence; and this is the theophany one experiences in the gods' arms. It alone is the true theophany: yet when it happens one is not aware of gods at all, but only of intensified particulars, the feelings of laurels or the stillness of air. The other theophany is the one that occurs in poetry: the theophany by which a poet, naming the gods, movingly fashions an image for the immediate theophanic experience. The poetic image, which "names" or signifies the experience, arises only where the experience itself is lacking, and indeed inaccessible. "Real" theophany is nameless because its overwhelming power completely absorbs knowing in being; naming the gods, therefore, as an act of knowing, is inevitably a measure of one's distance from the gods named. Inevitably, too, the distance is one that haunts the poetry, and theophanic poems acknowledge it by a subtle rhetorical estrangement. Such poems remember the gods, summon them, and anticipate them, but they almost never represent theophany in the simple present tense. No poem can contain the god it calls.

Poetry, then, turns to theophany only when poets cannot. When the gods enter a theophanic poem, they appear there as the forms of the poet's imaginative desire. Their theophany is not the revelation of imaginative power but the expression of a wish for it—a wish they are meant, strangely, both to signify and to grant. As a result, theophanic poems always carry a residue of irony or uncertainty, no matter how full their representation of theophany may become. "Brot und Wein" speaks of the gods in abundant, familiar, and loving detail, but it can sustain no more than an erring and patient hope for their real return. Rimbaud's "Génie," though it signifies an apocalyptic release of vision, leaves the poet to shift as he can amid rages and boredoms, his force and feelings weary ("forces et sentiments las"), able only to hope for a realization of his god's visions in breath, body, and day. Likewise, Keats's "Ode to Psyche" is above all else a wooing poem, a plea, never made sure of fulfillment, for the goddess' presence to sanctify the poet's imagination. The gods in these poems, and others like them, appear under the aspect of a radical ambiguity. On the one hand, they alienate imagination in the act of representing it, and their named presence acts to defer the coming of the nameless visionary power that the poet seeks. On the other hand, as signs for that power, the gods remain figures of reassurance that the power is real, and perhaps attainable.

The distinctive form of the theophanic poem is determined by this ambiguity. Clearly, the effort of the poem must be to resist the ambiguity and to coax or extort a recovery of power from the gods' named presence. To accomplish that, the relationship between the gods and the mind that confronts them must be subtly weakened. When the poet first names the gods, he invests them with an almost mesmeric power over his imagination. This is so because the first act of naming is always a recognition of the gods' absence, and it evokes an overpowering nostalgia for the drunkenness (Hölderlin's "Dem Sonnengott") or vertigo (Keats's "Ode to Psyche") of original theophany that binds up the mind's creative energy. The release of that energy depends on the replacement of fascination by doubt: the mind's self-doubt about its visionary potency, and the projection of that doubt onto the gods, which issues in the characteristic posit that the gods' return is uncertain, or perhaps impossible, because the poet has come too late to receive them. It is perfectly possible to stop at this point, and to write a kind of anti-theophany, a poem that names the gods only to lament that they will never be found again; Rilke does just this in one of the *Sonnets to Orpheus* (1.24). In theophanic poems, however, the poet's doubt leads away from itself by assuming blindly the burden of its desire and bringing forward a series of images for the theophany that may be denied it. These images are not images of the gods alone, and sometimes not images of the gods at all; they give central place to a number of metonyms for divine presence which embody the transfigurations that the gods would bring if they came.

The appearance of these images, or more exactly their appearance against the background of possible imaginative barrenness, represents the emergence of imaginative strength out of the confused potentiality of desire, and has the effect of making theophany seem plausible, or even imminent. In fact, the images' discontinuity with the mind's self-doubt will most often create the illusion that the sought-for theophany is in the process of taking place, even though the images are only there because it is still withheld. The absent gods accordingly find a presence to answer the poem's plea for the power they represent. To the extent that a theophany seems to emerge in or through the poem's images, that presence is the poem's own.

II

It will be useful to take certain poems as paradigmatic examples of the theophanic pattern. Keats's "Ode to Psyche," already invoked twice, is a transparent instance. At the climax of the poem, the poet's promise to build

Psyche a sacred grove "in some untrodden region of my mind" undergoes a virtual fusion with the presence of the grove itself. Psyche's place of dwelling—or indwelling—is to be made of images, "branchèd thoughts" that "murmur in the wind" instead of pines; and it is precisely a grove made of images that the poem gives her:

> Far, far around shall those dark-clustered trees
> 　Fledge the wild-ridged mountains steep by steep;
> And there by zephyrs, streams, and birds, and bees,
> 　The moss-lain Dryads shall be lull'd to sleep;
> And in the midst of this wide quietness
> A rosy sanctuary will I dress
> With the wreath'd trellis of a working brain.[13]

Keats never abandons the fiction that he needs Psyche's presence to create this sanctuary at a later moment; yet her absence enables his desire for her to become so fertile in the imagery of theophany that the sought-for presence begins to appear as both emergent and a little superfluous. Interestingly, the "Ode on a Grecian Urn" presents much the same process in reverse, as the gradual ebb of Keats's imagination reduces the "men or gods" in "wild ecstasy" of the first stanza to the "marble men and maidens" of the last. In this sense the "Ode on a Grecian Urn" might be called the photographic negative of a theophanic poem.

A second paradigmatic instance is "Brot und Wein," a poem in which Hölderlin simultaneously declares that the gods are absent—"über dem Haupt droben in anderer Welt"—and that we who feel their absence embody the condition of their return in that very feeling. This is possible because the feeling, though it originates in a sense of desolate emptiness, leads continually towards images of divine presence. Throughout the poem, the perception of the gap in reality left by the gods' departure involves a rhetorical question which momentarily reinstates the world as it was in the gods' day—reinstates it through imagery: "Aber die Thronen, wo? die Tempel, und wo die Gefässe, / Wo mit Nektar gefüllt, Göttern zu Lust der Gesang?" (st. IV). Such images are only the merest flicker of divinity, but the point of them is that they measure the maximum distance between men and the gods. Divine absence does not exist as an absolute; it entails presence through the mediation of memory and desire. Out of this saving connection grows the feeling in which divine absence is transformed into a sign of imminent presence: a feeling of partial fullness, of ordinary human ("menschlich") joy as opposed to joy "with spirit" ("mit Geist"). This human joy arises when the imagination perceives links between earth and heaven within the human world. Hölderlin identifies the objects through which these links are disclosed as the gods' gifts; his epitomes for them are bread and wine:

> Brot ist der Erde Frucht, doch ists vom Licht gesegnet,
>   Und vom donnernden Gott kommet die Freude des Weins.
> Darum denken wir auch dabei der Himmlischen, die sonst
>   Da gewesen und die kehren in richtiger Zeit.
>
> (st. VIII)

The human condition is precisely to accept the gods' gifts and stand gratefully between despair and the highest joy. Yet this "between-ness" (which might remind one of Hölderlin's influence on Heidegger) can also sway back and forth between actual despair and a prophetic rapture that begins to resemble theophany.

Such a vacillation takes place at the end of the poem, where the desolate recognition that men are mere "heartless shadows" ("herzlos, Schatten") without the gods leads into a moment of vision that transfigures the shadow metaphor into a glimpse of theophanic presence. The scene of the vision is the underworld, the world of Shadows, which appears as an ironic signifier for the human world while remaining at a distant remove from it. Into this dark lower world, Dionysus enters bearing a torch, and at once a light breaks from the eyes and smiles of "blessedly wise" men: "Selige Weise sehns; ein Lächeln aus der gefangnen / Seele leuchtet, dem Licht tauet ihr Auge noch auf." The transfer of light from torch to smiles carries alienation from the gods to the height of virtual theophany: the god is not present, he is among "them," the dead, yet it is our faces that light up. In the same way, the god "softens the sleep of the Titan in earth"—thereby signifying a partial reconciliation between earthly and heavenly principles—but the softness attaches to us, as our eyes "thaw" to the light. The poem closes with the image of Cerberus being put to sleep: the "envious" dog, the chthonic element in man that is incommensurate with divinity, is extinguished as the light comes forth.

Hölderlin provides a more emphatic version of poetic theophany in his lyric "Dem Sonnengott," where an experience of genuine divine presence turns out to be less vital than the compensatory presence the poet summons through imagery. The poem begins in the painful gap left by the departure of the "young enchanting god," whom the poet has just seen, but who has gone off to be with "pious folk, who still revere him":

> Wo bist du? trunken dämmert die Seele mir
>   Von aller deiner Wonne; denn eben ists,
>   Dass ich gesehen, wie, müde seiner
>   Fahrt, der entzückende Götterjungling
>
> Die jungen Locken badet' in Goldgewölk;
>   Und jetzt noch blickt mein Auge von selbst nach ihm.
>
> (ll. 1–6)[14]

Despite his confused longing, the poet's anguish at the god's absence at once becomes the medium for a new theophany. More exactly, the anguish sponsors a new theophany by changing its allegiance from heaven to earth, and becoming an analogue in pain to the "human" joy of "Brot und Wein." Divine presence is too dazzling; it "darkens" the soul, and by the time one recognizes it, it is gone. Divine absence, however, like the music, mist, and dream which the poem will use to signify it, is an intangible that can immediately be felt as presence. Intuiting this, the poet declares his love for the earth, and in so doing converts the "drunken" reeling brought on by the god's appearance into a "sleep" that is identical with the process of image-making. The images that follow, brought forward to represent the earth under the aspect of the poet's love, then combine to intimate the god's return, an effect underscored by Hölderlin's use of the present tense to carry future meaning:

> Dich lieb ich, Erde! trauerst du doch mit mir!
>   Und unsre Trauer wandelt, wie Kinderschmerz,
>   In Schlummer sich, und wie die Winde
>   Flattern und flüstern im Saitenspiele
>
> Bis ihm des Meisters Finger den schönern Ton
>   Entlockt, so spielen Nebel und Träum um uns,
>   Bis der Beliebte wiederkömmt und
>   Leben und Geist sich in uns entzündet.
>
> (ll. 9–16)

Notable here is the way these lines repair the bond of dialogue, the shared presence involved in the self addressing an other, which the poem begins by breaking. In the first stanza, all that remains of the sun-god's presence is the unanswered vocative "du" with which the poet addresses him, and this modulates before long into the "ihm" that has left the poet behind. The absence of the god is declared as the absence of the second person singular. This recession of the other is healed over immediately when the poet substitutes the earth for the god as the object of his love: "Dich lieb ich, Erde!" "Dich" has explosive force here, forcefully underscored by its position in the stanza, because with it the poet addresses a present other for the first time; and the poem transforms the shared presence of address into a miraculous mutuality by balancing the modulation from "du" to "ihm" with a parallel movement from "dich" to "unsre" and "uns." The poet and the earth very nearly enter into an alliance *against* the god, which at the same time seems to assure his return as "the beloved."

A final paradigmatic instance, this one more intricate than the others, can be provided by a late poem of Rilke, one of his many about the gods. It requires quotation in full:

> Jetzt wär es Zeit, dass Götter träten aus
> bewohnten Dingen . . .
> Und dass sie jede Wand in meinem Haus
> umschlügen. Neue Seite. Nur das Wind,
> das solch ein Blatt in Wendug würfe, reichte hin,
> die Luft, wie eine Scholle, umzuschaufeln:
> ein neues Atemfeld. Oh Götter, Götter,
> Ihr Oftgekommenen, Schläfer in dem Dingen,
> die heiter aufstehn, die, an dem Brunnen
> die wir vermuten, Hals und Antlitz waschen,
> und die ihr Ausgeruhtsein leicht hinzutun
> zu dem, was voll scheint, urserm vollen Leben.
> Noch einmal sei es euer Morgen, Götter.
> Wir wiederholen. Ihr allein seid Ursprung.
> Die Welt steht auf mit euch, und Anfang glänzt
> An allen Bruchstelln unsere Misslingens . . .[15]

Rilke's stance in this poem resembles Hölderlin's in "Brot und Wein" and "Dem Sonnengott"; here, too, the experience of the gods' absence is interpreted as a sign of their return. The resemblance calls to mind Rilke's praise of Hölderlin as the one among poets for whom absence is a plenitude, not emptiness: "Ach, was die Höchsten begehren, du legtest es wunschlos / Baustein auf Baustein: es stand. Doch selber sein Umsturz / irrte dich nicht" (*SW*, II, 94).[16] "Jetzt wär es Zeit," however, exchanges the ordinary human feelings which assure the gods' return in Hölderlin for an ecstasy of anticipation which gradually becomes an ecstasy of presence. The poem does this by carrying the implicit paradox of all theophanic poems to an extreme, and openly putting theophany out of reach. Theophany comes as a wind, or not at all; and the wind blows where it lists. Assumedly, this uncertain and perhaps even random coming and going of theophany should provoke anxiety about the gods' return, but that is precisely what fails to happen. Instead, Rilke subjects the gods to an imagery that represents their movements as a rhythm of recurrence, a rhythm in which the return of divine presence is both inevitable and imminent. This subtle bias towards presence is aligned with the poem's complete avoidance of all images for the gods' absence. Even the opening sentence, which reveals that the gods have not yet come back, appears in the form of a surmise that they are about to step forward. Unlike Keats and Hölderlin, who introduce images of absence in order to transcend them, Rilke has no need to confront absence directly because his poem is situated beyond the point where the absence of the gods is a problem. From the very first word, the enlivening "now" ("jetzt"), the poem is set on the threshold where absence crosses over into presence, and where, accordingly, absence and presence are hard to distinguish from one another. This placement gives the temporality of recurrence its own particular "sacred ground," one as appropriate for it as Keats's pastoral grove is appropriate for the Psyche whom he sees "by my own eyes inspired."

"Jetzt wär es Zeit" unfolds as a formal, quasi-ritual movement from desire to apostrophe to petition, a pattern which is predictable enough. Yet the movement is oddly articulated, and most strongly marked by its leisureliness, by the ample space it leaves between its phases—and most particularly the space it leaves between desire and apostrophe. The desire that moves the poet is clearly urgent, and tinged by a contemptuous impatience with "lived-in things" ("bewohnten Dinge"); yet Rilke is seemingly in no hurry to translate desire into prayer. Instead, he allows the desire to amplify itself, deferring a possible movement towards fulfillment in favor of making images for fulfillment. This might seem a feint at the substitution of images for presence which constitutes poetic theophany; but it is not that. These images are denied all illusion of presence because of the subjunctive mood in which they appear; and they do nothing to suggest the imminence of theophany, let alone its recurrence. The images simply focus the poet's longing on the apocalyptic moment in which the gods are supposed to come forward; they remain images in alienation, images at a distance from their object. In Hölderlin, the binding of desire to such images would modulate into momentary despair; "besser zu schlaffen," we read in "Brot und Wein," "[als] so zu harren, und was zu tun indes und zu sagen / Weiss ich nicht" (st. VII). Rilke, though, excludes the emotions of alienation from his poem just as he excludes all images of absence, and for the same reason: the exclusion is a sign that the gap between desire and the gods is already closing. The foreclosure of despair establishes a threshold in which desire has begun to cross over into fulfillment, and desire is thereby free to heighten itself without running the risk of a collapse into anxiety. Both absence and despair, it is true, continue to constitute a faint background to the poem, more or less in the mode of feelings that have been repressed. Unlike repressed feelings, however, they do not manage to make a disabling return to the foreground —only the gods make returns; and the only moment of the poem that the excluded feelings influence directly, the moment of petition, transforms them completely.

When the poem enters into its apostrophe, the imagery of recurrence proceeds to take it over. Addressed at last, the gods are named as "the often come" ("Ihr Oftgekommenen"), which identifies them with the principle of return, and named again as "Sleepers in things / who wake serenely" ("Schläfer in dem Dingen, / die heiter aufstehn"), which identifies them with the movement from sleeping to waking rather than with the rhythm to and fro. As the apostrophe continues, the immanence of theophany suggested by these namings begins to appear as an imminence, as Rilke fills the poem with a detailed, sensuous imagery of the gods' awakening. The getting-up serenely, the washing of faces and necks at a spring, and the setting of rest on our full life, all combine to suggest a movement of divine generosity in which gods, not men, purify themselves and make oblations. The result is what Rilke calls the gods' morning, a Götterdämmerung which is a rising, not a fall; and the intimation of its presence, memorably heightened by the unexpectedly homely image of the gods' washing, is so strong that when the poem shifts from apostrophe to petition, the renewed note of longing comes almost as a shock.

The poem's petition is concentrated into a single line—"Noch einmal sei es euer Morgen, Götter"—and is followed by an apparent pang of doubt or anxiety: "Wir wiederholen. Ihr allein seid Ursprung." Most likely, this brief shadowing of the poem by excluded emotions is a necessary gesture of respect towards the gods' otherness, a conscious refusal to usurp so much power through imagery that theophany becomes solipsism. ("Dem Sonnengott" does the same thing when it binds the poet to the earth.) Yet Rilke's acknowledgment of human limitation is less a renunciation of the apostrophe's sense of presence than it is a succinct restatement of the poem's central myth of relationship: that men and the gods are old acquaintances, bound together in the cyclical rhythm of the gods' sleep and waking. The alternation of "repetition" ("Wiederholung"), where the mind lives in things and walls them up, with "origin" ("Ursprung"), where the gods knock the walls down, is the poem's primal fact, the ground on which its unclouded desire is sure of fulfillment. Doubt is not resumed here, but transfigured, turned into a generative principle; and this, in turn, leads to a climactic redoubling of the sense of presence. In the poem's final lines, Rilke brings forward an image of "beginning" ("Anfang") as it shines, apparently like morning dew, in the cracks of a rock. The image belongs to the archetypal pattern of the gods' return, and the sentence that provides it is written in the generic present. But the sentence, like its counterpart in "Dem Sonnengott," is syntactically indistinguishable from the simple present, and it self-reflexively situates itself in the simple present with its image of gleaming beginning and the associated healing of our "broken places" ("Bruchstelln"). As the poem ends, "Die Welt steht auf"—the world wakes up—in whatever tensual mode the reader desires. Even more, perhaps, than the "Ode to Psyche," "Jetzt wär es Zeit" closes with an imagery that constitutes a vision while representing its advent in some other moment.

III

Theophanic poetry is by its very nature a highly self-conscious form, so it is hardly surprising that the basic pattern of poetic theophany is strongly influenced by a reflexive awareness of its dependency on images. This influence comes from two different dimensions, or definitions, of the image: the image as word, and the image as trope. In the first instance, the poet invoking the gods shows an awareness that the aim of his invocation is not literally a presence but an inscription, a written proxy for a presence that remains inaccessible. The poem, as a result, must find a visionary impetus so strong that its words will seem privileged to act as divine Words in little, each one a miniature logos. The transition from doubt to advent, divine absence to virtual presence, is therefore often aligned with an effort to show that a process is taking place, in which the words that intimate theophany take on a magical or sacred power that identifies them with the things they name. In the second instance, the poet is aware that the gods he invokes are simultaneously tropes for a visionary power that originates within him, and traditional tropes for powers that are not his own. Consequently, the theophanic pattern tends to incorporate a rhythm in which the poet first gives the gods what is "theirs," usually by investing them with their traditional attributes, then makes them "his" by veering away from those attributes. Sometimes, this ends in a reduction of the gods to spirits of place, with the place left to signify the self in the presence of theophany.

The poems chosen as theophanic paradigms all pay some attention either to the verbal or to the tropic dimension of their images. To begin with the word: one of the striking features of the "Ode to Psyche" is that its goddess' name recedes from the poem as her presence grows stronger there. The only occasion on which Keats affirms Psyche's presence by naming her is the moment when he recalls recognizing her in the forest. This act of naming takes on the quality of a sacred ritual, because it is presented, quite super-fluously, in the form of a riddle:

> The winged boy I knew;
> But who wast thou, O happy, happy dove?
> His Psyche true!

The answer, which the poet knows in advance, has a complex effect. To begin with, it alone constitutes the vision in the forest as a theophany of Psyche, an act it underscores by disjoining Psyche herself from the composite presence of "Two fair creatures" twined together with which the vision begins. In addition, the riddle ritual shows the utterance of the goddess' name as originating in her miraculous presence, thereby taking the name out of the conventional catalogue of "faint Olympians" and inserting it into the immediacy of sacred visitation. Thereafter, Keats holds Psyche's name back from the poem, as if to write it down again would be a sacrilege; the name is replaced by continually varied epithets and periphrastic phrases. "Psyche" has become a numinous word, spoken in address to a present god; and the imagery built around the deliberate absence of the word appears as a series of metonyms for it, infused with the divine presence that it carries.

Hölderlin and Rilke go considerably further than Keats does in defin-ing theophany verbally. In fact, both "Brot und Wein" and "Jetzt wär es Zeit" contain identifications of theophany with the origination of words or sentences. In Hölderlin, the presence of the gods coincides with the action of naming the things one loves with words that "rise into being like flowers" ("Worte, wie Blumen, entstehn") (st. v). As Paul de Man points out, Hölderlin's use of "entstehen," with its distancing prefix, identifies the origination of new words with a movement away from something, a negation.[17] The new words, therefore, will intimate in their arising both their origin in divine absence and their shift to divine presence. This rootedness in an initial absence links the originating words with another form of word, which holds their place prophetically while the gods remain away. This, called by Hölderlin "the flowing word" ("das strömende Wort"), is "sleepless" through the long nights of a world without divine companionship; yet its source lies in those very nights, that very absence—as well it might in a poem where absence, deeply felt, is an augury of presence. This, in turn, intimates a blending of the flowing word with the words of "Brot und Wein" itself, which also arise in the absence of theophany in order to prefigure theophany.

In "Jetzt wär es Zeit," a pair of double meanings beguilingly identifies the coming of the gods with the writing down of a new poem. The gods, we remember, are to knock down the walls of the poet's house and leave him a "neue Seite": a new side. Yet "Seite" means "page" as well as "side." Likewise, the wind of theophany is to be "thrown in turning" by "such a leaf"—"solch ein Blatt." But "Blatt" means both "leaf of a tree" and "leaf of a book." By punning in this way, Rilke simultaneously affirms and denies that the theophany announced in his poem *is* his poem. At the same time, he provocatively suggests that theophany itself is a kind of punning, a punning on existence which his own puns echo. After all, a pun simply shows that one word has two sides; and what the gods do when they come is to "shovel" the air over from one side to another. Only the new side turns out, apocalyptically, to be a new heaven and new earth, paradoxically— punningly?—fused into one thing and one word: a new "breathfield," "neues Atemfeld."

The tropic pattern in theophanic poetry can be said to reflect the necessity for the poet to bind a free or open figure to himself as a subject. The "Ode to Psyche" offers an especially striking instance of the "veering" by which this binding is accomplished because Keats's goddess belongs to a time "too late for antique vows," and the poet is therefore forced to invest her with all the paraphernalia of a traditional deity before he takes it away from her. The point to be stressed is that he *does* take it away, that the imagery of his promise to be her voice, her lute, and so on, is not at all continuous with the imagery of his sacred grove. Quite the contrary: one set of images is a negation of the other, in which the direction of signification is definitely reversed. When Keats writes, "Let me be thy choir, and make a moan / Upon the midnight hours," we understand that the poet will signify the goddess. But when he describes the "wide quietness" that opens "in some untrodden region of my mind," we understand that the goddess will signify the poet—or, more exactly, that the landscape will signify the poet, because the goddess has been completely absorbed into the pastoral imagery, which in turn is a trope for the self.

The same condensation of divinity into locality into selfhood appears at the close of "Jetzt wär es Zeit," where theophany appears as a covering on the rocks of "our failures" ("unsere Misslingen"). (Wallace Stevens' "The Rock," which is a theophanic poem in every way except that it has no gods, does exactly the same thing.) "Jetzt wär es Zeit" is less eager than the "Ode to Psyche" to give the gods what is theirs before taking them to itself, but it does allow them a sacred spring, and catches them in the act of transferring what is theirs to what is ours, as they load their rest on "what seems full, our full life." It is probably "Dem Sonnengott" that, among the paradigm poems, displays the most radical veering of imagery away from its affiliation with the gods, the other. In its first half, as the poet tries to recover from the shock of his original theophany, the poem recalls the sun-god in entirely traditional terms, as "the charming youthful god" who "laved his young locks in golden clouds" ("Die jungen Locken badet' im Goldgewölk"). When the god's real presence has faded away, however, the earth-centered imagery that builds a theophany from his absence is a specific negation of the appearances that have made the poet's soul "darken with drunkenness." The golden clouds around the god's head are replaced by the "dream and mist" that swirl around "us"—the poet and the earth—and the sungod's light is internalized as the "life and spirit" that "take fire in us."

Both the verbal and the tropic patterns are essentially supplemental forms in theophanic poetry. They appear as a kind of surplus of transformation, as gratuitous metonyms for the shift from absence to presence on which theophanic poems depend. Perhaps the reason that these poems so often call on such extra resonance is that their position as visionary works is intrinsically weak. Geoffrey Hartman, commenting on the passage in *The Fall of Hyperion* where Keats bears the vision of Saturn and Thea as a "load" on his "mortality," remarks on the oddity of a poet's having to support the divine images that ought to support him.[18] The remark holds good of theophanic poetry in general: the fact is that the theophanic poet relies on supplemental patterns because in supporting the load of the gods he needs all the help he can get. It ought to be added, though, that the supplemental patterns are not interchangeable. The verbal pattern is a deadly serious business, and at its most intense the exaltation of the word can virtually consume the poet who authors the word. Lawrence's striking poem "Name the Gods!" is an instance of this: a poem that breaks into halves, the first a refusal to name the gods "because they have no form nor shape nor substance," the second a description of theophany which disintegrates the poet's syntax and compels him to break his silence by naming Priapus. The tropic pattern, on the other hand, is a thing of great fluidity, and even has both comic and erotic dimensions. Heine's "Die Götter Griechenlands" from *Die Nordsee* has the poet giving the gods their own because they are underdogs, exiles, and exploded myths. "Ich hab Ihr niemals geliebt, Götter," the poet informs his ragtag divinities, but he is moved to fight for them when they appear to him as dead, night-wandering shadows ("tote, nachtwandelnde Schatten"). And the comedy of this turns into a kind of visionary farce in Rimbaud's "L'Aube," where the poet chases frantically after the goddess of dawn and starts to take her veils off, one by one.

IV

In an essay called "Positive Negation," Angus Fletcher argues that the experience of transition from one state of being to another finds its characteristic representation in metaphor, and that the threshold of transition, the moment of breakthrough, is characterized by the emergence of a personification.[19] This scheme seems to apply with particular appropriateness to theophanic poems. The transition, in these works, belongs to the imagination: from self-doubt and visionary weakness to self-possession and visionary strength. The metaphor is the petitionary situation: the imagination as petitioner to the god. The personification, of course, is the god appealed to. The distinctive feature in theophanic versions of this pattern is the crucial fact that the personification is reflexive. The god to which the imagination appeals is an objectified aspect of the imagination itself. The form of the poem, therefore, is implicitly introspective, and this internalization of the "liminal" structure that Fletcher identifies seems to be a key to the specific form of transcendence that the imagination draws from poetic theophany. As we know, the god in the poem never answers the imagination's prayer; instead, the prayer itself becomes its own answer. Yet this conversion of the god's unsettling silence into the poem's self-affirming language is also, insofar as the poem creates its own theophany, the language of the god himself. And this recognition—which in its own right seems to isolate a metaphorical identification of poet with god, poem with oracle, at the heart of the theophanic form—inevitably raises an essential question. If the imagination, in prayer to its personification, finally answers *itself*, what happens to the personification in the process?

If the poems we have looked at are any guide, the answer is that as poetic theophany grows imminent, the personification, the god, loses its initial ambiguity as a sign. The blend of alienation and reassurance that sets the task of the theophanic poem tends to dissolve as the poem's thrust towards presence de-centers its gods. By the time the poem closes, the gods' role is to *identify* the imagination's situation as liminal: to mark the site of a threshold across which theophany is everywhere. In general, this act of delineation occurs in conjunction with an imagery of openness and potentiality, which projects theophany beyond the borders of the poem. Thus the "Ode to Psyche" closes with the image of a casement open to receive Eros; "Brot und Wein" ends with releases of light; and "Jetzt wär es Zeit" both opens into futurity with its final ellipsis and recalls, with its image of glistening dew, the pivotal, liberating image of the gods' washing. In each case, what appears is an origin, as in Rilke's poem: a healing of broken places, a time of waiting fertilized by signs of change, the promise of an endlessly recurrent wedding night.

In transforming the gods into what one might call the threshold markers for theophany, the theophanic poem works in two, apparently contradictory ways. On the one hand, it elaborates the imagery that metonymizes theophany in order to heighten the illusion of presence. As a rule, the elaboration draws on the primal characteristic of the gods—the fact that they literally em-body, give body to, an imaginative potential—to appear as an emphasis on bodiliness, both in the gods and in the landscape. On the other hand, the poem remains mindful that figures on a threshold stand *before* something, and tends to attenuate the gods so that the condition their presence signifies, the nameless theophany in which they are no longer visible, begins to come forward.

By emphasizing the bodiliness of the gods, as Rilke does when he shows them washing, the poet seems to insist that the imaginative power they represent can, like them, take on body, become real and palpable. Most often, however, this reassuring intimation is heightened by one even more reassuring—the one in Rimbaud's "L'Aube." More often than not, the gods in a theophanic poem are distinctly charged with eroticism. Keats's Psyche, Rimbaud's Génie, Pound's Aphrodite, and all the gods in Lawrence are obvious examples. Even in the relatively chaste "Brot und Wein" the flowing word is said to be sleepless *like lovers.* The point of this close bond between theophany and the erotic seems to be a suggestion of a turning outward in the gods' presence, a radical openness to communion which is the negation of their original remoteness. Rimbaud's "Villes," an exuberant orgy of theophanies that "rise up" in response to "the eternal birth of Venus," embodies this in the erotic generosity of Venus and, surprisingly, of Diana:

> Là haut ... les cerfs tettent Diane. Les Bacchantes des banlieues sanglotent et la lune brûle et hurle. Vénus entre les cavernes des forgerons et des ermites.
>
> (*Oeuvres*, p. 276)

Here as elsewhere, it is the gods' own eroticism that draws them down to us. We literally attract them, as Leda does in poems by Rilke, Lawrence, and Yeats; and because we attract them, we can hope to seduce them into granting our imaginative desire, or else to be seduced by them into transcendental rapture.

Often enough, the landscape of theophany shares the erotic quality of its gods. "Villes," replete with colossi and craters, masts and gorges, and "seraphic centauresses" that "revolve among the avalanches," is an ebullient example; the "Ode to Psyche" is a more subtle and evocative one. More generally, theophanic landscapes are defined by the presence of privileged recesses or enclosures, most often situated amidst a larger expanse that veers away into indefiniteness or virtual infinity. The enclosures, suggesting sanctuaries, retreats, or womblike repositories of potential vision, signify a natural tendency in the landscape to accept theophany. The infinite expanse, complementing that suggestion, seems to signify the unbounded region or openness into which theophany can project consciousness. In "Villes," the craters, chalets, platforms within precipices, castles of bone, and the caves of smiths and hermits are among the sacred recesses, while the mountain on which the theophanies occur offers access to the abyss, to the burning sky, and to the Aphroditean sea "au-dessus du niveau des plus hautes crêtes." "Jetzt wär es Zeit" offers the poet's house, waiting to be torn apart into the "new side" of pure openness; "Dem Sonnengott" offers the swirl of mist and dream; the "Ode to Psyche" centers on the rosy sanctuary amid wild-ridged mountains. In the *Pisan Cantos*, Aphrodite's eyes appear within the suddenly privileged space of Pound's tent, and seem to contain a bound-lessness that expands around him; while in Hölderlin's "Der Rhein," lovers under the visitation of the gods find themselves "zu Hause" in a protected grove while others wander rapturously out of the "cool forest" towards the evening light. Naturally enough, the privileged recesses in these landscapes are often lovers' retreats, which the surrounding expanse seems to shelter.

The tendency of these richly endowed landscapes to absorb the gods that sanctify them has already become apparent. This recession of divinity in poems that do nothing but solicit divinity certainly seems like an oddity at first glance, but it is already clear that the identity of the gods as threshold figures makes such a recession nearly inevitable. Since the illusion of pres-ence created by a theophanic poem is meant to run seamlessly into a return of genuine "nameless" theophany, the gods of the theophanic poem must tend to resume the anonymity, the invisibility, that they possess in that transcendental condition. What this generally means in terms of the poetry is that the gods ultimately undergo disembodiment. Initially, they appear as external forms that alienate visionary power from the self and, at the same time, make that power accessible by signifying it. This is the point in which their bodiliness, their eroticism, is valuable. But when the mind recovers the power alienated in the gods, it tends to take the gods back into itself, where they do not appear as before, but are transmuted into metonyms of vision-ary strength. Often enough, this relocation of divinity is carried out by the appearance of a light, an "illumination," within the self: the hymeneal torch in "Ode to Psyche," the shining eyes and smile in "Brot und Wein," the glisten of beginning in "Jetzt wär es Zeit." "Dem Sonnengott" probably goes furthest in this respect, when it metaphorically identifies its poetic theophany with a dream that catches fire. The gods, then, like Rimbaud's génie, are essentially migratory figures: one takes them on as "affection and future, strength and love," by greeting them, then sending them on their way.

Perhaps the best way to sum up the peculiar texture and rhythm of theophanic poetry is to say that its underlying principle is a proliferation of transcendences. The poems invoke the gods by name in order to forget the names of the gods; they evoke theophany with images in order to find their way towards a theophany beyond images; and they do both only insofar as they can surmount the fear that they can do neither. The import of these transcendental movements is a radical denial of the common Romantic insistence that the absence or diminishment of vision is absolute and irreparable; that the best one can do for the loss of a visionary gleam is to find compensation for it elsewhere. The most prominent of Romantic compensations is, of course, the Wordsworthian one: an imaginative memory that animates the self's past heightenings. Theophanic poems offer a refuge for the imagination that cannot accept the Wordsworthian remedy. Through the interior dialogue that the gods initiate, the imagination can recover a lost vision by signifying that vision on the threshold of resumption.

Notes

1 [Editor's Note] Readers of this essay may find it helpful to consult Friedrich Hölderlin, *Poems and Fragments*, trans. Michael Hamburger, enlarged edn (Cambridge: Cambridge UP, 1980) and *The Selected Poetry of Rainer Maria Rilke*, trans. Stephen Mitchell (New York: Random House, 1984).
2 *Poetical Works*, ed. Thomas Hutchinson, rev. Ernest de Selincourt (London: Oxford U. Press, 1969).
3 *Natural Supernaturalism: Tradition and Innovation in Romantic Literature* (New York: Norton, 1973), pp. 385–90.
4 "Parzenlied," *Goethes Werke in Zwölf Bänden*, ed. Helmut Holtzhauer (Berlin and Weimar: Aufbau Verlag, 1966), III, 434.
5 Hölderlin, "Hyperions Schicksalslied," *Werke und Briefe*, ed. Friedrich Beissner and Jochum Schmidt (Frankfurt am Main: Insel, 1969), I, 229.
6 Rilke, "Welche Stille um einen Gott!" *Sämtliche Werke*, ed. Ernst Zinn (Wiesbaden: Insel, 1957), II, 468.
7 "Da ich ein Knabe war," *WB*, I, 230.
8 "Brot und Wein," st. V, *WB*, I, 309.
9 *Oeuvres de Rimbaud*, ed. Suzanne Bernard (Paris: Garnier, 1960), p. 308.
10 Canto LXXXI, *The Cantos of Ezra Pound* (New York: New Directions, 1970), p. 520.
11 "Da ich ein Knabe war," ll. 21–33.
12 Paul de Man, "Intentional Structure of the Romantic Image," in Harold Bloom, ed., *Romanticism and Consciousness* (New York: Norton, 1970), pp. 65–77, deals with a similar problem in commenting on "Brot und Wein."
13 *Poetical Works*, ed. H. W. Garrod (London: Oxford U. Press, 1956).
14 *WB*, I, 225.
15 *SW*, II, 185; the ellipses are Rilke's.

16 [Author's Translation] "Ah, what the highest desired, you built without a wish, / stone upon stone: it stood. Yet its collapse / left you unbemused."

17 "Intentional Structure of the Romantic Image," pp. 66–67.

18 "Spectral Symbolism and Authorial Self in Keats's *Hyperion*," in *The Fate of Reading*, by Geoffrey Hartman (Chicago: Chicago U. Press, 1975), pp. 57–73.

19 "'Positive Negation': Threshold, Sequence, and Personification in Coleridge," in *New Perspectives on Wordsworth and Coleridge*, ed. Geoffrey H. Hartman (New York: Columbia U. Press, 1972), pp. 133–64.

58

ROMANTIC HELLENISM

Timothy Webb

Source: *The Cambridge Companion to British Romanticism*, ed. Stuart Curran (Cambridge: Cambridge University Press, 1993), pp. 148–76.

I

Like "Romanticism" itself, Romantic Hellenism is a cultural and literary phenomenon whose existence is widely in evidence yet which remains elusive, problematic and difficult to define with inclusive rigor. Like Romanticism, it has often been simplified and misrepresented; contrary to general belief, it achieved expression in forms that were diverse, paradoxical, sometimes self-contradictory, and often controversially or adversarially related to received modes and ideas. Like Romanticism, it never achieved articulation as a coherent philosophy; it never generated a school of practitioners who might have advertised themselves as Romantic Hellenists; it was never consciously or programmatically identified by those who seem to have pursued or embodied it most creatively. Again like Romanticism, it is a retrospective label that yokes together for historical convenience a wide range of manifestations and examples centered in and around what we now call the Romantic period but with roots that go far back into the eighteenth century.

In England Romantic Hellenism is a powerful but inconstant presence that expresses itself in a variety of ways. Since it is a tendency rather than a tangible ideology, it can not be argued for or articulated, although the relevance of the Greek model is specifically formulated by Shelley in the preface to *Hellas* where – in the face of a temporizing British foreign policy toward the Greek struggle for independence, he provocatively claims, "We are all Greeks" – in his essays on Christianity, on the manners of the ancient Greeks and on Greek sculpture; and, more narrowly, by the painter Benjamin Robert Haydon in his celebratory essay on the Elgin Marbles. Among English writers it emerged most richly and variously in the work of the second generation of Romantic poets; it never achieved a comparable status in the imaginative world of their predecessors. Insofar as it represented an openness and a creative susceptibility to the Greek example rather than a less personally focused interest in Greek art and literature, it was largely resisted by Wordsworth, Coleridge and Southey, who preferred the northern and the Christian to a phenomenon they regarded as southern and pagan. It also seemed to provide a challenge or a provocation to those who subscribed to the values of the patriotic and the English, since it could be seen as a foreign importation that represented a danger to all such traditional allegiances, whether in religious codes or architecture or poetic diction. It could be used as an escape from the urgencies of the eye and an endorsement of the *status quo* or as a subversive and challenging source of alternative values. In some of its manifestations, it involved the recovery of classical models and coincided with and was stimulated by that artistic phenomenon known as "Neoclassicism"; yet those who subscribed to such ideals did not see themselves as traditionalists or conservatives but "felt the excitement of a radical departure." It received an impetus and a point of focus in the Elgin Marbles, which were removed with Turkish permission from the Parthenon at Athens and exhibited in London by stages in 1807, 1812 and more permanently after they had been purchased for the nation in 1816. For some years it ran coincident to the course of philhellenism, that is, the movement dedicated to the recovery of Greek political independence; Shelley's *Hellas* prophetically celebrated "the great drama of the revival of liberty" and Byron died in this cause while preparing for the inevitable conflict (*Poetry and Prose*, p. 410). In architecture, there was a Greek Revival that began by coexisting with other styles such as the Gothic (Chippendale achieved similar equality of taste by designing chairs in the modes of Greek and Gothic, as well as Chinese); but by 1803 the Greek example "was the very criterion of architectural distinction" and remained a recurring influence on public buildings until the 1840s.[1] To some extent it was a European phenomenon; although there were national variations and the French and German versions were by no means identical to the English, the new discoveries, insights and theories could largely be exchanged and transmitted through the international currency of translation. Most obviously and most potently perhaps, it informed a number of major creative works: the mythological poems of Keats, especially *Endymion*, "Hyperion," "Lamia" and some of the odes; the second cantos of Byron's *Childe Harold's Pilgrimage* and *Don Juan*, and some of his Turkish tales; Shelley's *Prometheus Unbound* and *Hellas*, his mythological poems, especially "The Witch of Atlas," and his translations of the Homeric Hymns and Plato; and, in the sphere of art, John Flaxman's illustrations of Homer and Aeschylus and his designs for the pottery of Thomas Wedgwood.

The common factor to all these varieties of Romantic Hellenism is an interest in Greece or the Grecian model and a desire to appropriate it for present purposes. This interest expresses itself sometimes negatively and sometimes positively; sometimes as a nostalgic yearning to escape into another place and another age apparently more golden than the present and sometimes as a desire to make the lessons of the past immediately relevant to the urgencies of contemporary life; sometimes as an emphasis on the differences between Greece and England, sometimes as a suggestion of analogies; sometimes as radical, sometimes as conservative; sometimes as admiration for Athens, sometimes as cultivation of Spartan virtues; sometimes as geographically specific, sometimes in terms of a landscape and a sense of place both distanced and idealized; sometimes as an inhibiting awareness of the Greek tradition, sometimes as anxious homage to the giant examples of antiquity and sometimes as creatively critical engagement with a tradition that is fragmented and suggestively open to interpretation, development and revision. If Homer could be many things to many readers, so too could the Greek example. The fascination of Romantic Hellenism is in its endless variety, in the scope it offered for views that are radically opposed. Throughout the eighteenth and early nineteenth centuries the image of Greece and of the Greek achievement was constantly refined, revised, refuted or reinterpreted through a complex and continuous process of redefinition.

Such a process of definition and redefinition is well-recognized by modern writers, particularly when they engage with the classical tradition as translators or interpreters or as originators who wish to relate creatively to the work of the past. The challenge for writers of the Romantic period was not substantially different. They were closer perhaps to the excitement of the rediscovery of Greece and to its gradual substitution for the supremacy of Roman civilization and values. They were more inclined to register this shifting of the balance as a pretext for liberalization; some, later, were prepared to find in the unknown an intimation of harmonizing possibilities. Yet, even if our own pressing concerns may have caused us to exaggerate the problematic, the difficult, the burden of reading and interpretation, as we deconstruct the achievements of Romanticism, we are now sensitively attuned to registering more precisely than before those troubled discords in the history of Romantic Hellenism understated by earlier critics that point towards a continuity between Romantic and modern. The discords and the harmonies must be understood as they relate to each other; the positive achievements can now sometimes be seen as less radiantly self-confident and more defiantly and precariously worked for, while the doubts, hesitations and contradictions can be frankly acknowledged.

Like ourselves, writers and artists of the Romantic period were confronted not only with the enigma of the fragment but with the urgent question of how they should relate to a tradition that, for all its appearances of comforting familiarity, might often have been "unimaginably different" and that gave expression to a system of values that might be uncongenial, if it could be reconstructed. The Greek legacy comprised a canon of literature that was variously defined, but it also included a much more extensive series of texts in the form of art and architecture and especially in what Shelley called "sculpture's marble language" (*The Revolt of Islam*, line 573) that could not be so easily translated and that, like Homer, Aeschylus, Plato and Thucydides, were subject to the necessities and pressures of translation and interpretation. How the Romantics attempted to make sense of this extended language and how they translated it into artistic form are best illustrated by a number of suggestive examples.

First, there are two contrasting instances provided by the German art historian Johann Joachim Winckelmann and his translator, the Swiss artist and aphorist Henry Fuseli, who was a friend of William Blake. Winckelmann (whose work was directly known to Blake and Shelley) was one of the most significant figures in the history of Romantic Hellenism. Through books such as *Gedanken über die Nachahmung der Griechischen Werke in der Mahlerey und Bildhauerkunst* (*The Imitation of the Painting and Sculpture of the Greeks* [1755; translated by Fuseli, 1765]) and *Geschichte der Kunst des Alterthums* (*History of Ancient Art* [translated into French in 1766, 1781, 1790–1803 but not completely into English until 1880]), Winckelmann initiated "a new organ for the human spirit," according to Hegel, and opened up a new continent according to Goethe, who compared him to Columbus.[2] His combination of the analytical and the poetic inspired a fresh understanding of the principles and the achievements of Greek art, notably of sculpture, and helped to tilt the balance of European taste from Rome towards Greece. Winckelmann's feeling for Greek sculpture was influenced by his environmental theory stressing a connection between the climate of Athens and its democratic institutions. Although he invested emotionally and intellectually in the superiority of the Greek example, his discovery of the neglected artistic virtues of Greece was conditioned and in part compromised by the fact that it took place in Italy. His intuitive and imaginative approach is clearly illustrated by his account of the *Torso Belvedere* (1759; translated by Fuseli, 1765) which is in effect a prose poem. In the conclusion to *History of Art* he suggestively explains the pleasure and the challenge of such imaginative reconstruction by comparing himself to "a maiden, standing on the shore of the ocean" who "follows with tearful eyes her departing lover with no hope of ever seeing him again." The art-historian as Ariadne embraces his readers and fellow interpreters of the classical tradition in a wistful analogy that focuses on the compensating faculty of desire: "Like that loving maiden, we too have, as it were, nothing but a shadowy outline of the object of our wishes, but that very indistinctness awakens only a more earnest longing for what we have lost, and we study the copies of the originals more attentively than we should have done the originals themselves if we had been in full possession of them." Winckelmann admits that the "authority of antiquity predetermines our judgments" and that our imaginative projections can be as perilously self-justifying as "an interview with spirits" that we encourage ourselves to see "when there is nothing to be seen," but he finally asserts that "he who always proposes to himself to *find much* will by *seeking* for much perceive something."[3] So his great history ends with a curious dying fall and the surge of its poetic prose is strangely qualified and rendered hesitant by the indeterminacy and obliqueness of its final claim.

For all his gifts, Winckelmann was a historian rather than a creative artist. The alternative perspective is provided by Fuseli in his chalk and sepia wash sketch "The Artist in Despair over the Magnitude of Antique Fragments" (c. 1778–80). Here Fuseli presents an image of the frailty and insufficiency of the modern creator when confronted with the weighty remains of a tradition that is alien, enigmatic and overwhelming. Unlike Winckelmann, Fuseli's artist is not stimulated by *Sehnsucht* or a nostalgia for a golden and superior past; instead, the somewhat androgynous figure, no longer a yearning Ariadne, sits disconsolate and threatened, disproportionately miniscule beside a giant left foot surrealistically surmounted by a giant right hand with index finger pointing meaningfully upward. Perhaps this is evidence of personal neurosis but it might also be seen as a symptom of a cultural crisis that was experienced especially by writers and artists for whom the Greek achievement was both an unreachable ideal and a system that could not now be reassembled or understood as a whole. Fuseli's artist experiences, it would seem, that burden of the past that has been increasingly identified with the artistic self-consciousness of the modern writer.[4] That burden can also be identified in Keats, nowhere more acutely or with greater existential profundity than in "The Fall of Hyperion" where, confronted by the Muse, he struggles with a sense of his own inadequacy to translate the Greek myth into effective poetic form in a contemporary world of misery, heartbreak and challenging political change. That life-or-death dialogue is conducted on the steps of a temple that dwarfs the poet and troubles his sense of poetic identity and purpose; this daunting edifice is a nightmare version of those peaceful Grecian temples pictured by Claude and Poussin that Keats associates elsewhere with the "happy pieties" of old religion and that in the "Ode to Psyche" he vows to reconstruct in his own mind.[5]

The difficulty of imagining the past is at the center of Keats's "Ode on a Grecian Urn." This urn is a product of that rediscovery of the art of Greek pottery that was stimulated by the collecting of Greek vases in Sicily, translated into prints by the work of artists such as D'Hancarville, Tischbein, Thomas Kirk and Henry Moses, and disseminated and commercialized by the business acumen of Josiah Wedgwood through the agency of Flaxman's interpretations. The urn itself is a silent "historian" and the poet makes strenuous efforts to interpret its "legend." The urn Keats describes with such precision of detail does not correspond to any specific model but has been compositely assembled from a variety of sources including the Sosibios Vase of which Keats made a drawing. The aesthetics of its composition may seem to conform to the practices of eighteenth-century art, as does the attribution to the urn itself of a conveniently epigrammatic lesson for the reader or the observer. Yet, as more recent criticism has demonstrated, the quotable sonority of the last lines overlays and even conceals a textual and interpretative enigma that cannot easily be resolved. At the center of the poem which at first sight appears to conclude with such emphatic and unhesitant finality we confront an absence and a silence both troubling and unresponsive. The "historian" can offer no further evidence. Like all historians and histories, it necessarily leaves room for further interpretation.

In his mythological poems Keats frequently exhibits an extraordinary imaginative ability to reconstruct "the realm . . . / of Flora, and old Pan," or the "Fauns and Dryades / Coming with softest rustle through the trees" or "the swift bound / Of Bacchus from his chariot"; yet such intimations of joy were difficult to sustain and were often followed or challenged by "A sense of real things" that "like a muddy stream, would bear along / My soul to nothingness" ("Sleep and Poetry," lines 101–2; "I stood tiptoe," lines 153–4; "Sleep and Poetry," lines 334–5, 157–9). Keats responded to this sense of uncertainty in several ways: in the preface to *Endymion* he gave voice to a sense of failure and inadequacy – "I hope I have not in too late a day touched the beautiful mythology of Greece, and dulled its brightness" – while he increasingly acknowledged the limitations of the "leaf-fringed legend" ("Ode on a Grecian Urn," line 5) and aspired to "a more naked and grecian Manner" (*Letters*, I, 207). Here one can sense not only the struggle with himself but the transition from one model of Greekness to another: mythological self-indulgence is replaced by the less compromising example of the Elgin Marbles he had first seen at the British Museum in 1817 when they caused him "a most dizzy pain / That mingles Grecian grandeur with the rude / Wasting of old Time" ("On Seeing the Elgin Marbles," lines 11–13).

Finally, and by way of contrast with Keats, there is the case of Shelley at Pompeii. Shelley had many reservations about the ancient Greeks and he was well aware of the limitations of Athenian democracy, yet he also regarded the Greeks as the founders of much that was best in Western civilization, "glorious beings whom the imagination almost refuses to figure to itself as belonging to our kind" (*Prose*, p. 219). In his "Essay on the Manners of the Ancient Greeks" he sympathetically explains, without necessarily approving, the strong homosexual element in Athenian society and its significance for an informed understanding of the works of Plato, particularly *The Symposium* which had been treated with euphemism and evasion by its most recent translator: "There is no book which shows the Greeks precisely as they were; they seem all written for children, with the caution that no practice or sentiment highly inconsistent with our present manners should be mentioned, lest those manners should receive outrage and violation" (*Prose*, p. 219)[6]. One of the dangers of Romantic Hellenism was the tendency to translate the ancient Greeks into replications of ourselves; so Barthélemy (author of *Les Voyages du jeune Anacharsis en Grèce* [1788]) "never forgets that he is a Christian and a Frenchman," while Wieland "cherishes too many political prejudices" (in the *History of Agathon* [1766–67; 1794]) (*Prose*, p. 219). The otherness of the Greeks must be acknowledged, whatever the discomforts or the shock to propriety: "For the Greeks of the Periclean age were widely different from us. It is to be lamented that no modern writer has hitherto dared to show them exactly as they were." Although Shelley acknowledged this unbridgeable gap between the Greeks of the classical age and the inhabitants of modern Europe, he also believed that the Greeks had achieved a unity of being and a coherence of existence that had since been lost, largely under the influence of Christianity.[7]

In January 1819, when he was living at Naples, he visited the nearby city of Pompeii (first excavated in 1748), which was the subject of an illustrated study by J. P. Gandy and William Gell (1817–19) and of Macaulay's Cambridge prize poem of 1819, which had inspired powerful personal responses from Goethe, Chateaubriand and Madame de Staël among many others, and which would later be treated by Lamartine and Leopardi.[8] Like a number of significant Romantic Hellenists (including Winckelmann and Goethe), Shelley never reached Greece, and his experience of Italy with its "warm and radiant atmosphere which is interfused through all things" strongly influenced his views of classical Greece and helped to shape poems such as *Epipsychidion* with its Elysian isle exotic and erotic "Under the roof of blue Ionian weather" (line 542). His response to "the city disinterred" was conditioned by his belief (misguided in fact) that Pompeii had been a Greek settlement, and he translated Italian into Greek through an intense act of imaginative interpretation: "This scene was what the Greeks beheld. They lived in harmony with nature, & the interstices of their incomparable columns, were portals as it were to admit the spirit of beauty which animates this glorious universe . . . If such is Pompeii, what was Athens?" (*Letters*, II, 73).

Although Shelley makes a central and creative use of the volcano in other poems such as *Prometheus Unbound* and "Ode to Naples," in this case he seems unaware of the ironies in his celebration of the Greek ideal. His readiness to make this imaginative reconstruction owes much to his strong desire to reanimate the past and in particular to approach the ruins of classical antiquity not as signs of man's destructive tendency but as indications of a potential as yet unfulfilled: so in *Laon and Cythna* (revised as *The Revolt of Islam*) his Greek hero Laon identifies the "dwellings of a race of mightier men" (line 759) in the "broken tombs and columns riven" (line 754) of an Argolis still subject to Ottoman rule, and interprets the language of these ruins to signify that "Such man has been, and such may yet become! / Ay wiser, greater, gentler, even than they" (lines 766–7). But even this attempt to apply the lessons of antiquity reaches its climax with an image of volcanic eruption in which the multitude is compared to "a sulphurous hill" that "shall burst and fill / The world with cleansing fire" (lines 785–8). The more pastoral tone of the letter on Pompeii with its emphasis on harmonious environment may have been influenced by Schlegel's enthusiastic account of the performance of Greek drama "which could only be exhibited under an unobstructed sky."[9]

The supposed Greek city was attractive to Shelley because it represented a radiant alternative to the "Cimmerian gloom" and smoke that characterized so many modern cities, most notoriously London, which even provided a point of comparison for the infernal city ("Hell is a city much like London" [*Peter Bell the Third*, line 147]). Shelley's reconstruction of the Greek *polis* starts from a perspective that encourages him to concentrate not on its political organization or the details of its architecture but on its relationship with the natural world. It would not be easy to find an example of a city that had less in common with a "*populous manufacturing dissipated town*" (*Letters*, I, 197) such as Nottingham with its "famine-wasted inhabitants" (*ibid.*, I, 213) or, more surprisingly, Keswick, where "tho the face of the country is lovely the *people* are detestable" (*ibid.*, I, 223). In Keswick the "manufacturers with their contamination have crept into the peaceful vale and deformed the loveliness of Nature with human taint"; otherwise, "the Christian Heaven (with its Hell) would be to *us* no paradise, but such a scene as this!" (*ibid.*, I, 200–1). Here, as so often in Shelley, the Elysian possibilities intimated by the landscape are denied and subverted by the contaminating presence of man. By contrast, the very emptiness of Pompeii provides scope for a concentration on the harmonizing possibilities (rather like Wordsworth's view of London from Westminster Bridge as a city, still, glittering, and smokeless); it is purified, temporarily at least, both of the disfiguring social and political symptoms of modern capitalist society and of "the poor, loveless, ever-anxious crowd" (Coleridge's phrase) that presses uncomfortably upon the imagination and the social conscience. It would be unjust to complain that Shelley lacked such a conscience since the evidence of his life and his work demonstrates the opposite so fully and so clearly, yet it is worth observing how his Hellenizing tendency pulls him away from the facts of nineteenth-century urbanization towards an idealized alternative where he can people with his wishes vacancy and oblivion. This preference led him to live in Italian cities such as Pisa, to celebrate the republic of Athens as a model for poetic and philosophical creativity in the preface to *Prometheus Unbound*, to compose the *lontani* (or long-distance perspectives) of "Lines Written among the Euganean Hills"; it also inspired him to create in the "Ode to Naples" (1820) a poem that built upon the positive experience of visiting the ghost town of Pompeii, linked it to the history of the Elysian city of Naples (itself a Greek foundation as Shelley intimated by calling it "Metropolis of a ruined Paradise"), and bound the present to the past and the future by celebrating the recent news of the proclamation of a Constitutional Government at Naples.

II

The roots of Romantic Hellenism are distinct from that revaluation of the classical tradition associated with the Renaissance. Although precise origins are hard to establish, the growth of Hellenism received much of its impetus from a series of discoveries or rediscoveries, the most significant of which may have been the gradual recognition of Greece itself, together with a slowly developing challenge to the reigning authority of a culture largely centered on Rome. This redistribution of cultural forces can be traced back in part to English and French travellers in Greece in the late seventeenth and early eighteenth centuries who provided a new impetus towards an understanding of the Greek achievement in terms not of an idealized and abstract set of landscapes but of topographical and social specificity.[10] By the early nineteenth century, Greece was no longer as remote and unfamiliar as it once had been, and the Napoleonic Wars made it even more attractive to those who were unable to pursue the more traditional itineraries of the Grand Tour. Byron's friend Hobhouse reported, "Attica . . . swarms with travellers . . . and . . . a few more years may furnish the Piraeus with all the accommodations of a fashionable watering-place," while in 1814 C. J. Blomfield declared anonymously in the *Quarterly Review*: "No man is now accounted a traveller, who has not bathed in the Eurotas and tasted the olives of Attica" (*Quarterly Review* II [1841]:458). This emphasis on the empirical experience of Greece reached its culmination and its greatest publicity in the figure of Byron who prided himself on his personal knowledge of the plain of Troy where he stood "*daily*, for more than a month" and "venerated the grand original as the truth of *history* (in the material facts) and of *place*." (*Letters and Journals*, VIII, 21–2).[11] Byron insisted on his direct personal knowledge in presenting the Grecian world in a perspective that was often bifocal: for instance, Scotland and Homer are combined in the line "And Loch-na-gar with Ida looked o'er Troy." Topographical certitude enabled him to deflate the untroubled simplicities of Wordsworth's picturesque presentation of Greece as a land of lush pastoral variety "Under a cope of variegated sky"; it also allowed him to defend the accuracy of Pope's translation by matching it against particulars such as the "glow" of the night sky at Troy (*Letters and Journals*, IV, 325–6). Byron was all too acutely aware that the plight of Greece offered opportunities to unscrupulous dealers in sentimental patriotism and its tokens; he himself had once considered purchasing the island of Ithaca and he had been offered the plain of Marathon for about nine hundred pounds. His contempt for the depredations of Lord Elgin and the collaboration of the English art-lover is given full expression in *The Curse of Minerva* and in *Childe Harold's Pilgrimage* (1812). The second canto of *Childe Harold* makes a virtue out of authenticity and poetic capital out of Byron's travels across the map of Greece; here and in the Turkish tales he combines exoticism with a sense of history and of place and a responsiveness to contemporary political realities. These poems have achieved a more durable celebrity than many other records of first-hand experiences in Greece and the Levant, but they are the products of a continuing tradition that included travel writers and writers of verse such as William Falconer (whose *The Shipwreck* [1762] Byron particularly admired); topographers such as William Gell (whose *The Itinerary of Greece* [1811] was reviewed by Byron); and architects and archaeologists such as James Stuart and Nicholas Revett whose meticulously illustrated *Antiquities of Athens* (five volumes between 1762 and 1830) initiated a new era in the study of classical architecture and left its mark on English churches and public buildings.[12]

Byron's uncompromising commitment to fact also led him to remind his readers that the language of modern Greece was Romaic. He translated several poems from the Romaic including the "War Song" of Constantine Rhigas, the patriotic poet and revolutionary who had been executed by the Turks in 1798. He also included lists of modern Greek authors and examples of Romaic with translations in the notes to *Childe Harold*. This emphasis on language sometimes allowed him to exploit the contrast between ancient and modern by drawing attention to the linguistic difference. In the second canto of *Don Juan* the eponymous hero is washed ashore on one of the "wild and smaller Cyclades" where he attracts the attention of Haidée, much as Odysseus encounters Nausicaa in Homer. The parallel is both developed and deliberately counterpointed in a variety of ways, not least by Byron's strong assertion of physiological imperatives and by his insistence on Juan's linguistic difficulties as he is addressed "in good modern Greek, / With an Ionian accent, low and sweet" (lines 1198–9). "Being no Grecian" (line 1202) Juan does not understand but, as every public schoolboy would certainly have known, "Grecian" could mean not only a Greek but a classical scholar; here Byron brings into play both the ambiguity of the word and the ambivalent attitudes of the academy towards the language of the Greeks (according to C. J. Blomfield, it was "one of the most barbarous dialects of modern Europe" [*Quarterly Review*, II (1814):459]). One of the effects of this insistence on Romaic is to place the events of the narrative very tangibly in a society that is a contemporary reality rather than a literary reconstruction or an abstract ideal. Byron's decoding of the Greek language is related to his demystifying of Greek mythology; both are part of a philosophy that insists on the value of the present and the immediate, on life experienced directly rather than refracted through literature, and on the strength of the vernacular rather than the more exclusive attributes of the classical language.

A like concentration on authenticity marked a number of books on Homer that approached his poems in the light of the growing awareness of the new contexts provided by comparative anthropology and by a direct investigation of the facts of place. The anthropological and the sociological are well exemplified by the Scottish professor Thomas Blackwell, whose *Enquiry into the Life and Writings of Homer* (1735) argued that the "naturalness" of Greek life was too crude to be socially desirable but was a perfect medium for the production of epic poetry: "Neither . . . does it seem to be given to one and the same Kingdom, to be thoroughly civilized, and afford proper Subjects for Poetry." Blackwell's *Enquiry* stressed the naturalness of Homer's society and its influence on forms of expression that contrasted with "the Prattle, and little pretty Forms that enervate a polished Speech." Modern poets with epic ambitions were forced to strain if they wished to achieve similar effects: "We are obliged to adopt a set of more *natural* manners, which however are foreign to us, and must be like plants raised up in hot-beds or greenhouses." Blackwell's conclusion that "we may never be a Proper Subject of an Heroic Poem" set out the terms of a problem that would continue to resonate for the poets of the Romantic period just as his views on language would find an echo in the preface to *Lyrical Ballads*. His *Enquiry* eventually helped to bring about that gradual shift of taste that reluctantly acknowledged the primitive and the brutal in Homer and that ultimately rejected Pope's versions of the *Iliad* (1715–20) and the *Odyssey* (1715–26) in favor of George Chapman's translations, not least because Chapman achieved a spirited diction and versification that seemed more forcefully appropriate than "the milkiness of the best good manners" ("Critical Remarks on Pope's Homer" published in *Gentleman's Magazine*, 1785; text cited in ERM, p. 178). Such interpretations depended on a primitivistic approach to Homer and his heroic code of values. Poets became increasingly troubled by the battle-scenes of the *Iliad* and some tried to subvert the traditional connection between war and epic. Robert Southey was uncomfortably in accord with these responses to Homer when, in 1814, he claimed that "Book after book of butchery, however skilfully performed is unsuitable to the European state of mind at present." He speculated that "if Homer were living now, he would write very differently" and would address himself "more to our feelings and reflecting faculties." This response, which included not only the *Iliad* but the *Odyssey* with its "raw head and bloody-bone-monster" [the Cyclops], must have been sharpened by the long course of the Napoleonic Wars and by the Romantic emphasis on the subjective which in the view of critics such as Schlegel distinguished the moderns from the ancients.[13]

Such insights presented themselves from time to time during the eighteenth century but in England the influence of Pope's translation had helped to occlude their sharper edges; even William Cowper, who severely criticized the "good christian meekness of Pope," was incapable of capturing Homer's "smartness and acrimony" in his own version of 1791 (ERM, p. 178). No English poet or translator succeeded in capitalizing on the ideas of Blackwell, or of Robert Wood whose *Essay on the Original Genius of Homer* (1767) exercised an inspirational effect on the German scholar F. A. Wolf, whose own epoch-making *Prolegomena ad Homerum* appeared in 1795, two years after the German translation of the *Iliad* by Johann Voss. Unlike Blackwell, Robert Wood approached Homer from a perspective largely, though not exclusively, empirical; in his *Essay* he concentrated partly on authenticating Homer's imagery and partly on the social context that produced his poetry. Like Blackwell, he made no attempt to "civilize" Homer, or to "half chris-ten" him: "most of Homer's heroes would, in the present age, be capitally convicted, in any country in Europe, on the Poet's evidence." The contrast and the coincidence between Wood and Blackwell is symptomatic of the larger course of Romantic Hellenism: one centered his enquiry around empirical observation while the other observed Greece from the perspective of Aberdeen; yet the joint effect of their writings was to reinterpret the Homeric achievement and to place a new emphasis on the bardic, on the otherness of Homer, on the gap that separated him from the society of contemporary western Europe, and on the topographical and social circum-stances that gave birth to epic poetry.

Such developments in interpretation were often the result of a series of personal initiatives, sometimes even of improvisations, and many of them were self-delighting or self-defining rather than calculated to contribute to a large pattern of research. Yet when we consider them retrospectively, it is clear that by the end of the eighteenth century, if not even before, the understanding of Greece and the Greek tradition had been radically altered, extended and enriched by an incremental process of adjustment and read-justment. The narrowly focused activities of editors and of classical scholars had been challenged by the new perspectives of the travellers, the topo-graphers, the collectors, and the pioneers of that science that would become archaeology (some of whom tried to combine the insights of empirical observation with the practices of traditional scholarship). Though there was much here that was speculative or inaccurate, there was also a linking sense of immediacy and of freshness. By the turn of the century it was possible to feel with some confidence that much more was known about Greece than in the time of Milton or of Pope. The cultural supremacy of Rome had been challenged by Greece; although the first generation of Romantic poets (with the striking but ambivalent exception of Blake) would not transfer their allegiance, Shelley and Keats had no hesitation in preferring Greece, while Byron was politically and emotionally committed to the ideal of Greek independence from Turkish hegemony but less convinced of the virtues of ancient Greek literature and mythology and intolerant of that Platonic philosophy of love and "intellectual beauty" Shelley wished to mediate to his English contemporaries. Byron's philhellenism continued to coexist with a preference for the models of Augustan literature that looked back to the examples of Horace and Virgil and that had been largely discounted by Blake, Shelley and Keats. This is another of those paradoxical conjunc-tions or configurations that mark the history of Romantic Hellenism.

This developing understanding of Greece was also registered in a series of artistic phenomena that made a major impact on taste by transmitting the results of discovery or collecting or scholarly reconstruction to a wider sphere. A major figure in this process was Winckelmann who provided a new focus to the taste for the antique. Winckelmann may have been a Columbus among art-historians but, for all his originality, his reading of Greek art was informed by an ideology that was perhaps as much an expression of neoclassical principles as an anticipation of Romanticism. Like his contemporaries, Winckelmann was much impressed by the apparent whiteness of Greek sculpture (it was the nineteenth century that discovered that statues had been brightly painted). This induced him to emphasize the purity and classical serenity of Greek art and it coincided with his desire to celebrate what he called "a noble simplicity and sedate grandeur in Gesture and Expression": "As the bottom of the sea lies peaceful beneath a foaming surface, a great soul lies sedate beneath the strife of passions in Greek figures." So the contortions and struggles of the *Laocoon* reminded him of "simplicity and calmness" and the *Torso* displayed "not even a hint . . . of violence or lascivious love" (ERM, pp. 121, 126). Although he significantly shifted the terms of approach, Winckelmann was in some ways conditioned by the limitations of eighteenth-century taste; his preference for calmness has something in common with the flavor of Joseph Spence whose widely read Roman-orientated and mythological handbook *Polymetis* (1747) excludes the gods of the underworld from its garden setting. For all his delight in the representation of the body, Winckelmann's example tended towards the repression or the erasure of the violent or the problematic so that for many of his disciples, whether readers, writers or artists, the Greek tradition came to imply sedateness without struggle and calmness without conflict. It was this misrepresentation that eventually provoked Nietzsche to complain: "Our classicists lack a genuine pleasure in the violent and powerful aspects of the classical world."[14]

The deficiencies of Winckelmann's criteria and the standards of the neoclassical were brought under scrutiny by the appearance in England of the Elgin Marbles. After a Select Committee hearing in 1816 the Marbles were purchased by Parliament for £35,000, which occasioned a Cruikshank cartoon in which John Bull is pictured "buying *Stones* at the time his numerous family want *Bread*!!" but which inspired Haydon to pronounce "an Aera in public feeling" and to claim: "Were the Elgin Marbles lost, there would be a great gap in art as there would in philosophy if Newton had never existed."[15] As their criteria for establishing the financial and artistic value of the Marbles, the Select Committee had chosen the *Apollo*, *the Torso Belvedere* and the *Laocoon*. But the giant and fragmentary presence of the Marbles seemed to cast doubt on some of the criteria by which they had been evaluated, Richard Payne Knight, mythographer and arbiter of taste, who gave evidence to the Committee, embodied those standards under challenge. Knight was a member of the Society of Dilettanti (or art-connoisseurs) that had sponsored the work of Stuart and Revert and in 1812 also supported an Ionian expedition by William Gell in the hope that his researches would eventually contribute to "the Improvement of National Taste." His views were supported by other Dilettanti and collectors who, like himself, had based their collections on neoclassical principles.

Such opposition soon proved ineffectual. In 1816 Hazlitt registered the immediate impact of the Marbles with the hope that they would "lift the Fine Arts out of the Limbo of vanity and affectation . . . in which they have lain sprawling and fluttering, gasping for breath, wasting away, vapid and abortive" he reported, "Already these Marbles have produced a revolution in our artists' minds" (*Works*, XVIII, 100–1). Haydon became dissatisfied with the *Apollo* and found fault with its "hard, marbly, puffed figure" while Flaxman declared that "the Apollo in comparison with the Theseus was a dancing master" (Haydon, *Diary*, I, 247, II, 15). Hazlitt condemned the *Apollo* and its supercilious air in terms that reveal he associated it with the French (who had displayed it in the Louvre during the Napoleonic era) and with the classicism of the eighteenth century: "The Apollo Belvedere is positively bad, a theatrical coxcomb, and ill-made; I mean compared with the Theseus." He also observed that there was "no alliteration or antithesis" and commented: "The limbs have too much an appearance of . . . balancing and answering to one another, like the rhymes in verse. The Elgin Marbles are harmonious, flowing, varied prose" (*Works*, XVII, 148; X, 222, 169). It would seem that the *Apollo* was to be equated with the heroic couplets of the Augustans and with a classicism that was now stilted, restricted and outmoded when matched against the fluent openness of the Marbles and that primitive strength that was less obviously polished but more expressive of heroic energies. Keats, who first saw the Marbles in 1817 in the ebullient company of Haydon, produced a sonnet in which he told Haydon that at first he could not "speak / Definitively on these mighty things" but, though he may have been overcome by the weight and pressures of antiquity like Fuseli's artist, he later crystallized a desire to achieve an equivalent effect in literature by writing in "a more naked and grecian manner." The giant figures of "Hyperion" and "The Fall of Hyperion" may have been inspired partly by Milton's practice of "placing" the protagonists of his epic, partly by the rocky suggestiveness of Scottish landscape and partly by Keats's experience as a dresser at Guy's Hospital of the configurations and attitudes of pain, but the controlling and shaping influence is that of the Elgin Marbles. Keats's figuring of poetry as "might half-slumb'ring on its own right arm" ("Sleep and Poetry," line 237) is also, almost certainly, a recollection of the statue of Theseus (or Dionysus) he must have seen when he visited the Marbles at the British Museum. Such images are blended with others that may have been suggested by the work of classicizing artists such as Claude and Titian – like most poets, Keats was eclectic in his absorbing of influences – yet without this direct experience of the Greek example his later mythological poetry would lack some of its muscularity and its formidable sense of fragmentation and alienation. As these poems show, Keats internalized from his encounters with Greek art a sense of strength, power and authority that demanded imitation, but he also experienced a sense of tension that undermined any complacent inclination to celebrate the nicely balanced harmonies of "classical" sculpture, together with an unnerving intimation of his own diminutive stature as a poet.

Shelley was originally much less curious about art than was Keats. Unlike Keats and Hazlitt and Haydon, who were centered in London, he seems to have adhered very closely to Winckelmann and the ideals of neoclassicism. Unlike his wife Mary, he did not go to see the Elgin Marbles before he left England, but the Italian experience inspired him to visit the collections of Rome, Naples and Florence where he had access to the most celebrated examples of Greek sculpture such as the *Apollo* and the *Torso Belvedere*, the *Laocoon*, the *Niobe*, a dazzle of Venuses including the *Venus de Medici*, and the *Discobolos* (rediscovered in 1781). Although some of the statues were Roman or Greco-Roman copies of lost originals, they all seemed to embody an immediate Greekness, and they stimulated in Shelley an intensity of appreciation inspired and directed by Winckelmann's influential mixture of the analytical and the poetic. The intimate connection between Greek sculpture and his experience of Italy is made clear in one of his letters to Peacock from Rome, where he describes the synaesthetic effect of seeing the statues of Castor and Pollux on Monte Cavallo: "the sublime and living majesty of their limbs & mien . . . seen in the blue sky of Italy, & over looking the City of Rome, surrounded by the light & the music of that chrystalline fountain, no cast can com[m]unicate" (*Letters*, II, 89). Shelley's particular responsiveness to Greek sculpture can be traced in a series of short prose essays on the figures of Niobe, Laocoon, Mercury, Bacchus and many others; it also exercised a shaping influence on the mythological invention of his later poems (see *Prose*, pp. 343–53; for a corrected text, see E. B. Murray, "Shelley's *Notes on Sculptures*," *Keats-Shelley Journal*, XXXII [1983]: 150–71).

This Romantic rediscovery of the uses of Greek mythology is much more than a reordering of aesthetic preferences; in the work of lesser poets such as Leigh Hunt or Barry Cornwall or even Thomas Love Peacock it may have been largely decorative or superficial or simply fashionable or even, as Schlegel put it, a mere antiquity slop-shop, yet for Shelley and Keats it was energized and inventive and often gave expression to their deepest concerns. The rediscovery of the virtues of Greek art was paralleled by the publication of a series of handbooks in which Greek mythology had been welcomed, domesticated and made available to the general reader. These included books by John Lemprière (1788) and John Bell (1790); detailed explications and commentary on Greek texts, especially the works of the neo-Platonists, by Thomas Taylor, the "English Pagan," including *The Mystical Initiations; or Hymns of Orpheus* (1787); a privately issued "Account of the Worship of Priapus" by the art-collector Richard Payne Knight which formed the basis for the more discreet *Inquiry into the Symbolic Language of Ancient Art and Mythology* (1818); and the publications of William Godwin whose *Pantheon or Ancient History of the Gods of Greece and Rome* (issued in 1806 under the name of "Edward Baldwin") was primarily intended for children. This interest in Greek mythology can be seen as part of a more widely based concern to investigate the origins and significance of the mythological. The researches of syncretic mythologists were based on the premise that "beneath the seemingly disparate and heterogeneous elements of ancient universal mythico-religious and historical traditions there lay a harmonious tradition";[16] the results were speculative and often fanciful as, for example, in the work of Jacob Bryant whose *New System; or, An Analysis of Ancient Mythology* appeared in 1774. Often there was a tension between a need to see all mythologies as ultimately consistent and in accord with the Christian interpretation of history, and a recognition of diversity that was troubling or exhilarating depending on one's point of view. Some investigations suggested that behind the classical stories of love there lay the unacknowledged potency of sexual forces in man and in nature. Payne Knight, for example, provided an account of Priapus that was more favorable to the fertility rituals he discovered than to the repressive and oppressive practices of organized religion.[17]

Not all poets would have been fully aware of all these debates and researches yet they provide an essential context for the reading of Romantic receptions of mythology. For some poets the Grecian emphasis ran against the grain of the English tradition; so in 1804 Joseph Cottle declared in the preface to the second edition of *Alfred*, an epic poem defiantly focused on an English national hero: "whoever in these times founds a machinery on the mythology of the Greeks, will do so at his peril." In their different ways, both Wordsworth and Coleridge resisted the temptation and both recognized a danger not only to their poetic standards but to received ideas. Wordsworth paid tribute to the mystical origins of Greek mythology in *The Excursion* (IV.718–62), and the unimaginative and selfish commercialism of his own age caused him once to exclaim with wistful provocativeness that he would rather be "A Pagan suckled in a creed outworn." In spite of such intimations, he was more at home with the visionary dreariness of the north than with the "pleasure-ground" that he associated with Greece; his own recasting of "pastoral" is in part a rebuke to sentimental simplifications of landscape and to what he regarded as the pagan luxurance of the south. Coleridge had learned at school that Greek influences could produce poetic diction that was formulaic or evasive and separated from the native thew and sinew of Englishness (*Biographia*, I, 10); his more profound objection was to the limitations of the Greek imagination when compared to the

Hebraic Bible. He was out of sympathy with the contemporary taste for mythology that he associated with Deists and atheists. The mythologists tended to decode religion not as divinely ordained but as "the imaginative product of early man"; their interpretations were often literalist and reductive and substituted the rational for the mystical. The multiplicity and inventiveness of the mythological imagination pointed to origins that were human rather than divine: "the same phenomena were reflected in as many versions as there were cultures, religions, and individual poets or myth-makers."[18] Like the later Blake but for different reasons perhaps, Coleridge found in the Bible not only the truth and the moral foundation that was lacking in Greek mythology but a superior and more satisfying form of expression. The structures of the Christian imagination allowed greater purchase and greater freedom of operation for the religious sensibility. Just as Wordsworth was ultimately repelled by the "anthropomorphitism of the Pagan religion," so Coleridge observed that the Greeks "changed the ideas into finites, and these finites into *anthropomorphi*, or forms of men." This emphasis on form led to that statuesqueness that appealed to Shelley and Keats but that Coleridge interpreted as damagingly limited when compared to the more suggestive open-endedness of the Christian: "With them the form was the end. The reverse of this was the natural effect of Christianity; in which finites, even the human form, must, in order to satisfy the mind, be brought into connection with, and be in fact symbolical of, the infinite; and must be considered in some enduring, however shadowy and indistinct, point of view, as the vehicle or representative of moral truth." So Coleridge preferred Gothic architecture to Greek or Greco-Roman; following Schlegel, he admired the sublimity of the Gothic cathedral "where all distinction evades the eye" and equated it with *Hamlet* as opposed to the *Antigone* of Sophocles, a polarity further explored in a comparison between York Minster and the Pantheon.[19]

That Coleridge's evaluation reverses precisely the preferences of Shelley is highly suggestive: in aesthetic terms, Shelley's taste may have been more conservative but its implications involved a challenge and a threat to that system of values espoused and articulated by Coleridge and Wordsworth. Shelley preferred the Greco-Roman temple to the Christian cathedral just as he celebrated the positive potential of Greek mythology as embodied in sculpture and in literature and lamented those Christian prejudices that had turned "the wrecks of Greek mythology, as well as the little they understood of their philosophy, to purposes of deformity and falsehood" (*Prose*, p. 274). Shelley was horrified by the cruel God of the Old Testament whom he attacked in *Queen Mab*, and he found in youthful divinities such as Bacchus and Mercury an attractive alternative to Jehovah: for him the countenance of a statue of Bacchus "has a divine and supernatural beauty as one who walks through the world untouched by its corruptions, its corrupting cares; it looks like one who unconsciously yet with delight confers pleasure and peace" (*Prose*, p. 348). Shelley's Greek gods also display a sexual energy that is associated with a celebration of the body and of physical love. His Venus Anadyomene is characterized by "inextinguishable desire" and her smile and the "tongue lying against the lower lip as in the listlessness of passive joy, express love, still love" (*Prose*, p. 348). Shelley does not miss the opportunity to suggest a contrast: "Her pointed and pear-like bosom ever virgin – the virgin Mary might have this beauty, but alas! . . ."

Keats, too, was repelled by the excesses of Methodism and of evangelical Christianity represented, for example, by Hannah More's *Cheap Repository*, designed to counteract the effect of Thomas Paine's *The Age of Reason*, that had sold two million copies when it was first published in 1795. His 1816 sonnet "Written in Disgust of Vulgar Superstition" vividly expresses his sense of how "the mind of man is closely bound / In some black spell" while the contrasting virtues of his Pan and Apollo take on a much sharper definition and a new relevance when examined in the context of the sonnet. These antitheses were feelingly enumerated by Leigh Hunt, the radical journalist and poet of mythological propensities, who was a friend of both Shelley and Keats: "[The Greeks] dealt in loves and luxuries, in what resulted from the first laws of nature, and tended to keep humanity alive . . . [the Christians] have dealt in angry debates, in intolerance, in gloomy denouncements, in persecutions, in excommunications, in wars and massacres, in what perplexes, outrages, and destroys humanity" (*Examiner* [May 4, 1817]: 274). Keats would have agreed with Schlegel that the Greeks had invented the "poetry of gladness," and he gratefully identified in them "the Religion of the Beautiful, the Religion of Joy."[20] Shelley emphasized the laughter of the Greek gods and their enjoyment of "delight which nothing can destroy" (*Prose*, p. 347), and discovered in the Homeric Hymn to Mercury, which he translated, a poem that was "infinitely comical" (*Letters*, II, 218). The hymns and odes of both poets often employ the patterns of religious ritual to express a set of values that is heterodox and suggests an alternative to prevailing Christian structures. In both cases, the Greek world defines itself at least in part by its negative relationship to Christianity; it is held in tension by an opposite whose existence is understood but not always expressed. This is particularly true for Shelley: the full significance of his vision of Greece becomes clearer when it is set against Christianity, Praxiteles against Michelangelo, Paestum or Pompeii or the Greek temples against York Minster and the Gothic, Mercury and the Witch of Atlas against God the Father. That such preferences were ideologically charged and potentially subversive would have been evident to many contemporaries. Wordsworth responded to Keats's performance of the ode to Pan from *Endymion* by commenting: "a Very pretty piece of Paganism."[21] He was dismissing not only a poem which had little in common with his own poetic austerity but an influence that was in opposition to the Christian code.

III

A knowledge of classical literature, and in particular of the Greek language, was a widely recognized badge of exclusivity both among those who possessed it and those who did not. The classical languages were associated with the privileges of the ruling class, and Greek, in particular, was the preserve of a relatively small social group. Byron was aware of this and there were times when he was sharply critical of the narrow values of classicism; yet, when it suited him, he could also take advantage of it. So he wrote with an admiration at once patronizing and ostensibly baffled of the achievements of Keats who "without Greek / Contrived to talk about the Gods of late, / Much as they might have been supposed to speak" (*Don Juan*, XI.60.3– 5). Keats's apparent solecisms were not easily forgiven by some of the reviewers in the *Quarterly* and *Blackwood's* who criticized his intrusion into the world of Greek mythology as if it were a social impropriety; in contrast, even those reviewers who were shocked by Shelley's politics and his morality were prepared to concede the traditional solidity of his classical learning. Shelley himself reacted more generously by offering to teach Keats Greek and Spanish if he came to Italy. Keats had been taught Latin but not Greek at his grammar school, but in 1818 in a letter to his friend Reynolds he announced his intention of learning Greek, because he longed to "feast upon old Homer." Keats's feelings about the Greek language may be revealed by his description of the banquet in "Lamia": "Soft went the music the soft air along, / While fluent Greek a vowelled undersong / Kept up among the guests" (lines 199–201). There are intimations here of that kind of liberated musicality Keats identified with the nightingale who could sing "of summer in full-throated ease" (line 10). This vowelled expressiveness of the "warm south" can be contrasted to the "gabble" of Gaelic and to the deficiencies of the French language which is "perhaps the poorest one ever spoken since the jabbering in the Tower of Ba[bel]" (*Letters* I, 338, 155).

Through such slight but suggestive details we can sense the intensity of Keats's imagining and the power of the attraction he felt towards that world of Greek antiquity into which he had been admitted only in part by the chance of his education. There were many others who were convinced that the status not only of the Greek language but of classical studies in general was unjustified on intellectual and cultural grounds and who believed that it formed part of an exclusive and repressive system concerned with the perpetuation of the *status quo*. The problem can be traced back to the eighteenth century, where Romantic Hellenism had its roots. Prominent among those who had been excluded from an intimacy with the classics were such major influences on the emerging novel as Defoe and Richardson, neither of whom had the advantage of the public school education provided for Shelley and Byron at Eton and Harrow and both of whom vigorously rejected the ethos and influence of antiquity as they understood it. It is not an accident that the novel seems to have had its roots among the lower middle classes, and among women, most of whom had only a limited knowledge of the classics, since its insistence on the vernacular, the immediate, and a tangible social reality seems to place it at a distance from much of the poetry of the period, which so self-consciously locates itself in a tradition that is imported as well as national and that evolves its own specialized diction. This division is particularly sharp in the eighteenth century since so much of its best poetry defines itself directly or indirectly by its relation to classical models. Fielding is a notable exception among the novelists since he makes use of his classical poetics and his sense of the value of tradition and precedent to orientate his readers and to define and legitimize the virtue of his own enterprise as a writer of epic in prose. Yet Fielding's classicism may be one of his least significant contributions to the English novel. Much more significant was the position of women who were a central and increasingly powerful force both in the development of the novel and in its consumption as readers. With a few notable exceptions such as Elizabeth Carter, who translated Epictetus, most women had little or no knowledge of Latin while Greek was a still rarer acquisition; many would have been alienated by certain aspects of its system of values. The case against epic was put by Samuel Richardson who, like Defoe, strongly disapproved of the morality of the *Iliad* and the *Aeneid* and interpreted them from a perspective that had much in common with the world of feminine values that formed the center of his fiction; according to this reading, the example of Homer and Virgil was largely responsible for "the savage spirit that has actuated, from the earliest ages to this time, the fighting fellows, that, worse than lions or tigers, have ravaged the earth, and made it a field of blood."[22] Instead of this patriarchal and militaristic society with its premium on masculine *virtue* (or brutality), Richardson preferred to explore the dynamics of feminine psychology, the sharply focused conflicts of domestic life and the fierce complexities of sexual behavior.

Among those who criticized the exclusivity of the classics was Thomas Paine, who argued in *The Rights of Man* that an insistence on the classics was based on a desire to restrict intellectual curiosity. An unquestioning respect for the traditions of Greece and Rome was an obstacle to the proper perception of historical progress: "We do great injustice to ourselves by placing them in such a superior line." If the mists of antiquity could be dispersed, the ancient Greeks and Romans might find that the true advantage was not with them and that they should admire the moderns rather than the other way round." Paine may have experienced the anxiety of influence, but he proclaimed his unhesitating allegiance not to the system of the past but to the imperatives of individualism and subjectivity: "I followed exactly what my heart dictated. I neither read books, nor studied other people's opinions. I thought for myself."[23] Here the Rousseauistic language of the heart is smoothly but defiantly transmuted into the programmed assertion of intellectual independence.

Paine's friend William Blake declared an independence not only intellectual but imaginative: "We do not want either Greek or Roman models if we are but just & true to our own Imaginations," he declared in the preface to *Milton* in which he negotiated a fresh relationship not only with the predominant presence of Milton in English epic poetry but with the Greek and Roman models with which Milton himself had engaged. Los, the principle of the poetic imagination, gives voice in *Jerusalem* (10.20–1) to a resistance that is perhaps more inclusive but that represents, among other things, the response of the contemporary poet when threatened by the giant models of antiquity: "I must Create a System, or be enslav'd by another Mans / I will not Reason & Compare: my business is to Create." For Blake the struggle was exceptionally complex since it involved the sphere of art as well as that of literature. Under the influence of his patron William Hayley, he began to learn Greek (together with Hebrew and Latin), and in January 1803 he reported that he could read the language "as fluently as an Oxford scholar" (*Poetry and Prose*, p. 696). This was one manifestation of a predilection for the Greek example he had programmatically associated with his philosophy as an artist when in 1799 he defined "the purpose for which alone I live" as "in conjunction with such men as my friend [George] Cumberland, to renew the lost Art of the Greeks."[24] In 1800 he wrote prophetically to Cumberland about "the immense flood of Grecian light & glory which is coming on Europe" and predicted that even the "once stupid" inhabitants of London would "enter into an Emulation of Grecian manners" (*Poetry and Prose*, pp. 678–9). His own practice as an artist was influenced both by Greek models and by the mediating influence of his friend Flaxman who translated the world of Greek literature into a simple linearity that seemed to conform to the neoclassical principles articulated by Winckelmann and appealed to Blake.

Yet the restlessness of Blake's temperament and the ambivalence of his relations both with tradition and with authority prevented him from accepting the influence of classical models with any sustained tranquillity. Rather like Samuel Richardson, he compounded Greece and Rome and implicated both of them in the effects of militarism: "The Classics, it is the Classics! & not Goths nor Monks, that desolate Europe with Wars" ("On Homer's Poetry," *Poetry and Prose*, p. 267). This contagion of the negative influence could be detected at work in English literature: "Shakespeare & Milton were both curb'd by the general malady & infection from the silly Greek & Latin slaves of the Sword" (preface to *Milton, Poetry and Prose*, p. 95). Blake's critique characteristically included both the political and the aesthetic implications and consequences: "Rome & Greece swept Art into their maw & destroyd it . . . Grecian is Mathematic Form. Gothic is Living Form" ("On Virgil," *Poetry and Prose*, p. 267). This judgment not only suggests the effects of a false philosophy but links it to that inertia caused by an unimaginative and mechanical adherence to a code. Blake went further still in the aphoristic declarations accompanying the *Laocoon* in 1820. Here he identified the cultural conditions of the classical world as antagonistic to the artist and the imagination: "There are States in which all Visionary Men are accounted Mad Men such are Greece and Rome Such is Empire or Tax" (*Poetry and Prose*, p. 271). The vehemence of this accusation may derive some of its energy from Blake's consciousness of the homage he had once paid to Homer and of the debt he owed as a practicing artist to the achievement and the example of the Greeks. At this stage of his life he turned instead to the Bible, proclaiming that "The Old & New Testaments are the Great Code of Art" (*ibid.*, p. 271). The Bible is now invested by Blake with those imaginative virtues the classics frustrated and denied: "The Whole Bible is filld with Imagination & Visions from End to End & not with Moral Virtues that is the business of Plato & the Greeks & all Warriors The Moral Virtues are continual Accusers of Sin & promote Eternal Wars & Dominency over others" ("Annotations to Berkeley's *Siris*," *Poetry and Prose*, p. 653). Such uncomfortable attempts to reject or resist the power of classical influence or to deny its existence may reveal a characteristic instability in Blake, but they also point to an acute problem with power, authority and precedent and the true value of the classics experienced by a number of his contemporaries and their successors. In many of these cases Greek and Latin were regarded as equally at fault, interchangeable and almost synonymous.

Surprisingly, perhaps, Shelley was at first one of these, and his happy acknowledgment of Greek influence in *Hellas* was only achieved after a struggle and a long process of discovery. Although Shelley had read *The Enquirer* (1797) in which Godwin propounded the linguistic and moral claims of a study of the classics, he was unimpressed; as he told Godwin in 1812, "it certainly is my opinion . . . that the evils of acquiring Greek & Latin considerably overbalance the benefits." His primary argument was political: "Was not the government of republican Rome, & most of those of Greece as oppressive & arbitrary, as liberal of encouragement to monopoly as that of Great Britain is at present? And what do we learn from their poets? as you have yourself acknowledged somewhere 'they are fit for nothing but the perpetuation of the noxious race of heroes in the world'" (*Letters*, I, 316). This attack on the heroic principle brings Shelley close to Richardson and to Blake, and his association of Greece and Rome with the values of militarism again aligns him with Blake: "witness the interminable aggressions between each other of the states of Greece, & the thirst of conquest with which even republican Rome desolated the Earth" (*ibid.*, I, 317). Nor could the young Shelley admit a plausible case for the virtues of classical literature: "Did Greek & Roman literature refine the soul of Johnson, does it extend the thousand narrow bigots educated in the very bosom of *classicality*?" (*ibid.*, I, 318). What Shelley had in mind was the prescriptive philosophy set out in passages like the following from Johnson's preface to the *Dictionary of the English Language*: "Illiterate writers, will at one time or another, by public infatuation, rise into renown, who, not knowing the original import of words, will use them with colloquial licentiousness, confound distinction, and forget propriety." As Olivia Smith has pointed out, Johnson's statement "associates an ignorance of the classical languages with sexual immorality and the breaking down of class division."[25] Unlike some of those who argued against Johnson and those models of literacy that minimized the native power of the English language, Shelley did not insist on the alternative strength of the vernacular and its accessibility to a less privileged reading public. Yet the absoluteness of his radical politics prevented him from acknowledging any merit in a system of knowledge associated with a "despotism" in literature and with self-interest and expediency in politics.

Godwin replied at length and emphasized the value and relevance of the Greek and Roman historians, yet his endorsement does not acknowledge that the question was problematic (for Godwin's recommendations, see Shelley, *Letters*, I, 340–1). The interpretation of history was open to strong readings as a report to the Privy Council indicated in 1813 when it noted that in Godwin's own histories of Greece, France and England "every democratic sentiment is printed in italics."[26] Even an admiration for Greece did not always imply a sympathetic interest in the French Revolution or a concern for the rights of man. Flaxman, for example, had no difficulty in reconciling his neoclassical figurings of Greek mythology with conservative politics; the frigidities of his sculpture and the decorative simplicity of his designs do not suggest an affinity with turbulent or revolutionary energies.[27] Thomas Taylor, whose translations and commentaries on Plato and the neo-Platonists helped to shape the intellectual world of Romantic poetry and its richly symbolic narratives, engaged with Paine in *A Vindication of the Rights of Brutus* (1792); he specifically contrasted the connective particles of his version of Pausanias (1794) with contemporary France, which exhibited "anarchy and uproar, licentious liberty and barbaric rage, all the darkness of atheism, and all the madness of democratic power" (*The Description of Greece, by Pausanias* [London, 1794], preface). In particular, as Godwin must have known, Greece provided materials for those who, in an age of revolution, preferred an interpretation that was pointedly antidemocratic.[28]

Such factors must have influenced Shelley, who was not prepared to accept Godwin's collapsing of Greek and Roman into synonymous terms. Unlike Godwin, he could never fully accept the Roman virtues although he accorded them high praise in the *Defence of Poetry*. He continued to attribute to Roman civilization those negative qualities that had originally alienated him from the classical tradition as a whole, and he considered the Roman example inferior to that of Greece because the actions and forms of Roman social life "never seem to have been perfectly saturated with the poetical element." In contrast, Greek society came to embody for him that ideal balance between the social form and the life of the imagination that he analyzed and celebrated in the *Defence*. Shelley's interpretation of classical Greece posits a significant shift in the social structure: "The study of modern history is the study of kings, financiers, statesmen, and priests. The history of ancient Greece is the study of legislators, philosophers, and poets; it is the history of men, compared with the history of titles. What the Greeks were was a reality, not a promise" (*Prose*, p. 219).

Shelley's emotional and intellectual commitment to such a version of the Greek ideal had only become possible because he had been able to exempt Greece from those implications of code, system, privilege and even repression that had come to be included among the connotations of "the classics." Whatever its limitations and its "imperfections" in historical reality, Greece became for Shelley, as for many other Romantic Hellenists, a symbol of freedom, whether political, literary or intellectual. To some extent, this utopian reading of Greek history had been foreshadowed by a sequence of eighteenth-century works: these included Samuel Johnson's *Irene*, Thomson's *Liberty*, Glover's *Leonidas*, Collins's "Ode to Liberty," William Young's *The Spirit of Athens*, and poems by Warton, Gray and Falconer. Of all these writers, only William Falconer had direct knowledge of Greece, yet the strong libertarian emphasis of their interpretations was activated rather than impeded by such abstract engagement. Shelley, in his turn, imagined a country, or perhaps a city, of the mind "Based on the crystalline sea / Of thought and its eternity" (*Hellas*, lines 698–9; see "Ode to Liberty," lines 61–90). This translates abstraction itself into a strength and an intellectual continuity, but the libertarian emphasis was rarely divorced from more immediate political considerations whether directly or by implication. It can often be read not only as an overt identification with certain aspects of the Greek tradition or the Greek political cause but as a comment on or a reaction to the current disposition of British and European politics.

Almost too obviously, perhaps, the popularity of *Leonidas* during the period of the Napoleonic threat was based on an English capacity to identify with the Greeks and to interpret the French as the successors of the Persians. The battle of Marathon in which the Greeks had repelled the Persian invasion exercised such a special attraction, according to James Mill, that "even as an event in English history" it eventually became more important than the battle of Hastings.[29] When Marathon features in "The isles of Greece" (*Don Juan*, canto III, 689ff), Byron's most plangent expression of Greek patriotic feeling is ironically qualified by a "complex act of poetic ventriloquism" when it is delivered by a poet who is a "sad trimmer," and it is directed, at least in part, towards the politics of England.[30] Both *Childe Harold* and Turkish tales such as *The Giaour* were concerned with the contiguities and contrasts of Western and Eastern culture and carried a reflexive significance for the British reader. It is not surprising, therefore, to find that reviewers of *The Revolt of Islam* quite correctly perceived that

Shelley's epic was more centrally concerned with British politics and British standards of morality than with the conflict between Greece and the Ottoman Empire which provides one of its major narrative threads. Here, as so often in the more interesting examples of Romantic Hellenism, the materials are open to interpretation and dispute. Even in its apparent abstraction, the Greek example remains a potential to be realized, a model to be engaged with for the reader or interpreter, a vital and contentious site for the exercise of the contemporary imagination.

Notes

1 J. Mordaunt Crook, *The Greek Revival: Neo-Classical Attitudes in British Architecture* (London: John Murray, 1972), p. 97. For a list of Greek Revival buildings, see p. 98. For Gothic and classical and their coexistence, see Butler, *Romantics, Rebels and Reactionaries: English Literature and its Background 1760–1830* (Oxford University Press, 1981), pp. 17–18.

2 Hegel is cited by Walter Pater in his essay on Winckelmann, *The Renaissance: Studies in Art and Poetry* (1873; reprinted, London: Macmillan, 1928). Goethe's remark can be found in *Conversations of Goethe with Eckermann*, trans. John Oxenford (London and Toronto: Dent and Dutton, 1930), p. 173 (February 16, 1827).

3 *Winckelmann: Writings on Art*, ed. David Irwin (London: Phaidon, 1972), p, 144.

4 See *Henry Fuseli 1741–1825* (London: Tate Gallery, 1975), plate 10. In fact, the fragments are Roman and come from the Colossus of Constantine.

5 For temples in Keats, see Ian Jack, *Keats and the Mirror of Art* (Oxford: Clarendon Press, 1967). For alternative religions, see Homer Brown, "Creations and Destroyings: Keats's Protestant Hymn, the 'Ode to Psyche,'" *Diacritics* 6 (Winter 1976): 49–56.

6 The translator of *The Symposium* was Floyer Sydenham whose translation of the complete works of Plato was finished by Thomas Taylor and eventually published in 1804. Only one complete edition of Plato in a modern language and only one in Greek had appeared since 1602, although the Renaissance had produced approximately thirty. Shelley insisted that those who did not know Greek "ought not to be excluded by this prudery to possess an exact and comprehensive conception of the history of man."

7 See Timothy Webb, "Shelley and the Religion of Joy," in *Studies in Romanticism* 15 (1976): 357–82.

8 See Mario Praz, "Herculaneum and European Taste," in *Magazine of Art* 33 (1939): 684–93, 727; see also Wolfgang Leppmann, *Pompeii in Fact and Fiction* (London: Elek Books, 1966).

9 August Wilhelm Schlegel, *Vorlesungen über dramatische Kunst und Literatur*. Delivered at Vienna, 1808, published 1809–11; translated into English as *A Course of Lectures on Dramatic Art and Literature* by J. Black in 1815. The reference is to lecture 3 where Schlegel directly relates the openness of Greek theatre and the publicity of its transactions to the ideals of Greek democracy. See also the more general account in lecture 1 of the formative influence of natural environment: "The whole of their art and their poetry is expressive of the consciousness of this harmony of all their faculties. They have invented the poetry of gladness."

10 For travelers, see: C. A. Hutton, "The Travels of 'Palmyra' Wood in 1750–51," *Journal of Hellenic Studies* 47 (1927): 102–28; S. H. Weber, *Voyages and Travels in Greece, the Near East and Adjacent Regions previous to the year 1801*, Catalogue of the Gennadius Library, American School of Classical Studies at Athens, 1953; Paul Fussell, Jr., "Patrick Brydone; the Eighteenth-Century Traveller as Representative Man," *Bulletin of the New York Public Library* 66 (1962): 349–63; James M. Osborn, "Travel Literature and the Rise of Neo-Hellenism in England," *Bulletin of the New York Public Library* 67 (1963): 279–300; Fani-Maria Tsigakou, *The Rediscovery of Greece: Travellers and Painters of the Romantic Era* (London: Thames and Hudson, 1981); Richard Stoneman, ed. *A Literary Companion to Greece* (Harmondsworth: Penguin, 1984).

11 For Troy, see Terence Spencer, "Robert Wood and the Problem of Troy," in *Journal of the Warburg and Courtauld Institutes* 20 (1957): 75–105. For topographical authenticity, see Webb, *English Romantic Hellenism 1700–1824* (Manchester and New York: Manchester University Press and Barnes and Noble, 1982); pp. 8–9, hereafter cited as ERH.

12 The English travelers were Charles Perry, Richard Pococke, Robert Wood, Richard Chandler, J. B. S. Morritt, E. D. Clarke and (after Byron's excursion) Edward Dodwell, T. S. Hughes and H. W. Williams. Topographical poets included Thomas Lisle, W. R. Wright, J. D. Carlyle, Richard Polwhele, Charles Kelsall and William Haygarth. Other notable topographers included William Leake. For Byron's review of Leake, see *Collected Miscellaneous Prose*, ed. Andrew Nicholson (Oxford: Clarendon Press, 1991), pp. 48–50.

13 *New Letters of Robert Southey*, ed. Kenneth Curry, 2 vols. (New York and London: Columbia University Press, 1965) II. 105. Schlegel wrote: "The Grecian idea of humanity consisted in a perfect concord and proportion between all the powers, – a natural harmony. The moderns . . . have arrived at the consciousness of the internal discord which renders such an idea impossible; and hence the endeavour of their poetry is to reconcile these two worlds between which we find ourselves divided, and to melt them indissolubly into each other," *A Course of Dramatic Lectures*, 1.16–17. For attitudes to war in epic poetry, see Stuart Curran, *Poetic Form and British Romanticism* (Oxford and New York: Oxford University Press, 1986), ch. 7.

14 Cited in Howard Mills, *Peacock: His Circle and his Age* (Cambridge University Press, 1969), p. 23. See also: "If the world at large ever discovered how unmodern the classics really are, the classicists would lose their jobs as teachers."

15 *The Diary of Benjamin Robert Haydon*, ed. Willard Bissell Pope, 5 vols. (Cambridge: Harvard University Press, 1960) II, 76; "On the Judgment of Connoisseurs being preferred to that of Professional Men," cited in Jack, *Keats and the Mirror of Art*, p. 35.

16 A. J. Kuhn, "English Deism and the Development of Romantic Mythological Syncretism," *PMLA* 71 (1956): 1094. See also Butler, *Romantics, Rebels and Reactionaries*, pp. 129–37 and Frank E. Manuel, *The Eighteenth Century Confronts the Gods* (Cambridge: Harvard University Press, 1959). Shelley's debts to the syncretic mythology are suggestively explored by Stuart Curran, *Shelley's Annus Mirabilis: The Maturing of an Epic Vision* (San Marino, California: Huntington Library, 1975).

17 "The crucial fact about the Classicism of Shelley and Peacock is that it does evolve into paganism – not so much an aesthetic as an ideological cult, an interpretation of man's oldest beliefs which stresses first that they are inventions, and second that they belong to a natural rather than a supernatural order. What is more . . . the cult of sexuality is celebratory and joyous; it shows up in its most

unfavourable light the authoritarian, ascetic and life-denying tendencies of Hebraic Christianity," Butler, *Romantics, Rebels and Reactionaries*, p. 131.

18 Butler, *Romantics, Rebels and Reactionaries*, p. 82.

19 *Coleridge's Miscellaneous Criticism*, ed. Thomas M. Raysor (London: Constable, 1936), p. 148; see also pp. 191–3, 149–50.

20 William Sharp, *The Life and Letters of Joseph Severn* (London, 1829), p. 29.

21 Cited in Robert Gittings, *John Keats*, corr. edn. (London: Heinemann, 1970), p. 167.

22 *Selected Letters of Samuel Richardson*, ed. John Carroll (Oxford: Clarendon Press, 1964), p. 134.

23 *The Complete Writings of Thomas Paine*, ed. Philip S. Foner (New York, 1945), I, 123. For an account of Paine's views, see A. Owen Aldridge, "Thomas Paine and the Classics," *Eighteenth-Century Studies* I (1967–8): 370–80. See also, *Complete Writings*, I, 406.

24 *The Letters of William Blake with related documents*, ed. Geoffrey Keynes, 3rd edn. (Oxford: Clarendon Press, 1980), p. 6.

25 Olivia Smith, *The Politics of Language 1791–1819* (Oxford: Clarendon Press, 1984), p. 13.

26 Ford K. Brown, *The Life of William Godwin* (London and Toronto: Dent and Dutton, 1926), p. 227.

27 For Flaxman's attitude and his refusal to meet the French painter Jacques-Louis David because his hands were "dyed beyond purification," see Hugh Honour, *Neo-Classicism* (Harmondsworth: Penguin 1968), p. 71.

28 See, for example, John Gillies, *History of Ancient Greece* (1786) which insists on "the incurable evils inherent in every form of Republican policy" and emphasizes "the inestimable benefits, resulting to Liberty itself, from the lawful domination of hereditary Kings, and the steady operation of well-regulated Monarchy" (from the Dedication to George III). See also William Mitford, the "Tory Historian of Greece" whose history appeared in five volumes between 1784 and 1810. Byron detected in his work "wrath, and partiality" while Coleridge took note of Mitford's zeal against democratic government.

29 *The Collected Works of John Stuart Mill*, ed. J. M. Robson *et al.* (Toronto University Press, 1963), 11, 273.

30 *Poetical Works*, v, 701n. See also *Childe Harold*, II.836ff.

59

THE ROMANTIC CALLING OF THINKING: STANLEY CAVELL ON THE LINE WITH WORDSWORTH

Edward Duffy

Source: *Studies in Romanticism* 37 (1998), 615–45.

> Everyman has to learn the points of compass again as often as he awakes, whether from sleep or from abstraction.
>
> —Henry David Thoreau, *Walden*

More than a decade ago, Jerome McGann's *The Romantic Ideology* offered itself as an example of what Stanley Cavell calls "philosophical criticism": i.e. "a mode of criticism [that] can be thought of as the world of a particular work [or of a particular culture] brought to consciousness of itself."[1] The culture brought to light in McGann's book was less romantic literature itself than its professionalization in a literary academy, given to "an uncritical absorption of Romanticism's own self-representations,"[2] and thus endlessly replicating a German ideology that evades real material contradictions by displacing them into a supposedly independent or prior world of Ideas. For the exposition of these "dramas of displacement and idealization" (McGann 1), Marjorie Levinson's account of "Tintern Abbey" has become a model of clarity. According to Levinson, Wordsworth's "textual procedures transform lived contradiction into the appearance of aesthetic complexity."[3] These verbal procedures contrive to overlook fissure, scandal and impasse so as to secure the insight of "heterocosmic affirmation" (Levinson 12) and the satisfactions of "achieved form" (Levinson 1).

If the burden of this position is that professional students of romantic literature must be more guarded against the seductive constructions of their subject, then Cavell's counter example from the neighboring discipline of philosophy is that of a thinker finding himself unguardedly drawn toward romantic texts when, against the grain of his own professional commitments, he hears them directly addressing his condition, as if they know where to find him and how to find him out. At the outset of *In Quest of the Ordinary*, Cavell thinks out loud about his progress toward romanticism: "In the first of the lectures collected here, I note a perplexity that began making its presence felt to me some ten years ago. As I was trying to follow the last part, part 4, of my book *The Claim of Reason* to a moment of conclusion, my progress kept being deflected by outbreaks of romantic texts. ... After completing the manuscript, I would from time to time ask myself for some account of this interference. What is philosophy for me, or what has it begun showing itself to be, that it should call for, and call for these, romantic orientations or transgressions?"[4] This philosopher finds himself drawn to texts like Wordsworth's "Immortality" ode and Coleridge's "Ancient Mariner" because in them he finds allegories of what constantly provokes and drives his own thinking: the interlocked claims of skepticism and the ordinary. By "skepticism," Cavell initially means the "astonished" finding of modern philosophy that when any human subject would approach either the external world or other minds, it runs up against an unbreachable line, behind which what would be known either as the thing in itself or another's innerness must withhold itself. Commencing with Descartes' methodical doubt, this philosophical history achieves a strained extremity of statement in Hume, and then (as Cavell tells the story) comes to an unstable and not totally satisfying "settlement" in Kant. The Kantian settlement falls short of complete satisfaction because it makes the possibility of knowing dependent on the *conditions* of our knowledge, conditions schematized in the categories of the understanding. It makes do with recovering a world of our own making and imposition. Its elaborate architectonic does save knowledge but only on the condition that something called the thing-in-itself be turned out of doors as *necessarily* inaccessible. This is a settlement of things to which at least a piece of Cavell replies with a sardonic "thanks for nothing" (*IQ* 53).

But that is not the end of the story of skepticism as Cavell tells it. Going on from Kant, he reads Wittgenstein as an "inheritor of the task of Kant's transcendental logic, namely to demonstrate, or articulate, the a priori fit of the categories of human understanding with the objects of human understanding, that is, with objects," but an inheritor who would lead the world-disclosing authority of Kantian condition back home to the ordinary or "everyday" use of words.[5] In his career in philosophy, Cavell eventually comes to testify that this Wittgensteinian appeal to the everyday "home" (*TN* 32) of our every word was "counting on" something more satisfyingly worked out in the look and sound of Emerson and Thoreau's prose as their writings address "the problematic of the day, the everyday, the near, the low, the common" (*TN* 81) with nothing more fundamental to "go on" than the "writer's faith"[6] that (in Cavell's constant emphasis) our *every word* bespeaks "some intimacy between language and world" (*TN* 81)—or some "intimacy lost"[7] in which our "terms as conditions" (*IQ* 27) are seen not to "limit" but "to constitute our access to the world."[8]

From the standpoint of the writer's faith, what most effectively but ever so casually blocks our access to the world is what, still thinking of Wittgenstein but quoting Hamlet, Cavell calls "your philosophy" (*MW* xxvi). In Cavell's account of it, the work which *Philosophical Investigations* sets itself is, by grammatical investigations, to bring up to the light of perspicuous representation the terms or conditions of our existence. But necessary to this "clearing up the ground of language on which we stand" is a complementary work of destruction: specifically, the dismantling of an entire edifice of philosophical construction.[9] To "your philosophy," then, Cavell's Wittgenstein would apply what he calls his "therapies" (*Investigations* §133), internal to which is an endlessly called for diagnosis of how the philosophical impositions of our thinking—what Cavell calls "the desire for thought, running out of control" (*TN* 54)—deaden us to the world delivered to us in our terms and conditions.

The nearly terminal patient addressed by Wittgenstein's therapies is that hardly uncommon cast of mind that takes the essence of thought to be *logic*, "a *super*-order between—so to speak—*super*-concepts" (*Investigations* §97; Wittgenstein's emphases). To illustrate what Wittgenstein, the practitioner of grammatical investigations, mocks as philosophy's "disabling sublimizings" (*TN* 55), take this one example of his "relentless project to . . . de-sublimize thought" (*TN* 71). Appositely enough, this exemplary counter to your philosophy's drive toward "sublim[ing] the logic of our language" (*Investigations* §38) articulates the beginnings of an inquiry into the language game of *games*. To the easy and "logical" assumption that card games, board games and athletic games *must* possess some one thing (a logical entity professionally known as a universal) common to them all, a voice in the *Investigations* fairly shouts back, "Dont think, but look" (*Investigations* §66). Look at how we competent users of the language cast the net of the word *game* so confidently, widely and methodically not because of one essential feature common to all its applications, but because, in our form of life, the word has extended itself along a weave of "family resemblances" much as "in spinning a thread we twist fibre on fibre. And the strength of the thread does not reside in the fact that some one fibre runs through its whole length, but in the overlapping of many fibers" (*Investigations* §67). One desired result of such a grammatical investigation is to bring up to the light the tissues of relation that constitute the schema or *holdings* of a word; one major obstacle to pursuing or even seeing the point of such an investigation is the preconceived and specifically philosophical idea that such tissues of relation are only various wrappers behind any and each one of which there lurks the unalloyed prize of the one common thing that justifies their one common name.

That such words of ours as have fallen victim to "philosophical pre-occupation" (*MW* 238) promise (false) generalizing ascents but leave us foundered in "disabling sublimizings" (*TN* 55) is worked out in a powerfully compressed metaphor in Remark 107 of the *Investigations*:

The more minutely [my translation for *genauer*, rendered by Anscombe as *narrowly*] we examine actual language, the sharper becomes the conflict between it and our requirement. (For the crystalline purity of logic was, of course, not a *result of investigation*: it was a requirement.) The conflict becomes intolerable; the requirement is now in danger of becoming empty.—We have got on to slippery ice where there is no friction and so in a certain sense the conditions are ideal, but also, just because of that, we are unable to walk. We want to walk: then [Cavell's translation, for the significance of which see *TN* 55] we need *friction*. Back to the rough ground!

Wittgenstein refigures the transcendence of our crystalline "requirement" into ice underfoot so as to bring out how the drive toward sublimity must, if successful on its own terms, disable that "taking steps" (with, by, and from every word) which Cavell proposes as his picture of philosophical work in progress. Our words of philosophical ambition would shake from their heels any remnant of the rough ground, which provides the traction not ready to foot in the uniformly slick and precisely *a-poretic* surface of the crystalline. Such words would fly upward to the dictates of "our requirement," and "just because of that," writes Cavell, they are "in danger of becoming empty" (*TN* 56). Impressed into such service, our words are in danger of declining into "frozen slides of the motion of our ordinary words, becoming the language of noone, unspeakable moments which refuse the value of the experience of ordinary words, their shared memories" (*TN* 64).

Cavell can never get (and would never wish to get) skepticism definitively behind him because, by his accounting, skepticism is "the *discovery* of the everyday, a discovery of exactly *what* it is that skepticism would deny" (*IQ* 170; Cavell's emphasis) as it seeks to bring about an epistemological utopia (a nowhere) where, in wish and fantasy, "the connection between my claims of knowledge and the objects upon which [they fall . . . would occur] without my intervention, apart from my agreements."[10] This avoidance of the human is, Cavell insists, all too human: "We understandably do not like our concepts to be based on what matters to us (something Wittgenstein once put by saying 'Concepts . . . are the expression of our interests' (§570); it makes our language seem unstable and the instability seems to mean what I have expressed as my being responsible for whatever stability our criteria may have, and I do not want this responsibility; it mars my wish for sublimity" (*CH* 92). Having found that we have all too "casually" pledged our epistemological allegiance to the raised banner of sublimity, we fall into the grip of feeling that to do their work our words must not be our words. Kicking against the pricks of these poor things of our own, we try to "unleash" them "from our criteria . . . to unleash our voices from them"; we seek to "abdicate such responsibility as we have over" them (*CH* 22). We seek to empty our words of ourselves.

To get this tangled drama of avoidance perspicuously clear, Cavell repeatedly stages the play of the mind in the act of finding that its own regnant idea of intellectual rigor is driving it toward a scene of self-recognition where the ghostly selections of its "requirement" are to see themselves as blindly devoted to emptiness. In the trenchant accents of a Greek chorus, Cavell concludes "in a word" that "the motive to skepticism" is "this emptiness itself. Anything short of the ideal is arbitrary, artificial, language at its most mediocre. I must empty out my contribution to words, so that language itself, as if beyond me, exclusively takes over the responsibility for meaning" (*TN* 56). In aversion to this imposed ideal, Cavell dates the dawning of his philosophical calling from the moment when he found himself attracted to the "stubborn, accurate superficiality" (*IQ* 129) of first Austin and then Wittgenstein and so went on to see his way clear toward what he would call Emerson's stand and "mastertone" of a *partiality* to the human voice, a partiality such that Cavell, with arrogance aforethought, would announce himself as a recovering voice of philosophy out to turn around this philosophy's "drive to the inhuman" (*IQ* 26) and the "monstrous" (*IQ* 141) by making "the recovery of the (of my) (ordinary) (human) voice" both his own business and that of his profession (*IQ* 26).

To Cavell as to Wittgenstein before him, the goal of his thinking is "perspicuous representation," but the incentive to get on the way of this thinking begins with finding oneself stopped dead on a plane of ice, where there is no footing, no possibility of going on. "Philosophy begins in loss, in finding yourself at a loss" (*TN* 114). It begins with the acknowledgement that precisely there where you thought your thought was getting to the bottom of things, it was plunging you ever deeper into the disabling pit of a *selva oscura*, the terminus of whose darkly descending way is, as in Dante's hell, the coldly imprisoning fixity of ice.

In his reading of the "Ancient Mariner," Cavell sees the poem's frozen antarctic wastes as an objective correlative of the mariner's initial way of being (or not being) in the world. For Cavell, the deep freeze of these latitudes caps "an enactment . . . of skepticism's casual step to the path of intellectual numbness" (*TN* 57). Keeping the albatross steadily in sight as decisive for the mariner's condition, Cavell nonetheless reads the reputedly gratuitous and perverse act of killing it not as the mariner's original transgression but as the fated consequence of his casual repudiation of the ordinary, as this is allegorized in the mariner's ship "having passed the line [and found itself] driven to the cold Country"—the latter a topography of the rigidly frozen mindlessness we're all headed for when we seek to sublime the logic of our language beyond the terms or "lines" of "the forms of life which grow language" (*CR* 170). Cavell's mariner, then, is a representative user of our possibilities for thinking, who has let himself become "enchanted by a way of thinking" (*IQ* 47) that drives him toward a condition of icy emptiness, fixation and loss of progress "not through ignorance . . . but through a refusal of knowledge, a denial, or a repression of knowledge, say even a killing of it" (*IQ* 51). The mariner is each and all of us, who at some time will be bewitched by a picture of knowing as "a harmony, a concord, a union, a transparence," and so come to view "our actual successes in knowing [as] poor things" (*CR* 440).

In Cavell's reading of the "Ancient Mariner," the poem's action commences with a disowning of knowledge and drives on toward an evisceration of the human. In counterpoint with this loss at sea, Cavell hears Wordsworth's "Immortality" ode as tuned in the key of a *natality* ode drawn toward the founding "strength" of (re)birth. Precisely because this "text of recovery" acknowledges that the hour of splendor in the grass is gone, it would find a way of letting time lapse toward the possibility of "a newborn Day" (*IQ* 75), where the initial "visionary gleam" is not said to fade *out*, but to fade *into* something identified as "the light of common day." By the light of this interpretation, then, the poem describes not so much vision's loss as its migration toward the low and near, a migration to be managed by what Cavell trusts can be a happier disillusionment in which "the vision is preserved in the way it is forgone" (*IQ* 75). That our childhood, as it were, abandons us does not mean that the only remaining way for us to recall or participate in it would be to dead-end ourselves into a "sack of nostalgia" (*IQ* 74). Nor does it mean that we are to let go of childhood in a "lapse of memory" (*IQ* 74). Rather, the abandonment of our childhood—its leaving of us and our leaving of it—proposes a "success of forgoing" (*IQ* 74), an *activity* "of bearing childhood as gone, as having become what we are, sharing our fate" (*IQ* 73–74). One's childhood is gone, and I am left here bearing it on this edge of time and called to acknowledge it. Condemned thus to the fact and meaning of *this* childhood—sentenced to "being the odd one one is, one's having that to recollect and imitate that one has" (*IQ* 75)— one is called away from any forlorn effort to get even for this, and called toward such "mornings of mourning" as would lead one to accept the verdict of reality and time, and so refit oneself for life.

If the ordinary in the light in which we routinely live has become a world of death to which we have become dead, then Cavell hears Wordsworth calling for a replacement or transfiguring of this ordinary with "lively origination, or say birth; with interest" (*IQ* 75)—that interest which Wordsworth so uncommonly interested himself in, and which Cavell computes as analogous with Thoreau and Emerson's equally alarming appeals for us "to take an interest in our lives,"[11] as if the open secret shared by these nineteenth-century thinkers is that our condition is such that "nothing (now) makes an impression on us" (*TN* 92) because we have succumbed to a death-like "torpor" where, in Wordsworth's diagnosis, our craving for "gross and violent stimulants"[12] constitutes an exact and numbingly redundant set of symptoms for how, as he says in a famous sonnet, "For this, for everything, we are out of tune; / It moves us not." For Cavell, the "drama of concepts" (*IQ* 37) played out in the "Immortality" ode departs from an aggrieved sense of abandonment in a world gone dead, and goes on to a call for "interest," the latter a turning toward what, amid all the debris of our life, still remains charged with attraction for us, its call on us the sign and promise of our "heaven-born freedom."

In directing interest and giving thought to the ordinary terms of our existence, Cavell's Wittgensteinian investigations, Emersonian essays and romantic readings would bring up to "complete clarity" not only *what* the terms or conditions of our existence are, but (*Investigations* §242) *that* these terms express the interests and indeed the necessities of the life-form of us talkers. Our attunements in language register what, at the level not of opinions but of forms of life, counts for us, and one cardinal, say hingeing, necessity of the form of life of us talkers is paradoxically the necessity of our freedom. For if there is to be any counting or criteria or grammar at all—if, that is, there is to be any language at all—then we have to be the ones originating it, all our countings a matter of what counts or matters for us. Cavell succinctly and powerfully develops this paradox of our necessary freedom in a reading of Emerson's "Fate," which he understands as bent on resituating in language the twin Kantian standpoints of freedom and necessity. Bearing down on a short and seemingly lightweight run of Emersonian sentences, Cavell makes them yield the provocative contention that although we are "victims of meaning," with the "character" of our language wording our world into intelligibility and so laying down before us what Cavell calls the "fatefulness of the ordinary," it is still the case that our "Lordship" (of a language that is no one else's but our own) "polarizes" this subjection to language. If we are fated to the ordinary and thus victims of meaning, we still "have a say in what we mean, [and] our antagonism to fate, to which we are fated, and in which our freedom resides, is as a struggle with the language we emit, of our character with itself" (*IQ* 40). In addressing itself to the "old knots of fate, freedom, and foreknowledge," the character of Emerson's "Fate," then, "is meant to enact" an attractively penned (and pent) "struggle against itself, hence of language with itself, for its freedom" (*IQ* 40).

If the emphasis of Wittgenstein's *Investigations* falls on bringing up to "total clarity" the "language of life" (*CH* 21), by a contrast mostly of emphasis, the nineteenth-century writing exemplified in the sentences of Emerson would raise itself up as a standard for the animating "life of language" (*CH* 21). With the genius of Emerson's writing said by Cavell to spring "from an Intuition of what counts to a Tuition of how to recount it" (*TN* 102), such writing is less interested in the assertion of any determinate theses or propositions than in giving voice and expression to the "*partiality*" of thinking as such, "what Kant calls (and Freud more or less calls) its incentive or interest (*Triebfeder* [a German word that, in this case of thinking, speaks of the trigger or spring for our drive toward intelligibility])" (*CH* 42). What Cavell calls the "constitution of Emerson's writing," then, is conceived to be a series or course of words edifyingly laid out before its thinking readers in the hope of "attracting [this thinking of theirs] to its partiality" (*CH* 42). For our partiality—what counts or matters for us—is "the life of language," what animates it and brings it to life.

Perhaps nowhere does Cavell so dramatically represent this undergirding of the grammar of our life-forms by our shared partialities of incentive and interest than in one highly charged and carefully staged moment of self-fashioning in the writing of *The Claim of Reason* 94–95. The scene is an argument about the natural and the conventional. But then, in a groundbreaking access to and of desire, there rises up before the eye and progress of the argument two pages of densely packed and breathlessly performed parenthesis, in which the language philosopher represents himself as drawn irresistibly to the question why we ever so much as begin to articulate the world into such conceptual constellations as we find in widest commonality around us spread. Cavell's answer (which he computes as fragments toward an "economics" and an "aesthetics" of speech) is that everything given us in the counts and recountings of our shared language traces what has mattered or counted for us. Around this axis, the lathe of the strenuous tongue shears out a continually reforming "constitution" of words. Since we count only what counts or matters to us, the play of our re-countings should be keyed to this question of what matters to us. They should be pitched toward what Cavell calls "the achievement [or "exit"] of desire" (*IQ* 28).

In reference to *Walden*—a book that "takes it upon itself to tell all and say nothing" (*CR* 95)—Cavell puts the point more openly (still in 95–96 of *The Claim of Reason*): "If we formulate the idea that valuing underwrites asserting as the idea that interest informs telling or talking generally, then we may say that the degree to which you talk of things in ways that hold no interest for you . . . is the degree to which you consign yourself to nonsensicality, stupify yourself. . . . I think of this consignment as a form not so much of dementia as of what amentia ought to mean, a form of mindlessness. It does not appear unthinkable that the bulk of an entire culture, call it the public discourse of the culture, the culture thinking aloud about itself . . . should become ungovernably inane." In Cavell's account of it, then, Thoreau's ambition "to be a track-repairer somewhere in the orbit of the earth" (*SW* 98, in "Sounds," *Walden*) is precisely not the pushing of a private agenda. To the contrary, Thoreau's draw toward *resolution* as "[comprising] both hardening and melting, the total concentration of resources and the total expenditure of them" (*SW* 109) is directed toward "speaking of necessaries, and speaking with necessity" (*TN* 81), as these necessities will be found to be encrypted in our ordinary and publicly shared language, the face value of whose every word is a fragment of our natural history and thus an open secret about what (in Cavell's brashly unfashionable emphasis) the human has *naturally* set its heart on.

For Cavell, the achievement of desire has become the one pressing philosophical task, a task signally taken on by Emerson and Thoreau but also to be found in Wittgenstein. Take the latter's remark that "it is what human beings *say* that is true and false; and they agree in the *language* they use" (*Investigations* §241). The point of this apparently flat piece of information is that the agreement in question is not agreement in opinions but in forms of life. It is agreement in what matters. And discovering the depth of this systematic *Übereinstimmung* or "mutual attunement" was not, Cavell insists, "Wittgenstein's intellectual goal." It was his "instrument" (*CR* 30), because "nothing is deeper than the fact, or extent, of [this] agreement itself" (*CR* 32). It is the bedrock organon—what we have to go on—for exposing false necessities and discovering what really counts for us. So, in Wittgenstein's description of philosophy as "[leaving] everything as it is" (*Investigations* §124), Cavell hears not reassurance for the temperamentally conservative but the most radical requirement for "the most forbearing act of thinking (this may mean the most thoughtful) to let true need, say desire, be manifest and be obeyed" (*TN* 45).

In Cavell's accounting of romanticism, its practitioners are drawn or attracted to an urgently practical and never ending *finding* of one's self not as some fixed (and fixating) noumenal essence but as the incessantly onward *activity* of finding what, as a presence not to be put by, rightly and strongly attracts us. Again *Walden* is an apposite example. To Cavell, this is a book whose edification would put the manifestly distracted minds and even more scattered wills of its readers on the spot. It would call on its neighbors and readers "who are said to live in New England" to get (back) on track by exposing themselves to this writing's exemplarily different way of inhabiting or settling or "repeopling" the woods (and the words) of this new world. A romanticism that is thus "in quest of the ordinary" is not out to force an intellectual fix. As epitomized in Wordsworth's "wise passiveness" and emblematized in Cavell's emphasis on the openingly receptive hand of acknowledgement, it is turned outward to the conditions of our human experience, waiting for it to be declared in these conditions where we find ourselves—what, not as stasis but as a stance or standpoint, is our position or interest in all this. Or as it is put by the query from *Walden*, which Cavell placed as the epigraph to his *The World Viewed*: "Why do precisely these objects which we behold make a world?"[13]

Our attunements expressed through our criteria bear witness to what has mattered to us, what we have found *worth* saying. How we count points to what counts for us; and by this directive or route, Cavell would affiliate the writers he directly and philosophically inherits with modern prophets and romantics like Rousseau, endlessly preaching that we have fouled our own nest not by ignorance but by alienation, not, that is, by some blank deficit of knowledge but by the creation and pursuit of a pack of false necessities, in whose tumultuously raised cry we have become hounded strangers to ourselves, every one his own albatross, and so every one called to his own redemption. No wonder, then, that the academic tent or meeting Cavell says he would be most at home in would be something called the "Department of Redeeming" (*Q&A* 238) an institutional address where a philosopher like him could one day teach romantic literature as "texts of recovery" and another give more or less straight *Ethics 303* lectures on how the rational basis of moral argument consists not in any as yet unrealized purchase on universally demonstrable truths but in methods whose point and aim is "a knowledge of our own position, of where we stand; in short to a knowledge and definition of ourselves" (*CR* 312). The specifically romantic agenda of this Department of Redeeming would be, as Cavell resolves, "to find what degrees of freedom we have in this condition [of bondage to emptiness and false necessities], to show that it is at once needless yet somehow, because of that, all but necessary, inescapable, to subject its presentation of necessities to diagnosis, in order to find truer necessities" (*IQ* 9). This "romantic quest which [Cavell] is happy to join" is in the business of recovering what William Blake calls in several places "the lineaments of gratified desire," as these will be endlessly articulated by whatever, according to the economics and esthetics of speech, we have found worth saying.

In her forcefully compressed manifesto of New-Historicist critical aims, Marjorie Levinson writes that she would "compel a tired organic apparatus to reveal its fabulous fusions" (Levinson 10). Despite protestations to the contrary, this mission statement sounds suspiciously like a renouncing of Wordsworth and all his works. Uncannily, though, Levinson's words read like a virtual transcription of Cavell's clearly appreciative description of the romantic literary work as both a "book of losses" and a "text of recovery." A transcription, however, with all the values reversed. For precisely where Cavell posts the acknowledgement of loss as a necessary condition for recovery, Levinson detects a feint of avoidance such that any succeeding claim to recuperation must, in any true and strict accounting, turn out to be just so much bunk and false consciousness. To Levinson, Wordsworth is a writer who, through spousal fairy tales of communion, would "restore continuity to a socially and psychically fractured existence" (5) so that where there was "[deadlock] at the practical level" (5) or "unworkable, unspeakable loss, there is [the supplement of] redemptive, figural definition" (4).

The "resolution" into which Cavell happily but demandingly sees *Walden* crystallizing shares with the "fabulous fusions" of Levinson the sense of a scatter of elements here buckling into definition and integrity. This sameness in difference (the difference between, say, working through an *ambivalence* and clarifying an *ambiguity*) suggests why it is so difficult to keep steadily in mind the world of difference between them. Levinson can talk the characteristic romantic act of ingathering down into an apparatus for manufacturing fabulous fusions because, all her claims to the practical notwithstanding, she overintellectualizes this deeply practical act. Her formulation of these things is just made for holding up to scorn an imposed and totalizing *intellectual* coherence, which, it should go without saying, is manifestly inadequate to the dense and complicated play of historical contradictions it would presume to master or explain. By way of contrast, Cavell describes his route to romanticism as the eventual finding that his life in philosophy was calling on this movement not for clear and distanced certainties to appease the mind and conveniently obviate action, but for a series of testaments to the kind of quest falling to the lot of any of us who at any time might find ourselves newly awakened to the need for a clearance onward toward autonomous acts turned around the axis of our real need—find ourselves called on for a here-I-stand resolution about just what, in the acknowledgement of pervasive dereliction and ruin, we and our energies are to be in the service of. In the terms of Wordsworth (invoked in Cavell's first book) Cavell finds in romanticism not some idealizing opium of the dispossessed, but one sternly challenging exemplar after another about what one is to do when one finds that it's just our human fate to have become "A moral agent, judging between good / And evil not as for the mind's delight / But for her safety, one who was to *act*" (Cavell quoting Wordsworth [1805 *Prelude* 8.668–70] in *MW* 314; Wordsworth's emphasis).

Cavell's coming to romanticism as the still present cultural place most exemplarily in quest of a recovery of and to the track of our desire does not deliver us from historical mischance. It nails us to it. For it unfolds into a cleared space of acknowledgement an endless set of things, conditions, terms, histories and responsibilities which, having been called to and charged with, we have manifestly not lived up to. In contrast with this resolutely practical (and dauntingly rebuking) picture of what romanticism would be about, the account given of it in materialist New-Historicism is not, for all its talk of Praxis, practical enough. It turns struggles for conviction about courses of action into instances of what Cavell memorably calls "meaning our lives up" (*MW* 145). It pictures romanticism as blindly and hopelessly driven toward "a transcendental displacement of human desire" (McGann 26) when, in Cavell's patient reading of the same cultural project, the imperative is to put together "constitutions of words," in which, by the passage "from an Intuition of what counts to a Tuition of how to recount it" (*TN* 102), desire would be found and released—and found and released in a mode of thinking and writing, where every word is placed and constellated with others of its kind so as to bear witness to what we as a form of life have found needed the telling, what we have found worth the candle of remarking and conceptualizing.

2

To be myself practical about all that depends on this turning of our inquiry from the panoptic coherence of a theory of our lives to the utterly specific imperatives of acknowledgement and resolution, I turn to some practical criticism of one of the two official spots of time in Book II of *The Prelude* (1805). That spot of time is what is usually called the "gibbet mast" episode (a naming of it which I will be contesting). With my reading of this passage, I hope to show that this representatively powerful stretch of Wordsworth's writing, though untouched by any of Cavell's direct attention, nonetheless *answers* to his thinking with effects and yields of disclosure, which have been unavailable to, indeed blocked by, our current professional investments. What Wordsworth's autobiographical account of a little boy lost in northern England most generally answers to (and casts light back on) is Cavell's intuition that the incentive of this romantic/ autobiographical/lyrical writing is toward a constitution of words, which would be both "[an account] book of our losses" and "a text of recovery." And, as intimated by the punning title of *In Quest of the Ordinary*, the one by way of the other, as if an autopsy performed on the actual ordinary remaining to us after our casual slaughters of the everyday could, at the last, come to count as the first step on the way of an auguring quest, not dead set on flying *up* above the track of where we find ourselves, but instead turned to the business of "going *on*" (*SW* 136; CH 10) with an ordinary that unendingly comes round to us in a thinking, that is now to be (re)conceived and (re) born as a staying of the course of whatever attractions we find, upon investigation, to have been apportioned to us as the near and the common.

(My claim that this segment of Wordsworth's writing *answers* to Cavell's intuition about what this kind of writing is for might be more practically, say testably, entered by saying that this episode yields up something of the character of its mystery and the mystery of its character to such "master-tone" tuitions of Cavell's own writing as *character* and [secular] *mysteries* themselves, and also [to give only a partial list]: *abandonment, finding, losing, way, bottom, ground, casual, casualty, going on, down, up, steps, lasting, hand, reading, writing, standing, thinking, re-membering, empty, death, (re)birth, exposed, near, common, low, high, ordinary, interest.*)

The first spot of time finds a five-year old Wordsworth in the tutelary company of an adult. Accompanied by "honest James," this child, whose hand can scarcely "hold a bridle," rides into the hills, becomes separated from his "encourager and guide," loses his increasingly fearful and stumbling way, and with mounting panic comes to the remains of a murderer's gibbet. This memorial of mortally inflicted and capitally atoned violence strikes terror in the boy, but once arrived at the "bottom" it marks, he does not dwell on it. No sooner is he brought to a stand before the gibbet than he "forthwith" applies himself to "reascending the bare Common" where he sees the spot of time proper: a "naked pool" set starkly beneath the hills; a beacon high above on a summit; and in between a young woman drawing water in a pitcher.

And here the narrative ends, seemingly in the middle of things. Wordsworth manifestly found his way home and lived to tell the tale. But the narrative gap about how precisely this rescue came to pass indicates that, however this little boy lost was in fact found, Wordsworth's recollection of it is set on substituting for any empirical, matter-of-fact finding of him the memorably lasting sight of what, when thus lost, he saw before him: the "visionary dreariness" that "invested" the pool, girl and beacon. The complex of pool, girl and beacon reflects the boy's present condition back to him. It finds him out. It pictures the way he has just now discovered things to be with him: a five-year old far from home and "by some mischance" separated from his adult guide and protector. The indefiniteness of "by some mischance" is again remarkably incomplete reporting, but it very economically renders the effect of abruptness with which the boy is in a twinkling plunged back into a totally stripped and unsponsored childhood. For it is in a far different mood that Wordsworth remembers this boy starting out on his excursion into the hills. Manfully astride his horse, the boy was then nothing if not cocky. Running on "proud hopes," he was already riding for a fall into the condition of an unaccommodated foundling, fearfully alone and abandoned to the elements.

Within the boy's nascent semiotic capacities, the naked pool "[lying] beneath the hills" captures the stricken condition of one abruptly overwhelmed and profoundly exposed: the condition of a Jobean infant *redivivus*, who has to suffer again, and with full awareness, the experience of coming naked into the world. By itself, the pool starkly presents what is here to be dealt with; it measures the depths from which this boy seeks deliverance. But in conjunction with the memory's other two main elements, it also points a way out of these depths. Along with the sighting of the water-bearing girl, the pool points upward to the hard labor of effecting such deliverance by taking steps on one's own—steps, which, in succession to the girl's difficult but persistent progress, would orient themselves by the preeminently stationed beacon, the latter a stand-in for the protectively commanding presence of the lost "encourager and guide." Clearly, it is the distraught and disoriented mind of the child that has, as it were, come upon (or invented) these three *données* of pool, girl and beacon into the synthesis of their mutually sustaining saliency. As disoriented as it is—or precisely *because* it has been so abruptly knocked off its high horse—this mind is indeed "lord and master . . . outward sense / But the obedient servant of her will."

(Historically, Penrith Beacon was one of several housings for the signal fires that, in times past, might at a moment's notice flare up along the edgy border between England and Scotland. Seeing the beacon in this light, we might think of it as calling the embattled girl and the lost boy to arms. Or, elaborating a figure from Alan Liu, one might say that the beacon "supervises" their moves.[14] The humbly pedestrian complement of this aerial perspective is that of a young traveler upon the moor coming to the alarmed acknowledgement that he has there lost his way and must now look up to the beacon as a telling landmark by which to recover his bearings.)

Reticent about just how the boy came to be separated from James, the narrative is Wordsworthianly prolix about the boy's "dismounting" his horse and going "down" the rough and stony moor to a "bottom." All this apparent finickiness about the ups and downs of this experience will insistently have its say because (to borrow a term from Michael Riffaterre) this story's semiotic matrix is a stripped and Joseph-like abandonment to the pit or the depths, a spatially structured matrix whose draw time no more than space is allowed to escape. Scholarship has established that the Penrith execution dates from no more than eight years before Wordsworth's boyhood encounter with it.[15] But Wordsworth's confusion of this relatively recent scene with the grimly gibbeted remains of an execution carried out a century earlier at Hawkshead leads him to paint a distinctly opposite picture. Wordsworth does not simply, and misleadingly, state that the initial inscription on this mound occurred "in times long past." With a sensitive subjection of his syntax and verse rhythm to the perspective of a young boy, the poet presents this recurrent act of inscription as if the push toward it is issuing from some archaic origin, as "still from year to year / By superstition of the neighborhood / The grass is cleared away; and to this hour / The letters are all fresh and visible." (The last line-and-a-half describes a counter movement out and up into the clarified resolution of written characters. As such, this writing about writing anticipates the saliently raised "pre-eminence" of the beacon.) Arrived at more than one kind of "bottom," the boy is understandably spooked by all the terrors compacted into the letters of the murderer's name. So he confronts these characters as if they were coming after him from a deep backward and abysm of time. This is not factually the case, but it is powerfully true to the boy's experience of this scene of guilt and harsh retributive justice.

In perhaps the finest historicizing of Wordsworth's work, James Chandler has shown how the spots of time enact a "disciplining" of the poet's mind, a correction of that mind's course antithetically provoked by its obstinately entertained delusion about the "freedom of the individual mind," unmoored from any limiting conditions of place and history.[16] Chandler positions Wordsworth's struggle for this mental discipline between the French Ideologues' exclusive reliance on the individual intellect's "private stock of reason" and Edmund Burke's counter championing of the prescriptive "prejudices" encoded into England's unwritten constitution of itself. Building on Chandler's demonstration that the drama of this long poem is one about thinking and specifically about the fantasy of a privatized thought, I would like to propose that, whatever immediate demons of French Ideologues and Revolutions Wordsworth may have been wrestling with in Book II of the 1805 *Prelude*, his passage through this crisis in the growth of his mind finds its fullest—say its most philosophical or most thoughtful—accounting in Cavell's diagnosis of the all too human phenomenon of "the desire for thought, running out of control" (*TN* 54) as it seeks to "sublime the logic of our language" (*Investigations* §38) beyond the finitude of those forms of life which "grow language" (*CR* 170). I propose, that is, to set the mental traveling of *The Prelude*—its repeated passages of error and return—against the background of the forms and practices of "correction," called for by what Cavell, following Wittgenstein, seeks to flush out into the open as the *fantasy* of a private language, the fantasy of a way of saying and thinking that could disown our attunements in forms of life and still pretend to be called thinking and not an empty mindlessness.

As Chandler points out, Wordsworth's expressly philosophical approach to the spots of time of Book II replays the plot of loss initiating the composition of *The Prelude* as a whole. In both passes through this masterplot, the writer acknowledges that precisely as a function of claiming an absolute independence of life or intellect, he has come to a standstill, not knowing which way to turn. So when, after a series of false starts in Book I, the writer of *The Prelude* gives out with the grievous question "was it for this [that I was granted the life to be exemplified in the spots of time]," Chandler is surely right to affirm that the "this" referring to Wordsworth's loss of progress "is precisely the situation over which poetry triumphs to come into being" (Chandler 188). But an aspect of this impasse to which Chandler gives insuffient weight is the great Wordsworthian theme of *interest*. For the difficulties *The Prelude* negotiates at its outset dramatize the dispiriting loss of progress attendant on that lack of true interest, deftly emblematized by Wordsworth in the hectically irresolute catalogue of aborted poetic projects, with which he puts paid to one of the more potentially numbing requirements of the epic genre.

The Prelude, then, only gets its subject underway when the writer's deficit of interest dialectically provokes its counter of reanimating memories of childhood. Further along in Wordsworth's journey, when this chronicler of himself finds himself bewitched by "some charm of logic" that makes "an emptiness / [Fall] on the historian's page, and even on that / Of poets" (11.90–92), it is a logic-induced emptiness which creates the gravity well, along which the newly stalled Wordsworth finds himself drawn toward the spots of time as features of himself and his history, which he finds he must now own up to and account for if he is ever to get *back* on the way of his thinking and writing. From first to last, then, *The Prelude is* interested in that "going on" or "taking steps" which, for Cavell, constitutes thinking. Here at the decisive turning point in the poem's heroic action, it shows its representatively lost author confidently recovering his bearings and again getting on his way against all in "your philosophy" that would stall, fixate or suffocate his inclination to take an interest in, and so give thought to, his life.

Chandler represents Wordsworth's turnaround as a matter of his now appreciating as "mysteries of passion" (84) what formerly, as a self-divided English *philosophe* or ideologue, he dismissed as groundless prejudices from

209

"the weak being of the past" (10.823). The Cavellian idea of receiving words and the forms of life these words articulate—epitomized for him in Emerson's "all I know is reception"—does not contradict this reading of a poet temporarily severed from his roots but then restored to his native English stock of thinking. On the contrary, Cavell's repeated emphasis on the human as a species whose nature is custom or "the social" is profoundly receptive to the idea of "second nature" invoked in the title of Chandler's book. But when Cavell refers to custom as "second nature," we may be confident that, unlike most new-historicists and post-structuralists, he is not putting *nature* under erasure as just an empty counter to get something pertinent said about the real thing of custom or convention. Quite the contrary. For, as already mentioned, Cavell follows Wittgenstein in stressing that our "forms of life" grow out of our *natural* circumstances and responses. He argues that this key Wittgensteinian term is not only, or even mainly, about the "horizontal" differences between, say, French and English. It is also, and most originally in Wittgenstein, about the "vertical" differences in "natural history" between the human life form and, for example, that lion about whom Wittgenstein famously observes that if he could talk we couldn't understand him (*Investigations* 223).

Reminding ourselves of the necessary agreements or attunements that condition a form of life should make dawn an aspect of Wordsworth's work as not beating what might all too easily be construed as a know-nothing retreat into Burkean *pre-judice*, but as being (as I would like to put it) progressively about the very different business of bringing us all back, with interest, to those common *judgments*, which, as encoded into the language of the ordinary, are always already indicative of the natural attractions and authentic necessities of the life form of us talkers. (I am preceded here by Charles Altieri's trenchant assertion that Wordsworth is "not a poet of nature but *the* poet of philosophical grammar," but the way I hear Cavell, Wittgenstein and Wordsworth in conversation with one another, it strikes me that precisely *because* Wordsworth is the poet of philosophical grammar, he must also be a poet of [our] nature.)[17]

To the degree that Wordsworth the young ideologue worked to cut himself off from the form-of-life "background against which our criteria do their work, even make sense" (*CR* 83), he found himself driven toward a forced and disabling repression of forms of life. This is Wordsworth's autobiographical way of finding himself in the position of one of those astonished casualties of philosophy, whom Wittgenstein was forever trying to get simply to see their loss of progress so that he could then call them back to the "language-game which is [a word's] original home" (*Investigations* §116). Detoured into "your philosophy" and become sharply aware of its not affording satisfaction or progress, Wordsworth found himself, in Cavell's phrase and emphasis, "*having to remember*" (*MW* 314) a tale of first loss when he first became unsettlingly at home with *loss*, on terms of familiarity with it.

Although the five-year old's abrupt plunge into a condition of being lost and disoriented strikes considerable traumatic power, it cannot by itself account for the incident's manifest staying power. For that, the gathering idea or term of *loss* is needed, Limned at the "twilight of rememberable life" (1799 *Prelude* 1.298), this child, prompted by very real stumblings and terrors, found himself *conceptually* ready (as, by contrast, a newly weaned infant would not be conceptually ready) to have something happen to him that he himself could count as being lost. So in Wordsworth's present enterprise of remembering his adult self as lost to and in philosophy, Wordsworth is drawn back *to* this archaic history as something to be drawn *on* as the founding scene of loss deposited in his memory bank. On this spot of personally hallowed time and ground, there arises for Wordsworth not so much the fact of loss as his initiation into the publically expressed and exposed *condition* of loss—what on the ground of our agreements in forms of life we "say together" (as the word *con-dition* says) so as to make answer to this calling out of *loss* everything from losing your keys or your place or your balance, to whatever we may still be able to mean by a lost soul or a lost generation.

In *The Prelude*, Wordsworth would give an account of himself by thinking through his budget of experience. What his accounting of that experience comes to is that he is lost or abandoned. That what he is pre-eminently exposed to is his mortality becomes clear in the second spot of time, centered around the sudden death of his father.[18] There the 13-year old becomes an actual, say an officially counted, orphan. In the first spot of time, a still younger Wordsworth temporarily, but with strikingly abrupt force, suffers the fate of a foundling. Both spots are emblems of unaccommodated humanity; they both "stand for [Wordsworth's] humanity" (*IQ* 114) as subject to mortality not as a contingent event but as a necessary condition of what we are—what, by the nature of our natality and finitude, we are ineluctably exposed to. If the conviction of loss is the recurring occasion for taking thought about oneself—if it is "the incentive to thinking" —then this taking thought must remain faithful to the condition of its own existence and action. In the language which the 1850 *Prelude* offers in summary of the Snowdon vision, the "naked pool" is a ground of "sense" that will conduct toward a pertinently "ideal form" of accounting only if that pool of human condition is fully assumed or taken on, only if it is from this, and only this, experience that one draws the figures to enter into one's account.[19] (Bearing down on his master theme of acknowledgement, Cavell puts it this way: only the "actual" is the "womb, contains the terms, of the eventual . . . Wittgenstein's insight is that the ordinary has, and alone has, the power to move the ordinary, to leave the human habitat habitable, the same transfigured" [*TN* 46–47].)

Since to Wordsworth no less than to Cavell nothing is more "actual" than our losses and our disappointments, both of his recovering spots of time rise up before the blocked progress of his autobiography as radical scenes of loss and abandonment. They reach the Wordsworth writing about the "imagination, how impaired and how restored" just where he finds himself: lost in and to "your philosophy." Both spots rehearse, what Cavell kerygmatically announces in Thoreau as that "morning of mourning, [that] dawning of grief" (*T* 54) which (in Cavell's reading of Freud) is the one thing endlessly needed to refit our fixated selves for life and progress in the world.

Wordsworth's recounting of his founding experience of loss carries a recuperative power because at the iconically condensed finding of himself in the verticality of pool, girl and beacon, there rings out as internal to this condition a call to go on beyond where he is in the taking of steps toward the finding and recovering of himself. For the constellation of pool, girl and beacon is not simply what the boy is (called); this reading or calling out of the boy also provocatively calls its subject out to an answerable style of response, to his own upright show of character. This is most striking in the embattled gait and bearing of the girl. Her progress up the wind-struck hill epitomizes the boy's own exposed condition, but her bearing of herself also counts as an example calling on him to take steps of his own—steps which cannot but be taken on his own but also steps which can do no better than take their bearings from the perspicuously raised up standard of a public beacon, newly urgent and pertinent to this untraveled traveler suddenly finding himself at sea. This spot of time provides a concrete autobiographical instance, then, of what Cavell finds the "Immortality" ode to be calling for from us adults: i.e. a "recovering from the loss of childhood by recovering something of, or in, childhood (in particular, recovering its forms of recovery)" (*IQ* 73).

The girl is the element in the spot exerting the strongest draw on Wordsworth's interest and attention. Once James has fallen out of view, she is the only (other) living human here, and the only component of the memory that was of just that day. When "long afterwards" the young man Wordsworth "roamed about / In daily presence of this scene," the beacon and pool were still there, but the girl was long gone. There for Wordsworth for that one specular moment, she then moved on into her own life, while the adult who would compose *The Prelude* found himself, as it were, stuck with her, like a fate. Unlike the pool or the beacon, the girl makes Wordsworth *have* to remember her. Her presence to him circa 1776 was as ephemeral (and as powerful) as the wind, but the boy who saw her that day persistently found himself having to remember her bearing of water, as if the travail she experienced in that aversive posture toward the forces of wind and gravity constituted an intimate double or other to him, something that was not yet finished with him, something that had more to say to him or bring forth about him.

If this girl forms the human gravitational center of this spot of time, then it is truly remarkable how neglected and virtually unthought of she is in

contemporary critical discourse. Typical of such neglect is the way a sophisticated reader like Alan Liu will make this spot of time crucial in his account
of Wordsworth's poetry, but barely mention the girl. Her only appearance
in his lengthy book is short, parenthetical, and dismissive: she is a "relic"
of "Maryology," a piece of "religiosity" in what Liu routinely names the
"gibbet mast scene" (Liu 390). There are exceptions—notably Thomas
Weiskel and Jonathan Wordsworth[20]—but most professional readers of this
scene fall in line with Jonathan Bishop's influential assertion that the girl,
pool and beacon are only "accidental concommitants" of the gibbet.[21]

Both in Wordsworth's first rendition of the spot and in his repetition
of how he would need colors and words unknown to man to paint it right,
it is the girl who holds climactic pride of place in series with the pool and
the beacon. And while the second mentions of the beacon and pool are
just deictically abbreviated repetitions, such is not the case for the girl. Her
second time around, she has matured into the "woman," but even more
significantly the entire second mention of her is performed with a meas-
urable quantum of variation, the effect of which is that the apparent
redundancy of "the woman, and her garments vexed and tossed / By the
strong wind" comes across not as fewer words and diminished information
value but as an increment of *concentration*, a concentration of emphasis just
made for the subject/author's gathering of his attention toward that one
positional spot within the spot, occupied by the figure of the girl.

Although I am claiming that it is new light on Wordsworth to see this
scene's pitcher-bearing girl as the writer's *doppelgänger*, it is not as though
contemporary criticism has not repeatedly read what it calls the gibbet mast
episode as self-reflexive of the writing in which it occurs. But this noting of
self-reflexivity has been fixated on the "unknown hand's" recurrent engrav-
ing of the murderer's name into monumental letters. J. Douglas Kneale's
Monumental Writing: Aspects of Rhetoric in Wordsworth's Poetry gives the
most thoroughly singleminded expression to this approach.[22] For Kneale,
the murderer's "literary remains" (Kneale 142) underwrite a "posthumous
text" (142) which, in recognition of "the proleptic displacement of a life by
letters" (144) "gives and takes away a life in letters" (147). In our current
critical climate, such readings of absence (which New Historicists like
Levinson have appropriated for their own purposes [Levinson 6–13])
gather conviction and often claim their origins in Paul de Man's contention
that all of Wordsworth's autobiographical poetry is epitaphic "even if it
obliges us to imagine a tombstone large enough to hold the entire *Prelude*."[23]

By itself, the anonymous hand behind the monumental letters may indeed
suggest how our words can be turned from life, "becoming the language of
noone" in what Cavell repeatedly arraigns as "your philosophy" or "the
desire for thought running out of control." But if this is so, then the writing
of this epitaph characterizes only what the writing in which it is exhibited
(say, gibbeted) is out to effect a recovery *from*. Seen as a figure for your

philosophy's death-dealing inscription of itself into one (ordinary) human life, this plot of ground does, as we say, have Wordsworth's name on it. Its monumental letters knew just where to find Wordsworth as he came to that crossroads in the recounting of his life, when he was set on the convention-ally "philosophical" task of making our words conform to the requirement of a subliming logic. But this is hardly what, at the last, Wordsworth would be about with his words. On the contrary, it is, as James Chandler says of the initial impasse out of which *The Prelude* grew, "the situation over which poetry triumphs to come into being" (Chandler 188). The analogy between Wittgenstein and Wordsworth strikes me as patent. In the growth of Wordsworth's mind, the turning (back) to the true thinking of what he calls Imagination (and Wittgenstein calls perspicuous representation) begins in the same experience of loss at which Wittgenstein spotted the beginnings of a philosophical problem. "A philosophical problem," writes Wittgenstein, "has the form: 'I don't know my way about'" (*Investigations* §123). To find yourself abandoned in the way "your philosophy" has of inflicting loss is therewith to experience the "incentive to thinking" (*CH* 19–20) and to experience it in such a way and on such occasions that what we call thinking will have to be reconceived as a reception or acknowledgement of the conditions for our knowing or saying anything at all—something Cavell sees exemplified in what he calls Emerson's "abandonment of and to language, and the world" (*IQ* 175). A condition of abandonment not only brings on the incentive to thinking; it also keeps one persistently on the way of this thinking.

Received in the light of the way Cavell both trusts and distrusts our words, the monumental letters found next to the gibbet need not mark some absolute end-game of language. Instead, they may be more concretely taken as there placed by this writing so as themselves to place just where Wordsworth found himself when he subjected this language of ours to your philosophy's emptying and deadening work, murdering to dissect. In aversion to this possibility of our words for the death-in-life of a terminal and lived emptiness, Wordsworth would have his autobiographical writ-ing exemplify how the "mystery of words" (*The Prelude* 5.621) can also make "breathings for incommunicable powers" (3.187). He would, that is, give himself over to what Thoreau calls the "volatile truth" of our words, which in Thoreau's words, "is instantly translated" out and up from the "literal monument" of their inadequately "residual statement" (*SW* 27; "Conclusion," *Walden*).

In Wordsworth's first spot of time, the "volatile truth" of our words makes its appropriately fleeting appearance when, confronted with the dead letter of the monumental epitaph, the boy is "forthwith" (I will put it) *translated* toward an active taking of steps which draw near to their finding end in a hieratic female figure, the emphatically aversive dynamism of whose posture—vexed, tossed and uphill in a strong wind—suggests the difficult task of delivering up the volatile life of our words—words which, it bears repeating, are always calling for just this maieutic labor of bringing them (back) to (our) life, because we are always turning this rumored bread of life into stones, as with perfect symmetry we "refuse the value of the experience of ordinary words" (*TN* 64) and force on them a "frozen emptiness of sublimity" (*TN* 56).

The pitcher-bearing woman is both preserved in, and quickening of, Wordsworth the rememberer. As housed in his memory, she has drawn the water forth and would bring it home. Her labors are at first, or at bottom, just the ordinary "woman's work" of the day, but over the course of Wordsworth's remembered life with this laboring image, its travail comes to be powerfully amplified into intimations of the womanly burden and mystery of bearing a child. The woman exhibits a bearing and carriage, which (as I have tried to suggest) draws to itself such terms as *labor, travail,* and *delivery.* She resonates with the issue of life and generativity, resonates that issue all the way out toward the endless human task of conceiving and bearing our humanity.

I trust I am not alone in sensing the interlocked importance of the fact that this figure is a woman and that her bearing is what I would characterize as hieratic. But I fear that I may find myself quite alone when I suggest as a possible key to this ceremonious collapsing of the sacred and the reproductive the Biblical "type-scene" of the young woman thankfully found at a well, a well which is, writes Robert Alter, "obviously a symbol of fertility."[24] But bear with me.

In the type-scene Alter defines, the woman at the well is not just any woman. Like Isaac's Rebekah, she is the future betrothed, the beloved and necessary medium for accomplishing the promise of an elect human generation. I would put my intuition (or fantasy) about this Biblical type-scene's pertinence to Wordsworth this way: In and through this woman's persistence as that which most profoundly names him—this woman as in effect *his* type-scene—Wordsworth finds that he has become imaginatively wedded to her. And the here delivered fruit of this imaginative union is the way the poet's letting the image of the woman call upon him calls him back to that calling, which Shakespeare has one of his characters call a laboring in the mind (*A Midsummer Night's Dream* 5.i.73). As remembered in *The Prelude,* then, the girl becomes the heraldic *mise en abyme* not for the static and spatial form of this work but for what, time after time, is calling for the work of this form and its kind. The pitcher-bearing woman intimates what, on and by the way of this writing, has been found to be this writing's incentive. She announces what all along has been calling *The Prelude* out into its character as a self-naming constitution of words.[25]

A picture of Wordsworth laboring to give articulated birth to himself in letters bears a striking resemblance to what Cavell will have to say about Emerson's writing as a representative corpus or "constitution" out to show its "partiality" toward the task of giving birth to the human and the social. Briefly, Cavell's "This New Yet Unapproachable America" receives Emerson's "Experience" as a work of mourning for the author's son and namesake, dead at five. Cavell's intuition about the work of mourning performed by "Experience" is that it labors to bear up under the edict of Waldo's terminal separation by bringing forth on this continent and for these shores a body or constitution of words, within which the quickening life and promise of Waldo (and so the promise of "this new, yet unapproachable America") would be kept, buried or guarded (the latter the root of tuition). According to Cavell, the essay has an "idea of itself as pregnant" (*TN* 103), which leads to "Emerson's imagining his giving birth somehow as a man" (*TN* 104), as if "coming to terms were a coming to term" (*TN* 21). So in the course of reading the famously aphoristic and fragmentary essays of this writer who founded thinking for America, we find ourselves being counseled to "*bear* with these distractions, with this coetaneous growth of the parts, they will one day be *members*, and obey one will" (*TN* 100; first emphasis mine, second Emerson's). For reading Emerson—coming to terms with him—is a process in which, as Cavell puts it, " 'parts' become 'members' . . . a process in which remembering (a name for philosophy's work) is given its origin in dismemberment" (*TN* 21).

Remembering my own (but surely not just my own) sense of *The Prelude* as beginning in fragmentary snapshots of unbidden memory and building itself up into an explicit claim to epic representativeness, I conceive the progress of Wordsworth's epic poem as having or requiring a gestation like Emerson's embryonic development toward his "constitution of words." *The Prelude* gets on the way of its progress only when its author/subject finds himself at a loss in that distraction and dismemberment of purpose, which is the self-reproaching referent of the poem's intiating cry, "Was it for this?" And from there, the poem is a work in progress of remembering, where the composing of a self out of these *disjecta membra* is not, as said, undertaken for the sake of constructing a theory about oneself, but in the spirit of "seeking to know what you are made of and cultivating the thing you are meant to do" (*CH* 7).

As set on the way from the pool to the beacon, the woman bearing some ordinary waters of life becomes a Wordsworthian figure of desire or a figure of Wordsworthian desire, and specifically a figure of his desire for taking thought—for giving an account (of himself), for re-membering himself. Like Emerson in "Self-Reliance," this memorably persistent double of Wordsworth "stands for humanity" (*IQ* 114). But if she stands for what "The American Scholar" calls Man Thinking, then she stands up for the inflection of this thinking toward its feminine or patient matrix from within which we might find it in ourselves to "stop to think (say not for action but for passion), as if to let our needs recognize what they need" (*CH* 20). She offers a picture of thinking and coming to our senses which is, one might say, literally "unknown to *man*" (my emphasis). But if this woman "more near" stands for our humanity in and as she can stand or bear it, she also stands for it in the way her own upright and uphill bearing calls on a represent-atively human Wordsworth to take a correspondently upright and thinking stand toward his experience of being lost and cast down. She calls on him to take steps of his own so as to find his own way home—*home* as in Wittgenstein's "the home of a concept."

In the one-tone-off oddity of Emerson's phrase, "the mysteries of human condition," Cavell hears the finding that our life is had only on condition, and that we are thus, each and all, called to be as receptive to the condition(s) in which our histories, social and natural, have left us, as the "naked pool" of the first spot is, *exempli gratia*, open to all the climatological givens it finds itself embedded in and at the mercy of. Wordsworth's "naked pool" sug-gests the necessary but forbidding aspect of the great Cavellian mastertone of acknowledgement. The other, more inviting, aspect of this mastertone shines down from the border beacon as a figure for the lights afforded by the terms and conditions of the (our) ordinary (language). A literal landmark to both the woman and the boy, the beacon supervises the space in which that boy lost himself and then found himself in the laboriously wayfaring figure of the woman. It articulates the "bare common" where *in principio* the boy found himself at a loss, and with his work cut out for him. If a literal landmark is what the boy then made of this communally edified structure, this boy's life clearly did not end with its five-year old impressions of the beacon, pool, and woman. Further on, when the grown man seeks to remember himself as lost to and in "your philosophy," the persistently remembered beacon stands ready to become the "lost guide" of the ordinary, an ordinary which would command and deliver what alone can provide the criterial signposts by which we initiates into a form of life may get our-selves back on the way of a thinking, acknowledged to be over rough and "logically" untidy ground, but, for all that, endlessly attractive, not just because it affords our life-form a needed friction and orientation, but more basically, because it holds out the promise that, with any and every word, we might find ourselves stepping on our transport to the track and the release of our desire.

3

I have kept largely in reserve the most sustained New Historical reading of Wordsworth, a reading which, as it happens, places the spots of time at the origin of the work of Wordsworth's art. In his *Wordsworth: The Sense of History*, Alan Liu would have it that when the matter of the French Revolution opened the author of the 13-book *Prelude* to the invasive other of history, it brought on a flood whose cresting in Books 9 and 10 anti-thetically provoked or "[made] possible the intensity of the poem's [programmatically evasive] lyrical self-consciousness in Books 11–13"

(Liu 361). But Book 13's "decisive close . . . on a crescendo of impersonal Mind is unconvincing based on everything the poet has so far told us about his shifting sense of self" (Liu 400). So the 13-book mobilization of Wordsworth's poem must preveniently represent its author/subject as "corrected," a task assigned to the spots of time.

Liu rightly attributes the "It" resounding throughout Wordsworth's claim of access (atop Snowdon) to an impersonally imperial intellect, and brilliantly shows how this impersonality (recent Cavell will call it "neutrality")[26] counts as the answer to the poem's initiating question, "Was it for this?" The experience of this life was not, Liu hears Wordsworth claiming, granted for the distracted personal maunderings of the first part of Book I. It was granted for *this*, for this access to an authoritative claim on [in Kant's terms] a universal, objective and necessary Reason, which, in antithesis to the imperial power of Napoleon and in acknowledgement of Wordsworth's draw toward the ordinary, is precisely not "simple empire [but] the empire of the simple" (Liu 448).

But to Liu, Wordsworth manages this speciously evasive recuperation by a tactical retreat into "simple autobiography," the latter derisively equated with "Revelation" and "marking the transformation of history into personal history, and French empire into the mind's empire" (Liu 361). As with Marjorie Levinson's strictures on Wordsworth's "fabulous fusions," this justifiable insistence on the autobiographical in Wordsworth reads like a virtual transcription of Cavell on the relations of language, mind and subjectivity . . . but again with the values reversed. To a Cavell who has only recently become explicitly autobiographical, "the philosophical methods of Wittgenstein and Austin demand a systematic engagement with the autobiographical" (*Pi* 6), because on questions like "what we should say when?" these philosophers knew that they had no better authority than their own lives. In Cavell's pithy phrasing, these are thinkers who must always be "laying their bodies on the philosophical line, and living to tell the tale" (*Pi* 10).

According to Liu, Book II of *The Prelude* performs an autobiographical "correction [of desires]" whose achievement in and by the spots of time represents the Archimedean point on which Wordsworth turns his empire of the mind toward its closure in the "It" of the necessary, the universal and the objective. Liu has legitimately enough taken this phrasing of a "correction of desires" from the second spot of time, and I would like, as it were, to listen to that Wordsworthian phrasing with a Wittgensteinian acoustic. For the "*correction*" of those of us (essentially, all of us) who are *out*, *away*, or *astray* is, as already conveyed, incessantly called for in both Cavell and Wittgenstein's philosophical practice. A Cavell alive to both the manner and content of Wittgenstein's standing order back to language games as "the home of a concept" speaks of this tonality in the *Investigations* as its "voice of correction" (*TN* 38). The correction in question, however, is not coming down from any power superior to the individual masters of a language. Instead, the kind of correction endlessly in force (or at play) in Wittgenstein and Cavell is one dictated by the network of *our* criteria, on which I, but I no more than anyone else, am the authority.

What, at Cavell's Wittgensteinian leading, I am trying to get open is the seriousness and depth of Wordsworth's call for a wise passiveness, as that appeal looks toward Cavell's "argument of the ordinary" and its imperative of acknowledgement as he variously hears them in Thoreau's call to be still in this wretched nervous nineteenth century, in Wittgenstein's pleading to his reader "Don't think, but look," in Emerson's presentation of himself as sitting at the feet of the common as at the feet of his guru or master (*SW* 147). Taking up Emerson's reiterated cry for "patience, patience" (which "[Emerson] seeks as the most active of intellectual conditions),"[27] Cavell makes the case for our radical and defining need for that "philosophical power of passiveness that Emerson characteristically treats in considering what he calls attraction, as important to him as gravity is to Newton" (*TN* 114). As interpreted by Cavell in *Conditions Handsome and Unhandsome*, the most unhandsome part of our condition is the "evanescence and lubricity of all objects, which lets them slip through our fingers then when we clutch hardest" (*CH* 38). To Cavell, this clutching hand anticipates Heidegger's thinking and imagery about representative thinking. It emblematizes an "interpretation of Western conceptualizing as a kind of sublimized violence" whose overcoming "will require the achievement of a form of knowledge both Emerson and Heidegger call reception" (*CH* 39). This reception is "the reverse of the unhandsome in our condition" (*CH* 41). It is the "handsome" or "attractive" part of that condition, "what Emerson calls being drawn and what Heidegger calls getting in the draw, or draft, of thinking" (*CH* 41). Into the draft of a thinking which seeks less a theory of our lives—"meaning them up"—than something *The Prelude*'s approach to the spots of time exemplifies in a beloved woman's way of "convers[ing] with things" (199)— those same "things" whose "laws [lying] / Beyond the reach of human will or power" Wordsworth shortly before announced as the "light" then found ready to "guide or cheer" him when his own clutching philosophical hand had wrought him into a state of "eclipse."[28]

That New Historicist criticism is blind to the "philosophical power of passiveness," so prominent in Cavell and so pertinent to Wordsworth, may be illustrated by Liu's commentary on a Charles Le Brun depiction of Mary Magdalen, Wordsworth's two-line misreading of which he makes into something of a visual frontispiece for his thesis about *The Prelude*'s programmatic "transform" of the sublime of Revolutionary history into a false lyrical beauty.

The two lines from Wordsworth catch this Revolutionary tourist in the act of gravitating to the beauty of the Magdalen while turning away from the rubble of the Bastille. Liu's analysis of the painting is a finely discriminating act of art criticism, and deftly woven into the larger fabric of his argument. He is clearly right to call Wordsworth's rendering of the painting a misreading (Liu 369). Doubtless influenced by what a Magdalen penitently weeping at Jesus' feet is expected to be doing, Wordsworth depicts her as sorrowing, when she is clearly not in sorrow but caught up in some ecstatic rapture. This Magdalen "is not in the aspect of sentimental sorrow, but in the act of being dramatically ravished or violently transported" (Liu 369). Given all the fine things Liu has to say about the painting and about Wordsworth's (mis)appropriation of it, I find myself at a loss at how grossly or roughly *Liu* misreads it. In only one example of an extremely violent language, he calls the experience the Magdalen is undergoing "a rape of beauty by the sublime" (Liu 369). But a rapture is not a rape. The attitude given expression in the Magdalen's face is one of rapt openness, and her visual intertext is the obedient virgin of the Annunciation receiving the Word delivered to her and standing ready to bring it to full term. By contrast, Liu sounds like he is talking about a Ledaean body out of Yeats, frighteningly "caressed / By the dark webs, her nape caught in his bill." But when Yeats wrote this in a poem originally entitled "Annunciation," he at least knew that he was envisioning a way of generating worlds that was the precise opposite of the attitude of reception enshrined in the traditional Annunciation scene and its derivatives.

LeBrun's Magdalen is an emblem of wise passiveness. Prototypically a "heart that watches and receives," her attractiveness to Wordsworth (and the point of her enraptured beauty's stark juxtaposition to the violence of Revolutionary thought and practice) is that she herself is so alive and responsive to what (to quote Thoreau again) rightly and strongly attracts her. In its fervently active and eroticized posture of reception, the painting may be thought of as an icon for what Cavell calls that handsome/attractive/receptive part of our condition when we find ourselves "stopping to think (say not for action but for passion), as if to let our needs recognize what they need" (*CH* 20).

To New Historicist work with its pervasive air of power and violence, this picture of the mind as radically receptive will appear soft-headed or wishful. But the investigations of Wittgenstein and Cavell, I am claiming, make dawn an aspect of this radical receptivity, which demands intellectual rigor and contests just who in these regions of knowing and thinking and acknowledging may be in the grip of the deepest and most disabling fantasy. As in the Emersonian paradox that "he who has more obedience masters me" (*IQ* 116), the empire of the simple is, in Cavell, a mastery granted only to those having great obedience, stillness, or waiting, only to those willing to let the words of their experience and the experience of their words make an impression on them and tell them all they know. This promise of an *imperium* of expression, founded on a persistent listening, is the all but stifled voice, from which the concerted mastertones of Cavell's philosophical authorship would elicit an uncanny attunement back to the form of life which the thought-provoking texts of romanticism have left us to be remembered in. That our currently regnant arbiters of these texts of recovery do not seem very much on the *qui vive* for this voice, that its tonalities are all but lost on them, is something to think about.

Notes

1 Stanley Cavell, *Must We Mean What We Say? A Book of Essays* (Cambridge, MA: Harvard UP, 1969) 313; hereafter *MW*.

2 Jerome J. McGann, *The Romantic Ideology: A Critical Investigation* (Chicago: U of Chicago P, 1983) 1.

3 Marjorie Levinson, *Wordsworth's Great Period Poems: Four Essays* (Cambridge, MA: Harvard UP, 1986) 4.

4 Stanley Cavell, *In Quest of the Ordinary: Lines of Skepticism and Romanticism* (Chicago: U of Chicago P, 1988) x; hereafter *IQ*.

5 Stanley Cavell, *This New Yet Unapproachable America: Lectures after Emerson after Wittgenstein* (Albuquerque: Living Batch P, 1989) 80; 33; hereafter *TN*.

6 Stanley Cavell, *The Senses of Walden: An Expanded Edition* (San Francisco: North Point P, 1981) 104; hereafter *SW*.

7 Stanley Cavell, *Themes Out of School: Effects and Causes* (Chicago: U of Chicago P, 1984) 33; hereafter *T*.

8 Stanley Cavell, *Conditions Handsome and Unhandsome: The Constitution of Emersonian Perfectionism* (Chicago: U of Chicago P, 1990) 22; hereafter *CH*.

9 Ludwig Wittgenstein, *Philosophical Investigations*, trans. G. E. M. Anscombe (New York: Harper, 1953) §118; hereafter *Investigations*. In conformity with the standard practice for citing *Philosophical Investigations*, I give the section number for Part I and the page number for Part II.

10 Stanley Cavell, *The Claim of Reason: Wittgenstein, Skepticism, Morality, and Tragedy* (Oxford and New York: Oxford UP, 1979) 351–52; hereafter *CR*.

11 Morris Eaves and Michael Fischer, ed., "Questions and Answers," *Romanticism and Contemporary Criticism* (Ithaca: Cornell UP, 1986) 230; hereafter *Q&A*.

12 W. J. B. Owen and Jane Worthington Smyser, *The Prose Works of William Wordsworth* (Oxford: Clarendon, 1974) 1.128–29; hereafter *Prose Works*.

13 Stanley Cavell, *The World Viewed: Reflections on the Ontology of Film* (Cambridge, MA: Harvard UP, 1979); hereafter *WV*. The sentence from *Walden* is from "Brute Neighbors."

14 Alan Liu, *Wordsworth: The Sense of History* (Stanford: Stanford UP, 1989) 100.

15 William Wordsworth, *The Prelude 1799, 1805, 1850*, ed., Jonathan Wordsworth (New York: Norton, 1979) 9.

16 James K. Chandler, *Wordsworth's Second Nature: A Study of the Poetry and Politics* (Chicago: U of Chicago P, 1984).

17 Charles Altieri, "Wordsworth's 'Preface' as Literary Theory," *Criticism* 17 (Spring, 1976): 128. Wittgenstein's sense of our natural reactions as expressed or worked out in language and form of life points to a dimension of the natural, different from (though not incompatible with) the sense of the natural championed by eco-romanticists such as Jonathan Bate in his *Romantic Ecology: Wordsworth and the Environmental Tradition* (London: Routledge, 1991). I share Bate's exasperation with Alan Liu's exaggerated but still characteristic New Historical claim that "there is no Nature" (Liu 38). Someone needed to say, "'Nature' is a term that needs to be contested, not rejected. It is profoundly unhelpful to say

'There is no nature'" (Bate 56). But it seems to me that Bate is imagining a dimi-nished, alienated, and too narrowly "green" nature, when, in assertions like the following, he draws an either/or line between romantic thinking and what that thinking must find itself called to think its way through: "The Romantic Ideology is not . . . a theory of imagination and symbol . . . but a theory of eco-systems and unalienated labor" (10). Romanticism is, to my mind, both of these things, and it is so in the nature of things, in the nature of human labor with and among things.

18 See David Ellis, *Wordsworth, Freud and the Spots of Time: Interpretation in The Prelude* (Cambridge: Cambridge UP, 1985) 17–34.

19 In her study of the 1805 five-book *Prelude*, Sybil S. Eakin shows how its inter-mediate placement of the Snowdon material *before* the concluding spots of time frames the latter and serves to draw out their maturing significance regarding "the power of the mind." Although the phrasing I have used shows up only in the 1850 version, its "sense conducting to ideal form" remains a formulation succinctly pertinent to the first spot's similarly vertical structure of pool, woman and beacon. One might even surmise that, once drawn into intimate composi-tional conversation with the Snowdon vision, the verticality of the first spot of time played no small part in the fact of Wordsworth's discourse going on to this kind of summarizing statement about what as an image of the mind Snowdon was about. (See Sybil S. Eakin, "The Spots of Time in Early Versions of *The Prelude*," *SiR* 12 [Winter 1973]: 389–405.)

20 Thomas Weiskel, *The Romantic Sublime: Studies in the Structure and Psychology of Transcendence* (Baltimore: Johns Hopkins UP, 1976) 175–85. Jonathan Wordsworth, *The Prelude 1799, 1805, 1850* (578–79). Weiskel's reading of this scene is forceful, subtle and suggestive, but, in considering the girl in isolation from the pool and beacon, he sees her as an image of militant repression and regression. "The vision [i.e. of her] occurs in flight from the characters" (179) of writing at the site of the gibbet, but not in the recuperative sense of a turning away from the dead letter. On the contrary, for Weiskel this flight represents a further turn of the screw of death-dealing repression. Defensively *seen* but not *read* by Wordsworth, she fights the visionary poet's battle "against the fact that things may come to signify" (180). As will emerge, this is a reading of this female figure very different from my own.

21 Jonathan Bishop, "Wordsworth and the 'Spots of Time,'" *ELH* 26 (March 1959): 56.

22 J. Douglas Kneale (Lincoln, Neb.: U of Nebraska P, 1988). See also: Robert Young, "'For Thou Wert There': History, Erasure, and Superscription in *The Prelude*" in Samuel Weber, *Demarcating the Disciplines: Philosophy Literature Art* (Minneapolis: U of Minnesota P, 1986) 103–28; Mary Jacobus, *Romanticism, Writing and Sexual Difference* (Oxford: Clarendon, 1989) 16–27.

23 Paul de Man (eds. Burt, Newmark, Warminski), *Romanticism and Contemporary Criticism: The Gauss Seminar and Other Papers* (Baltimore: Johns Hopkins UP, 1993) 82.

24 Robert Alter, *The Art of Biblical Narrative* (New York: Basic Books, 1981) 52.

25 For *mise en abyme*, see Michael Riffaterre, *Fictional Truth* (Baltimore: Johns Hopkins UP, 1990) 22. In using this term, I wish to recover its technical use in heraldry from what Derrida and his epigones have, as it were, ruinously subjected it to. As Riffaterre puts it, a literary *mise en abyme* is (like the coat of arms placed, in small, within a coat of arms) "a mini-narrative encapsulating the narrative that contains it, a specularity, a mirroring of text by subtext remin-iscent of the Romantic conceit of the oak tree potential within the acorn."

26 Stanley Cavell, *A Pitch of Philosophy: Autobiographical Exercises* (Cambridge, MA: Harvard UP, 1994) 34–35; hereafter *Pi*.

27 Stanley Cavell, *Philosophical Passages: Wittgenstein, Emerson, Austin, Derrida* (Oxford and Cambridge, MA: Blackwell, 1995) 38; hereafter *Pa*.

28 I am rushing over, or through, the enormously important and anxiously tangled subject of the masculine and the feminine in our (whose?) economies of thinking, a subject drumming more and more insistently through Cavell's most recent work. The (en)gendering of our knowledge, for example, strikes me as the major preoccupation of his latest book on the movies. The subject of this book is the "unkown woman" of some Hollywood melodramas of the thirties and forties, and in pursuit of this subject, Cavell keeps returning to "the male philosopher's feminine voice (not by me identified with a general female feminine voice)," or (in another phrasing) keeps trying to hear tell of this "'forgotten,' misplaced feminine voice, letting it out, uttering it." See *Contesting Tears: The Hollywood Melodrama of the Unknown Woman* (Chicago: U of Chicago P, 1996) 34, 192.

60

INTRODUCTION

Tilottama Rajan

Source: *Dark Interpreter: The Discourse of Romanticism* (Ithaca, NY: Cornell University Press, 1980), pp. 13–26.

The work of art, according to Hegel, is "something made, produced by a man who has taken it into his imagination . . . and issued it by his own activity out of his imagination."[1] Hegel's statement about the purely formal or epistemological ideality of the work of art indicates why the ideals of the Romantic movement are so closely bound up with a belief in the transforming power of aesthetic activity, urged by Shelley and Schiller among others.[2] Art, as the power to invent, is paradigmatic of man's capacity to take existence itself into his mind and rewrite it according to the images of desire. Indeed the historical and etymological connection of the term "Romanticism" with "romance" points to a view of literature as an idealizing rather than a mimetic activity, a mode of consciousness that envisions the unreal and the possible across the barrier of the actual. Yet implicit in this belief that the mind can create the unreal must be a doubt as to the reality of a mental creation. Poetic language, as Paul de Man comments, is intentional in structure: because it is a product of consciousness rather than a reflection of external nature, it shares in the nothingness of consciousness rather than in the substantiality of things. As an attempt to transcend its own nothingness, the poetic image is doomed in advance, because it is "always constitutive, able to posit regardless of presence but, by the same token, unable to give a foundation to what it posits except as an intent of consciousness."[3] It is against this knowledge that we must read the Romantic attempt to deny the gap between fiction and actuality through an aesthetics which claims the identity of beauty and truth or mind and nature. We associate with the Romantics (particularly Coleridge and Schelling) a belief in the unity of consciousness and nature which, in turn, leads to an organic view of poetry as a natural and therefore real construct. But this view emerges as an essentially defensive reaction to an insight into the intentionality of poetic language which is present even in such writers as Coleridge and Schelling.

224

Even the more idealistic theorists of the period are not unaware that experience contradicts the language of affirmation. Jean-Paul Richter, who tries to argue for the identity of mimesis and idealization in the face of an obvious discrepancy between mental representations and things as they are, suggests that art is not just an imitation but a "corrective" imitation of reality. Poetry, according to him, "should neither destroy nor repeat but decipher reality":

> Poetry represents that highest life which is eternally lacking in all our reality ... she paints the future drama on the curtain of eternity. She is no flat mirror of the present, but the magic mirror of the time which is not yet. . . . We return to the principle of poetic imitation. If in poetic imitation the copy contains more than the original or even produces its opposite—pleasure from poetic sorrow, for example—this occurs because a double nature is being imitated: an outer and an inner one, *each the mirror of the other*.[4]

But there is in this argument, which bases itself on the doubleness of reality, a hiatus which invites us to deconstruct or see through the confident claim for the authority of poetic idealization. Jean-Paul begins by distinguishing an "inner" from an "outer" and merely apparent reality. He then manages to assume the monistic identity of the actual and the ideal, when in fact he has already used a dualistic separation of the two to restore figuratively a beauty which is clearly not present in life. The deliberate blurring of a vocabulary of transcendence into one of immanence allows him to conceal the extent to which he doubts the reality of his own idealism. To define literature as a decipherment rather than a straightforward imitation is already to constitute the Romantic text on two levels. It is to introduce a lacuna between historical appearance and eschatological innocence that may equally well become a lacuna between aesthetic appearance and existential reality.

It is often assumed (for instance by M. H. Abrams, Northrop Frye, and Ernest Lee Tuveson) that the high claims made for imagination as the guarantor of man's innocence over his corruption constitute what is truly revolutionary in the Romantic movement. In transferring the creative initiative from God to man, and in replacing revelation with imagination, the Romantics are thought to have overthrown a Christian pessimism which denied man direct access to the ideal. But in fact, a case can be made for saying that it is precisely this claim of a natural supernaturalism based on the imagination which is the most conservative element in a literature that stands on the edge of modernism, in a universe already recognized as discontinuous rather than organic. The Romantic rhetoric of affirmation avoids breaking with the past, and simply restates with reference to imagination the optimistic humanism urged by the Enlightenment with reference to reason. The compensatory, conservative nature of Romantic sacraments such as the marriage between mind and nature or the identity of beauty and truth is nowhere more evident than in Wordsworth. In both *The Prelude* and *The Excursion* he turns away from the disruptive horror disclosed by the French Revolution to a nature that exists in the past, even though he concedes in the latter poem that his vision of an organic universe may be a fiction of what never was ("Preface" to *The Excursion*, ll. 50–51).[5] In *The Prelude* itself the mythical status of this nature, and hence the compensatory motivation of the mind that imagines it, are repeatedly denied by an argument which speaks of the pastoral communion with nature as something "impaired" and then "restored," remembered and not imagined. But the poem also deconstructs its own assumptions by associating nature itself with the cataclysms of historical experience, which are described in natural metaphors of flood and deluge that make chaos and discontinuity at least as primary as organic unity (x.81–83). Paradoxically it is such recognitions, rather than the post-Enlightenment faith in human perfectibility through a secular conversion of the patterns of providence into those of aesthetic theodicy, which prove to be the truly subversive element in Romanticism.

My concern is not with the Romantic awareness of temporality, or of what Heidegger calls *Geworfenheit*. It is more specifically with the effect of this awareness on Romantic poems, considered reflexively as works that are trying to come to terms with the status of their own discourse, and hence with the function of man's imagination in relation to external reality. At certain critical points the Romantics deconstruct their own affirmative postulates. Jacques Derrida uses the term "deconstruction" to indicate the procedure of textual analysis by which the critic dismantles or takes apart the paraphrasable meaning of a text, in order to disclose within that text the gaps in logic which reveal the author's subconscious awareness of or commitment to a system of assumptions opposite to the one he explicitly endorses. Crucial to this procedure is the assumption that the text itself provides us with the tools we are to use in deconstructing it. To deconstruct a text is thus to assume that it is a disunified and contradictory structure tacitly involved in contesting its own meaning. The radicalism of deconstructive criticism in relation to other theories of multiple meaning such as the New Criticism has been well described by Derrida's translator, Gayatri Spivak, who notes that Cleanth Brooks equates complexity with a polysemy that does not disrupt the organic unity of the text. In a deconstruction, on the contrary, the critic attempts to "spot the point where a text covers up" its own self-contestation and hence sees "the text coming undone as a structure of concealment, revealing its self-transgression, its undecidability." She emphasizes that it is not a question "simply of locating a moment of ambiguity or irony ultimately incorporated into the text's system of unified meaning but rather a moment that genuinely threatens to collapse that system".[6] Such a moment occurs in the passage by Jean-Paul already cited.

Deconstructive criticism assumes not only that texts are self-negating from a thematic point of view, but also that they betray a semiotic anxiety about the tendency of literature to put what it says in doubt. There is nothing new about the view that the Romantics had doubts about their own imaginative logocentrism. But the status accorded these doubts in much of the most influential criticism is intermediate rather than terminal, and such criticism therefore does not call into question the view that the Romantics ultimately saw imagination as a transcending act. Bloom[7] and Frye emphasize the mythopoeic and visionary drive of Romantic language even in defeat. Abrams sees dejection and angst as a vital part of a dialectic of contraries which is meant to transcend rather than end in opposition. He does not regard Romantic poetry as what Schiller called a "naive" poetry, the product of a state of unorganized innocence. But he does see the typical Romantic work as capable of absorbing its own doubts without becoming discontinuous with its own assumptions. He does, therefore, tend to see the poetry of the period as committed to the "organized" or complex naiveté envisioned by Schiller as occurring in the future through a Coleridgean reconciliation of opposites in a dynamic unity.

Abrams, of course, is concerned more with the phenomenology of consciousness than with the status of discourse. But insofar as he makes assumptions about discourse, he remains committed to a logocentric reading of Romanticism derived from a philosophy of organicism. It is not unlikely that in determining the role of doubt within the dialectic of hope, he has in mind a model of the text which derives from the New Critical view of the poem as a complex harmony: an organic structure whose unity is strengthened rather than undermined by the presence of irony, ambiguity, and paradox. Such a view of poetry, because it makes the poet into the great reconciler, sustains rather than questions the constructive authority of imagination. While de Man may be wrong in arguing that *no* poetry can survive the self-contestation of irony and remain logocentric, the difficulty he senses about the potential contradiction between organic and ironic views of the poem seems valid with reference to *Romantic* poetry:

> As it refines its interpretations more and more, American criticism does not discover a single meaning, but a plurality of significations that can be radically opposed to each other. Instead of revealing a continuity affiliated with the coherence of the natural world, it takes us into a discontinuous world of reflective irony and ambiguity. . . . This unitarian criticism finally becomes a criticism of ambiguity, an ironic reflection on the absence of the unity it had postulated.[8]

Critics such as Abrams and Earl Wasserman, in other words, take into account the darker side of Romanticism, but do not always recognize how far these elements threaten traditional Romantic postulates. The darker elements in Romantic works are not a part of their organic unity, but rather threaten to collapse this unity.

What is equally important from the point of view of this study is that Abrams finds in German philosophy a theoretical support for an idealism not always carried to its dialectical completion by the poets. He therefore regards as an anachronism the readings of those critics who "looking back at earlier literature through the gloomy contemporary perspective . . . [argue] that Romantic writers could not really have meant what they claimed, hence that they must have been self-divided, or even unconsciously committed to the negations of the positives they so confidently asserted."[9] My own argument arises, in part, from a sense that the definitions of discourse developed by modern theorists such as Derrida, Heidegger, Sartre, and de Man[10] can already be found in the work of certain Romantic theorists, and that a deconstructive reading of Romantic poems is historically valid to the same degree as is a logocentric reading. But more important, the model of discourse eventually developed by the Romantic countertradition discussed in the next chapter, while fundamentally different from the one attributed to the Romantic period by critics such as Abrams and Frye, is also significantly different from the one developed by a criticism directed to the deconstruction of logocentric humanism. In other words, the current debate between organicist and deconstructionist critics over the nature of Romanticism was originally waged by the Romantics themselves and was not resolved in favor of either side. Thus it is Schiller, Schopenhauer, and Nietzsche who can provide us with a vocabulary with which to interpret a wide variety of Romantic poems, considered as allegories of the aesthetic act and the operations it performs. This vocabulary, while theoretically autonomous in its potential applicability outside the Romantic period, shares with the vocabulary derived by Abrams from Hegel and Schelling the advantage of being historically grounded within it.

Earlier criticism of Romantic poetry emphasized the validity of the period's transcendental claims for art, without giving full weight to the self-questioning consequent upon the fact that the history of Romantic poetry is that of "a syntax that proved inadequate to the demands placed upon it."[11] From the discontinuity Bostetter noted between an overly optimistic (even if complex) concept of art and a basic fidelity to the facts of existence arises a series of self-frustrating literary structures which German Romantic theorists characterize as ironic or sentimental. But contrary to Bostetter, the Romantic encounter between the theory of art and the poetry of experience is formative as well as frustrating. Poems such as *The Fall of Hyperion* and *The Triumph of Life* are involved in questioning the aesthetic assumptions with which they begin, and in moving toward a concept of art which permits the liberation, for conscious use by the poet, of areas of experience that had previously to be repressed or sublimated in accordance with a more naive view of the function of imagination. On the other hand, it is incorrect to argue that Romanticism is, from its inception, a movement of self-demystification. Paul de Man, who deduces a conscious aesthetic of failure from Romantic choices of literary forms, tends to minimize two related problems. He underestimates the degree to which Romantic poetry is conditioned by the period's belief in art as a transcending act to *evade* sentimentally the recognition of its own temporality. He also does not consider the extent to which such evasion, which distinguishes Romantic writers from modern writers such as Samuel Beckett and prevents Romantic texts from achieving pure irony, is a double-edged phenomenon. The Romantic evasion of the temporality of art is not just an act of bad faith, but ultimately a gesture that raises legitimate questions about the productive role of illusion in life.

The attempt of Romantic poetry to revise its sense of its own goals and limits is thus a complicated one. Serge Doubrovsky suggests that the "function of literature in every age" may be "precisely to constitute itself within the philosophy that is always more fundamental, more inward, more closely linked to human experience than the 'official' metaphysic of that same age."[12] What is offered in this book is, to some extent, a "deconstruction" of the official Romantic metaphysic of the imagination (endorsed by such modern critics as Abrams and Frye), and an argument that Romantic texts are themselves involved in probing beneath the assumptions about their own language which they incorporate as their surface content. From this point of view, the history of Romantic poetry and aesthetics can be seen as the gradual bringing to light of a counterplot within the apparently utopian narrative of Romantic desire, through the confrontation of recognitions initially hidden in the subtexts rather than the texts of works.[13] But it is also necessary to recognize that the text cannot simply be replaced by a subtext, and that the official content of a work does not cease to exist because it is undermined from within. It is because the doubts buried in subtexts are not necessarily "truer" than the affirmations urged in texts that Romanticism is less decisive in its commitment to self-irony than de Man sometimes supposes.[14] The limitations of deconstruction as a method of approaching Romantic poetry arise not only from its limitations as a critical position rather than a temporary critical tactic, but also from the Romantic poet's sense of the limits of demystification as an attitude to life.

Two texts not discussed subsequently may serve to illustrate the problematical duality of surface and depth present in Romantic conceptions of aesthetic discourse. The text which eventually became Book I of *The Excursion* began as a short, bare narrative of unrelieved distress. Wordsworth added to it a pantheistic gloss so different from the substance of the poem that at one point (in the D version) he was compelled to split his text into two separate poems, "The Ruined Cottage" and "The Pedlar." The providential vision of nature that emerges from "The Pedlar" reinterprets and sublimates the vision of nature as a bleak, amoral force, similar to

229

Shelley's "Power," which emerges from "The Ruined Cottage." Coleridge's *Rime of the Ancient Mariner* is similarly a work whose stylistically hybrid quality throws into relief a fault or break in the poem's inner space, which divides idealization from truth. The gloss (added in 1817) is an attempt to ameliorate the much earlier narrative through a selective mimesis of the latter, which excludes its ambiguities and horrors, makes the mariner's return to the soul's own country seem more certain than it is, and absorbs purgatory into theodicy. In the cases of both Wordsworth and Coleridge, there is a contradiction between argument and narrative: the text includes a subtext which can be used to take it apart. And in both cases, the chronological priority of this subtext reveals the genesis of an affirmative rhetoric in an anxiety it cannot wholly dismiss.

This peculiar coexistence of one discourse with another that radically contradicts it can be explained only as a result of inconsistent views of how poetry ought to represent the world it depicts. The naturalistic narrative of "The Ruined Cottage" is a product of the belief that poetry should be mimetic, while the psychological biography of the Pedlar is written with a sense that the function of a narrator is correctively to idealize experience by pretending to be innocent of it. That Wordsworth was not unaware of this dichotomy is evident from the fact that he kept revising the text in such a way as to bring out the very heteronomy between the idealistic and mimetic aspects of discourse which he tries to hide. It is also evident from the fact that he elevates the naive figure of the Pedlar to the status of a guide, yet denies his discourse the confirming authority of the first-person narrative used in *The Prelude*, and thus skeptically distances the reader from a "retelling" or "representation" of experience that may be perceived as unreliable. In Coleridge's poem, similarly, the gloss claims for language the power of transcending life. Yet this power is constantly put in question by the fact that the act of speech as it appears in the narrative itself is an act of disclosure and not of idealization: a retelling in which the Mariner must return obsessively into the very core of darkness he is supposed to have mastered.

Coleridge's inclusion of two texts (the gloss and the narrative) thematizes the process by which art "represents" experience, and exposes a lacuna between aesthetic form and existential content that exists less obviously in the texts discussed in subsequent chapters. From a poem's choice of a literary genre or mode of discourse it is often possible to infer the assumptions it is making about the nature of the aesthetic medium. Yet the status of these assumptions in Romantic texts is frequently put in doubt by the inclusion of a secondary discourse that splits the work into conflicting strata of awareness. Keats's late romances, which couple realistic and grotesque elements with romance, and in which romance functions as a metonymy for the idealizing power of aesthetic illusion in general, typify a tendency to reflect upon the conventions of a naive art by attaching them to conventions that make radically opposite assumptions. While the ambivalence of

Romantic poems is sometimes reflected in a stylistic heteronomy within the poem, at other times it is expressed less obviously through an ambiguity in the illocutionary force attributed to the argument of the text. Both *Prometheus Unbound* and Coleridge's conversation poems uneasily hypostatize mental representation, by using modes of discourse that claim the status of affirmative statement for a vision that is elsewhere conceded to exist only in the subjunctive mood of desire.

My own feeling that we need to return behind existing readings of Romantic poetry to the theoretical nexus in which both idealistic and deconstructive theories have their genesis[15] arises from this sense of a doubleness or ambivalence in Romantic texts for which modern critical schools have so far been unable to invent a terminology. Romantic poetry is certainly not what Schiller calls a naive poetry, a poetry free of doubt and irony. Long before Derrida and de Man, D. G. James complained that Shelley's poetry is neither on this side nor on that, but inhabits a split in its own interpretation of existence: "Thus we complain chiefly, not that he does not show us what he thinks, but that what he shows and what he thinks cannot be reconciled."[16] Such a comment lays the groundwork for a deconstructive reading of Romanticism. Indeed, the characteristic of the Romantic text seems to be that it exists on two levels of awareness, often to the point of self-contradiction. But what the critic is to make of this self-contradiction is the crucial problem, and the guidance provided by the poetry itself is less clear than the main schools of criticism suppose. Because Romantic poetry itself conceives of its function (not simply its status) as both mimetic and idealistic, the fundamentally idealistic reading followed by organicist criticism is difficult to sustain. But on the other hand, the relationship between the mimetic and idealistic levels as surface and depth seems to vary from one text to another, and the idealistic level is not always the less "fundamental" and less "inward." It thus becomes a simplification to dismiss Romantic idealism as a willful blindness to an awareness concealed in the subtexts of poems—the view tacitly taken by proto-deconstructionists like Bostetter. Equally, it becomes a simplification to see all doubt as a deliberate strategy—the view taken by recent deconstructionists who attempt to rehabilitate Romantic writers by suggesting that they were really more modern than their skeptical critics.

Romantic literature is better seen as a literature involved in the restless process of self-examination, and in search of a model of discourse which accommodates rather than simplifies its ambivalence toward the inherited equation of art with idealization. The first chapter of this book attempts to trace the working out of such a model dialectically, through a series of critical texts beginning with Schiller's *On Naive and Sentimental Poetry* and culminating in Nietzsche's *Birth of Tragedy*. These texts, in turn, provide a vocabulary to describe and relate the contradictory aesthetic postures assumed by Romantic poetry in its parallel attempt to reassess its own status. In focusing on some of the major work of three writers—Shelley, Keats, and Coleridge—I have attempted to be illustrative and not exhaustive. The inclusion of works so heterogeneous as conversation poems, romances, and mythological narratives suggests something of the range of the texts that, despite surface dissimilarities, can be seen as reflecting on the status of their own discourse. But since this is intended to be a theoretical and not a historical study of Romanticism, I have avoided including a number of works, such as *The Rime of the Ancient Mariner* and *Childe Harold's Pilgrimage*, discussion of which would only have resulted in the repetition of conclusions already reached with regard to works of Keats and Shelley. For similar reasons, and because of the work already done on him by Geoffrey Hartman, David Ferry, and Frances Ferguson, I have limited myself to brief discussions of Wordsworth in the course of a chapter on Coleridge. In discussing three authors (one early Romantic and two late Romantic poets) I try to provide a biography of the oeuvre, as it were, and to see individual poems as related moments in the journey of each aesthetic consciousness. But in excluding three other major poets, I assume that they too would yield to the same kind of approach, and I try to indicate at the end of the book the lines that such study might follow.

Finally, a word should be said about the theoretical vocabulary employed here. The use of words such as "naive" and "sentimental" or "Apollonian" and "Dionysiac" does not simply involve exchanging one set of terms for another, putting a Romantic vocabulary derived from German idealism in place of the more traditional Blakean terms "innocence" and "experience," or the orthodox Christian antithesis of Edenic and fallen man. On the contrary, it is a way of indicating an important shift in the Romantic conception of the structure of human experience. The traditional vocabulary of Romantic criticism, which provides secular equivalents for the stages of providential history, tacitly hypostastizes the state of innocence by identifying it with Eden, and thus legitimizes the notion of art as a corrective illusion, designed to repair the ruins of our first parents. The vocabulary of Schiller and (to a greater extent) Schopenhauer and Nietzsche not only secularizes, but also *internalizes* innocence as a psychic defence, and thus recognizes it as partly a fictive projection of the sentimental consciousness. The far-reaching consequences of this recognition for the way the mind conceives of aesthetic discourse will be the subject of the following chapters.

Notes

1 G. W. F. Hegel, *Aesthetics: Lectures on Fine Art* (1835), trans. T. M. Knox (Oxford: Clarendon, 1975), I, 162.
2 I refer to Shelley's "A Defence of Poetry" and Schiller's letters *On the Aesthetic Education of Man*. Among critics who have argued for the centrality of imagination to Romantic utopianism are M. H. Abrams (*Natural Supernaturalism: Tradition and Revolution in Romantic Literature* [New York: Norton, 1971],

pp. 117ff.), Northrop Frye (*A Study of English Romanticism* [New York: Random House, 1968], pp. 20ff.), Ernest Lee Tuveson (*The Imagination as a Means of Grace* [Berkeley and LosAngeles: University of California Press, 1960]), and Harold Bloom (*The Visionary Company* [New York: Doubleday, 1961], p. xiv; "The Internalization of Quest Romance," in *The Ringers in The Tower* [Chicago: University of Chicago Press, 1971], pp. 13–36).

3 Paul de Man, "The Intentional Structure of the Romantic Image," in *Romanticism and Consciousness*, ed. Harold Bloom (New York: Norton, 1970), p. 69. The notion of intentionality was originated by Brentano and Husserl, but de Man's use of the term probably derives from Sartre. In defining consciousness itself as "intentional" (i.e., as consciousness *of* something from which it is separated by the act of having to conceive this thing) Sartre emphasizes that consciousness is a *nothing* or lack in relation to the being outside itself. In applying this concept to the image, he notes that "an image, too, is an image *of* something," and is not the thing itself from which it is divided by the act of having to image it (*Imagination: A Psychological Critique* [1936], trans. Forrest Williams [Ann Arbor: University of Michigan Press, 1972], p. 133). For a further discussion of the idea that language can only *intend* and cannot *incarnate* what it describes, see Sartre, *The Psychology of Imagination* (1940), trans. Bernard Frechtman (New York: Washington Square Press, 1968), p. 5; and also *Imagination*, p. 4.

4 Jean-Paul Richter, *Horn of Oberon: Jean-Paul Richer's "School for Aesthetics"* (1812), trans. Margaret R. Hale (Detroit: Wayne State University Press, 1973), pp. 309, 24. Italics mine.

5 Unless otherwise indicated, all references to Romantic poems supplied in the text are to the collected editions listed in the Selected List of Works Cited.

6 Jacques Derrida, *Of Grammatology* (1967), trans. Gayatri Spivak (Baltimore: The Johns Hopkins University Press, 1976), pp. lxxiii–lxxv. Deconstruction holds that language is inherently self-undermining and that the text is a self-consuming artifact. It thus sets itself in opposition to almost the entire past tradition of semiotics, which Derrida labels *logocentric* because it invests language with the authority to signify truth. The logocentric tradition assumes that language has the capacity to "make present" the truth which it "re-presents" through linguistic signs, and that this direct correspondence between the signifier and the thing signified is guaranteed either by some transcendent source or (as in Romanticism) by the true voice of feeling. In a literary sense, it is thus possible to speak of a logocentric *poetics of presence*, which assumes that literature can make present that which it signifies, can make real that which it imagines. In contrast, Derrida argues that language is a product of *différance*, and cannot be viewed logocentrically: the prime characteristic of language is that the signifier does not make present the thing signified, and that words are thus the *deferral* rather than the communication of a truth which they indicate but simultaneously undermine. In a literary sense, the consequence of Derrida's view of language would be a *poetics of absence*, in which the text would be a perpetual contesting and canceling of its own meaning, and hence a projection of its own nothingness.

Derrida's use of a deconstructive method of criticism arises from his general characterization of language as *différance* rather than *logos;* I make no such assumptions about the structure of language, and hence do not see deconstruction as a method valid with reference to all texts. Self-contestation is not an inherent feature of literary works, and deconstruction is a critical procedure applicable only to those texts which do contest their own meaning. There are, in other words, logocentric poems, although they do not fall within the range of this study.

7 Harold Bloom, *Shelley's Mythmaking* (1959; rpt. Ithaca: Cornell University Press, 1969).

8 De Man, *Blindness and Insight: Essays in the Rhetoric of Contemporary Criticism* (New York: Oxford University Press, 1971), p. 28.

9 Abrams, *Natural Supernaturalism*, p. 446.

10 See Appendix A for further discussion of the relation of Derrida and de Man to Heidegger and Sartre.

11 Edward Bostetter, *The Romantic Ventriloquists: Wordsworth, Coleridge, Shelley, Keats, Byron* (1963; revised ed. Seattle: University of Washington Press, 1975), p. 5.

12 Serge Doubrovsky, *The New Criticism in France* (1966), trans. Derek Coltman (Chicago: University of Chicago Press, 1973), p. 279.

13 The word "subtext" was first used by Stanislavski to indicate that part of a play which is not made explicit in the dialogue, but emerges between the lines. I use the word in a slightly different sense, to indicate a subversive and repressed text which is not consistent with the explicit text, in relation to which it stands as the subconscious to the conscious. I assume first that the subtext is not something that a reader infers from between the lines but something which can be found *in* the words of a poem, and second that the author is not wholly in control of his subtext. Where he is in control of a "second" text within the poem, I would use the term "countertext" or "co-text."

14 To be fair, de Man does sometimes recognize the "tenacious self-mystification" of Romantic writers with regard to "the truths that come to light in the last quarter of the eighteenth century" ("The Rhetoric of Temporality," in *Interpretation: Theory and Practice*, ed. Charles Singleton [Baltimore: The Johns Hopkins University Press, 1969], p. 191). But latterly he has seemed to view this tendency of Romanticism to relapse into illusions it sees through as something inherent in language, which cannot deconstruct except in relation to something constructed. Thus Romanticism, according to him, is not divided between text and subtext. "[It] is not a demystification. It is demystified from the start," as is all language (*Blindness and Insight*, p. 18). I would see the tendency mentioned above as something specific to Romanticism: an upsurge of the idealistic impulse, rather than simply an intermission in the drama of irony. That is to say, I would give the self-mystificatory tendencies in Romanticism more importance than does de Man.

15 The link between deconstructive criticism and the philosophy of Schopenhauer and Nietzsche is discussed in the next chapter. Organicist criticism derives even more clearly from Romantic philosophy: particularly that of Coleridge and Schelling.

16 D. G. James, *The Romantic Comedy* (London: Oxford University Press, 1948), p. 96.

Part 10

SUBJECTIVITY, PSYCHOLOGY, AND SOCIOLOGY

61

CHRISTABEL:
THE WANERING MOTHER
AND THE ENIGMA OF FORM

Karen Swann

Source: *Studies in Romanticism* 23 (1986), 533–54.

The first questions Christabel asks Geraldine refer to identity and origins: "who art thou?" and "how camest thou here?" Geraldine's response is oblique; in effect she replies, "I am like you, and my story is like your own":

> My sire is of a noble line,
> And my name is Geraldine:
> Five warriors seized me yestermorn,
> Me, even me, a maid forlorn: . . .
>
> They spurred amain, their steeds were white:
> And once we crossed the shade of night.
> As sure as Heaven shall rescue me,
> I have no thought what men they be;
> Nor do I know how long it is
> (For I have lain entranced I wis)
> Since one, the tallest of the five,
> Took me from the palfrey's back,
> A weary woman, scarce alive. . . .
>
> Whither they went I cannot tell—
> I thought I heard, some minutes past,
> Sounds as of a castle bell.
> Stretch forth thy hand (thus ended she),
> And help a wretched maid to flee.
>
> (ll. 79–104)[1]

Geraldine's tale echoes and anticipates Christabel's. Christabel is also first introduced as the daughter of a "noble" father; she, too, experiences things she "cannot tell," calls on Heaven to rescue her, crosses threshholds and falls into trances. But in contrast to the story "Christabel," often criticized for its ambiguities, Geraldine's tale presents sexual and moral categories as unambiguous and distinct: villainous male force appropriates and silences an innocent female victim. This difference effects a corresponding clarification of genre. Geraldine translates "Christabel" into the familiar terms of the tale of terror.

Geraldine's translation would appear to establish the identity of the woman. Ultimately, however, her story complicates the issue of feminine identity by suggesting its entanglement, at the origin, with genre. How one takes Geraldine depends on one's sense of the "line" of representations she comes from. For Christabel, but also, for any absorbed reader of circulating library romances, Geraldine's story of abduction works as a seduction— Christabel recognizes Geraldine as a certain type of heroine and embraces her.[2] More guarded readers appropriate Geraldine as confidently as Christabel does, but they see her quite differently. Charles Tomlinson, for example, reads "Christabel" as "a tale of terror," but in contrast to Geraldine's own story casts her in the role of villain, while for Patricia Adair, Geraldine is betrayed by her very conventionality: she tells her story in "rather unconvincing and second-rate verse which was, no doubt, deliberately meant to sound false."[3] Geraldine is "false" because she comes from an ignoble line of Gothic temptresses, or, in the case of other critics, because she can be traced back to the ignoble Duessa and to a host of other predatory figures. Tellingly these sophisticated readers, who employ literary history to read Geraldine as a figure of untruth, are the worst ruffians—they either refuse to hear the woman's story of her own abduction, or assume that her protests are really a come-on.

Geraldine may be Christabel's ghost or projection as many critics have suggested, but only if we acknowledge that Christabel produces herself as a received representation—a feminine character who in turn raises the ghosts of different subtexts, each dictating a reading of her as victim or seductress, good or evil, genuine or affected. I will be arguing in this essay that "Christabel" both dramatizes and provokes hysteria. The poem explores the possessing force of certain bodies—Geraldine's, of course, but also bodies of literary convention, which I am calling "genres." Particularly in Coleridge's day, debates on literary decorum allowed the gendering of structure in a way that seemed to assuage anxiety about the subject's relation to cultural forms. Questions involving the subject's autonomy could be framed as an opposition between authentic, contained "manly" speech and "feminine" bodies—the utterly conventional yet licentiously imaginative female characters, readers, and genres of the circulating libraries. In "Christabel," Coleridge both capitalizes on and exposes culture's tactical gendering of formal questions. The poem invites us to link the displacing movement of cultural forms through subjects to the "feminine" malady of hysteria and the "feminine" genres of the circulating library; at the same time, it mockingly and dreamily informs us that hysteria is the condition of all subjects in discourse, and that the attribution of this condition to feminine bodies is a conventional, hysterical response.

I

If Coleridge were thinking of dramatizing hysteria in a poem, he might have turned to Burton's account of "Maids', Nuns', and Widows' Melancholy" in *The Anatomy of Melancholy*, a book he knew well. According to Burton, hysterics "think themselves bewitched":

> Some think they see visions, confer with spirits and devils, they shall surely be damned, are afraid of some treachery, imminent danger, and the like, they will not speak, make answer to any question, but are almost distracted, mad, or stupid for the time, and by fits. . . .[4]

The malady befalls barren or celibate women; among these, Catholic noblewomen who are forced to remain idle are particularly susceptible. Most of the symptoms Burton catalogues are touched on in the passage quoted above. Hysterics have visions and are afraid "by fits"—the "fits of the mother" or womb ("the heart itself beats, is sore grieved, and faints . . . like fits of the mother" [p. 415]). The symptom which most interests Burton, though, is the inability of hysterics to communicate their troubles: they "cannot tell" what ails them. This fact becomes a refrain of his own exposition: "and yet will not, cannot again tell how, where, or what offends them", "many of them cannot tell how to express themselves in words, or how it holds them, what ails them; you cannot understand them, or well tell what to make of their sayings" (p. 416).

They "cannot tell," and *you* cannot "well tell" what to make of them: the phenomenon of their blocked or incomprehensible speech seems to produce similar effects in the writer. And indeed, Burton's impetous and fitful prose in many respects resembles the discourse of the hysteric, into whose point of view he regularly tumbles ("Some *think* they see visions," but "they *shall* surely be damned" [my italics]). Far from resisting this identification, Burton makes narrative capital from the slippage, as here, when he allows himself to become "carried away" by sympathy for the Christabel-like afflicted:

> I do not so much pity them that may otherwise be eased, but those alone that out of a strong temperament, innate constitution, are violently carried away with this torrent of inward humours, and

> though very modest of themselves, sober, religious, virtuous, and well given (as many so distressed maids are), yet cannot make resistance . . .

and then, as if shaking off a "fit," comically pauses to reflect on his own indecorous "torrents":

> But where am I? Into what subject have I rushed? What have I to do with nuns, maids, virgins, widows? I am a bachelor myself, and lead a monastic life in a college: *nae ego sane ineptus qui haec dixerim*, I confess 'tis an indecorum, and as Pallas, a virgin, blushed when Jupiter by chance spake of love matters in her presence, and turned away her face, *me reprimam*; though my subject necessarily require it, I will say no more.
>
> (p. 417)

Protesting all the while his ignorance of women, the "old bachelor" coyly figures himself as a virgin whose body betrays her when desire takes her unawares. He also takes the part of the apparently more knowing and self-controlled Jupiter, but only to suggest that the latter's fatherly indifference is an act. For whether he is an artful or artless seducer, Jupiter himself appears only to rush into speech "by chance"—the "chance," we suspect, of finding himself in such close proximity to his virginal daughter. The woman whose desire is written on her body is like the man who makes love the "matter" of his discourse: both attempt to disguise desire, and become the more seductive when desire is revealed in the context of their attempts to suppress it.

The story of Pallas and Jupiter is placed at a strategic point in Burton's chapter. It punctuates his resolve to check the torrents of his narrative, a resolve immediately and engagingly broken when, more "by chance" than design, he finds he has to say something more ("And yet I must and will say something more"). This time he is prompted by his commiseration with all distressed women to launch an attack on "them that are in fault."

> . . . those tyrannizing pseudo-politicians, superstitious orders, rash vows, hard-hearted parents, guardians, unnatural friends, allies (call them how you will), those careless and stupid overseers . . .

those fathers and parental substitutes (particularly the Church), who "suppress the vigour of youth" and ensure the orderly descent of their estates through the enforced celibacy of their daughters (p. 418). An "old bachelor" who leads a monastic life in a college; whose own discourse, like the discourse of the hysteric, seems to be the product of a strained compromise between lawless impulses and the claims of order; who might himself be said to be possessed by spirits and the dead language in which they wrote, ends his

240

discussion of "maids', nuns', and widows' melancholy" by championing those who "cannot tell" against the ungenerous legislators of the world.

There are suggestive correspondences between Burton's chapter on hysteria and "Christabel." Christabel is a virtuous Catholic gentlewoman whose lover is away, possibly at the behest of her father, out of whose castle she "steals" at the beginning of the poem. Whether or not he is responsible for blighting love affairs,[5] Sir Leoline has affinities with both of Burton's father-figures: like the "pseudopoliticians" he is intimately linked with repressive law; like Jupiter, his relation to his daughter is somewhat suspect. Moreover, the poem's descriptions of Christabel's experiences—first with the possibly supernatural Geraldine and later, with a traumatic memory or scene which comes over her by fits and bars her from telling—and its insistent references to a "mother" who at one point threatens to block Geraldine's speech ("Off, wandering mother!" [l. 205]), follow Burton's account of the characteristic symptoms of hysteria. But Coleridge may have appreciated most the comic slippages in Burton's narrative between the slightly hysterical scholar whose business it is to "tell" and the women who are the matter of his discourse. When he came to write "Christabel," Coleridge told the story through narrators who are as enigmatic as the women they tell about—we cannot "well tell" if they are one voice or two. More than any detail of the plot, the participation of these narrators in the "feminine" exchanges they describe, and the poem's playful suggestion that hysteria cannot be restricted to *feminine* bodies, marks the kinship of "Christabel" and Burton's text.

II

Who is Geraldine and where does she come from? Possibly, from Christabel. In the opening of the poem Christabel has gone into the woods to pray for her absent lover after having had uneasy dreams "all yester-night"—"Dreams, that made her moan and leap, / As on her bed she lay in sleep," we are told in the 1816 version of the poem. In the woods *two* ladies perform the actions of moaning and leaping which, yester-night, *one* lady had performed alone:

> The lady leaps up suddenly,
> The lovely lady, Christabel!
> It moaned as near, as near can be,
> But what it is she cannot tell—
> On the other side it seems to be,
> Of the huge, broad-breasted, old oak tree.
>
> (1816: ll. 37–42)

For a moment we, too, are in the woods, particularly if, like the poem's "first" readers, we already know something of the plot. Does "the lady" refer to Christabel or Geraldine? Is her leaping up the cause or effect of fright? The next lines supply answers to these questions, and as the scene proceeds "it" resolves into the distinct, articulate character Geraldine. For a moment's space, however, we entertain the notion that an uneasy lady leaped up suddenly and terrified herself.

Burton says of hysterics, "some think they see visions, confer with spirits and devils, they shall surely be damned." Geraldine is such a "vision." She appears in response to what Burton implies and psychoanalysis declares are the wishes of hysterics—to get around patriarchal law, which legislates desire. In the beginning of the poem Christabel "cannot tell" what ails her, but critics have theorized from her sighs that she is suffering from romance, from frustrated love for the "lover that's far away," for the Baron, or even, for the mother.[6] Geraldine, who appears as if in answer to Christabel's prayer, "steals" with her back into the castle, sleeps with her "as a mother with her child," and then meets the Baron's embrace, allows the performance of these wishes. Moreover, like an hysterical symptom, which figures both desire and its repression, Geraldine also fulfills the last clause of Burton's formula: although much is ambiguous *before* she appears, it is not until she appears that Christabel feels "damned," and that we are invited to moralize ambiguity as duplicity, the cause of "sorrow and shame" (ll. 270, 296, 674).

As well as answering *Christabel's* desires, however, Geraldine answers the indeterminacy of the narrative and the reader's expectancy. The wood out-side the Baron's castle is not the "natural" world, as is often declared,[7] but a world stocked with cultural artifacts. Before Geraldine ever appears it is haunted by the ghosts of old stories: familiar settings and props function as portents, both for the superstitious and the well-read. The wood and the midnight hour are the "moment's space" where innocence is traditionally put to the test, or when spirits walk abroad; other details—the cock's crow at midnight, the mastiff's unrest, the contracted moon—we know to be art's way of signifying nature's response to human disorder. These so-called "Gothic trappings" ensnare us because they mean nothing ("Tu-whit, tu-whoo") and too much: like the sighs we seize on as evidence of Christabel's inner life, they gesture to an enigma, something as yet hidden from view. Geraldine makes "answer meet" to these suspensions of the narrative, not by providing closure, but by representing indeterminacy:

> There she sees a damsel bright,
> Drest in a silken robe of white,
> That shadowy in the moonlight shone:
> The neck that made that white robe wan,
> Her stately neck, and arms were bare;
> Her blue-veined feet unsandal'd were,
> And wildly glittered here and there
> The gems entangled in her hair.
>
> (ll. 58–65)

Precipitating out of the Gothic atmosphere, Geraldine promises to contain in herself an entrapping play of surfaces and shadows; with her appearance suspense resolves into a familiar sign of ambiguity.

Geraldine is a fantasy, produced by the psychic operations of condensation and displacement. On the one hand, her function is to objectify: she intervenes in moments of interpretive crisis as a legible representation—a "vision," a story, and a plot. At the same time, though, she, the story she tells, and the plot she seems to set in motion are all displacing performances of ambiguities she might at first promise to "answer" more decisively. After she pops up, two women dramatize the implied doubleness of the daughter who "stole" along the forest keeping her thoughts to herself (l. 31). Very little else changes. Prompted by an uneasy dream one women "stole" out of her father's castle; two women return to it "as if in stealth" (l. 120), and by the end of Part I Christabel has simply resumed "fearfully dreaming," at least according to the narrator (l. 294). The spell that becomes "lord of her utterance" (l. 268) that night does no more than render explicit the inhibition of her "telling" already operative in the opening scene of the poem, where her silence was obscurely connected to the brooding, dreaming "lord" of the castle, the father who loved the daughter "so well." By the end of the poem we have simply returned to where we began: Christabel is "inly praying" once again, this time at the "old" Baron's feet, and once again Geraldine is on "the other side" (l. 614).

While it proposes an answer to the question "who art thou?" this reading only makes Christabel's second question to Geraldine more problematic: Geraldine is a fantasy, but she does not seem to "come from" any locatable place. The many source studies of the poem have shown that her origins are as much in literature as in Christabel: she first appears to the latter as a highly aestheticized object, and first speaks, many readers think to her discredit, in a highly encoded discourse. A material, communally available representation, she could have been dreamed up by any of the characters to whom she appears in the course of the poem—by the uneasy dreamer Christabel, but also by the Baron, into whose castle she steals while he is asleep, and, Christabel suggests, dreaming uneasily (l. 165), or by Bracy, whose dream of her seems to "live upon [his] eye" the next day (l. 559). She could even be part of *our* dream. For in "Christabel" as in all of his poems of the supernatural, Coleridge plots to turn us into dreamers—to "procure" our "willing suspension of disbelief," our happy relinquishment of the reality principle. In "Christabel" as in dreams there is no version of the negative: questions raise possibilities that are neither confirmed nor wholly dismissed ("Is it the wind . . . ? / There is not wind enough . . ." [ll. 44–45]). Tags drift from one "lady" to another, suggesting the affinity of apparent adversaries; signs are familiar yet unreadable, laden with associations which neither exclude each other nor resolve into univocality.

Geraldine intervenes into these several dreamlike states as a figure of the imaginary itself—a figure whose legibility derives from its status within the Symbolic order. She obeys the laws which structure all psychic phenomena, including dreams, jokes, and hysteria, the malady which allowed Freud to "discover" these very laws. The latter, however, do not explain why *particular* representations become collectively privileged. Why, at moments when they brush with the (il-)logic of the unconscious, do subjects automatically, even hysterically, produce certain *gendered* sights and stories?—produce the image of a radically divided woman, or of two women in each other's arms; and produce the story of a woman who seduces, and/or is seduced, abducted, and silenced by a father, a seducer, and/or a ruffian? This story, including all the ambiguities that make it hard to "tell," is of course the story of hysteria as told by Burton, and later, painstakingly reconstructed by Freud from its plural, displacing performances on the bodies of women. Even the common reader would know it, however, for it describes all the permutations of the romance plot—a form largely, but not exclusively, associated with a body of popular, "feminine" literature.

If a body like Geraldine's pops up from behind a tree when all the witnesses are in the woods, it is no accident: everyone thinks feminine forms appropriately represent the dangers and attractions of fantasy life. Coleridge, who dramatized the highly overdetermined romance/hysteria plot in "Christabel" and happily flaunted feminine bodies when it suited him, was no exception. But I want to argue, first by looking at his generic play, and then by examining his treatment of the family romance, that in "Christabel" he was also mockingly obtruding a conspiracy to view, allowing us to see "feminine" genre and gender alike as cultural fantasy.

III

"Christabel's" narrators are themselves hysterics. The poem's interlocutor and respondent mime the entanglement of Geraldine and Christabel—I call them "they," but it is not clear if we hear two voices or one. Like the women they describe, they are overmastered by "visions." Repeatedly, they abandon an authoritative point of view to fall into the story's present; or they engage in transferential exchanges with the characters whose plot they are narrating. In the opening scene, for example, one of them plunges into the tale to plead to and for Christabel: "Hush, beating heart of Christabel! / Jesu, Maria, shield her well!" As if she hears, a stanza later Christabel cries out, "Mary mother, save me now!" (ll. 53–54, 69). Further on, the sequence is reversed when the speaker seems to take up Christabel's speech. She has just assured Geraldine that Sir Leoline will "guide and guard [her] safe and free" (l. 110); although the narrators generally are not as trusting as Christabel, one seems inspired by her confidence to echo her, twice: "So free from danger, free from fear / They crossed the court: right glad they were" (ll. 135–36, 143–44).

These narrators create the conditions and logic of dream: like them, and because of them, the reader is impotent to decide the poem's ambiguities from a position outside its fictions. Furthermore, the poem's "fictions" seem to be about little else than these formal slippages. The repressed of "Christabel's" dreamwork is almost too visible to be seen—not a particular psychic content but literary conventions themselves, like those which demand that narrators speak from privileged points of view, and important for this argument, bodies of conventions or "genres." "Christabel" obtrudes genre to our notice. The Gothic atmosphere of the first stanza, with its enumerations of ominously coincident bird and clock noises, goes slightly bad in the second—partly because of the very presence of the shocking "mastiff bitch," but also because both mastiff and narrator become heady with coincidence: making answer to the clock, "Four for the quarters, and twelve for the hour . . . Sixteen short howls, not over loud," she becomes an obvious piece of Gothic machinery (ll. 10–13). A similar generic disturbance occurs between Part 1, told more or less in the "tale of terror" convention, and its conclusion, which recapitulates the story in a new convention, that of sentimental fiction. Suddenly Christabel "means" "a bourgeois lady of delicate, even saccharine, sensibility": "Her face, oh call it fair not pale, / And both blue eyes more bright than clear, / Each about to have a tear" (ll. 289–91). As suddenly, the narrators are exposed in a desperate act of wielding genre, using convention to force legibility on a sight that won't be explained.

Once we become aware of these instabilities, no stretch of the poem is exempt. In life women might faint, dogs might moan, and fires might flare up without anyone remarking it; if these coincide in story, they mean something. When they coincide in the overloaded, tonally unsettling Part I of "Christabel" they simultaneously draw attention to themselves as elements of a code. Although we may think of genres as vessels which successive authors infuse with original content, "Christabel's" "originality" is to expose them as the means by which significance is produced and contained.

This analysis raises the issue of the generic status of "Christabel." What is its literary genre? But also, what genre of psychic phenomenon does the poem aspire to—is it like a dream, as we first proposed, or like a joke? The latter question may not immediately seem important, since jokes and dreams have so much in common: like hysteria, they work by condensation and displacement to bring the repressed to light.[8] But for the poem's first readers, at least, it clearly mattered which was which. The reviewers of 1816 fiercely protested the poem's "licentious" mixing of joke and dream, categories of psychic phenomena which they translated into literary categories: was "Christabel" a bit of "doggrel," a wild, weird tale of terror, or a fantastic combination of the two? (Modern readers, less tuned to genre play, have decided the question by not hearing the jokes.)[9] Coleridge's contemporaries recognized that jokes and dreams demand different attitudes: if one responds to "Christabel" as though it were just a wild weird tale, and it turns out to be a joke, then the joke is on oneself. "Christabel" frightened its reviewers, not because it was such a successful tale of terror, but because they couldn't decide what sort of tale it was.

"Christabel" made its first readers hysterical because it is not one genre or another but a joke on our desire to decide genre. As such, it turned a "merely" formal question into a matter of one upsmanship. Most of the critics responded by redirecting the joke, giving the impression that it was on the poem and the author. Coleridge, they claimed, mixed the genres of joke and dream, not as a joke, but in a dream. What is telling is their almost universal decision to recast these issues of literary and formal mastery into the more obviously charged and manageable terms of sexual difference. According to them, the poem was, after all, just one of those tales of terror which ladies like to read ("For what woman of fashion would not purchase a book recommended by Lord Byron?" asks the *AntiJacobin*[10]); the author, variously described as an "enchanted virgin," an "old nurse," a "dreamer"— by implication, a hysteric—simply could not control the discourses that spoke through him like so many "lords" of his utterance.[11]

Gendering the formal question, the reviewers reenact the scene of Geraldine's first appearance: then, too, a variety of characters responded to indeterminacy by producing a feminine body at once utterly conventional and too full of significance. In critical discourse as in fantasy life, it seems, feminine forms—the derogated genres of the circulating library, the feminized body of the author, or the body of Geraldine—represent the enigma of form itself. Female bodies "naturally" seem to figure an ungraspable truth: that form, habitually viewed as the arbitrary, contingent vessel of more enduring meanings, is yet the source and determinant of all meanings, whether the subject's or the world's.

Displacing what is problematic about form onto the feminine gender ultimately serves the hypothetical authenticity and integrity of masculine gender and "manly" language. Look, for example, at the opening lines of the passage Hazlitt selects as the only "genuine burst of humanity" "worthy of the author" in the whole poem—the only place where "no dream oppresses him, no spell binds him"[12]:

> Alas! they had been friends in youth;
> But whispering tongues can poison truth;
> And constancy lives in realms above;
> And life is thorny; and youth is vain;
> And to be wroth with one we love
> Doth work like madness in the brain.
> And thus it chanced, as I divine,
> With Roland and Sir Leoline.
>
> (ll. 408–15)

Hazlitt was not alone in his approbation: many reviewers of the poem quoted this passage with approval, and Coleridge himself called them "the best & sweetest Lines [he] ever wrote."[13] They are indeed outstanding—the only moment, in this tale about mysterious exchanges among women, when an already-past, already-interpreted, fully-breached male friendship is encountered. For those of us who don't equate "manliness" with universality and authenticity, this unremarked confluence of masculine subject-matter and "genuine" discourse is of course suspicious: it's not *simply* purity of style that made this passage the standard against which all other Christabellian discourse could be measured and found "licentious," "indecorous," "affected"—in short, effeminate.

But here, we are anticipated by the passage itself, which exposes "manliness" as a gendered convention. When the narrator begins this impassioned flight, we assume he speaks from privileged knowledge: why else such drama? Several lines later, though, he betrays that this is all something he has "divined," something that may have chanced. "Chancing" on a situation that really spoke to him—a ruined manly friendship—the narrator has constructed a "divination" based on what he knows—about constancy (it isn't to be found on earth), life (it's thorny), and youth (it's vain). Although he is more caught up in his speech than she, his voice is as "hollow" as Geraldine's. His flight or "genuine burst of humanity" is a fit of the mother, and a mocking treatment of manly discourse on the part of Coleridge, whose later accession to the going opinion was either a private joke or a guilty, revisionary reading of his licentious youth. If this tonal instability was lost on "Christabel's" reviewers, it can only be because, like the narrator himself, they were reading hysterically: a "vision" of autonomous male identities caused them automatically to produce a set of received ideas about manly discourse.

"Christabel" exposes the conventionality of manly authenticity and the giddiness of manly decorum; in the same move, it suggests that attributing hysteria to feminine forms is a hysterical response to a more general condition. In the poem as elsewhere, "the feminine" is the locus of erotic and generic license: this can have the exciting charge of perversity or madness, or can seem absolutely conventional, affected. "Christabel" contrives to have these alternatives redound on the reader, who continually feels mad or just stupid, unable to "tell" how to characterize the verse at any given point. Here is Christabel "imprisoned" in the arms of Geraldine:

> With open eyes (ah woe is me!)
> Asleep, and dreaming fearfully,
> Fearfully dreaming, yet, I wis,
> Dreaming that alone, which is—
> O sorrow and shame! Can this be she,
> The lady, who knelt at the old oak tree?
> And lo! the worker of these harms,

> That holds the maiden in her arms,
> Seems to slumber still and mild,
> As a mother with her child.
>
> (ll. 292–301)

Geraldine's arms, the scene of the close embrace, and the conclusion as a whole, which recasts part I as a sentimental narrative—all in some sense work to imprison the significances of the text. Yet the scenario only imperfectly traps, and closes not at all, the questions which circulated through part I. Identity is still a matter of debate, and still hangs on a suggestively ambiguous "she" ("Can this be she?"). Even the women's gender identities and roles are undecidable, their single embrace "read" by multiple, superimposed relationships. Geraldine, a "lady" like Christabel, is also sleeping with Christabel; a "worker of harms," a ruffian-like assaultor of unspecified gender, she is also like a "mild," protective mother. If in keeping with the sentimentality of this section of the poem, the mother/child analogy is introduced to clean up the post-coital embrace of the women, it redounds to suggest the eroticism of maternal attention. These ghostly stories, all already raised in the text of Part I, work to create the compellingly charged erotic ambivalence of "Christabel"—ambivalence about becoming absorbed into a body which may be "the same" as one's own, or may belong to an adversary, a "worker of harms," and which is associated with, or represented by, the maternal body.

Christabel's situation, including, perhaps her feminine situation, is contagious. The narrator, who seems overmastered by the very spell he is describing, can only direct us to a "sight" ("And lo!"), the significance of which he "cannot tell." His speech breaks down before the woman who is "dreaming fearfully, / Fearfully dreaming," before the form that may conceal "that alone, which is."

The narrator circles round but cannot tell the enigma of form, of the body or sign that is at once meaningless and too full of significance. His own discourse repeats the paradox of the "sight," and becomes a locus of the reader's interpretive breakdown. His lament strikes us as coming from "genuine" distress at the remembrance of Christabel's or horrible predicament. But particularly in context, the lines—

> With open eyes (ah woe is me!)
> Asleep and dreaming fearfully,
> Fearfully dreaming, yet, I wis,
> Dreaming that alone which is—

raise the ghost of a sentimental style that as a matter of course suppresses all distressing sights and implications, while coyly directing the reader to what's not being said. To decide the narrator's credibility—is he bewildered or merely "affected," effeminate; could he even be camping it up?—it is necessary to bring genre to bear, to decide whether Gothic or sentimental romance is a determining convention. This is simultaneously to recognize that the voice we have been hearing cannot be authentic—if mad, it speaks in the tale of terror's legislated mad discourse; that genres are constructs which produce meaning for the subject; and that genres, like fantasy, reproduce the indeterminacies they at first appear to limit or control. Our relation to Christabel's narrators is like theirs to Christabel: the enigmatic form of their discourse turns us into hysterical readers, subject to the possessing, conventional bodies that that discourse raises in us.

IV

"Christabel's" romance plot suggests that our culture's hysterical relation to feminine forms—or its hysterical feminization of form—has its origins in the family romance. The poem invites us to distinguish between paternal and feminine orders of experience. The father's sphere is the Law—a legislative, symbolic order structured according to a divisive logic:

> Each matin bell, the Baron saith,
> Knells us back to a world of death.
> These words Sir Leoline first said,
> When he rose and found his lady dead:
> These words Sir Leoline will say
> Many a morn to his dying day!
>
> And hence the custom and law began
> That still at dawn the sacristan,
> Who duly pulls the heavy bell,
> Five and forty beads must tell
> Between each stroke—a warning knell,
> Which not a soul can choose but hear
> From Bratha Head to Wyndermere.
>
> (ll. 332–44)

The Baron's response to a traumatic event is to commemorate it. Every day, punctually, he relives the loss of "his lady," spacing and controlling the recurrences of his sorrow. By institutionalizing the observance, he turns a private grief into a public ceremony. The compulsive becomes the compulsory: the sacristan "duly" pulls his bell, and "not a soul can choose but hear."

Separation is something of a habit with the Baron. Three other times during the poem he attempts to stabilize his relation to a disturbing person or event by opening out a "space between" (l. 349). In the past, the narrator "divine[s]," Sir Leoline had been "wroth" with Lord Roland (ll. 412–13).

Wrath and the threat of madness precipitate a separation which leaves each scarred (ll. 421–22). The speaker "ween[s]" these scars will never go away and seems to guess right, since the Baron's memory of that friendship revives when Geraldine appears on the scene and tells her story:

> Sir Leoline, a moment's space,
> Stood gazing on the damsel's face:
> And the youthful Lord of Tryermaine
> Came back upon his heart again.
>
> (ll. 427–30)

For a second time the Baron experiences maddening confusion, here obscurely related to the striking together of "youthful lord" and "damsel," known and new, past and present, revived love and recognized loss. Once again he becomes wrathful ("His noble heart swelled high with rage" [l. 432]), and introduces a "law" of deathly separation: he will "dislodge" the "reptile souls" of Geraldine's abductors "from the bodies and forms of men" (ll. 442–43). Finally, for a third time the Baron meets "[swelling] rage and pain" (l. 638) and "confusion" (l. 639) with division: in the last stanza of the poem, "turning from his own sweet maid," he leads Geraldine off (l. 653).

The Baron's customs and laws divide and oppose potential "sames" or potentially intermingling parts of "the same." In contrast, femininity bewilders the narrator because one can never tell if identities and differences are constant, "the same": "Can this be she, / The lady, who knelt at the old oak tree?" (ll. 296–97); "And Christabel awoke and spied / The same who lay down by her side— / Oh rather say, the same . . ." (ll. 370–71). Tales, glances, and verbal tags circulate between Christabel and Geraldine throughout the poem: each is a "lady," each makes "answer meet" to the other. These exchanges could be said to obey the law of "the mother." Her function has puzzled some critics, who have found it hard to reconcile her angelic guardianship of Christabel with her likeness to Geraldine.[14] Coleridge, however, intended "Christabel's" mother to be a punning, rather than a stable, character. Referring simultaneously to the malady of hysteria, the womb whose vaporish fantasies were thought to block the hysteric's speech, and the female parent, "the mother" is an exemplarily vagrant sign, whose shifts of meaning obey the very "laws" which determine the characteristic displacements of hysteria.

The mother escapes the Baron's divisive categories. Neither opposites nor "the same," Geraldine and Christabel are identically self-divided, each subject to a "sight" or "weight" whose history and effects she "cannot tell." The Baron might attempt to redress such duplicity by dislodging offending "souls" from the "bodies and forms" they occupy. The "mother," however, is neither spirit nor body. Dying the hour Christabel was born, she inhabits her daughter as an already-dislodged form, or in psychoanalytic terms, as an alien internal entity or fantasy.[15] At times Christabel feels this "weight" as the fully external, "weary weight" of Geraldine (l. 131), at times as an inner "vision" which "falls" on her. Where the Baron imagines parenthood bestowing on him all the privileges of ownership ("*his own* sweet maid"), possession by the "mother" breaks down privilege, including that of an original, controlling term. The "weight" or "sight" is both within and without, both the fantasy that cannot be told and the representation that makes it legible.

The Baron also remembers the mother by a weary weight, but he gets someone else to heft it: every morning his sacristan "duly pulls the heavy bell" which "not a soul can choose but hear." Obviously the organizations we have been calling the father's and the mother's exist in some relation to one another. A feminist reading of this relation might charge the Law with producing hysterics, women who "cannot tell" what ails them because the Law legislates against every voice but its own. The *Baron* stifles the daughter by his oppressive, deathly presence: stealing back into his castle with Geraldine, Christabel passes his room "as still as death / With stifled breath" (l. 171). "The mother"—the malady of hysteria—symptomatically represents the daughter's internalization of patriarchal law. This reading is supported by Burton, who laid the daughter's troubles on the pseudopoliticians, and by Geraldine, who identifies the curse that prevents Christabel from "telling" as masculine prohibition: the sign which seals them both up is a "lord" of utterance and an "overmastering" spell.

A plot as popular as this one, however, is probably overdetermined. "Christabel" invites at least two other readings of the relation between hysteria and the law. First, that hysteria produces the Law: repeatedly, the Baron opens out a space between himself and perceived threats in order to "shield" himself from overmastering confusion or madness. Second, that the Law is just one form of hysteria. According to the narrator, the Baron's cutting efforts leave him internally scarred. The space between is also a mark within, from which no "shield" can protect him. Like the hysteric he is always vulnerable to a recurrence of "swelling" confusion, a revival of the already-internalized mark, to which he responds with another legislative cut. The Law resembles hysteria in its defenses and effects: it attempts to decide irresolution by producing something "on the other side," and its cuts leave the legislator subject to recurrences.[16]

"Christabel" invites us to decide there is only one significant "sight"— Geraldine's bosom; and to infer that it is women who can have no discourse within the law. But at the same time it allows us to see hysteria as the coincidence of superimposed fields: as a metaphysical condition of the speaking subject, as a malady historically affecting women who suffer under patriarchal law, and as a fantasy of patriarchal culture—a representation which figures the subject's alienation from the symbolic order on the bodies of women. Christabel and Geraldine, who enter the Baron's castle while he sleeps, enact their "own" fantasy and his dream.

To account for the power of this dream, we might try tracing it back to the origin. At the moment the Baron is about to cast off his only child, a protesting narrator invokes the mother:

> Why is thy cheek so wan and wild,
> Sir Leoline? Thy only child
> Lies at thy feet, thy joy, thy pride,
> So fair, so innocent, so mild;
> The same, for whom thy lady died!
> O by the pangs of her dear mother
> Think thou no evil of thy child!
> For her, and thee, and for no other,
> She prayed the moment ere she died:
> Prayed that the babe for whom she died,
> Might prove her dear lord's joy and pride!
> > That prayer her deadly pangs beguiled,
> > Sir Leoline!
> > And wouldst thou wrong thy only child,
> > Her child and thine?
>
> > > (ll. 621–35)

These lines refer us back to the opening of part II, where custom and law were instituted in response to a "lady's" death. This "lady" was also a mother, the narrator reminds us here; her death was simultaneous with a birth, her "pangs"—at once labor and death pangs—were beguiled by prayers, her suffering mingled with joy.

The Baron's law is an interpretive moment: he decides to read the occasion as a death only. His action anticipates his later disavowal of Christabel, which occurs almost as if in response to the narrator's reminder that she is "[thy lady's] child and thine"; and it resonates with Geraldine's response when, diverted from her plot for a moment as love for Christabel and longing for the mother rise up in her, she collects herself by flinging off the latter ("Off, wandering mother!" [l. 205]). In each case, a feminine body comes to represent a threat to the wishfully autonomous self "Christabel," with its punning allusions to "the mother," invites us to speculate that the "law" of gender, which legislates the systematic exclusion of feminine forms, is connected to the experience of maternal attention. In this view, representations of feminine bodies as sites of non-self-identity all take revenge on the maternal body, which, in its historical role as the first "worker of harms," is the agent through which identity is constituted on a split. The mother "wounds" with her love, constituting the subject as originally, irreducibly divided, marked by the meanings and desires of the Other.

This reading, however, may play into the hands of the patriarchs. Historically, they have used maternity to ground a question of origins; they have used gender to naturalize what is in fact a function of genre—of constructs which are only meaningful within an already-originated cultural order. To suggest that misogyny can be traced to experience of the mother, to attribute it to blind revenge for the subject's condition, is to give it a sort of tragic weight. It's also to forget the tone of "Christabel." The urbane ironist and even the apparently less controlled patriarch of that poem suggest that the projects of culture are at once more political and more finessed than what we've just described. The Baron's exclusion and readmission of women amounts to a kind of play. He guards his fantasied autonomy by opening out spaces between—between bodies, genders, generations. He lives in a deathly, "dreary" world, until his "dream" of radically split women reanimates it with desire. With the appearance of Geraldine, the threat of abduction—a threat for every subject in discourse—can be rewritten, flirted with, in dreams of seduction which repeat, at a safe distance, the "confusions" of first love. That night, a fantasized feminine body—single yet double, like the mother's when pregnant with child, or the hysteric's when inhabited by the vaporish conceptions of an origin which is never *her* origin—performs exchanges with another body like her own. These women figure but only imperfectly contain impropriety, allowing its threats and attractions to return to the Baron's world as a taint. Geraldine moves from Christabel's bed to his arms, supplanting the daughter who had supplanted the mother; for a moment, she produces in him the illusion that one can "forget . . . age" (l. 431) and all that has intervened, and recapture the fantasied past, when exchanges traversed the laws of self-identity and even the laws of gender.

V

Coleridge, who capitalizes on the potential of feminine bodies to eroticize masculine discourse, is himself a pseudopolitician; at the same time, like the hysteric he seems to counter the Law. Drawing together matters of form and desire, his discussion of meter in the Preface to "Christabel" nicely illustrates this double relation to the symbolic order. On the one hand, the principle the author lays down is strikingly consonant with the Baron's tolling "custom and law":

> I have only to add that the metre of Christabel is not, properly speaking, irregular, though it may seem so from its being founded on a new principle: namely, that of counting in each line the accents, not the syllables. Though the latter may vary from seven to twelve, yet in each line the accents will be found to be only four. Nevertheless, this occasional variation in number of syllables is not introduced wantonly, or for the mere ends of convenience, but in correspondence with some transition in the nature of the imagery or passion.

"Christabel's" metrics are figured in the poem as the ringing of the Baron's clock and matin bell. Coleridge's "principle," however, is designed to accommodate, not just the Baron, who would institute unvarying repetition, but also the movement of desire, "transition[s] in the nature of the imagery or passion."

Coleridge's meter, or more broadly, his joking treatment of gender and genre, can thus be seen as a compromise between the Law's reificatory strategies and the potentially wanton, disruptive liveliness of passion—a compromise which ultimately benefits the ironist who acquiesces to the laws he also exposes as interested. Yet Coleridge's play, which mocks the law of gender/genre by too faithfully reinscribing its conventions, also opens up the possibility of a more radical collapse between the positions of patriarch, hysteric, and ironist: it exposes the wantonness of the Law, and allows one to discover the laws of desire; it suggests that the Law itself may be inseparable from the operations of desire. When Bracy the Bard hears the Baron's deathly matin bell, he declares. "So let it knell!"—

> There is no lack of such, I ween,
> As well fill up the space between.
> In Langdale Pike and Witch's Lair,
> And Dungeon-ghyll so foully rent,
> With ropes of rock and bells of air
> Three sinful sextons' ghosts are pent,
> Who all give back, one after t'other,
> The death-note to their living brother;
> And oft too, by the knell offended,
> Just as their one! two! three! is ended,
> The devil mocks the doleful tale
> With a merry peal from Borodale.
>   (ll. 348–59)

Bracy's accession echoes Christabel's words at the end of Part I, when she announces her obedience to Geraldine's request: "So let it be!" (l. 235). Bracy is in league with the hysteric, and Coleridge with them all—and all submit to the Law. When Christabel steals into her father's house with Geraldine, we "cannot tell" if her silence is the absolute solicitude of a dutiful daughter or a sign of subversive intent: does hysteria come from too much or too little respect for the father? In a sense it doesn't matter, since the effects are the same for the Baron and us: her very unreadability draws out and mocks his and our possessing desire to decide meaning. Her strategy resembles Bracy's—apparently without doing anything himself, he simply "lets" the law mock its own voice. It echoes through hollow, rent spaces, which in dutifully returning its knell, elude its efforts to control the significance of an event. "Telling" notes become the occasion of ghostly echoes, which in turn generate Bracy's lively ghost stories; finally, as if by way of commentary, the "devil" makes merry mockery of the whole phenomenon. The passage describes in little the narrative tactics of "Christabel." By too-dutiful accession to the laws of gender and genre, "Christabel" exposes their strategies to view, letting the Law subvert itself.

Notes

1 Quotations from "Christabel" and its preface are taken from *Coleridge's Poetical Works*, ed. Ernest Hartley Coleridge (1912; rpt. Oxford: Oxford U. Press, 1969).

2 See Susan Luther, "'Christabel' as Dream Reverie," *Romantic Reassessments* 61, ed. Dr. James Hogg (Salzburg: Institut fur Englische Sprache und Literatur, Univ. Salzburg A5020, 1976), for the argument that Christabel is a reader of romances.

3 "'Christabel'" (1955), rpt. in *The Ancient Mariner and Other Poems: A Casebook*, eds. Alun R. Jones and William Tydemann (London and Basingstoke: Macmillan, 1973), p. 235; *The Waking Dream: A Study of Coleridge's Poetry* (London: Edward Arnold, 1967), p. 146.

4 *The Anatomy of Melancholy*, ed. Holbrook Jackson (New York: Random House-Vintage Books, 1977), p. 416. Future references to this edition appear in the text.

5 In "Sir Cauline," the ballad from which Coleridge took the name Christabel, this is the case; that Christabel's lover is dismissed by her father.

6 See for example Roy Basler, *Sex, Symbolism, and Psychology in Literature* (New Brunswick: Rutgers U. Press, 1948), p. 41; Gerald Enscoe, *Eros and the Romantics* (The Hague and Paris: Mouton, 1967), pp. 44–45; Jonas Spatz, "The Mystery of Eros: Sexual Initiation in Coleridge's 'Christabel,'" *PMLA* 90 (1975), 112–13; Barbara A. Schapiro, *The Romantic Mother: Narcissistic Patterns in Romantic Poetry* (Baltimore and London: Johns Hopkins U. Press, 1983), 61–85.

7 See for example Enscoe, p. 43; John Beer, *Coleridge's Poetic Intelligence* (London and Basingstoke: Macmillan, 1977), p. 187; and H. W. Piper, "The Disunity of *Christabel* and the Fall of Nature," *Essays in Criticism* 28 (1978), 216–27.

8 Or so Freud claims in *Jokes and their Relation to the Unconscious*, chapter VI ("Jokes, Dreams, and the Unconscious"), trans. James Strachey (New York: Norton, 1963), pp. 159–80.

9 For examples of the reviews, see *The Romantic Reviewed*, ed. Donald H. Reiman (New York and London: Garland, 1977), II, 666, 239. Modern critics sometimes notice tonal or generic instability as "falls" into Gothic trickery, into caricature of the Gothic, or into sentimentality; see for example Max Schulz, *The Poetic Voices of Coleridge* (Detroit: Wayne State U. Press, 1963), pp. 66–71; and Paul Edwards and MacDonald Emslie, "'Thoughts all so unlike each other': The Paradoxical in *Christabel*," *English Studies* 52 (1971), 328. The latter suggest these discrepancies are intended to shock.

10 *Romantics Reviewed* I, 23.

11 *Romantics Reviewed* I, 373; II, 866; II, 531. I discuss these reviews more fully in my essay "Literary Gentlemen and Lovely Ladies: The Debate on the Character of 'Christabel,'" forthcoming in *ELH*.

12 *Romantics Reviewed* II, 531.

13 *Collected Letters of Samuel Taylor Coleridge*, ed. Earl Leslie Griggs (Oxford: Clarendon Press, 1956–71), III, 435.

14 See for example Abe Delson, "The Function of Geraldine in *Christabel*: A Critical Perspective and Interpretation," *English Studies* 61 (1980), 130–41; and Enscoe, p. 46.
15 My understanding of fantasy here follows that of Jean Laplanche and J.-B Pontalis in their "Fantasy and the Origins of Sexuality," *International Journal of Psycho-Analysis* 49 (1968), 1–18.
16 My argument here is indebted to Richard Rand's discussion of the ubiquitous "mark" in "Geraldine," *Glyph* 3 (1978), 74–97.

62

WORDSWORTH AND THE LANGUAGE OF THE DREAM

Mary Jacobus

Source: *English Literary History* 46 (1979), 618–44.

I

The strange figure at the start of *The Prelude* Book V—"This Arab Phantom," "This Semi-Quixote . . . from the world of sleep" (V.140–42)—is at once the most dreamlike and the most literary of all Wordsworth's solitaries. Lodged between the phantasmal and the bookish, he occupies the same hinterland as those "old Men, / Old Humourists" of Wordsworth's childhood who "have into Phantoms pass'd / Of texture midway betwixt life and books" (III.609–13).[1] The intermediacy here (what kind of texture might this be?) is one that Wordsworth elsewhere emphasizes in its own right with his account of the imagination at work on stone and sea-beast to produce an "inter-mediate image," that of the semi-supernatural Leech-gatherer.[2] Such shocks of indeterminacy mark many of the climactic moments of arrest and recognition in *The Prelude*, when the limits of comprehension and of language are reached together, and the invisible world is disclosed. The tumultuous rhetoric of the Vale of Gondo passage—"Characters of the great Apocalypse, / The types and symbols of Eternity" (VI.570–71)—gestures towards a ghostly revelation beyond the scope of writing; if the face of nature could itself become an intelligible text, there would be no need of representation, and no need of nature either. Wordsworth's nostalgia for an original or apoca-lyptic plenitude in language (the word made Logos) hardly needs dwelling on. What does seem worth exploring is the troubling status of both books and writing in a poem which enlists them to "enshrine the spirit of the past / For future restoration"—"I would give," Wordsworth yearns in Book XI, "*as far as words can give*, / A substance and a life to what I feel" (XI.339–43; my italics). One might go further and ask why it is that a dream, the dream of the Arab Quixote, should become the means of confronting this anxiety; though it seems reasonable enough to lament the perishability of books ("shrines so frail"), it is an odd tack to start a Book on books with a dream that turns them, rather ludicrously, into a stone and a shell clutched by a crazed quester.

Wordsworth is engagingly eager to claim the Maniac's anxiousness as his own—

> I. methinks.
> Could share that Maniac's anxiousness. could go
> Upon like errand. . . .
>
>   (V.159–61)

—and the Arab Quixote, "craz'd / By love and feeling and internal thought" (V.144–45), is an extreme type of the poet himself, at work on his unending, backward-looking, recuperative task. Enlisting in the quest, he becomes a kind of Sancho Panza converted to the fantasies of his master. There is certainly an air of quirkiness in the "disquietude" shrewdly noted by Wordsworth's "friend" ("in plain truth, / 'Twas going far to seek disquietude," V.51–52); as if Wordsworth were indulging in a far-fetched line of thought under the auspices of Romance. How different from the unmediated prophetic note of his culminating invocation to words—the instrument of salvation, but only "as far as words *can*" save—at the end of Book V. Eloquent and elusive, even windily so (inspired by inspiration), the lines not only raise questions about the nature of that "texture midway betwixt life and books," but constitute a strange moment in themselves. Well-known as it is, the passage is worth another look:

> Visionary Power
> Attends upon the motions of the winds
> Embodied in the mystery of words.
> There darkness makes abode, and all the host
> Of shadowy things do work their changes there,
> As in a mansion like their proper home.
> Even forms and substances are circumfus'd
> By that transparent veil with light divine;
> And through the turnings intricate of Verse
> Present themselves as objects recognis'd,
> In flashes, and with a glory scarce their own.
>
>   (V.619–29)

I used the word "look" deliberately. Wordsworth writes like a man trying to net the wind in the "turnings intricate" of his own blank verse; for all its insubstantiality, his meaning can only be glimpsed if we actually look at the lines (and at the spaces between them) rather than read them. We have, so to speak, to *see*, not *feel*, how beautiful they are. The deadening of a text already slowed by its solemn rhythms allows us, paradoxically, to endow it with a living spirit—lodged in the interstices of the web, behind the veil, as a ghostly and unrepresentable presence. As always, Wordsworth's straining of language to its limits has its own fullness; if the motions of winds can never be embodied, if the mystery of words must remain ineffable, still, the veil of poetry irradiates and makes strange the objects it obscures (the rhetoric's infectious). The gap between word and thing, once opened, proves Wordsworth's richest source of meaning—"all the host / Of shadowy things do work their changes there"—and by a sleight of hand it is enshrined in the inter-text rather than the text: in "a mansion like their proper home" that "Tintern Abbey" helps us to gloss as the mind ("thy mind / Shall be a mansion for all lovely forms," 11. 139–40); not a memorial shrine for the dead, but a spacious and sanctified dwelling—less a pleasure-dome than a sacred edifice.

The precariousness of this edifice gives *The Prelude* both its characteristic plangency about poetic vision ("I see by glimpses now; when age comes on, / May scarcely see at all . . ." XI.338–39) and its moments of triumphant recoil on what cannot be seen ("an obscure sense / Of possible sublimity," II.336–37). It is just this precariousness, this anxious relation between representation and vision, writing and salvation, that I want to pursue as a way of getting at the dream of the Arab Quixote in terms other than those proposed by Wordsworth himself (who was, of course, bound to misinterpret his own—his "friend's"—"dream").[3] It's nothing new to say that the deepest imaginative experiences recorded in *The Prelude* are bound up with anxiety of one sort or another. But the relation between writing and anxiety is more obscure, as is the relation between "Books" and "Imagination," and I want to suggest that both the anxiousness and the bookishness—the literariness—of *The Prelude* are, like the anxiousness of the Old Cumberland Beggar, "vital": vital in the sense of energizing, impelling Wordsworth ever onwards in his time- and text-defying quest. I've already touched on the dual power of language to estrange and transfigure, on the flight that is also a salvage (one could reverse the order in each case, in the interests of a darker psychic reading), and the same duality is present in the co-existence of urgency and prolixity in *The Prelude*; Blake, after all, had done with it in a single aphorism ("Eternity is in love with the productions of time"). Writing about it and about it allows Wordsworth himself, while looking back over his shoulder at the fleet waters of the drowning world, to exit on a loud prophetic blast of harmony from what has been in many ways a profoundly elegiac poem ("I see by glimpses now . . ."). Writing as deferral postpones the promised End; it also defends against non-being by textualizing it. But, as we all know, the self is not to be written out so easily, remaining obstinately lodged in the inter-text, midway between life and books. What results is less a web of meaning than an enmeshing of absences—those shadowy objects glimpsed "through the turnings intricate of Verse." I want to follow one of the strands, not so much in the hope that it will wind to the centre of the labyrinth and back (where should such a centre lie?) as in the hope of tracing the process by which meaning is at once generated and unsettled in *The Prelude*. After what's been said by way of introduction, it won't be surprizing that my chosen thread leads from *anxiety* to *motion*, from *motion* to *spectre*, from there to *spectacle*, and finally back to *dream*. Whether visionary or nightmarish, the movement uncovers some of the problems of representation which must trouble with peculiar intensity a poem whose autobiographical project is to represent the growth of a poet's mind: the self that writes.

II

Wordsworth himself tells us that his friend's dream is the product of reading ("perusing . . . The famous History of the Errant Knight") and of thought ("On poetry and geometric Truth . . . he mused"). To put it another way, Romance has been crossed with Philosophy, Cervantes with Descartes. Even within the dream itself, interpretation has begun:

> The Arab told him that the Stone,
> *To give it in the language of the Dream*,
> Was Euclid's Elements; 'and this', said he,
> 'This other', pointing to the Shell, 'this Book
> Is something of more worth.' And, at the word,
> The Stranger, said my friend continuing,
> Stretch'd forth the Shell towards me, with command
> That I should hold it to my ear; I did so,
> And heard that instant in an unknown tongue,
> Which yet I understood, articulate sounds,
> A loud prophetic blast of harmony,
> An Ode, in passion utter'd, which foretold
> Destruction to the children of the Earth.
> By deluge now at hand.
>
> (V.86–99; my italics)

"What is a poet if not a translator, a decipherer?" asks Baudelaire. To interpret further is to risk introducing yet another substitution in an endlessly proliferating series.[4] But suppose one skews the passage sideways to look at "the language of the Dream" another way on. It's worth noticing, for instance, that Wordsworth gives only one line to the stone, but spends six on the shell—that utterance concerns him more than order. The disordering blast or destructive Ode restores originary speech to poetry in an apocalyptic Logocentricity which destroys the need of texts. Is this something to hold onto?—that *Dream*, lodged at the line-ending with *Stone*, may be working to trump the story certainties of Euclid with its own irrefutable logic? Pairing ("rhyming") *Book* and *word* and setting them in the same way against another, later pair, *Tongue* and *sounds*, produces the same suggestive trumping movement: for the reified book and the sign, we get the obliterating pentecostal harmony that makes all books redundant. No wonder the dreamer tells us that "A wish was now ingender'd in my fear / To cleave unto this Man" (V.115–16); the poet would be out of business in such an eternity. No wonder, too, that the blast is siren-music, a joyous, even seductive note woven in with its destructiveness: that it might engender a quite opposite wish.

This is reassuring: it bears out the nostalgia I suggested earlier, as I hoped it might. But let's stay with Wordsworth's equivocation a little longer. The piedpiper narrative as such need not detain us, for its hectic rhythms lead inexorably to the moment of awakening. What Wordsworth himself lingers on in the midst of his hurry is the production of meaning within the dream. As with the Arab Quixote—

> 'the very Knight
> Whose Tale Cervantes tells, yet not the Knight,
> But was an Arab of the Desert, too;
> Of these was neither, and was both at once. . . .'
> (V.123–26)

—a parade of pedantic exactitude creates uncertainty: "neither, and . . . both at once." Is this truth or fiction, dream or charade? Or is it the transaction between them that Wordsworth is enacting here? The two books are firmly labelled ("one that held acquaintance with the stars . . . Th'other that was a God, yea, many Gods . . . ," 104, 107), yet in testifying to his faith, Wordsworth undercuts the symbolizing process itself:

> 'strange as it may seem,
> I wonder'd not, although I plainly saw
> The one to be a Stone, th' other a Shell,
> Nor doubted once but that they both were Books,
> Having a perfect faith in all that pass'd.'
> (V.110–14)

Of course, such double perception is a common experience in dreaming, but "although I plainly saw . . . Nor doubted once" has the faintly comical ring of nonsense-verse like Lewis Carroll's, where absurd substitutions at once unsettle proprieties of naming and refer to the craziness of things ("He thought he saw ————: He looked again, and found it was ————"); properly speaking, book seems quite as inconsequential as stone or shell. What we are left with is the arbitrariness endemic in language, and the faith that is necessary if we are to engage in any act of representation or reading; so that the movement is from *Stone* to *Shell* to *Books*, and thence to (what should be capitalized personification, but has instead the intensifying adjectival "perfect"), *faith.* As Wordsworth writes in a theatrical context, "Delusion bold! And faith must needs be coy" (VII.307). Why coy? Presumably because it is in bad company. Showmanship and illusion, more restrained here than in the mountebank world of London, bring a more respectable belief. The passage from literal to metaphoric, from thing to word, becomes the chaste woman as opposed to the bold hussy—operating within the symbolic laws of language rather than on the streets of outrageous representation (compare Pope's noisy operatic Harlot in *The Dunciad:* "*O Cara! Cara!*" IV.45ff).[5] Or so Wordsworth would have us believe, for the purification of language from all taint of unchaste representationalism is the necessary fiction of *The Prelude* in general and the dream of the Arab Quixote in particular.

Meanwhile, what about that word, "anxiety"? One woman purified in the interest of Wordsworthian quietness is Mary of Buttermere—rescued from her fallen state in the popular theatre of Book VII where she figures as a seduced, abandoned, bigamously unmarried mother, and restored to innocence on her native ground: "Without contamination does she live / In quietness, *without anxiety*" (VII.352–53).[6] Here, "anxiety" seems almost synonymous with consciousness, perhaps even with desire, though obviously carrying overtones of disquiet—"disquietude," as Wordsworth's friend calls it. How, if at all, does it relate to the Arab Quixote's "Maniac anxiousness"? Under "anxiousness," the OED cites (in 1658) "An anxiousness about their everlasting state." In 1798, it is Southey on a father's anxiousness. This combination of anxiety about the future (shall I be saved?) and solicitude about one's offspring (are my children/books safe?) seems especially relevant to Wordsworthian usage. It's not a question of Angst, whether Freudian neurotic dread or Heideggerian metaphysical insecurity; rather, it is a movement comprising both salvation and salvage, desire and recuperation. For a poet, particularly, the question becomes: will I be saved if I write? will my writings survive? In a more general sense, all writing expresses a demand that can never be satisfied. Language inscribes loss; lack hollows being into desire; desire perpetuates itself in the symbolic articulations of language.[7] Desire, like the maniac's anxiousness, sets in motion. Wordsworthian usage elsewhere gives us the child of the spots of time, "scudding away from snare to snare . . . hurrying on, / Still hurrying, hurrying onward" (I.319–21), troubling the calm of nature with his "anxious visitation"; or seeing in the death of his father a correction of his earlier "desires" on "That day . . . when from the crag / [He] look'd in such anxiety of hope" (XI.371–72). Snaring wood-cock and wanting to go home for the Christmas holidays are innocent enough desires in themselves, if misplaced. What matters to Wordsworth is not their object; it is the power of the child's anxiety to set his imagination to work, creating spectral beings out of mountain winds ("Low breathings coming after me") or "indisput-able shapes" out of the mist to haunt him retrospectively like the ghost of Hamlet's father.[8] In this, the spots of time prefigure the movement of baffled desire in the crossing of the Alps, the movement which is for Wordsworth that of the Imagination itself: "Effort, and expectation, and desire, / And something evermore about to be . . ." (VI.541–42). The loud prophetic blast of harmony, then, stirs its hearer because it announces an End which is not an end, but a going beyond.

Vital or life-giving anxiousness in Wordsworth's poetry characteristically gives rise to both motion and spectrality: to intimations of a ghostly life beyond the image which at once blocks it out and conjures it into being (a process described by Coleridge as "the substitution of a sublime feeling of the unimaginable for a mere image").[9] This is tricky terrain, and exor-cisms may be necessary. So it proves in Book VIII of *The Prelude*, where Wordsworth pays tribute to the visionary Lake District shepherds of his childhood. "Call ye these appearances," be writes,

> A shadow, a delusion, ye who are fed
> By the dead letter, not the spirit of things,
> Whose truth is not a *motion* or a shape
> Instinct with vital functions, but a Block
> Or waxen Image which yourselves have made,
> And ye adore.
>
> (VIII.431–36; my italics)

The familiar opposition between "the dead letter" and "the spirit of things" makes this an exemplary passage for both Wordsworth and his readers; paganizing the image as the worship of golden calves, it Christianizes the symbol—as well it might. For what we glimpse is a different kind of appari-tion. The fractional pause at the end of the line—"Whose truth is not a motion or a shape"—picks up the spectrality of the "indisputable shapes" of mist recalled by the troubled boy; the "shape / Instinct with vital functions" comes as an afterthought, but here too there are spectral reminiscences: the "grim shape" of the cliff in the boat-stealing episode, "As if with voluntary power instinct," pursues the child "With measur'd motion, like a living thing" (I.407, 411). One begins to see what Wordsworth is up against when one looks back at the visionary shepherd himself, a few lines before. Com-ically befogged—"In size a giant, stalking through the fog, / His Sheep like Greenland Bears"—he is offered to us as a type of the Christian sublime:

> His Form hath flash'd upon me, glorified
> By the deep radiance of the settling sun:
> Or him have I descried in distant sky,

263

> A solitary object and sublime,
> Above all height! like an aerial Cross,
> As it is stationed on some spiry Rock
> Of the Chartreuse, for worship.
> (VIII.404–10)

"Call ye these appearances . . . A shadow, a delusion": no—call them rather the transcendental signifier, the word made flesh and redeemed for eternity. But once again, there's a disconcerting reminiscence. Though Wordsworth has invoked the authority of sacred texts, and added a cosy touch with his recollection of Thomson's *Seasons* (the shepherd of "Autumn" who "stalks gigantic" through "the general fog"),[10] it is his own account of the rout of religion from the Grande Chartreuse, in *Descriptive Sketches*, that troubles the surface here: "A viewless flight of laughing Demons mock / The Cross, by angels planted on the aerial rock" (ll. 69–70).[11] Presumably this strange, hybrid reanimation of precursor texts is what prompts Wordsworth's unguarded description of the shepherd as a "Creature, spiritual almost *As those of books*" (VIII.417–18; my italics)—an admission hastily retracted with "but more exalted far, / Far more of an imaginative form" and followed up by the strategic banishing of literary pastoral ("not a Corin of the Groves . . . But . . . a Man / With the most common," VIII.420–24).

Behind every aerial Cross is a flight of Demons; behind every text is a prior text. So much is clear. What is odd about the shepherd is that Wordsworth relies on a submerged Romantic topos (if it can be dignified by the term) which already brings disquiet with it: that of the Brocken-Spectre. Coleridge, who had climbed the Brocken on the Whitsunday of 1799 in search of the phenomenon/phantom, makes use of it as an image of that ideal self which art (Shakespeare's art) throws back at us.[12] But Coleridge's idealized "being of gigantic proportions, and of such elevated dignity that you only know it to be yourself by similarity of action" takes an altogether stranger form in De Quincey's "Apparition of the Brocken." Identified with the "Dark Interpreter" of *Suspiria de Profundis*, the Brocken-Spectre becomes an estranged portion of self, like Shelley's Jupiter or a Blakean Emanation. Though De Quincey uses mirror-language, the image is reflected back at him through a glass darkly:

> the apparition is but it reflex of yourself; and, in uttering your secret feelings to *him*, you make this phantom the dark symbolic mirror for reflecting to the daylight what else must be hidden for ever.
>
> Such a relation does the Dark Interpreter, whom immediately the reader will learn to know as an intruder into my dreams, bear to my own mind. He is originally a mere reflex of my inner nature.[13]

Before arriving at this discovery, De Quincey forces his spectral doppelganger to undergo a series of exorcizing rituals—making the sign of the cross, re-consecrating an anenome ("the sorcerer's flower") and a pagan stone ("the sorcerer's altar") to the service of the pentecostal Christianity celebrated at Whitsun. By putting the Dark Interpreter through his motions, De Quincey tries the faith and tests the obedience of the Brocken-Spectre, baptizing superstition for religion. But (like the unconscious), the Dark Interpreter has his own ways of evading the censor:

> as the apparition of the Brocken sometimes is disturbed by storms or by driving showers, so as to dissemble his real origin, in like manner the Interpreter sometimes swerves out of my orbit, and mixes a little with alien natures. I do not always know him in these cases as my own parhelion. What he says, generally is but that which *I* have said in daylight, and in meditation deep enough to sculpture itself on my heart. But sometimes, as his face alters, his words alter; and they do not always seem such as I have used, or *could* use. No man can account for all things that occur in dreams. Generally I believe this—that he is a faithful representative of myself, but he also is at times subject to the action of the god *Phantasmus*, who rules in dreams.[14]

The god *Phantasmus* typically makes his presence felt in meteorological disturbance ("disturbed by storms or by driving showers"). Dreams become treacherous deeps, unknown seas worked to turmoil by hurricanes. The weather of *The Prelude* is rarely so tempestuous, but "the characters / Of danger and desire" can make the earth "Work like a sea" (I.497–501). It is this sea-change that transforms the sublimely Christianized shepherd from the reflex of Wordsworth's ideal into its antithesis—the ghastly Discharged Soldier, for instance, or the reified Blind London Beggar, or the Arab Quixote; those Dark Interpreters who serve as a "symbolic mirror for reflecting to the daylight what else must be hidden for ever." In other words, the language of the dream.

"In dreams always there is a power not contented with reproduction, but which absolutely creates or transforms." Not Freud, but De Quincey again.[15] Language, too, absolutely creates or transforms ("as his face alters, his words alter"). Subjected to the god *Phantasmus*, the characters sculptured on the heart lose their fixity and disclose "the mysterious handwritings of grief or joy which have inscribed themselves successively upon the palimpsest of your brain."[16] It is an aspect of the Wordsworthian supernatural that the semantic rules of the Uncanny (*heimlich* becomes *unheimlich*, estranging the familiar) hold good, or bad, for a word like "motion." Chambers' mid-eighteenth-century *Cyclopaedia* offers an appropriately dynamic definition drawn from ancient philosophy: "The ancient philosophers considered *motion* in a more general and extensive manner. *They defined it, a passage out of one state into another:* and thus made six kinds of motion, viz. Creation, generation, corruption, augmentation, diminution, and lation, or local motion" (OED; my italics). There is something of the same spectrum of meaning in Wordsworthian usage (Creation at one extreme, "Tintern Abbey"'s glad animal movements at the other); but its oscillations on a different axis, between quiet and disquiet, give it a special role in relation to the unsanctified movements of the imagination. Primitive animism attends upon the motions of the winds, as well as visionary power; is perhaps necessary to them, as a religion of fear may provide the altar-stone for pentecostal Christianity. The other voice of the loud prophetic blast of harmony is death, the unassimilably alien aspect of spiritual life. So, "Those hallow'd and pure motions of the sense" (I.578) which link life and joy are set against "sounds / Of undistinguishable motion, steps / Almost as silent as the turf they trod" (I.330–32) which link life and death. There's the common suggestion of winds in both motions ("even in that tempestuous time," "Low breathings coming after me"), but it is the uncanny animation which makes one an intimation of the ghostly, the other, an intimation of immortality. Again, it is the spectral striding in the boat-stealing episode—"the huge Cliff . . . with measur'd motion, like a living thing, / Strode after me" (I.409–12)—which makes it a haunting; whereas in the invocation to "Thou Soul . . . That giv'st to forms and images a breath / And everlasting motion" (I.429–31), breath is part of the incommunicable inspiration of the Holy Ghost. The "motions that are sent he knows not whence" to the man "Incumbent o'er the surface of past time" (IV.260, 263) scarcely ruffle its surface, but to the child plundering the raven's nest,

> With what strange utterance did the loud dry wind
> Blow through my ears! the sky seem'd not a sky
> Of earth, and with what motion mov'd the clouds!
>   (I.348–50)[17]

My point is not that the Wordsworthian supernatural needs guilt to make it ghostly (Wordsworth himself tells us as much), but that motion becomes uncanny when it is unsettled from latinate abstraction into an indeterminate physicality—betraying us to the superstitiousness we think we have overcome.[18] To put it another way, if all language is dead metaphor, then a movement towards the literal ("a passage out of one state into another") may, in reminding us of that originating death, summon ghostly presences.

III

In Book V of *The Prelude*, Wordsworth praises "dreamers" (i.e., authors of Romances) as "Forgers of lawless tales! . . . Who make our wish our power, our thought a deed, / An empire, a possession" (V.547–48, 552–53). Making

thought a deed is one function of the Dark Interpreter, language. Its movements may be profoundly disquieting, since it puts us in possession of our
thoughts. But it is a disquiet central to the alliance of language and imagination; without such dream-work, what should the lawless forger be up to except
lying? The lies of blocks or waxen images, as opposed to truth-in-motion,
constitute a crucial antithesis to the Wordsworthian supernatural—the
Wordsworthian spectacular of static mirror-representation: "those mimic
sights that ape / The absolute presence of reality . . . as in mirror" (VII.248–
50). Spectacle, the tyranny of the eye ("a transport of the outward sense, /
Not of the mind," XI.188–89), furnishes the theatrical underworld of *The
Prelude*, that mingled threat to and seduction of the imagination called
London. It might as well have been called Vanity Fair; framed by
Wordsworth's puritan ethic, it offers the this-worldly profits of the eye in
place of the other-worldly spiritual gains of the mind. "Great God!" writes
Wordsworth, "that aught *external* to the living mind / Should have such
mighty sway" (VIII.700–02; his italics). When he wants to admit its legitimate
pleasures, he has to subsume spectacle into spectrality, animating the show
in the visionary cinema of the imagination. The Cave of Yordas, in Book
VIII of *The Prelude*, provides him with the chance for a retrospective trumping of London by a replay in the mind's eye; darkness becomes the screen
on which to project a world of internalized images, subverting instead of
aping "The absolute presence of reality" with their shadowy motion:

> Substance and shadow, light and darkness, all
> Commingled, making up a Canopy
> Of Shapes and Forms and Tendencies to Shape
> That shift and vanish, change and interchange
> Like *Spectres*, ferment quiet and sublime;
> Which, after a short space, works less and less,
> Till very effort, every *motion* gone,
> The scene before him lies in perfect view,
> Exposed and lifeless, *as a written book.*
>
> (VIII.719–27; my italics)

Wordsworth's simile arrests the familiar liveliness of shapes and spectral
motion in an alien stillness. The lifelessness of the printed page "lies in
perfect view" as an unintelligible blank. (There is a quietly submerged play
of another kind going on here: compare Pope's "Did the dead Letter unsuccessful prove? / The brisk Example never fail'd to move," *The Dunciad*,
I.193–94). Such seeing is dead—unless it opens onto the endless vista of
Romance: "Ships, Rivers, Towers, the Warrior clad in Mail, / The prancing
Steed. the Pilgrim with his Staff . . . A Spectacle to which there is no end"
(VIII.738–41). Spectrality saves spectacle for the imagination, as the
shadow redeems the substance; Romance, in turn, legitimizes the spectral.

The experience evoked in these lines is, of course, reading itself. Is this the "texture midway betwixt life and books"?—neither of the mind nor visible, but wrought by the mind's eye on the page, animating the dead letter until (in Wordsworth's magical phrase) it is "streaming, / Like a magician's airy pageant" (VIII.733–34)? Reading the writing rather than seeing it, we have enchantment, illusionism, "ferment quiet and sublime"—a sublimity which results from making the visible a little hard to see on the printed page.[19]

The Cave of Yordas saves the city from satire and gives it back to Romance. Book VII of *The Prelude* is demonic not only in its imagery— "what a hell / For eyes and ears! What anarchy and din / Barbarian and infernal" (VII.658–60)—but in its exuberant parody of Pandemonium, itself already parodic of Creation:

> A Universe of death, which God by curse
> Created evil, for evil only good,
> Where all life dies, death lives, and Nature breeds,
> Perverse, all monstrous, all prodigious things,
> Abominable, inutterable, and worse
> Than Fables yet have feign'd, or fear conceiv'd,
> *Gorgons* and *Hydras*, and *Chimeras* dire.
>
> (*Paradise Lost*, II.622–28)

In the same way, Wordsworth parodies the sanctified Apocalypse of the Vale of Gondo ("Characters of the great Apocalypse, / The types and symbols of Eternity," VI.570–71) with the rhetorical nadir of Book VII: "Oh, blank confusion! and a type not false / Of what the mighty City is itself . . ." (VII.695–96). The self-transcending natural legibility of the Alps is usurped by urban illegibility, a system of signs where "differences . . . have no law, no meaning, and no end" (VII.703–04). But why the difficulty in reading London? Is the text meaningless simply because Wordsworth's puritan ethic will have it so?—because Vanity Fair, though it may tempt the Pilgrim with his staff, must leave him finally unmoved? Or is it rather the mistrust of the do-it-yourself enthusiast for the ready-made, akin to the progressive parent's worry that Action Man will oust creative play?

> A work that's finish'd to our hands, that lays,
> If any *spectacle* on earth can do,
> The whole creative powers of man asleep!
>
> (VII.652–54; my italics)

One could furnish a doctrinal justification for Wordsworth's underworld easily enough. But an aesthetic, and above all, a literary reading gives access to the textual rather than moral structuring of Book VII. Wordsworth, the imaginative showman, confronts us with the misbegotten forms of a materialized imagination in order to dissociate his own creative vision from its fallen counterpart—rather as Blake depicts the malformed monsters of Urizenic creation, weighted and hunched with resentful and anguished physicality, by way of contrast to the freedom of an unfettered imagination. Bartholomew Fair is an infernal jumble of "out-o'-th'-way, far-fetch'd, perverted things"; a "Parliament of Monsters" like Milton's, "Where all life dies, death lives, and Nature breeds, / Perverse":

> Albinos, painted Indians, Dwarfs,
> The Horse of Knowledge, and the learned Pig,
> The Stone-eater, the Man that swallows fire,
> Giants, "Ventriloquists, the Invisible Girl,
> The Bust that speaks, and moves its goggling eyes,
> The Wax-work, Clock-work, all the marvellous craft
> Of modem Merlins, wild Beasts, Puppet-shows,
> All out-o'-th'-way, far-fetch'd, perverted things,
> All freaks of Nature, all Promethean thoughts
> Of Man; his *dulness*, madness, and their feats,
> All jumbled up together to make up
> This Parliament of Monsters.
>
> (VII.680–91; my italics)

Perverted Nature has undergone literary mediation at the hands of Dulness; the prototypes for these parodic activities are the scatalogical games of *The Dunciad*, themselves grubbily parodic of the Devil's party. Behind "The Bust that speaks, and moves its goggling eyes" is Pope's stuffed effigy of the poet—"senseless, lifeless! idol void and vain! . . . a copy of a wit" (*The Dunciad*, II.46–48), the man of straw by means of which Pope dissociates his own activities in *The Dunciad* from those of a grub-street hack. So what Wordsworth is doing in these freak-shows is saving himself for an art that is both natural and sublime—an art that can create, not a ventriloquist's dummy, but the visionary shepherd of Book VIII.

But there's more to it. Wordsworth's disapproving verdict, "Trivial objects, melted and reduced / To one identity" (VII.702–03), applies to a satiric mode as well as to a scene. Ostensibly, he is banishing from *The Prelude* the techniques of the eighteenth-century city-poetry which it has in fact appropriated. Book VII borrows its energy from the wit that blurs significant differences in the insurrectionary turmoil and apocalyptic unsoundness of Johnson's *London*—"and now a Rabble Rages, now a Fire," "falling Houses thunder on your Head" (ll. 14, 17)—or tumbles "Dung, Guts, and Blood, / Drown'd Puppies, stinking Sprats, . . . Dead Cats, and Turnip-Tops" (ll. 61–63) in an indiscriminate flood down the conduit of Swift's disgust at the end of "A Description of a City Shower." Though Wordsworth makes satire stand in for a mode of imagination, parodic poetry for ventriloquistic creation, his own creativity is itself Promethean—Promethean, that is, not only in its creation of misshapen clay mannikins ("all the marvellous craft/ Of modern Merlins"), but in its stealing of Promethean fire. He is deeply implicated in a theft that is also a gift, at once hubristic and humanistic. Parody not only steals energy from a prior text but, by a double movement, simultaneously distorts and empties it of its power. On one level Wordsworth assimilates into *The Prelude* the Juvenalian disreputability and indignation which its mode would seem to exclude; on another, he cancels and purifies it by reverting to the daemonic sublime. But in order to do so, he has to erase the ghost of an indecorous text: a ghost that is writing itself, surfacing —like the uncanny—where it should remain hidden. The Blind London Beggar is at once the spectre of spectacle (the two words have the same root meaning: *specĕre*, to look or see, and *spectāre*, to look) and the means of its exorcism. Like the "blank confusion" of Bartholomew Fair, he offers a version of what one might call the negative sublime, the mind overborne by an unintelligible illegibility.[20] An embodiment of absence, the blind beggar is the most threatening of all Wordsworth's Dark Interpreters; he "smites" the sight like an assault on vision itself—"once," writes Wordsworth,

> 'twas my chance
> Abruptly to be smitten with the view
> Of a blind Beggar, who, with upright face,
> Stood propp'd against a Wall, upon his Chest
> Wearing a written paper, to explain
> The story of the Man, and who he was.
>
> (VII.609–14)

Why is this view such a blow to the mind ("My mind did at this spectacle turn round / As with the might of waters," VII.615–16)? Is it because the label parodies, diminishes, and controverts all attempts at self-representation, and with it Wordsworth's entire project in *The Prelude?* No characters, no written paper, can inscribe being; and so the beggar is doomed to non-being. To death, in fact—his sublime archetype in Book II of *Paradise Lost.*

The "execrable shape" of Death with his "horrid strides" is the darkest and most shadowy—the most shapeless and unshapely—of all Shapes haunting *The Prelude:*

> The other shape,
> If shape it might be call'd that shape had none
> Distinguishable in member, joint, or limb,
> Or substance might be call'd that shadow seem'd,
> For each seem'd either; black it stood as Night,
> Fierce as ten Furies, terrible as Hell . . .
>
> (*Paradise Lost*, II.666–71)

Here, if ever there was one, is an example of "the conferring, the abstracting, and the modifying powers of the Imagination" which Wordsworth had illustrated with the "intermediate image" of his own Leech-gatherer.[21] But once again, Milton's presence in Book VII has been overlaid by Pope's, the daemonic or negative sublime dulled into word-bound pedantry. The "Spectre" who rises up with cane and birch among the crowd in Book IV of *The Dunciad* is that of the Grammar-school tyrant himself (Dr. Busby):

> Since Man from beast by Words is known,
> Words are Man's province, Words we teach alone.
> When Reason doubtful, like the Samian letter,
> Points him two ways, the narrower is the better,
> (IV.149–52)

As Pope's note informs us, "The matter under debate is how to confine men to Words for life" (IV.175n). Wordsworth embarks on the work of liberation through the Letter itself. The Arch-Grammarian may ponder the Digamma ("tow'ring o'er your Alphabet, like Saul, / Stands our Digamma, and o'er-tops them all," IV.217–18) but he cannot take both forks of the Samian letter ("The letter Y, used by Pythagoras as an emblem of the different roads of Virtue and Vice," IV.151n). Not so Wordsworth. By a sleight of hand, the Blind London Beggar becomes a symbol of spiritual life-in-death—

> on the shape of the unmoving man,
> His fixèd face and sightless eyes, I look'd
> As if admonish'd from another world.
> (VII.620–22)

—and his label, "a type, / Or emblem, of the utmost that we know"; know of what?—"Both of ourselves and of the universe" (VII.617–19). (Knowledge both of self and of Other, the knowledge that language puts us in possession of). Wordsworth originally wrote: "The whole of what is written to our view, / Is but a label on a blind man's chest" (MS X).[22] The change from aphorism to recognition vivifies the dead letter ("Did the dead Letter unsuccessful prove?" etc), but what really brings both it and the beggar alive, infuses them with the spirit of things, is not a brisk example but a single word—"*utmost*." Earlier, Wordsworth has mused on the "mystery" of the faces that pass him by: now he confronts the mystery of meaninglessness and converts it into a species of revelation. By its nature, language does not force us to choose all or nothing, one or the other. The label can be at once nothing and all, neither and both at once, like the Arab Quixote or Milton's Death ("each seem'd either"). "Archimedes said that he could

271

move the world if he had a point whereon to rest his machine. Who has not felt the same aspirations as regards the world of his own mind?" (Fenwick Note on "The Immortality Ode"). Wordsworth's lever for turning the mind round "As with the might of waters" is the sign itself; at once fixed and mysterious, like London's face, it allows a vital traffic between the visible and the invisible world.

Is this why Wordsworth produces with such pleasure the figure of the Sadler's Wells actor, "The Champion Jack the Giant-killer"?

> Lo!
> He dons his Coat of Darkness; on the Stage
> Walks, and achieves his wonders, from the eye
> Of living mortal safe as is the moon
> 'Hid in her vacant interlunar cave'
> Delusion bold! and faith must needs be coy;
> How is it wrought? His garb is black, the word
> INVISIBLE flames forth upon his Chest.
>
> (VII.302–09)

An engaging piece of mock-heroic? Yes, but something more. Though Wordsworth himself is coy, his ravishment spills over in the boldness of the delusion. One might suspect him of having been seduced, like Mary of Buttermere (though the forms of theatrical entertainment in his case, like those of marriage in hers, could be said to have licensed spectacle—whose proper place, after all, is on the stage).[23] But Wordsworth himself speaks of reading as going to the theatre: re-reading pages which once entranced him, he finds them now "Dead in my eyes as is a theatre / Fresh emptied of spectators" (V.574–75). His early literary tastes, like enjoying Sadler's Wells, may have been replaced by more grown-up entertainment; but the show-man's trick remains his own: "all the host / of shadowy things do work their changes there" (V.622–23). Only the flaming word labels the coat as invisible —making it, in Milton's unimaginable phrase (the phrase to which Pope gave new currency at the opening of the fourth book of *The Dunciad* with his last-ditch plea for Enlightenment), "darkness visible." It's not surprising to stumble on a visual pun in the context of burlesque. What is discon-certing is the glimpse of a different Miltonic text behind the Coat of Darkness (a gaping garment, or *trompe l'oeil* obfuscation?): *Samson Agonistes*. On the face of it, the allusion—"Hid in her vacant interlunar cave"—is so incon-gruous that we are reminded once more of *The Dunciad*; the court of Dulness is a literary solecism in its own right, and her reign is inaugurated by farce:

> There motley Images her fancy strike,
> Figures ill pair'd, and Similies unlike,

> She sees a Mob of Metaphors advance,
> Pleas'd with the madness of the mazy dance:
> How Tragedy and Comedy embrace . . .
>
> (I.65–69)

And of course Wordsworth *is* being sportive, offering us a motley imagery of his own. But still, the breach of decorum remains an unsettling performance: to make tragedy and comedy embrace, to draw the curtailment of Samson's (and Milton's) powers into the orbit of a shape-changer—this is real boldness.

The oscillation between tragi-comic possibilities in this moment of mock-heroic brings to light a hidden structure of thought—an obfuscated text—which proves to be the link between Sadler's Wells and the dream of the Arab Quixote, between London and Books. A brisk move at this point might be to tie the interlunar cave in with the texture midway betwixt life and books; it offers another intermediate image lodged in the interstices of poetic language, another instance of darkness visible. One could also ponder the metaphysics of presence and absence ("under-presence," as Wordsworth cunningly redefines it in Book XIII), or invoke the movement of visionary insight which celebrates Wordsworth's oblivious crossing of the Alps, when the light of sense goes out in flashes and reveals the invisible world. Or one could recapitulate on the problems of self-representation, of "character"; Mrs. Ramsay, in *To the Lighthouse*, experiences her inner self as "a wedge of darkness" lodged in the intervals between the strokes of the lighthouse beam (later, she is a triangular shadow in Lily Briscoe's picture, thrown by an invisible person—the shadow of presence, death, bringing her back to life in art). All this, and more, would bear on *The Prelude*. But it is Milton's text that yields most, with its memorable elegy for the poet's lost sight—

> The Sun to me is dark
> And silent as the Moon,
> When she deserts the night,
> Hid in her vacant interlunar cave . . .
>
> (ll. 86–89)

—and its tragic play on darkness, desertion, and silence, its moon that "speaks" when visible and so makes of Samson's own utterance an echoing silence: "Myself my Sepulcher," as the moon is buried in its interlunar cave. A symbol of death-in-life, Samson becomes a speaking absence, an embodiment of lack as well as sightlessness. Earlier, Milton has identified light and Logos and made him mourn his exclusion from both as a bereavement which amounts to death-by-word ("decree")—

> O first created Beam, and thou great Word,
> 'Let there be light, and light was over all';
> Why am I thus bereav'd thy prime decree?
>
> (ll. 83–85)

—and what follows, a lament for the siting of seeing in the eye, takes us directly to Wordsworth's lament for the frailty of books as the shrine of Imagination ("Why, gifted with such powers to send abroad / Her spirit, must it lodge in shrines so frail?" VII.47–48):

> Since light so necessary is to life,
> And almost life itself, if it be true
> That light is in the Soul,
> She all in every part; why was the sight
> To such a tender ball as th'eye confined?
>
> (ll. 90–94)

But (this isn't in any way to enter into argument with Samson) without sight there couldn't even be the particular word-blindness induced by the blind London Beggar's label; without the tyranny of the eye there couldn't be the contrary motion of the Wordsworthian supernatural; without a text, one's own or that of a precursor, there would be no signs for the imagination to work with, no dead letter to become characters of danger or desire, and no books to obliterate or save.

IV

Which brings us back to the dream of the Arab Quixote. Freud would presumably classify it as an instance of *"Träume von oben,"*

> That is to say . . . formulations of ideas which could have been created just as well in a waking state as during the state of sleep, and which have derived their content only in certain parts from mental states at a comparatively deep level. That is why these dreams offer for the most part a content which has an abstract, poetic, or symbolic form.[24]

His comment relates, in fact, to the famous source of Wordsworth's "dream," an actual dream of November 10, 1619 recounted in Baillet's *Vie de Descartes* (1691)—the third of three, and the least frightening (the others include apocalyptic whirlwinds and claps of thunder).[25] Like Wordsworth's, the dream concerns two books: a *Dictionary* which Descartes interprets while still asleep as standing "merely for the sciences gathered together," and "a collection of poems entitled *Corpus Poetarum*" which "marked more particularly and expressly the union of philosophy with wisdom"—a superior mode of knowledge ascribed to "*la divinité de l'enthousiasme, et . . . la force de l'imagination.*" The dream is well-known, and the topos a traditional one (the Book of Nature and the Book of revealed Scripture). But—like Wordsworth's—the text is usually read in terms of its own re-reading, the interpretation supplied by Descartes himself.[26] Predictably enough, he made sense of it in the light of his intense anxiety about the proper course of study to pursue, his ambition to create a unified system of knowledge, and his hopes for divine inspiration in the task. No less than Wordsworth's Arab Quixote, he was a visionary pitting himself against overwhelming odds. What Descartes himself (and his later readers) omit from the text is its nonsense—its inconsequential dream-play with vanishing books and lost texts. It might be called the dream of the vanishing texts; texts highly relevant, as it happens, to Wordsworth's "dream." The form of the dream is this: Descartes finds a book on his table, the dictionary, without knowing how it had come there, and then happens on a second with no less surprise. Opening it, he chances on the line "*Quod vitae sectabor iter*" ("What path in life shall I pursue?") and simultaneously a stranger presents him with some verses beginning "*Est et non.*" Descartes recognizes the author as Ausonius (a fourth century Christian poet) and begins to search for the poem in his *Corpus Poetarum,* but cannot find it; meanwhile the stranger questions him about the provenance of the book, the dictionary disappears and returns in a different form, and Descartes—still unable to find "*Est et non*"—offers to turn up "*Quod vitae sectabor iter*" instead, until he is deflected by some engravings in what proves to be an unfamiliar edition. Finally both man and books vanish.

What stands out in all this is the capricious behaviour of the books themselves. Baillet is inclined to put Descartes' dreams down to late-night drinking, but it sounds more like late-night reading. Whatever the cause, though, a later reader could not fail to be struck by the irritating mixture of corporeality and elusiveness in both books and texts. The book-as-object could hardly be more prominent. (A related fantasy inspires Pope's mischievous picture of the hack-poet at work in *The Dunciad,* surrounded in his poetic frenzy by unfinished writings and pillaged books, and driven finally to build a sacrificial pyre to Dulness out of "twelve volumes, twelve of amplest size;" book-burning always a dangerously attractive fantasy to bibliophiles, especially when it is the Moderns who go up in smoke). There is no evidence that Wordsworth himself had first-hand knowledge of Baillet's *Vie de Descartes*, and it has been suggested that Beaupuis narrated the dream to him under the trees of Blois in 1792. But this seems a long gestation period (the dream of the Arab Quixote was composed in February/March 1804), and at the time concerned Wordsworth was evidently more preoccupied with day-dreams inspired by Ariosto, Tasso, and Spenser than with philosophic dreams. Coleridge, however, was reading Descartes throughout the years 1797 to 1803 (especially during 1801), and, as usual, projecting a book on him.[27] It would be pleasing to think that Wordsworth not only discussed the dream with Coleridge, but read it himself—he was, after all, a bookish man as well as (by his own account) a bookish child. Moreover, had he done so, he would have been singularly, or rather, doubly receptive to Descartes's vanishing texts. His own poetic mission was similarly a source of anxiousness, while the first of Ausonius's lines ("*Quod vitae . . .*") meshes nicely with the neo-miltonic quest announced in the Glad Preamble ("The earth is all before me . . . I cannot miss my way," I.15, 19). As for "*Est et non*" (The Pythagoraean "Yea" and "Nay," or truth and falsity in human knowledge), Ausonius's verses mischievously provide a text-book example of the "neither, and both at once" principle at work in the dream of the Arab Quixote: light may be synonymous with day, but the fact of light doesn't prevent it being night after all; on this yes-and-no, writes Ausonius, "the whole throng of rhetoricians depends in its wordy contests."[28] Think of the Coat of Darkness and its inscription, "INVISIBLE"; think also of Aristotle's deconstruction of the form of words that defines the sun as "the brightest star that moves above the earth" (what becomes of the definition when it's hid in its intersolar cave?).

In a different context, Hillis Miller uses this Aristotelean example to expose what he calls "a blind spot"—the rhetorical *catachresis* or misnaming which makes all referentiality in language a fiction.[29] The dream of the Arab Quixote similarly uncovers the fiction on which both Wordsworth's poetry and the black-coated actor depend. Appropriately enough, *The Prelude* loses the philosopher and comes up with the romancer; instead of Descartes, for whom madness and rational discourse were incompatible, we find Cervantes and his fiction-ridden hero—the catachrazy hero, one might call him, in his mistaking of windmills for giants. We are back in the hinterland between "life" and "books." In a sense, the relation between the authors of Wordsworth's two literary sources is the relation also between stone and shell; one symbolizing abstract, deductive reasoning, the other, the ungrounded truth of the imagination (and maybe the two are not so distinct). For a philosopher attempting the impossible, Wordsworth substitutes the Romantic idealist—"not a man out of his senses," in Coleridge's phrase, but a man so possessed by imagination "as to make him disregard the evidence of sense."[30] He tilts with metaphors, and though Sancho Panza may stand for the reality principle, he can never be the real hero. Wordsworth's own fall-guy is the "dwarf Man" of Book V ("'tis a Child, no Child, / But a dwarf Man," V.294–95)—a moral paragon and miniature pedant, his path "chok'd with grammars" like the victims of Pope's spectral pedagogue. He too is a bookish child ("in learning and in books / He is a prodigy"), a good reader and speller: "he can read / The inside of the earth, and spell the stars" (V.319–20, 332–33). But unlike the young Wordsworth, he knows no fear, "Unless it leap upon him in a dream." This rather ponderous satire on infant self-possession gives way abruptly to the real theme of "Books," Romance. In a rush of generous impatience, Wordsworth wishes on him and all children the heroes of popular romance who figure on the London stage in Book VII and reappear in the visionary after-images of the Cave of Yordas:

> Oh! give us once again the Wishing-Cap
> Of Fortunatus, and the invisible Coat
> Of Jack the Giant-killer, Robin Hood.
> And Sabra in the Forest with St. George!
> The Child, whose love is here, at least, doth reap
> One precious gain, that he forgets himself.
>
> (V.364–69)

Or rather, Wordsworth wishes on him "faith," the simple belief of the Sadler's Wells audience. The first book-as-object that he represents himself as having coveted is "A little, yellow canvas-cover'd Book, / A slender abstract of the Arabian Tales" (V.483–84). The Arabian Nights, by a happy Romantic pun, give him the composite hero of the dream: an Arabian Knight (remember the sublime pun thrown up by the deep and gloomy breathing place of the Snowdon vision: "The Soul, the Imagination of the whole," XIII.65). Such accidents of dream-language are among the "precious gains" of self-forgetfulness. By contrast, Wordsworth was fully conscious of the continuity between the child's imagination and his adult self. What is *Don Quixote* but a grown-up's version of Jack the Giant-killer, a text recovered from his earliest school-boy reading and given a new layer of meaning?[31] Books become spots of time, recuperating memory into consciousness. creating a inter-space between past and present which bridges the gulf between the divided consciousness of the adult ("I seem / Two consciousness, conscious of myself / And of some other Being," II.31–33).

De Quincey, who elsewhere writes perceptively about the dream of the Arab Quixote, has this to say about books in contrasting "The Literature of Knowledge and the Literature of Power":

> of this let everyone be assured—that he owes to the impassioned books which he has read many a thousand more of emotions than he can consciously trace back to them. Dim by their origination, these emotions yet arise in him, and mould him through life, like forgotten incidents of his childhood.[32]

Like forgotten incidents, forgotten books mould the language of the dream; even if their custodian is dispatched into an infinitely receding distance on his burial mission, they have a habit of coming to the surface. At this point it seems worth risking a connection between Romance and dream.

Romance, one might say, makes superstition manageable; turns it into "faith." Equally, it stands for the autonomy of the imagination, bringing self-forgetfulness. Dreams, too, though they may induce a frightening solipsism or abyss of idealism, enclose the dreamer in his own mind: "I was the Dreamer, they the Dream," Wordsworth writes of Cambridge (III.28); the London crowd becomes "A second-sight procession, such as glides / Over still mountains, or appears in dreams" (VII.602–03); the calm of nature makes the child forget that he has bodily eyes:

> what I saw
> Appear'd like something in myself, a dream.
> A prospect in my mind.
>
> (II.369–71)

This is a different self-possession from that of the infant prodigy, and because one would expect such imaginative possession to be an intensely pleasurable experience in both reading and writing ("Visionary Power / Attends upon the motions of the winds . . ."), it is worth looking sharply at a well-known passage where Wordsworth develops the opposite view. In the third "Essay on Epitaphs" (1810), he writes of words as "too awful an instrument for good and evil to be trifled with," and goes on to elaborate a rather morbidly self-lacerating fantasy about being taken over and deranged by them:

> If words be not . . . an incarnation of the thought but only a clothing for it, then surely will they prove an ill gift; such a one as those poisoned vestments, read of in the stories of superstitious times, which had power to consume and to alienate from his right mind the victim who put them on.[33]

(The reference is to Hercules, driven mad with pain by the garments which his wife had smeared with poison, thinking it a love-potion; when he tore off his clothes, his skin came too.) What Wordsworth is really talking about here is other people's words—the second-hand, "tainted" language of the previous century. We are witnesses to a casting-out, as with Pope's caricature of the hack-poet Bays, resting on his borrowed laurels: "Next, o'er his Books his eyes began to roll, / In pleasing memory of all he stole . . ." (*The Dunciad*, I.127–28). But the anxiety of influence itself only makes manageable a larger and more inescapable anxiety: that our texts have always been written before, that the loud prophetic blast of harmony is pentecostal and speaks with many voices—"Had voices more than all the winds" (V.108)—and that in submitting to textuality, we put on inherited garments. The dream of the Arab Quixote is an attempt to launder them while still remaining enfolded in the texture of language.

But perhaps Wordsworth need not have worried. De Quincey, who thought that encyclopedias in general, and Newton's *Principia* in particular, "transmigrated into other forms," was certain that the Literature of Power (unlike the Literature of Knowledge) remained "triumphant forever as long as the languages exist in which they speak or can be taught to speak":

> Human works of immortal beauty and works of nature in one respect stand on the same footing: they never absolutely repeat each other, never approach so near as not to differ; and they differ not as better and worse, or simply by more and less: they differ by undecipherable and incommunicable differences, that cannot be caught by mimicries, that cannot be reflected in the mirror of copies, that cannot become ponderable in the scales of vulgar comparison.[34]

"The literature of power," he concludes, "builds nests in aërial altitudes of temples sacred from violation—in the mind, that inter-textual edifice which *The Prelude* tries endlessly to defend against the violations, seductions, and transformations enacted by the language of the dream.

Notes

1 Quotations are from the 1805 text of *The Prelude*, ed. Ernest de Selincourt and Helen Darbishire (2nd ed., Oxford, 1959).

2 1815 Preface; *The Prose Works of William Wordsworth*, ed. W. J. B. Owen and J. W. Smyser, 3 vols. (Oxford, 1974), III, 33. Cf. Wordsworth's letter of 14 June 1802 on the "feeling of spirituality or supernaturalness" aroused by the Leech-gatherer in *The Letters of William and Dorothy Wordsworth: The Early Years*, ed. E. de Selincourt, rev. C. L. Shaver (Oxford, 1967), p. 366.

3 The "dream"—long since identified as Descartes'—was attributed to Wordsworth himself in ms. versions from 1839 onwards; see J. W. Smyser, "Wordsworth's Dream of Poetry and Science: *The Prelude*, V," *PMLA*, 71 (1956), 269–75.

4 Baudelaire's remark is quoted by W. H. Auden in *The Enchafed Flood or the Romantic Iconography of the Sea* (N.Y., 1950, P. 61—itself one of the most extended "interpretations" of the dream of the Arab Quixote. More recent interpretations include Geoffrey Hartman in *Wordsworth's Poetry 1787–1814* (New Haven and London, 1971), pp. 229–31, and J. Hillis Miller. "The Stone and the Shell: The Problem of Poetic Form in Wordsworth's Dream of the Arab," *Mouvements Premiers: Études Critiques Offertes à Georges Poulet* (Paris, 1972), pp. 125–47.

5 Cf. also Pope's mischievously parodic purification in *The Dunciad,* the hack-poet's burning of his own works:

> "Go, purify'd by flames ascend the sky,
> My better and more Christian progeny!
> Unstain'd, untouch'd, and yet in maiden sheets;
> While all your smutty sisters walk the streets."
> (*The Dunciad,* I.227–30)

6 Wordsworth might well have wished to lay Mary of Buttermere to rest: her marriage to the bigamist and impostor, Hatfield, took place two days before his own marriage to another Mary on 4 October 1802. The story broke during October and Coleridge, who presumably knew about Annette Vallon and her child, made sure it received coverage in the London papers by supplying a succession of articles to the *Morning Post* during October, November and December; see *The Collected Works of Samuel Taylor Coleridge: Essays on His Times*, ed. D. V. Erdman. 3 vols. (London and Princeton, 1978), I, 357–416.

7 For an elaboration of the Lacanian theory summarized here, see Jacques Lacan, *The Language of the Self*, trans. Anthony Wilden (Baltimore, 1968).

8 Ernest de Selincourt and Helen Darbishire (*The Prelude*, p. 615) suggest Hamlet's "questionable shape" as the source of Wordsworth's phrase.

9 See *Seven Lectures on Shakespeare and Milton*, ed. J. Payne Collier (London, 1856), p. 65; repr. in *The Romantics on Milton*, ed. J. A. Wittreich. Jr. (Cleveland, Ohio), p. 201.

10 See "Autumn," ll. 726–30.

11 This section of *Descriptive Sketches* did not find its way into Book VI of *The Prelude* until 1816/19 (see 1850, VI.414–89 and *The Prelude*, pp. 198, 200 *app. crit.*)

12 *Seven Lectures on Shakespeare and Milton*, ed. J. Payne Collier, p. 101. Cf. also Coleridge's poem, "Constancy to an Ideal Object."

13 *Blackwood's Magazine*, 57 (June 1845), 749.

14 *Ibid.*, 749–50.

15 *Ibid.*, 750.

16 *Ibid.*, 743.

17 One might add the effect—chiasmus with a difference—of bringing the two semantic poles into close juxtaposition in the skating episode, with "The rapid line of motion" spinning one way, earth rolling "With visible motion her diurnal round." another (I.482, 486): glad animal movements brought into the same orbit as the motions of the spheres.

18 See "The 'Uncanny'" (1919), *The Complete Psychological Works of Sigmund Freud*, trans. and ed. James Strachey, 24 vols. (London, 1955), XVII, 250.

19 See Harold Bloom, "Visionary Cinema in Romantic Poetry." *The Ringers in the Tower* (Chicago, 1971). pp. 37–52.

20 Cf., however, the more subtle and complex reading of this episode and its role in Book VII offered by Neil Hertz, "The Notion of Blockage in the Literature of the Sublime," *Psychoanalysis and the Question of the Text*, ed. Geoffrey Hartman (English Institute Essays, 1978), pp. 62–85. See also Thomas Weiskell, *The Romantic Sublime: Studies in the Structure and Psychology of Transcendence* (Baltimore and London, 1976), pp. 136–43, 167–204 for an enterprising psycho-analytic account of the sublime in Wordsworth's poetry.

21 It is this passage which Coleridge uses to illustrate the mind's power "to reconcile opposites and qualify contradictions, leaving a middle state of mind more strictly appropriate to the imagination than any other, when it is, as it were, hovering between images"; *see Seven Lectures on Shakespeare and Milton*, ed. J. Payne Collier, p. 64–65: repr. in *The Romantics on Milton*, ed. J. A. Wittreich. Jr., p. 200.

22 See the forthcoming Norton edition of *The Prelude*, ed. Jonathan Wordsworth (N.Y., 1979). VII.617–20n.

23 See *OED* for the theatricality of "spectacle" and its restricted technical sense, "a piece of stage-display or pageantry as contrasted with real drama."

24 *The Complete Psychological Works of Sigmund Freud*, trans. and ed. James Strachey, XXI, 203.

25 See N. K. Smith, *New Studies in the Philosophy of Descartes* (London. 1952). pp. 33–39 for the translation of Baillet's account (*Vie de Descartes. Book II*, ch. i, pp. 81–86) from which quotations below are taken. The two Ausonius texts are from Book VII, *Eclogues* ii and iv respectively.

26 See, for instance, Georges Poulet, "The Dream of Descartes," *Studies in Human Time*, trans. Elliot Coleman (Baltimore, 1956), pp. 50–73.

27 For the suggestion that Beaupuis provided Wordsworth with his source, see Smyser, pp. 272–73; Wordsworth's preoccupations at this period are recorded in *The Prelude*, IX.450–64. The dating of the dream of the Arab Quixote is discussed by Jonathan Wordsworth, "The Five-Book Prelude of early Spring 1804," *JEGP*, 76 (1977), 1–25. For Coleridge's interest in Descartes see James Lindsay, "Coleridge's Marginalia in a Volume of Descartes," *PMLA*, 49 (1934), 184–95, and *The Letters of S. T. Coleridge*, ed. E. L. Griggs, 6 vols. (Oxford, 1956–71), II, 677–703.

28 See *Ausonius*, trans. H. G. E. White (London and Cambridge, Mass., 1919), I, 173.

29 See J. Hillis Miller, "Stevens' Rock and Criticism as Cure," *Georgia Review*, 30 (1976), 29–30.

30 See *Specimens of the Table Talk of the Late Samuel Taylor Coleridge*, ed. H. N. Coleridge (London, 1835), II, 87.

31 For Wordsworth's early reading, see *The Prelude*, ed. Ernest de Selincourt and Helen Darbishire, p. 540. As Geoffrey Hartman puts it, "the spirit of poetry [is born] from the grave clothes of Romance"; see "False Themes and Gentle Minds," *Beyond Formalism* (New Haven and London, 1970), p. 289.

32 "The Poetry of Pope," *The Collected Writings of Thomas De Quincey*, ed. David Masson, 14 vols. (Edinburgh, 1889–90), XI, 59–60. For De Quincey's discussion of the dream of the Arab Quixote, see *ibid.*, II, 268–70.

33 *The Prose Works of William Wordsworth*, ed. W. J. B. Owen and J. W. Smyser, II, 84–85.

34 *The Collected Writings of Thomas De Quincey*, ed. David Masson, XI, 58.

63

COLERIDGE, PRESCIENCE, TENACITY AND THE ORIGIN OF SOCIOLOGY

Thomas McFarland

Source: *Romanticism* 4 (1998), 40–59.

In 1795, in some theological lectures, Coleridge, at that time only 23 years old, posed a question, modified from a verse in the Bible:[1] 'If we love not our friends and Parents whom we have seen – how can we love our universal Friend and Almighty Parent whom we have not seen?'[2] More than a quarter of a century later, in his *Opus Maximum*, he asked the same question: 'If ye love not your earthly parent, how *can* ye love your father in heaven?'[3] All that time, from 1795 to 1820 or later, the question had been held in his mind. It was occupying his thoughts in his fledgling, though virtuoso, work of the mid-1790s; and it was occupying his mind as he set forth on what he considered 'the great object of my life',[4] that object being 'my Opus Maximum on which I chiefly rely for the proof that I have not lived or laboured in vain' (CL, VI, p. 541, January 1826).

It is extraordinary that a mental formulation should remain vital in anyone's mind for so long a period of time. It is even more extraordinary, however, that it not only remained in Coleridge's mind for more than a quarter of a century, but that it did not rest there inertly. On the contrary, it permuted and combined under constant reflection to eventuate in the most distinctive and vivid insistence of the entire *Opus Maximum*.

For the apex of that work, and perhaps the most original and powerful insistence in his entire edifice of thought, is Coleridge's derivation of the belief in God from the relationship of mother and child. Few before Coleridge had dwelt so insistently on the meaning of that relationship, but under his intense scrutiny the profoundest of meanings are uncovered to view. The 'first dawnings' of a baby's humanity will break forth in the eye that connects the Mother's face with the warmth of the mother's bosom, the support of the mother's Arms. A thousand tender kisses excite a finer life in its lips & there first language is imitated from the mother's smiles. Ere yet a conscious self exists the love begins & the first love is love to another. The Babe acknowledges a self in the Mother's form, years before it can recognize a self in its own.

(*Opus Maximum*, Fragment Two ff. 65–6)

Sounding, except for the elevation of his language, much like Spitz, Kohut, Winnicott, or other modern investigators of the pre-Oedipal situation of the child, Coleridge points out that

The infant follows its mother's face as glowing with love and dreaming protection it is raised heavenward, and with the word God it combines in feeling whatever there is of reality in the warm touch, in the supporting grasp, in the glorious countenance. The whole problem of existence is present as a sum total in the mother; the mother exists as a One & indivisible something, before the outlines of her different limbs and features have been distinguished by the fixed and yet half vacant eye, & hence through each degree of dawning light the whole remains antecedent to the parts . . .

(Fragment Two, f. 88)

If the 'whole problem of existence is present as a sum total in the mother', it follows inevitably that this primal experience leads to the idea of 'God'. We are reminded that for the greatest of nineteenth-century theologians, Schleiermacher, religion grew simply out of *Abhängigkeitsgefühl*, the feeling of absolute dependence. Nowhere is dependence more absolute than in the relation of infant and mother.

Yet the powerful elaborations of this line of thought in 1820 all issue from the question posed by Coleridge in 1795. As he says in the *Opus Maximum*:

that which the mother is to her child, a someone unseen and yet ever present is to all. The first introduction to thought takes place in the transfer of person from the senses to the invisible. The reverence of the Invisible, substantiated by the feeling of love – this, which is the essence and proper definiton of religion is the commencement of the intellectual life, of the humanity. If ye love not your earthly parent, how *can* ye love your father in heaven?

(Fragment Two, f. 79)

A second instance of Coleridge's extreme ideational tenacity reveals exactly what the example brought forth above reveals: first, that mental collocations persisted in his mind over a course of decades, and, secondly, that the extreme prolongation of his intellectual attention was matched by the depth of the philosophemes so retained. Thus, in the *Opus Maximum* he notes that

> Unlike a multitude of tygers, a million of men is far and more than one man repeated a million times. Each man in a numerous society is not simply co-existent, he is virtually co-organized with, and into, the multitude of which he is an integral part. And, for the same cause, this multitude is no mere abstraction, but is capable of becoming a true and living whole, a power susceptible of personal attributes, a nation.
>
> (Fragment Two, f. 15)

About fifteen years earlier, in a letter to Thomas Clarkson in October 1806 Coleridge had said that

> A male & female Tyger is neither more or less whether you suppose them only existing in their appropriate wildness, or whether you suppose a thousand Pairs. But Man is truly altered by the co-existence of other men; his faculties cannot be developed in himself alone, & only by himself. Therefore the human race not by a bold metaphor, but in a sublime reality, approach to, & might become, one body whose head is Christ (the Logos).
>
> (CL, II, p. 1197)

The two passages, each so beautifully articulated, and each modified to its own particular purpose fifteen years apart, dramatically illustrate the extraordinary persistence in Coleridge's mind of thoughts once taken up.

But the passages are more than a witness to Coleridge's intellectual tenacity. They witness as well his cultural prescience and intellectual depth. For they each incorporate the fundamental understanding by which alone the science of sociology is possible. It was an understanding that could not be grasped at all by others in Coleridge's time. For a single instance, the brilliant Harriet Martineau found it totally unintelligible. As she recalled of a meeting with Coleridge in 1832:

> He looked very old, with his rounded shoulders and drooping head, and excessively thin limbs. His eyes were as wonderful as they were ever represented to be; – light grey, extremely prominent, and actually glittering: an appearance I am told common among opium eaters. His onset amused me not a little. He told me that he (the last

person whom I should have suspected) read my tales as they came out on the first of the month; and, after paying some compliments, he avowed that there were points on which we differed (I was full of wonder that there were any on which we agreed): 'for instance,' said he, 'you appear to consider that society is an aggregate of individuals!' I replied that I certainly did; whereupon he went off on one of the several metaphysical interpretations which may be put upon the many-sided fact of an organised human society, subject to natural laws in virtue of its aggregate character and organisation together. After a long flight in survey of society from his own balloon in his own current, he came down again to some considerations of individuals, and at length to some special biographical topics, ending with criticisms on old biographers, whose venerable works he brought down from the shelf. No one else spoke, of course, except when I once or twice put a question; and when his monologue came to what seemed a natural stop, I rose to go.[5]

Martineau's amusement at Coleridge's incomprehensible remark was recorded in her autobiography in the 1870s; so even as late as that Coleridge's distinction was so radical as not to be understandable. It was not until the work of the French school of sociologists, beginning in the 1890s, that the distinction became available even to specialists. As the great social anthropologist Marcel Mauss said in 1938, after a third of the twentieth century had passed, 'Thanks to forty years of effort, our sciences have become phenomenologies. We know that two special realms exist: the realm of consciousness on the one hand, and the realm of collective consciousness and the collectivity on the other. We know that these two realms are in the world and in life, are in nature.'[6]

Mauss was the nephew of the greatest of all sociologists, Emile Durkheim. In his Latin thesis for the Sorbonne in 1892, Durkheim had identified Montesquieu as the first sociological thinker; and he later wrote a revealing essay on the sociological perspective of Rousseau's *Social Contract*. But neither Montesquieu nor Rousseau, immensely important figures though they were, even comes close to matching the point and profundity of Coleridge's grasping of the bedrock fundamental of sociological awareness. Durkheim's own thought was profoundly influenced by Rousseau's conception of the *volonté générale*, which for Rousseau replaces the initiating conception of the individual in the state of nature (indeed, Talcott Parsons says flatly that 'clearly the *conscience collective* is a derivative of Rousseau's "general will" and [Auguste] Comte's "consensus"');[7] and Durkheim begins his essay on Rousseau by pointing out that the state of nature does not refer to natural bliss but to the conception of the individual taken without reference to others. But even these epoch-making understandings do not contain the matchless sociological potentiality of Coleridge's awareness.

Indeed, Colerídge's vivid metaphor of the different meanings of plurality in tigers and humans contains exactly the same understanding as does Durkheim's own memorable formulation, in his great work on the division of labour, of *conscience collective*. The 'collective consciousness' is diffused throughout society, and

> the states which constitute it differ specifically from those which constitute particular consciousnesses. The specificity results from the fact that they are not formed from the same elements. The latter result from the nature of the organico-psychic being taken in isolation, the former from the combination of a plurality of beings of this kind.[8]

For Durkheim, as Steven Lukes notes, social facts (*faits sociaux*), as opposed to 'organico-psychic' facts restricted to the individual,

> exist 'outside individual *consciences*'. Thus, for example, domestic or civic or contractual obligations are defined, externally to the individual, in law and custom; religious beliefs and practices 'exist prior to the individual, because they exist outside him'; language and currency, as well as professional practices 'function independently of my use of them'.[9]

Durkheim himself used the term *conscience collective* interchangeably with *conscience commune*, and in *De la division du travail social* he says that the '*conscience collective* or *commune*' is 'the set of beliefs and sentiments common to the average members of a single society and forms a determinate system that has its own life.'[10] (We should note parenthetically that Lukes points out that the 'French word "*conscience*" is ambiguous, embracing the meanings of the two English words "conscience" and "consciousness". Thus the "beliefs and sentiments" comprising the *conscience collective*, are, on the one hand, moral and religious, and, on the other, cognitive. See Lukes, p. 4) Later on, Durkheim tended to replace the term *conscience collective* with a more supple term, *représentations collectives*. Of this latter phrase Lukes says:

> Durkheim started using this concept in about 1897, when he wrote (in *Suicide*) that 'essentially social life is made up of *représentations*'. Collective *représentations* are 'states of the *conscience collective*' which are 'different in nature from the states of the individual *conscience*'. They express 'the way in which the group conceives itself in its relations with the objects which affect it.' Much of Durkheim's later work can be seen as the systematic study of collective *représentations*. Thus his sociology of knowledge examines the

social origin and the social reference, and the social functions, of the forms of cognitive thought; his sociology of religion does the same for religious beliefs; and his projected sociology of morality would have done likewise for moral beliefs and ideals.

(Lukes, p. 6)

The reference just made to Durkheim's sociology of religion tends in its ramifications also to illuminate Coleridge's prescience. In the second of the tyger passages quoted above, Coleridge directs his brilliant grasp of sociological reality toward religion: 'the human race, not by a bold metaphor, but in a sublime reality, approach to, & might become, one body whose head is Christ (the Logos).' Coleridge certainly understood that the church was a *conscience collective*, not a gathering of discrete individuals; the Greek word *ekklesia* means a gathering of citizens, an assembly, not simply a crowd. As Coleridge said in *On the Constitution of the Church and State*, the Christian church is 'not like reason or the court of conscience, existing only in and for the individual'. On the contrary, it is 'an institution consisting of visible and public communities'. Nor for Coleridge was it simply a hodge-podge of individual needs; his elevated idea of a national church should not be reduced merely to '*a* religion': 'Religion, a *noun of multitude*, or nomen collectivum, expressing the aggregate of all the different groups of notions and ceremonies connected with the invisible and supernatural' (CS, p. 61). That formula is of course denigrative, but even there the religious is definitively constituted by the social.

Indeed, Coleridge's two tyger passages, the one converging on 'a true and living whole, a power susceptible of personal attributes, a nation'; and the other converging on 'one body, whose head is Christ (the Logos)', come together in their common service to his interlocked conception of church and state. Coleridge warns the reader not to 'confound the STATE as a *whole*, and comprehending the church, with the State as one of the two constituent parts, and in contradistinction from the Church' (CS, p. 107). This sameness in difference arises from the polar nature of Coleridge's characteristic conceiving. Specifically the church is the complementing opposite of the state:

The Christian Church, I say, is no state, kingdom, or realm of the world; nor is it an Estate of any such realm, kingdom or state; but it is the appointed Opposite to them all *collectively* – the *sustaining, correcting, befriending* Opposite of the world! the compensating counter-force to the inherent and inevitable evils and defects of the STATE, *as* a state, and without reference to its better or worse construction as a particular state; while whatever is beneficent and humanizing in the aims, tendencies, and proper objects of the state, the Christian Church collects in itself as in a focus, to radiate them back in a higher quality: or to exhange the metaphor, it completes and strengthens the edifice of the state, without interference or com-mixture, in the mere act of laying and securing its own foundations.

(CS, pp. 114–15)

Underlying all this thinking was Coleridge's position that 'Religion, true or false, is and ever has been the centre of gravity to a realm, to which all other things must and will accommodate themselves'. (CS, p. 70)

Mutatis mutandis, the same conclusion pertains to the most mature thought of Durkheim. Of Durkheim's four large works, the first three were published during his Bordeaux period in the 1890s, the *Division of Labor* in 1893, the *Rules of Sociological Method* in 1895, *Suicide* in 1897. But the fourth and last, the *Elementary Forms of the Religious Life*, was not pub-lished until much later, until 1912, when he was professor at the Sorbonne. It is not only his final and greatest work, but is one of the truly significant books in all of Western culture. For in *Les formes élémentaires de la vie religieuse* Durkheim demonstrates, once and for all, what religion is. He shows that religion does not depend primarily on a belief in God – for some religions, such as Buddhism, do not have such a belief – but on the division of sacred from profane; and that the substratum and regulating factor of religion is always social. Arguing that 'Society is a reality *sui generis*',[12] he says, conforming exactly to Coleridge's conceptions as set forth in his tract on Church and State, that

we arrive at the following definition: *A religion is a unified system of beliefs and practices relative to sacred things, that is to say, things set apart and forbidden – beliefs and practices which unite into one single moral community called a Church, all those who adhere to them.* The second element which thus finds a place in our definition is no less essential than the first; for by showing that the idea of religion in inseparable from that of the Church, it makes it clear that religion should be an eminently collective thing.

(p. 49)

At the end of his masterwork Durkheim sums up: 'nearly all the great social institutions have been born in religion. Now in order that these principal aspects of the collective life may have commenced by being only varied aspects of the religious life, it is obviously necessary that the religious life be the eminent form, and, as it were, the concentrated form of the whole collective life. If religion has given birth to all that is essential in society, it is because the idea of society is the soul of religion' (p. 419).

This was the conclusion toward which the thought of the great sociologist had been moving from its earliest origins. Indeed, his revered teacher at the *École normale supérieure*, the classicist Fustel de Coulanges, had in his eminent work *La Cité antique* challengingly taken up the fecundating and originating power of religion in the ancient city. Fustel was very important to Durkheim – as a matter of fact, Durkheim's Latin thesis was dedicated to Fustel – and of the great influence exerted by the teacher on the student a commentator has said in part:

> *The Ancient City* is a study of the central role of religion, in particular the ancestor cult, in Greece and Rome ('The religious idea was, among the ancients, the inspiring breath and organizer of society'), stressing the importance of sacredness in the explanation of their institutions and beliefs, and the pervasive predominance of ritual (religion 'signified rites, ceremonies, acts of exterior worship. The doctrine was of small account: the practices were the important part; these were obligatory and bound men . . .'). These were the very features which Durkheim's Sociology of religion was to emphasize. Its germs can be seen throughout Fustel's great work: for example in its account of ancestor worship (establishing 'a powerful bond . . . among all the generations of the same family, which made of it a body forever inseparable'); in its view of primitive religion as the source of 'all the institutions, as well as all the private law, of the ancients', the earliest forms being 'the most important for us to know'; in its hypothesis that there might be a connection between the ideas of economic value and of religious value; and in its general focus on 'the intimate relation which always exists between men's ideas and 'their social state'. And, like Durkheim, Fustel spoke of the 'truth' underlying the 'legendary forms' of religious beliefs: 'Social laws were the work of the gods; but those gods, so powerful and beneficient, were nothing else than the beliefs of men.'
>
> (Lukes, pp. 62–3)

Despite the germinating seeds planted by Fustel, Durkheim did not, as he autobiographically says, start thinking seriously about religion until 1895: 'It was not until 1895 that I achieved a clear view of the essential role played by religion in social life. It was in that year that, for the first time, I found the means of tackling the study of religion sociologically. This was a revelation to me. That course of 1895 marked a dividing line in the development of my thought, to such an extent that all my previous researches had to be taken up afresh in order to be made to harmonize with these new insights' (Lukes, p. 237). Durkheim goes on to say that his reorientation was entirely due to 'the studies of religious history which I had just undertaken, and notably to the reading of the works of Robertson Smith and his school' (Lukes, p. 237). Robertson Smith, however, had himself been influenced, in his study of Semitic clans of Arabia, by Fustel's *La Cité antique*. In any event Durkheim's overt attention, beginning in 1895, combined with the subliminal awarenesses of earlier years to eventuate in the power and depth of the *Elementary Forms of the Religious Life* in 1912.

But this paper is not intended to be a treatise on the magnificent contribution of Durkbeim; and in truth Durkheim has loomed so large solely because of the necessity of illustrating how deep Coleridge's tenacious conceptions run. Yet it is necessary to reiterate that Durkheim was not only the first true sociologist, but also the greatest of all sociologists. His life and career were approximately contemporary with those of Georg Simmel and Max Weber in Germany; and although Karl Jaspers expresses almost unbounded admiration for Weber, and although the Weber mystique has great currency in modern sociology – 'Weber is seen as a kind of Magus', says Donald Macrae, in his study of Weber for the Modern Masters series[13] – nevertheless Durkheim is even more important. Noting that 'In sociology Weber is canonized', MacRae nevertheless judges that 'Durkheim is by far the greater sociologist' (pp. 5, 6).

The fact, therefore, that Coleridge's deep-running tenacity expressly prefigures the sociology of Durkheim guarantees not only a constancy but a prescience of thought. It is to that deep-running and prescient tenacity that the paper will now return to present another example. The elaborations of *On the Constitution of the Church and State* having been adduced in the course of the foregoing illustration, it might be instructive, as witness to the cornucopian richness of Coleridge's mind, to summon that same treatise for the next illustration. In this work Coleridge sees the healthy society as determined by a continuing tension of polar opposites.

One of these oppositions is that between permanence and progression: 'the two antagonist powers or opposite interests of the state, under which all other state interests are composed, are those of PERMANENCE and of PROGRESSION' (CS, p. 24). Coleridge goes on to connect 'the permanence of a state with the land and the landed property' (CS, p. 24); whereas 'the progression of a state, in the arts and comforts of life, in the diffusion of the information and knowledge, useful or necessary for all; in short, all advances in civilization, and the rights and privileges of citizens, are especially connected with, and derived from the four classes of the mercantile, the manufacturing, the distributive, and the professional' (CS, p. 25). After further discussion, he says:

> That harmonious balance of the two great correspondent, at once supporting and counterpoising, interests of the state, its permanence, and its progression; that balance of the landed and the personal interests was to be secured by a legislature of two Houses; the first consisting wholly of barons or landholders, permanent and hereditary senators; the second of the knights or minor barons, elected by, and as the representative of, the remaining landed community, together with the burgesses, the representatives of the

commercial, manufacturing, distributive, and professional classes, – the latter (the elected burgesses) constituting the major number. The king, meanwhile, in whom the executive power is vested, it will suffice at present to consider as the beam of the constitutional scales. A more comprehensive view of the kingly office must be deferred, till the remaining problem (the idea of a national church) has been solved.

(CS, pp. 29–30)

With that last statement Coleridge moves toward the twin realities, Church and State, that provide the title of his discourse; and when he arrives at those twin realities, he subsumes them under the same polar schematism that he has inaugurated with the concepts of permanence and progression:

In order to correct views respecting the constitution, in the more enlarged sense of the term, viz. the constitution of the *Nation*, we must, in addition to a grounded knowledge of the *State*, have the right idea of the *National Church*. These are two poles of the same magnet; the magnet itself, which is constituted by them, is the CONSTITUTION of the nation.

(CS, p. 31)

That the complex of ideas here being elaborated runs deep may perhaps be demonstrated by a single testimony. In 1859, in his classic treatise, *On Liberty*, John Stuart Mill writes:

In politics, again, it is almost a commonplace, that a party of order or stability, and a party of progress or reform, are both necessary elements of a healthy political life . . . Each of these modes of think-ing derives its utility from the deficiencies of the other; but it is in great measure the opposition of the other that keeps each within the limits of reason and sanity. Unless opinion favourable to democracy and to aristocracy, to property and to equality, to co-operation and to competition, to luxury and to abstinence, to sociality and to individuality, to liberty and discipline, and all the other standing antagonisms of practical life, are expressed with equal freedom, and enforced and defended with equal talent and energy, there is no chance of both elements obtaining their due; one scale is sure to go up, and the other down. Truth, in the great practical concerns of life, is so much a question of the reconciling and combining of opposites, that very few have minds sufficiently capacious and impartial to make the adjustment with an approach to correctness, and it has to be made by the rough process of a struggle between combatants fighting under hostile banners.[14]

The entire passage is permeated by the precursorship of Coleridge's *Church and State*. Mill, of course, admired Coleridge's mind and habitually read Coleridge's writings with respectful attention – after all, in a famous essay he divided all Englishmen of his time into only two classes, Benthamites and Coleridgeans – and one can have little doubt that he is here working directly with the memory of Coleridge's treatise of 1830. That he can, by 1859, term the ideas 'almost a commonplace', is eloquent witness to how deeply they had rooted themselves in the cultural soil.

But if the polarities of *Church and State* rooted deeply and branched out broadly, they had also been growing slowly in Coleridge's mind over the years. For in 1811, almost two full decades before the treatise on church and state, Coleridge is mulling the very same ideas:

> Church and state [he says] – civil and religious rights – to hold these essential power of civilized society in due relationship to each other, so as to prevent them from becoming its burdens, instead of its supports; this is perhaps the most difficult problem in the whole science of politics . . . From the first ages of Christianity to the present period, the two relations of a natural being, to his present and future state, have been abstracted and framed into moral personages, Church and State: and to each has been assigned its own domain and its special rights.[15]

This passage of 1811 shows conclusively that Coleridge had been tenaciously holding to the primary polarity of Church and State, and its implications for social thought, for twenty years before the treatise that still thirty years later influenced Mill. And it constitutes a third vital instance, to be set beside the two just elucidated, of his extraordinary intellectual tenacity.

This paper has up till now brought forward three complex examples, not just one, in order to illustrate how characteristic of Coleridge was the tenacious retention of focal ideational clusters. In doing so, it has illuminated also two subsidiary features of Coleridge's mentation. He not only tenaciously retained philosophical emphases, but these emphases were, first, characteristically explored at great depth, and, secondly, were elaborated in far reaching ramification. Each emphasis was, so to speak, like Coleridge's favorite organic metaphor of a tree: it germinated long, grew slowly, put its roots down ever more deeply, and branched out into broad and complex foliage.

All this seems unmistakably clear on the basis of the multiple examples just explored. Yet the intellectual public's awareness of the palpable truth of Coleridge's intellectual tenacity has been compromised by three large factors. Working in synergy they have constituted a kind of snarling Cerberus, it might be said, blocking in this instance the gateway to understanding. The first factor is the fragmentary nature of Coleridge's work, which, until the inauguration and completion of the great *Collected Coleridge*, was made to seem even more fragmentary by the existence of scattered and piecemeal texts, with much of the witness to his mental effort remaining unprinted. The second is the special allusiveness of Coleridge's prose style, and its reference to a vast range of reading in five languages, a reading by no means matched by his commentators. As a single instance, the present writer has had occasion to point out more than once that no commentator on Coleridge has ever so much as approached his magisterial command of the philosophy of Kant, and to compound that deficiency some have even projected their own ignorance into their assumptions about their subject. The third factor is the prevalence, in the last quarter century, of aggressive and ill-informed dismissals, taking their impetus from a heightened aware-ness of Coleridge's psychological desperation.

These dismissals have had a resonating effect. Fruman's *Damaged Archangel* received over 100 reviews, most of them laudatory, almost none of them by scholars competent to judge. It was bemusing to see intellectuals of the calibre of Angus Fletcher, Hugh Kenner, and Christopher Ricks largely accept that manipulated stock; and it was also bemusing to note that reviewers never seemed to question their own credentials for judging in the matter. It was in this witch-hunting climate of opinion that E.P. Thompson could, in an orgy of fulmination and denunciation, roundly dismiss Coleridge as being 'wrong on almost everything' and of being 'a chameleon'.[16]

Whatever Coleridge was, a chameleon he was not. Indeed, it might even be said that the whole point of this paper is to demonstrate how baseless is such a charge. No one has ever been more constant in his opinions or more tenacious in his intellectual attitudes and viewpoints than was Coleridge. But he has in recent years been enveloped in a miasma of misconception, and grossly, even ludicrously mistaken views have sometimes prevailed.

To dispel, or begin to dispel, that miasma of misconception, therefore, an extended concluding example must be joined to the three already summoned. It will serve to illustrate still a fourth aspect of Coleridge's all-pervading intellectual tenacity. To the characteristics of lengthy retention, depth, and ramified elaboration already identified must be added, and explored, another characteristic noted in passing above: the persistence of thoughts once taken up. For thoughts once taken up into the blast furnace of Coleridge's mental activity were never discarded or wholly rejected; they might be modified or reshaped in their role in his systematic commitment, but they were never forced out of his concern. His often-quoted description of his philosophical aims is a paramount witness to this truth. For he says that his system is an attempt

> to reduce all knowledges into harmony. It opposes no other system, but shows what was true in each; and how that which was true in the particular, in each of them became error, because it was only

half the truth. I have endeavoured to unite the insulated fragments of truth, and therewith to frame a perfect mirror. I show to each system that I fully understand and rightfully appreciate what that system means; but then I lift up that system to a higher point of view, from which I enable it to see its former position, where it was, indeed, but under another light and with different relations; so that the fragment of truth is not only acknowledged, but explained.[17]

A fine example of Coleridge's uniting the insulated fragments of truth, of retaining an unpalatable fragment by viewing it in another light and with different relations, is provided by his disposition of the received concept of reason in which he had been brought up. That reason, the *raison* of the French Enlightenment, came to seem inadequate to him. Instead of rejecting it entirely, however, as other thinkers might have done, he retained it. But he cast it in another light and with different relations. He renamed it 'understanding'; and he substituted a more satisfactory conception of reason under the now vacated term 'reason', the binary linkage of reason and understanding having been suggested to him by the dichotomized conceptions of Tetens, Kant, and Jacobi.

Incidentally, Coleridge's attention to the binary linkage of reason and understanding is a prime illustration of his intellectual tenacity, for as he says in *On the Constitution of Church and State*, to return to the work we have been mining, 'It is now thirty years since the diversity of REASON and the UNDERSTANDING, of an Idea and a Conception, and the practical importance of distinguishing the one from the other, were first made evident to me. And scarcely a month has passed during this long interval in which either books, or conversation, or the experience of life, have not supplied or suggested some fresh proof and instance of the mischiefs and mistakes, derived from that ignorance of this Truth, which I have elsewhere called the Queen-bee in the Hive of Error' (CS, pp. 58–9).

That passage alone, with its reference to a continuing mental engagement of thirty years, provides vivid witness to Coleridge's intellectual tenacity. And it would be very possible, by further investigation, to illustrate the characteristics of depth and elaboration, as well as those characteristics of tenacity and persistence already evident in the passage on its face. But instead of embarking on the lengthy and rewarding possibilities attendant on such an investigation, we will choose as our fourth example a very similar situation, but one susceptible of somewhat briefer address, with regard to another Coleridgean collocation.

That collocation is constituted by the Coleridgean concern with imagination. Here, as with reason, Coleridge's tenacious involvement – his long-term preoccupation and elaboration – was elicited by dissatisfaction with the received view obtaining in his formative years. But instead of Enlightenment *raison*, the received view here was the conception of mind and its active power espoused by the tradition of Locke. Indeed, the situation in England in Coleridge's intellectually germinating period was that Locke and Newton formed an alliance that reigned supreme. As Godwin said in 1793, 'Locke and others have established certain maxims respecting man, as Newton has done respecting matter, that are generally admitted for unquestionable.'[18] As corollary to his espousal of these beliefs, Godwin found the mind to be completely passive. 'In volition', he said, 'if the doctrine of necessity be true, the mind is altogether passive' (Godwin, I, p. 323). 'Man', he said again, 'is in reality a passive, and not an active being' (Godwin, I, p. 310).

But Coleridge came to rebel against this view, and his rebellion, continuing over the decades, is itself a prime witness to his intellectual tenacity, both in its length and in its elaboration. In 1801 he rejected the tradition of Locke and Newton in this way:

> Newton was a mere *Materialist* – Mind in his system is always passive – a lazy Looker-on on an external world. If the mind be not *passive*, if it be indeed Made in God's Image, & that too in the sublimest sense – the Image of the *Creator* – there is ground for suspicion, that any system built on the passiveness of the mind must be false, as a system.
>
> (CL, II, p. 709)

Fourteen years later the same urgency obtained, for one of Coleridge's hopes for Wordsworth's *Recluse*, as he wrote in 1815, was that it should refute 'the sandy Sophisms of Locke, and the Mechanic Dogmatists' by 'demonstrating that the Senses were living growths and developments of the Mind & Spirit in a much juster as well as higher sense, than the mind can be said to be formed by the Senses' (CL, IV, p. 574). The tenacity so clearly attested by the dates of 1801 and 1815 continued unabated. Another seventeen years passed, and the matter was still occupying Coleridge's thoughts; for in 1832 he said, 'The pith of my system is to make the senses out of the mind – not the mind out of the senses, as Locke did' (TT, II, p. 179. 25 July 1832).

Coleridge's intellectual tenacity in rejecting the passiveness of mind extended to his engagement with the chief evidence for the activity of the mind, the imagination. And here he did exactly what he also did with reason. Instead of simply dismissing the tradition of mental imaging arising out of the conception of the mind's passivity, he retained it under the name 'fancy'; and he simultaneously urged his own view, under the name 'imagination', of the mind as made in 'God's Image', the 'Image of the *Creator*':

> The IMAGINATION then I consider either as primary, or secondary. The primary IMAGINATION I hold to be the living Power and prime Agent of all human Perception, and as a repetition in the finite mind of the eternal act of creation in the infinite I AM. The secondary

I consider as an echo of the former, co-existing with the conscious will, yet still as identical with the primary in the *kind* of its agency, and differing only in *degree*, and in the *mode* of its operation. It dissolves, diffuses, dissipates, in order to re-create ... It is essentially *vital*, even as all objects (*as* objects) are essentially fixed and dead.[19]

To that extrication of the vital and creative activity of mind, conceived in analogy with the creative activity of God himself, Coleridge subjoins the rejected Lockean conception of a non-creative passivity, here presented in another light and with different relations:

FANCY, on the contrary, has no other counters to play with, but fixities and definites. The Fancy is indeed no other than a mode of Memory emancipated from the order of time and space; and blended with, and modified by the empirical phenomenon of the will, which we express by the word CHOICE. But equally with the ordinary memory it must receive all its materials ready made from the law of association.

(B, I, p. 305)

The invocation of the 'law of association' places 'fancy' firmly in the tradition of Locke, and of Locke's epigone, Hartley.

Those famous passages were published in 1817. In only this one place does Coleridge overtly summon the theological analogue, under the rubric 'primary imagination'. But as the passage of 1801 against Newton attests, it was always the substratum of his conception. The fundamental division between imagination and fancy too had had a long provenance in Coleridge's ever-tenacious concern. Fifteen years before the formulation in the *Biographia Literaria*, in a letter of 1802, he expresses that division for the first time. The occasion, distinguishing Greek religious poetry from that of the Hebrews, refers to imagination and fancy in such casual terms as to suggest that they had long been current in his conceiving; at any rate, they are certainly current in this letter of 10 September 1802, where he refers to 'Fancy, or the aggregating Faculty of the mind – not *Imagination*, or the *modifying*, and *co-adunating* Faculty' (CL, II, pp. 865–6).

But Coleridge's tenacious concern had been current even before the fifteen-year span from 1802 to 1817. For his elaboration of the doctrine of imagination is actually a reshaping of his earlier preoccupation with necessitarian thought. Necessitarian thought was unequivocally espoused by three figures important in Coleridge's early intellectual background, Hartley, Priestley, and Godwin. It is a large subject, but perhaps a single quotation from each figure will serve to triangulate it for our present elucidation. Hartley, in his *Observations on Man*, said in 1749 that one of 'the consequences flowing from the Doctrine of Association' was 'that of the Mechanism or Necessity of Human Actions, in Opposition to what is generally termed Free-will'.[20] Priestley, in 1777, in *The Doctrine of Philosophical Necessity Illustrated*, argued from materialist hypotheses that 'every thing belonging to the doctrine of materialism is, in fact, an argument for the doctrine of necessity, and, consequently, the doctrine of necessity is a direct inference from materialism'.[21]

And Godwin , in 1793, in *Political Justice*, espoused necessitarianism and said that 'He who affirms that all actions are necessary, means, that, if we form a just and complete view of all the circumstances in which a living, or intelligent being is placed, we shall find that he could not in any moment of his existence have acted otherwise than he has acted' (Godwin, I, p. 285). Coleridge was profoundly immersed in this tradition. Indeed, in 1794 he wrote Southey that 'I am a compleat Necessitarian – and understand the subject as well almost as Hartley himself – but I go farther than Hartley and believe the corporeality of *thought* – namely, that it is motion –' (CL, I, p. 137). But as Coleridge continued to work out the implications of his own primary assumptions, he came increasingly into conflict with the necessitarianism of Hartley, Priestley, and Godwin. The line of thought and observation that led to their abjuration may be glimpsed in a letter of 1800 to Josiah Wedgwood:

> Both I & Mrs Coleridge have carefully watched our little one and noted down all the circumstances &c. under which he smiled & under which he laughed for the first six times – nor have we remitted our attention – but I have not been able to derive the least confirmation of Hartley's or Darwin's Theory.
>
> (CL, I, p. 647)

In a note of 1804, Coleridge rejects Hartley's doctrine of association in unequivocal terms: 'I am much pleased with this Suggestion, as with everything that overthrows & or illustrates the overthrow of that all-annihilating system of explaining every thing wholly by association.'[22]

Yet Coleridge did not simply abandon the concerns directed into his hopes for necessitarian theory. Rather, he modified the applicability of their doctrine, and rechanneled their energy into his theory of imagination, which rectified necessitarian defects. As he said in an anticipatory note of 1796, 'Doctrine of necessity rendered not dangerous by the Imagination which contemplates immediate not remote effects' (NB, I, no. 156). Both concerns, opposition to Hartleyan necessity, on the one hand, and the liberating theory of imagination, on the other, continued at the forefront of Coleridge's thought, until, in 1817, twenty-one years later, in the *Biographia Literaria*, he set forth the fullest elaboration of the doctrine of imagination alongside an extended refutation of Hartley:

It remains then for me, first to state wherein Hartley differs from Aristotle; then, to exhibit the ground of my conviction, that he differed only to err; and next as the result, to shew, by what influence of the choice and judgment the associative power becomes either memory or fancy; and, in conclusion, to appropriate the remaining office of the mind to the reason, and the imagination.

(B, I, p. 105)

In Chapter Seven of his work, Coleridge delivers body blows to what he calls 'Hartley's scheme'. He speaks of

the assumption, that the will, and with the will all acts of thought and attention, are parts and products of this blind mechanism, instead of being distinct powers, whose function is to controul, determine, and modify the phantasmal chaos of association. The soul becomes a mere ens logicum.

(B, I, pp. 116–17)

The soul would by the same token, says Coleridge, become 'worthless and ludicrous'; for

in Hartley's scheme the soul is present only to be pinched or *stroked*, while the very squeals or purring are produced by an agency wholly independent and alien.

(B, I, p. 117)

Thus 'Hartley's scheme' is absolutely rejected by Coleridge as antithetical to his commitment to what he calls 'the free-will, our only absolute *self*' (B, I, p. 114).

But Coleridge's involvement in these matters did not simply run from that date in 1794 when he declared that he understood necessitarianism almost as well as Hartley himself, to the date in 1817, lengthy though that span of almost a quarter of a century is, when he elaborated a comprehensive scheme of imagination specifically designed to rescue his thought from Hartleyan implication. It ran still further. For sixteen years later, on May 18, 1833, a note in the *Table Talk* shows that Coleridge is still tenaciously ruminating on the convolutions of necessity and freedom. 'In natural history', he says, 'God's freedom is shown in the law of necessity. In moral history, God's necessity or providence is shown in man's freedom' (TT, II, p. 231. 18 May 1833).

These four examples of Coleridge's tenacity, here rehearsed at length, should serve to identify that characteristic as a fundamental feature of his mental activity. As I have said elsewhere:

Coleridge did not change by abrupt repudiations and summary *voltes-face*; change, for Coleridge, was always a matter of evolving emphases and additional considerations. He was as tenacious of his primary beliefs as any thinker has ever been; and no intellectual life can have been more continuous and integrated in its development than was his.[23]

Not constant change, but continuity, was the hallmark of Coleridge's intellectual activity. Not constant rejection and beginning again, but continuing integration was his typical procedure. One may place against E.P. Thompson's agitated denunciations Coleridge's own beautifully articulated statement of this ideal:

> It is a maxim with me, to make life as continuous as possible, by linking on the Present to the Past: and I believe that a large portion of the ingratitude, inconstancy, frivolity, and restless self-weariness so many examples of which obtrude themselves on every man of observation and reflective habits, is attributable to the *friable,* incohesive sort of existence that characterizes the mere man of the World, a fractional Life made up of successive moments that neither blend nor modify each other – a life that is strictly symbolized in the thread of Sand thro' the orifice of the Hour-glass, in which the sequence of Grains only *counterfeits* a continuity, and appears a *line* only because the interspaces between the Points are too small to be sensible. Without Memory there can be no hope – the Present is a phantom known only by its pining, if it do not breathe the vital air of the Future: what is the Future, but the Image of the Past projected on the mist of the Unknown, and seen with a glory round it's head.
>
> (CL, V, p. 266)

This, then, is enough. Coleridge's distinctive hope of aligning past, present, and future into one cohesive witness to a meaningful life, which is so strikingly formulated in the preceding quotation, underlies the enormous constancy of his intellectual career. Informed by such constancy, that career, despite the fragmentations and neuroses of his psychic life, raised itself to a high place in the annals of culture. And the idiosyncratic constancy, which co-inhered so unexpectedly with the ruinous disintegration of his personal existence, manifested itself in a tremendous intellectual tenacity. It was a tenacity whereby thoughts once propounded evermore played a vital role in Coleridge's concern; and he himself may be finally defined, in simple fact, as nothing less than a hero of intellectual abidingness.

Notes

1 'For he that loveth not his brother whom he hath seen, how can he love God whom he hath not seen' (I John 4:20).
2 S.T. Coleridge, *Lectures 1795 On Politics and Religion*, ed. by Lewis Patton and Peter Mann (London: Routledge and Kegan Paul; Princeton: Princeton University Press, 1971). Volume I in *The Collected Works of Samuel Taylor Coleridge*, ed. by Kathleen Coburn, Bollingen Series 75.
3 *Opus Maximum*, Fragment Two folio 79.
4 *Collected Letters of Samuel Taylor Coleridge*, ed. by Earl Leslie Griggs (Oxford: Clarendon Press, 1956–71), VI, p. 861. Hereafter cited as CL.
5 *Coleridge the Talker; A Series of Contemporary Descriptions and Comments*, ed. by Richard W. Armour and Raymond F. Howes, new edition with addenda (1940: New York and London: Johnson Reprint Corporation, 1969), p. 297.
6 Marcel Mauss, *Sociology and Psychology; Essays*, trans. by Ben Brewster (London, Boston and Henley: Routledge and Kegan Paul, 1979), p. 3.
7 Talcott Parsons, 'The Life and Work of Emile Durkheim', in Emile Durkheim, *Sociology and Philosophy*, trans. by D.F. Pocock, with an introduction by J.G. Peristiany (New York: The Free Press, 1974), p. li.
8 Emile Durkheim, *Les Règles de la méthode sociologique, revue et augmentée d'une préface nouvelle* (2nd. edn.: Paris: Alcan, 1901), pp. 127–8.
9 Steven Lukes, *Emile Durkheim: His Life and Work; A Historical and Critical Study* (London: Allen Lane The Penguin Press, 1973), p. 11, hereafter Lukes.
10 Emile Durkheim, *De la division du travail social* (2nd. edn.: Paris: Alcan, 1902), p. 46.
11 S.T. Coleridge, *On the Constitution of the Church and State*, ed. by John Colmer (London: Routledge and Kegan Paul; Princeton, Princeton University Press, 1976), p. 116. Volume 10 in *The Collected Works of Samuel Taylor Coleridge*, ed. by Kathleen Coburn, Bollingen Series 75. Hereafter cited as CS.
12 Emile Durkheim, *The Elementary Forms of the Religious Life*, trans. by Joseph Ward Swain (London: George Allen and Unwin Ltd, 1915), p. 16, subsequent page references in the text.
13 Donald G. MacRae, *Max Weber* (New York: The Viking Press, 1974), p. 4, subsequent page references in the text.
14 John Stuart Mill, *On Liberty*, ed. by David Spitz, Norton Critical Editions (New York: W.W. Norton, 1975), p. 46.
15 S.T. Coleridge, *Essays on His Times*, ed. by David V. Erdman, 3 vols (London: Routledge and Kegan Paul; Princeton: Princeton University Press, 1978), I, pp. 172–3. Volume 3 in *The Collected Works of Samuel Taylor Coleridge*, ed. by Kathleen Coburn, Bollingen Series 75.
16 E.P. Thompson, *in The Wordsworth Circle*, 10 (Summer 1979), pp. 262–3.
17 S.T. Coleridge, *Table Talk; Recorded by Henry Nelson Coleridge (and John Taylor Coleridge)*, ed. by Carl Woodring, 2 vols (London: Routledge and Kegan Paul; Princeton: Princeton University Press, 1990), II, 147–8. 12 September 1831. Volume 14 in *The Collected Works of Samuel Taylor Coleridge*, ed. by Kathleen Coburn, Bollingen Series 75. Hereafter cited as TT.
18 William Godwin, *An Enquiry Concerning Political Justice, and its Influence on General Virtue and Happiness* (London: G.G.J. and J. Robinson, 1793) I, p. 20. Facsimile edn. published by Woodstock Books: Oxford and New York, 1992. Hereafter cited as Godwin.
19 S.T. Coleridge, *Biographia Literaria*, ed. by James Engell and W. Jackson Bate (London: Routledge and Kegan Paul; Princeton: Princeton University Press, 1983),

I, p. 304. Volume 7 in *The Collected Works of Samuel Taylor Coleridge*, ed. by Kathleen Coburn, Bollingen Series 75. Hereafter cited as B.

20 David Hartley, *Observations on Man, His Frame, His Duty, and His Expectations* (London: S. Richardson for James Leake and Wm. Frederick, 1749), I, p. 500. Scholars' Facsimiles and Reprints: Delmar, New York, 1976.

21 Joseph Priestley, *The Doctrine of Philosophical Necessity Illustrated, being an appendix to the Disquisitions relating to Matter and Spirit*, vol. ii. The second edition enlarged (Birmingham: Printed by pearson and Rollason, for J. Johnson. No. 72, St Paul's Church-Yard, London, 1782), p. xviii.

22 *The Notebooks of Samuel Taylor Coleridge*, ed. by Kathleen Coburn *et al.* (London: Routledge and Kegan Paul; Princeton: Princeton University Press, 1957), II, no. 209. Hereafter NB.

23 Thomas McFarland, *Romanticism and the Heritage of Rousseau* (Oxford: Clarendon Press, 1995), p. 94.

INDEX

INDEX

literary seduction of upper-class
women **III** 83
lower-middle-class origins **III** 66–7
McGann's politization of **III** 383
Mammon of formalism **II** 71
material turmoils **I** 316
measure of human happiness **II** 403
mythological poems **IV** 169, 173
nature and culture as two poles of
symbolic system **I** 301
need to cater to female taste **III** 87
negative capability **III** 69, 75–7
notion of spirit-creation **I** 357
observations on Shelley **II** 58
odes **II** 125
oppositions generated by semiotics of
vision **III** 317
parallels with Nietzsche **I** 349–58
philosophical emphasis on social
service **I** 296
play upon biblical language **II** 67
poetic credentials **III** 329
poetic independence **II** 61
poetical character **I** 354; **III** 381
poetry's absolute independence **II** 62
posterity's award **I** 295
power of art **I** 295
presence of classical gods **IV** 150
pressures and possibilities of rhyming
II 170
principle of self-concentration **II** 66
Promethean quest **I** 119
pursuit of worldly goods **II** 62
"radically presumptuous profligate"
II 78
reaction to comments on the marbles
I 335
reflections on women readers **III** 70
religious nostalgia **I** 294
resentment of power of women
readers **III** 71–2
rhyme field **I** 317
role of artist **I** 300–1
role of audience **I** 300–1
Romantic Hellenism **IV** 172
self-awareness **I** 248–50
self-concentration **II** 62, 73, 81
sexual and literary inadequacy
III 81
social functions of poetry **I** 295
social, sexual, and literary
inadequacy **III** 80–1
social value **I** 301

squabble between Tory traditionalists
and liberal reformers **II** 165
struggle to discover a self **I** 16
stylistic habits **II** 174
symbolic nature of art **I** 14, 298
thematic admission of tragic material
I 296
theoretical thinking about the nature
and social value of poetry **I** 298
theory of Negative Capability **II** 4
thought, prophecy, and labyrinthine
mystery **I** 297
tragic, hieroglyphic, and solitary
centre of art **I** 299
transforming descriptive and
meditative propositions **I** 202–3
uneasiness about authority of his
own authorship **III** 80
use of poetry **I** 293–307
Vale of Soul-Making **III** 382
wealth of the imagination **II** 57–88
whirling atmosphere **I** 319–20
writing as a woman **III** 87
'Keats Reading Women, Women
Reading Keats' **III** 4–6
Keble, John **I** 228–9
*Keen-Sighted Politician Warming his
Imagination, A* **II** 37
Keller, Helen **IV** 103, 124
Kermode, Frank **IV** 136
Kerrigan, John **III** 13, 238
Ketch, J. **II** 69
Kierkegaard, Soren Aabye **I** 134
kindliness, dualities of **I** 182
King Lear **I** 29, 319; **II** 126; **III** 290–1,
381
Kinnaird, John **II** 63
Kneale, J. Douglas **IV** 213
Knight, Richard Payne **I** 328;
IV 180–1, 183
Knights, L. C. **III** 262
knowledge, conditions of **IV** 196
Kramer, Lawrence **IV** 7–8, 150
Kramnick, Isaac **II** 25
Kubla Khan **I** 131, 268; **II** 8, 179–98,
355; **III** 131, 358; **IV** 30, 143

Laberius **II** 50
Lady of the Lake, The **III** 203, 208
Lake school of poetry **I** 74
Lamb, Charles **III** 289, 321
Lamia **I** 351
Landré, Louis **III** 179